WHERE LAW AND MORALITY MEET

Where Law and Morality Meet

MATTHEW H. KRAMER

OXFORD
UNIVERSITY PRESS

OXFORD
UNIVERSITY PRESS

Great Clarendon Street, Oxford ox2 6DP

Oxford University Press is a department of the University of Oxford.
It furthers the University's objective of excellence in research, scholarship,
and education by publishing worldwide in

Oxford New York

Auckland Cape Town Dar es Salaam Hong Kong Karachi Kuala Lumpur
Madrid Melbourne Mexico City Nairobi New Delhi Taipei Toronto
Shanghai

With offices in

Argentina Austria Brazil Chile Czech Republic France Greece
Guatemala Hungary Italy Japan South Korea Poland Portugal
Singapore Switzerland Thailand Turkey Ukraine Vietnam

Oxford is a registered trade mark of Oxford University Press
in the UK and in certain other countries

Published in the United States
by Oxford University Press Inc., New York

British Library Cataloguing in Publication Data
Data Available
Library of Congress Cataloging-in-Publication Data

Kramer, Matthew H., 1959-
Where law and morality meet / Matthew H. Kramer.
p. cm.
Includes index.
ISBN 0-19-927419-3 (hard cover : alk. paper)
1. Law and ethics. I. Title.
K247.6.K73 2004
340'.112–dc22

2004021135

1 3 5 7 9 10 8 6 4 2

Typeset by Kolam Information Services Pvt. Ltd, Pondicherry, India
Printed in Great Britain
on acid-free paper by
Biddles Ltd., King's Lynn

To the memory of Christina Margaret Kelly (1928–97)

Preface

I wish to thank the following people for their very helpful comments on portions of this book: Trevor Allan, Brian Bix, Gerard Bradley, Richard Bronaugh, Ian Carter, Jules Coleman, Sean Coyle, Rowan Cruft, Sylvie Delacroix, Neil Duxbury, William Edmundson, Timothy Endicott, John Finnis, Michael Freeman, Kenneth Himma, Brian Leiter, Margaret Martin, Mark McBride, Emran Mian, Michael Moore, James Murphy, Amanda Perreau-Saussine, Joseph Raz, Mark Reiff, Scott Shapiro, Nigel Simmonds, Walter Sinnott-Armstrong, Philip Soper, Nicos Stavropoulos, Hillel Steiner, Bart Streumer, Peter Vallentyne, and Wilfrid Waluchow. I likewise wish to thank John Louth and Gwen Booth and their associates at the Oxford University Press for their handling of my book. In the course of writing this volume, I have gratefully benefited from the computing expertise of Giles Agnew (at Churchill College, Cambridge) and Andrew Gerrard and Sarah Kitching (at the Cambridge University Law Faculty). As always, I am indebted to my father for his encouragement.

Very early versions of the first two chapters appeared in *Legal Theory* (2000 and 2002), published by the Cambridge University Press. An early version of the third chapter appeared in the *American Journal of Jurisprudence* (2003), published by the Natural Law Institute of the University of Notre Dame. An early and somewhat abridged version of the fourth chapter appeared in *Law and Philosophy* (2004), published by Kluwer Academic Press. An early version of the fifth chapter appeared in the *Oxford Journal of Legal Studies* (2001), published by the Oxford University Press. I am grateful to these journals for permission to publish revised versions of my articles as chapters in the present book. (The revisions are especially far-reaching in the first two chapters.)

I presented an abridged version of Chapter 3 as a lecture at the University of Notre Dame Law School in April 2003, and an abridged version of Chapter 8 as a lecture at Dartmouth College in April 2004. I express my warm thanks for the gracious hospitality extended to me at those two institutions.

Finally, I am grateful to the numerous undergraduate and LLM Jurisprudence students at Cambridge University who have come up with perceptive questions and observations concerning many of the matters discussed herein. I have profited immensely from them.

Matthew H. Kramer

Cambridge, England
April 2004

Contents

Introduction

As the title of this book suggests, the central topic to be investigated herein is the relationship between law and morality. That is, we shall be exploring some of the myriad ways in which law and morality interact and some of the many ways in which they remain disjoined. Such an exploration will continue my longstanding defense of legal positivism. On the one hand, by tracing a number of points of intersection between the legal domain and the moral domain, the chapters below will help to dispel the idea that legal positivists have somehow denied the existence of important law-morality connections. On the other hand, by highlighting the contingency of all or most of those connections, this book will have placed itself squarely within the positivist tradition.

Some of the controversies joined by my discussions have been carried on mainly among legal positivists themselves, who disagree with one another about the best ways of understanding and elaborating the insights of the jurisprudential tradition to which they are heirs. They disagree about the scope, the significance, the implications, and even the sustainability of legal positivism's insistence on the separability of law and morality; and they disagree about kindred matters such as the nature of law's conventionality. Those disputes figure saliently in this book, especially in Part I and in Chapter 7. At least as prominent in contemporary legal philosophy, however, are the abiding conflicts between positivists and natural-law theorists. Through a variety of arguments, natural-law thinkers have endeavored to establish that law and morality are ineluctably intertwined in important ways. Accordingly, any satisfactory defense of legal positivism must seek to counter the claims of natural-law theorists. The present volume (especially in Part II) will undertake just such a task, as it builds on some of my previous writings in response to the challenges of legal positivism's opponents.

Although the original versions of some of the chapters in this book were published as articles in journals, and although there is no sustainedly cumulative line of reasoning that runs throughout the book, this volume is more than a collection of essays. Every chapter focuses on some facet(s) of the theme announced in the volume's title, and the chapters form closely integrated clusters. Each chapter was written with this book in mind. Moreover, the original versions of the previously published pieces have been significantly revised to minimize repetition and to increase the coherence of the volume as a whole (and, at several junctures, to amplify arguments considerably in order to register the development of my substantive views). This Introduction will outline the three main parts of the book and will set the stage for the arguments that are presented there.

I. Inclusivism, Incorporationism, and Exclusivism

Chapters 1 to 4 sally forth into debates between Exclusive Legal Positivists on the one hand and Inclusive Legal Positivists and Incorporationists on the other. Before we glance at the background to those debates, the relevant terminology should be elucidated. Let us begin, then, with a thumbnail sketch of each of the three major positions just named (two of which are commonly found together).

Inclusive Legal Positivism, as understood throughout this book, consists in the following thesis: it can be the case, though it need not be the case, that a norm's consistency with some or all of the requirements of morality is a precondition for the norm's status as a law in this or that jurisdiction. While such a precondition for legal validity is not inherent in the concept of law, it can be imposed as a threshold test under the Rule of Recognition in any particular legal regime.[1] That test, which can be applied by the officials in such a regime to all of the legal norms therein or to only some subset of those norms, is one of the criteria which the officials use for ascertaining the law. Insofar as a threshold criterion of that sort does prevail in any particular legal system, then, some degree of moral worthiness is a necessary condition for the legally authoritative force of each norm that is validated as a law within the system. Inclusive Legal Positivism, which readily accepts the possibility of such a state of affairs, is inclusive because it allows that moral precepts can figure among the criteria that guide officials' ascertainment of the law. Inclusivist theorists reject the view that *every* criterion for law-ascertainment in *every* credibly possible legal system is focused on nonnormative matters of provenance. At the same time, the Inclusivists are positivists because they also reject the view that *every* credibly possible legal system relies on moral tests among its law-ascertaining criteria. An Inclusive Legal Positivist insists that such tests are contingent features, rather than essential features, of the systems of law in which they are applied.

Incorporationism, as understood throughout this book, consists in the following thesis: it can be the case, though it need not be the case, that a norm's correctness as a moral principle is a sufficient condition for its status as

---

[1] The phrase 'Rule of Recognition', which I use here and elsewhere, is of course taken from H.L.A. Hart. It refers to the array of criteria that empower and obligate the officials in a legal system to ascertain the existence and contents of legal norms in accordance with standards specified by those criteria (which are largely, if not exhaustively, ranked). The Rule of Recognition in any legal system is a framework of normative presuppositions that underlie the law-identifying behavior of the officials in the system. In Chapter 4, I explore the general nature of any Rule of Recognition in some depth.

a legal norm in this or that jurisdiction. Albeit the role of moral correctness as a sufficient condition for legal validity is not inherent in the concept of law, it can obtain under the Rule of Recognition in any particular legal regime. An Incorporationist theorist maintains that moral principles regularly regarded by officials as legally determinative are indeed legal norms, notwithstanding that they have perhaps never been laid down in any explicit sources such as legislative enactments or judicial rulings. When officials do regularly engage in a practice of treating the moral soundness of norms as a sufficient condition for the norms' legal authoritativeness, they have thereby incorporated moral principles into the law of their system of governance—even before some or all of the applicable principles have received any explicit recognition. An Incorporationist theorist, who unhesitatingly accepts the possibility of such a state of affairs, is nonetheless a legal positivist because he insists that the incorporation of moral principles into a legal system's array of norms is contingent rather than inevitable.

Whereas Inclusive Legal Positivism and Incorporationism are perfectly compatible and are typically conjoined, Exclusive Legal Positivism is opposed to each of them. Exclusive Legal Positivists maintain that the very nature of law is inconsistent both with the role of moral principles as legal norms and with their role as criteria for validating legal norms.[2] While gladly acknowledging that moral principles often get invoked in the adjudicative and administrative activities of legal officials, the Exclusivists contend that those principles are extra-legal standards. Such standards affect the decisions reached by the officials, but only because those decisions are not based solely on legal requirements.

Now, the three positions just recounted have hardly emerged from nowhere. Rather, each of them as a distinctive variant of legal positivism has developed in reaction to Ronald Dworkin's early critiques of H.L.A. Hart.[3] Although the details of Dworkin's criticisms and of subsequent rejoinders to those criticisms cannot be traced in any depth here, a few remarks will help to supply the context within which the arguments of this book's first four chapters can best be fathomed.

Among the many accusations leveled by Dworkin against Hart is that legal positivism cannot adequately take account of the role of moral principles as

---

[2] Some Exclusive Legal Positivists appear to allow that a moral principle can be a legal norm if it has been enacted or affirmed in some formal source such as a statute or a judicial ruling or an administrative regulation. See, e.g., Scott Shapiro, 'The Difference that Rules Make', in Brian Bix (ed.), *Analyzing Law* (Oxford: Oxford University Press, 1998), 33, 57, 58–9. To take account of such Exclusivists, then, my reference to the status of moral principles as legal norms should be paired disjunctively with a reference to the status of such principles as legal norms that have not been directly and explicitly grounded in any formal sources. Only such a disjunctive formulation would capture the substance of what every Exclusive Legal Positivist denies. To avoid stylistic clottedness, however, I have not altered my prose to reflect this complexity in the Exclusivist camp.

[3] Those critiques are presented most notably in Ronald Dworkin, *Taking Rights Seriously* (Cambridge, MA: Harvard University Press, 1978), chaps 2–4.

binding bases for decisions by judges in hard cases. (In his later work, Dworkin has—quite unpersuasively—extended his anti-positivist account of adjudication beyond hard cases to all cases. Even there, however, he provides the motivation for his discussion by adverting to the operativeness of moral principles in hard cases.[4]) Retorting to Dworkin's broadsides, legal positivists have either sought to explain how moral principles can enter into the law or else have denied that such principles do enter into the law. In issuing such retorts, the positivists have pursued the routes of Inclusivism and Incorporationism or the route of Exclusivism. The first two of those routes are combinable, of course, whereas the third of them is at odds with the other two.

Inclusive Legal Positivism is the position with the firmest grounding in Hart's own work. Well before Dworkin's onslaughts, Hart had happily acknowledged that the criteria for law-ascertainment in any particular legal system can include moral principles. He had chiefly in mind criteria that constitute restrictions on law-making power. That is, he had chiefly in mind the role of moral principles as hurdles or thresholds that pose necessary conditions for the status of any norm as a legal norm.[5] Embracing Inclusive Legal Positivism *avant la lettre*, Hart blazed a trail that has been followed by many of his positivist successors. Foremost among those successors heretofore is Wilfrid Waluchow, whose subtle elaboration of the Inclusivist position has been a riposte to Dworkin as much as to the Exclusive Legal Positivists.[6]

However, Dworkin's attacks on legal positivism have not focused primarily on the role of moral principles as law-validating criteria which require consistency with some or all of the demands of morality as a necessary condition for the legal

---

[4] See Ronald Dworkin, *Law's Empire* (London: Fontana Press, 1986), 15–30. For my doubts about the applicability of Dworkin's model of adjudication to easy cases, see my *In Defense of Legal Positivism* (Oxford: Oxford University Press, 1999) [hereinafter cited as *IDLP*], 173–6. See also Nigel Simmonds, 'Imperial Visions and Mundane Practices', 46 *Cambridge Law Journal* 465, 479–80 (1987).

[5] Among the germane passages in Hart's work are the following: *The Concept of Law* (Oxford: Clarendon Press, 1961) [hereinafter cited as Hart, *Concept*], 199; 'Positivism and the Separation of Law and Morals', in *Essays in Jurisprudence and Philosophy* (Oxford: Clarendon Press, 1983) [hereinafter cited as *Essays*], 49, 54–5; 'Lon L. Fuller, *The Morality of Law*', in *Essays, supra*, at 343, 361; 'Postscript', to *The Concept of Law* (Oxford: Clarendon Press, 1994) (2nd edn) [hereinafter cited as Hart, 'Postscript'], 238, 247–8, 250–4. Although I readily concede that 'the distinction between [Inclusive and Exclusive] versions of the positivist thesis was unknown when [Hart wrote *The Concept of Law*] and was therefore not part of the polemical context of the time' (Leslie Green, 'The Concept of Law Revisited', 94 *Michigan Law Review* 1687, 1706–7 (1996)), the passages cited here are strong evidence suggesting that Hart implicitly or explicitly embraced Inclusive Legal Positivism throughout his career.

My own previous writings in this area have stemmed from a perspective similar to that of Hart. See *IDLP*, 114–15, 152–61, 197–9; 'Coming to Grips with the Law: In Defense of Positive Legal Positivism', 5 *Legal Theory* 171, 190–200 (1999). A Hartian perspective also generally informs W.J. Waluchow, *Inclusive Legal Positivism* (Oxford: Clarendon Press, 1994). An Inclusive Legal Positivist stance is likewise largely what David Lyons defends in his 'Principles, Positivism, and Legal Theory', 87 *Yale Law Journal* 415, 423–6 (1977).

[6] See generally W.J. Waluchow, *supra* note 5; W.J. Waluchow, 'Authority and the Practical Difference Thesis: A Defense of Inclusive Legal Positivism', 6 *Legal Theory* 45 (2000).

validity of any norm. Instead of concentrating on such Inclusivist concerns, Dworkin has laid stress on the status of moral principles as legal norms that serve as grounds for judgments by legal officials in particular cases. According to him, positivists are unable to acknowledge that moral principles do partake of such a status in certain legal systems. Incorporationism has emerged as a juris-prudential doctrine directly in response to this throwing down of the gauntlet by Dworkin. Born of some important pioneering work by Philip Soper, and endorsed quite straightforwardly by Hart, Incorporationism has heretofore been most sustainedly and forcefully championed by Jules Coleman (who coined the appellation 'Incorporationism', though he has used it to cover Inclusive Legal Positivism as well and has recently abandoned the term in favor of the 'Inclusive' label).[7] By emphasizing that a Rule of Recognition can direct judges and other officials to invoke moral principles as binding legal touchstones for assessing the conduct of people, Coleman has essayed to accommodate Dworkin's strictures without accepting that any process of legal decision-making *must* involve a reliance on moral standards. While remaining a positivist, he has freely allowed that moral principles can be incorporated into the law as determinative bases for legal officials' decisions.

Exclusive Legal Positivism has likewise evolved in the context of Dworkin's challenges to positivist theorizing. However, instead of trying to accommodate and defuse those challenges by showing that the positivist model of law is consistent with the role of moral precepts as law-validating criteria or as legal norms, the Exclusivists have denied that moral precepts can play any such role. In other words, they have sought to rebut the Dworkinian challenge by arguing that moral principles cannot enter into the law; the operativeness of such principles in adjudication is not to be mistaken for their having become elements of the law. Joseph Raz is the leading advocate of this Exclusivist position, which he has adopted in support of his general conception of law's professed authoritativeness.

Though Exclusive Legal Positivism was originally in large part a rejoinder to Dworkin, it has become at least as much a rejoinder to Inclusive Legal Positivism and Incorporationism. Indeed, the debates over the philosophical merits of Exclusivism have in recent years been conducted almost entirely among legal positivists of differing stripes. Dworkin and his followers have not remained

---

[7] For Coleman's main contributions, see his *The Practice of Principle* (Oxford: Oxford University Press, 2001) [hereinafter cited as Coleman, *Practice*], chaps 6–10; 'Constraints on the Criteria of Legality', 6 *Legal Theory* 171 (2000); 'Incorporationism, Conventionality, and the Practical Difference Thesis', 4 *Legal Theory* 381 (1998); 'Second Thoughts and Other First Impressions', in Brian Bix (ed.), *Analyzing Law* (Oxford: Clarendon Press, 1998), 257, 258–78; 'Authority and Reason', in Robert George (ed.), *The Autonomy of Law* (Oxford: Clarendon Press, 1996), 287; 'Negative and Positive Positivism', in *Markets, Morals, and the Law* (Cambridge: Cambridge University Press, 1988), 3. For Soper's pioneering work in this area, see his 'Legal Theory and the Obligation of a Judge: The Hart/Dworkin Dispute', 75 *Michigan Law Review* 473, 509–15 (1977). For Hart's endorsement of Incorporationism, see Hart, 'Postscript', 265–6. For Coleman's recent abandonment of the 'Incorporationist' label, see Coleman, *Practice*, 67 n.3, 105 n.9.

wholly silent, of course,[8] but the more numerous and persistent battles have been fought among positivists rather than between them and their Dworkinian foes. Into those battles my first four chapters will plunge.

Whereas my third chapter will address some aspects of Raz's defense of Exclusivism, the first two chapters will concentrate instead on the defense of Exclusivism mounted during the past several years by Scott Shapiro. Though Shapiro is greatly indebted to Raz's seminal work, he has propounded some powerful and thought-provoking arguments of his own in furtherance of the Exclusivist cause. Those arguments improve upon Raz's lines of reasoning, in a key respect that makes Shapiro a more suitable target for my Inclusivist/Incorporationist rebuttals. After all, Raz's most interesting and complex efforts to vindicate his Exclusivist stance have been founded on his thesis that law invariably claims to be possessed of legitimate authority. Because I have elsewhere argued at length that that underlying thesis is false (*IDLP*, 78–112), the room for a rewarding engagement with Raz's Exclusivist lines of reasoning is quite limited. In regard to Shapiro, the situation is decidedly different. His commendable achievement has lain in marshaling arguments which are broadly similar to those of Raz but which do not depend on any attribution to law of an invariable claim-to-legitimate-authority. Instead, he has sought to reveal that an Inclusivist or Incorporationist Rule of Recognition is incompatible with the fulfillment of a function which virtually any legal positivist (including me) would ascribe to law: the function of guiding conduct. Were Shapiro's critiques of Incorporationism and Inclusivism correct, they would be very damaging indeed—since they would demonstrate that neither of those two doctrines can consistently be upheld by anyone who conceives of law's workings in the way in which nearly all Inclusivists and Incorporationists do. Accordingly, the task of repelling his critiques is of vital importance for anyone not enamored of either Exclusive Legal Positivism or natural-law theories.

Chapter 1 first defends Inclusive Legal Positivism against Shapiro's onslaughts, and then defends Incorporationism. As will become apparent, however, my defense of Incorporationism is directed against Coleman almost as much as against Shapiro. Although in most respects Coleman and I are allied in striving to deflect the Exclusivist blows that have been struck against Incorporationism— and although I am much indebted to his work—my discussion will maintain that his approach to the matter is regrettably misleading. Whereas Coleman dwells on the possibility of a legal system in which the only laws are incorporated moral principles, my discussion will highlight the credible possibility of legal systems in which the laws for dealing with hard cases are incorporated moral principles. To be sure, my drawing of this contrast between his extreme version of Incorporationism and my own moderate version does not amount to an outright rejection of his stance. On the contrary, as will be avowed and indeed stressed in my first

---

[8] See, e.g., Ronald Dworkin, 'Thirty Years On', 115 *Harvard Law Review* 1655 (2002).

few chapters, Coleman's extreme Incorporationism is correct. However, as will also be emphasized, the truth of his theses is accompanied by the misplacedness of their priorities and by their consequent unilluminatingness. Neither in response to Dworkin nor in response to Shapiro and Raz is it advisable for Incorporationists to resort to the boldness of Coleman's position. A milder version of Incorporationism will suffice to counter all the relevant challenges, and will illuminate the workings of credible legal systems. My discussion will not only defend Incorporationism, but will endeavor to ensure that it is a doctrine fully worth defending.

Chapter 2 expands on the arguments of the first chapter by replying to some criticisms from Shapiro and Coleman. Although retorts and counter-retorts would become wearisome if they were fixated upon minutiae, my replies to the criticisms by Shapiro and Coleman are concerned with major points of clarification and amplification rather than with tedious details. In addition to elaborating on my own Inclusivist and Incorporationist positions, the second chapter briefly contests Shapiro's understanding of Hart's ideas. Because of the immense importance of Hart's work for modern legal positivism, an effort to pin down the tenor of his pronouncements is a worthwhile enterprise. (For much the same reason, Chapter 5 will engage in a further exegetical effort relating to Hart's work—albeit in connection with a different set of specific issues.) To be sure, exegetical disputation never supplants philosophical argumentation. To establish that Hart did not hold a certain belief is hardly per se to establish that that belief is incorrect. Nevertheless, given that an unimpugned misattribution of a dubious view to Hart (by Shapiro) might itself lend some plausibility to the notion that that dubious view is integral to jurisprudential positivism, my rectification of the misattribution is a useful supplement to philosophical argumentation.

In any event, the main purpose of Chapter 2 is indeed to supply additional philosophical arguments in support of the Inclusivist and Incorporationist positions espoused in Chapter 1. My third chapter continues that endeavor, with an array of 'defensive' and 'offensive' lines of reasoning. In the aftermath of the first two chapters' ripostes to Shapiro, Chapter 3 examines some other Exclusivist attempts to expose the putative missteps of Inclusivism and Incorporationism. Whereas Raz has submitted that an Inclusivist or Incorporationist Rule of Recognition would be incompatible with law's claim to legitimate authority, and whereas Shapiro has contended that such a Rule of Recognition would be inconsistent with law's performance of its guiding function, Andrei Marmor maintains that any such Rule of Recognition would be at odds with the conventionality of law. Eleni Mitrophanous has joined in by arguing that an Inclusivist/ Incorporationist Rule of Recognition would give rise to a level of uncertainty that would preclude the existence of a genuine legal system. My third chapter addresses the challenges posed by Marmor and Mitrophanous, and it also parries some of Raz's queries. After those defensive maneuvers, the chapter proceeds to refine and amplify my Inclusivist/Incorporationist positions. It expands on an argument presented in Chapter 1 concerning the status of customary norms as legal norms, in order to underscore the superiority of Incorporationism over Exclusivism; and it adduces some additional considerations that favor my moderate rendering of Incorporationism over Coleman's extreme version. In short, the chapter pivotally strengthens the first main part of this book by reinforcing and extending the stands taken in the first two chapters.

Chapter 4 completes Part I by warding off the latest salvo from the Exclusivist camp. First, however, the chapter's opening main section reflects on some basic features of any Rule of Recognition. In particular, we shall probe the extent to which the Rule of Recognition in any legal system is uniform throughout the system, and we shall ponder two levels at which a Rule of Recognition can exist: a foundational level, and an epiphenomenal level. Armed with the analyses in that opening section, we shall then move on to investigate the latest Exclusivist broadside. In some long and sophisticated arguments, Kenneth Himma has submitted that neither Inclusivism nor Incorporationism is consistent with the role of the highest tribunal in any credible legal system. He maintains that, in light of that role, moral soundness cannot be either a necessary condition or a sufficient condition for the legal validity of any norm. Only what the highest tribunal does decide or would decide about the moral soundness of any norm N, rather than N's soundness or unsoundness itself, can ever be determinative of N's status as a law. So Himma reasons. My rejoinders vindicate Inclusive Legal Positivism and Incorporationism by revealing that Himma has overlooked the multiplicity and the hierarchical ordering of the criteria in any advanced Rule of Recognition. When the multiplicity and rankings of those criteria are kept in view, we can perceive that a norm's moral soundness or unsoundness can indeed be determinative of the status of the norm as a law or not. In so responding to Himma, my fourth chapter draws upon arguments advanced in the closing pages of my second chapter, where I highlight the ways in which the justificatory orientation of legal officials can fix the content of their Rule of Recognition. By reaffirming those arguments and expanding upon them, Chapter 4 shows that Inclusivism and Incorporationism are perfectly reconcilable with the fact that legal officials—including the judges on a legal system's highest tribunal—may often err in hard cases when arriving at moral determinations for the purpose of ascertaining the existence and contents of laws. Those officials in difficult cases can be adhering to an Inclusivist or Incorporationist criterion which they frequently misapply in such cases.

While the issues pondered in Part I of this volume may initially seem arcane, they in fact bear on many of the basic characteristics of any legal system. In the first place, Inclusivism and Incorporationism have been devised to undermine Dworkin's complaint that legal positivism cannot adequately account for the presence of moral principles in the law of some jurisdictions. Dworkin is quite correct in thinking that any satisfactory jurisprudential theory must be able to come up with a plausible account of that presence. He goes astray, however, by underestimating the resourcefulness of legal positivism—which, in its Inclusivist and Incorporationist forms, is able to explain perfectly well how moral principles can enter into the law. Each of those species of positivism can avoid the strained contortions to which the Exclusive Legal Positivists have to resort when confronting Dworkinian critiques. Having fended off Dworkin's assaults on legal positivism as a general theory, the Inclusivists and Incorporationists must likewise come to grips with the sundry objections pressed by the Exclusivists. According to those objections, the Inclusivists and Incorporationists cannot consistently acknowledge certain elementary properties of law: its claim to authoritativeness, its capacity to guide behavior, its conventionality, its regularity, its institutional stratification capped by some paramount tribunal(s). Countering the Exclusivist objections thus involves a reconsideration of each of those properties. Intrapositivist disputes between Exclusivists and Inclusivists/Incorporationists reach deeply into the layers of the conceptual structure that informs our legal and jurisprudential thought. Part I of this book will indeed plumb those layers, as it ventures to uphold the Hartian legacy by championing the variant of legal positivism that can best withstand Dworkin's onslaughts while not losing sight of any of law's essential features.

II. Once More unto the Breach

Chapters 1 to 4 mesh at least implicitly with legal positivism's insistence on the separability of law and morality. After all, Exclusivists maintain that law-ascertaining judgments and moral judgments are strictly separate rather than merely separable, whereas Inclusivists and Incorporationists hold that the two types of judgments are separable rather than inevitably separate. Indeed, largely because Inclusivism and Incorporationism tally so smoothly with the cardinal tenets of legal positivism, I throughout this book have opted for the nomenclature of 'Inclusivism' and 'Incorporationism' in preference to the phrase 'soft positivism' which Hart employed (Hart, 'Postscript', 250–4). Whatever Hart may have intended, his phrase suggests a watering down of the traditional message of legal positivism. Any such suggestion is wholly unwarranted, for—as will be observed in Chapter 7—it is Exclusivism, rather than Inclusivism or Incorporationism, that constitutes a departure from the main ideas associated with the positivist tradition. Inclusivism and Incorporationism stand firmly within that tradition by highlighting both the possibility and the contingency of some important connections between morality and law.

In Chapters 5 to 7, the positivist affirmation of the separability of law and morality is even more prominently present and more wide-ranging than in the first part of the book. Chapters 5 and 6 shift attention from the intrapositivist disputes of Part I to some of the chief points of contention around which the conflicts between positivists and their natural-law opponents have been waged.

Chapter 7 resumes the task of contesting some arguments put forward by legal positivists themselves, but it does so precisely in order to endorse the array of theses which positivists have typically advanced in opposition to natural-law theorists. On the whole, then, Part II is aimed at defending positivism against its enemies. Whereas Part I concentrates on selecting among the different versions of legal positivism that have vied with one another in recent years, Part II takes up the cudgels for the general legal-positivist project.

Chapter 5 presents a set of rejoinders to David Dyzenhaus's review of my book *In Defense of Legal Positivism*. Originally published in the journal that carried the review, my replies to Dyzenhaus have here been shorn of the more detailed points that were appropriate to that polemical context. The replies retained for my fifth chapter are concerned with major substantive matters. As has already been indicated, one portion of the chapter endeavors to correct Dyzenhaus's misreading of Hart's work. Most of my retorts to Dyzenhaus, however, are philosophical rather than exegetical. They focus in particular on his misunderstanding of the positivist model of law-ascertainment and his cognate misunderstanding of the positivist insistence on the separability of law and morality.

Of special significance for the insistence just mentioned is a distinction between the *actual motivations* of legal officials and the *reasons-for-action* that confront them. As will be seen, a failure to attend to that distinction has led Dyzenhaus to misconstrue my arguments concerning the factors that can underlie the adherence of legal officials to rule-of-law principles. The dichotomy between actual motivations and reasons-for-action is explored even more sustainedly in Chapter 6, which investigates the moralized conceptions of the rule of law that have been sophisticatedly propounded by Nigel Simmonds and by Soper (who are formidable foes not least because they are far from unremittingly unsympathetic to the legal-positivist enterprise). In Chapter 6, and indeed in Chapters 5 and 7 as well, the importance of discriminating among different senses or dimensions of morality will become manifest. Those different senses or dimensions yield distinct ways in which the rule of law has been presented by natural-law thinkers—including Simmonds and Soper—as morally pregnant. Of particular pertinence in this context are morality-contrasted-with-immorality and morality-contrasted-with-prudence. Some natural-law arguments have portrayed the rule of law as partaking of an inherent moral worthiness, while other such arguments have contended that the only perceptible reasons-for-action that militate in favor of legal officials' compliance with rule-of-law requirements are nonprudential. Chapter 6 will scrutinize and rebut several arguments of each of those types. While allowing that the rule of law is a necessary condition for the realization of some crucial moral desiderata, I shall deny that it is possessed of any intrinsic moral significance.

Whereas Chapters 5 and 6 grapple with a number of animadversions leveled at jurisprudential positivism by some of its leading adversaries, Chapter 7 will aim to dispel some misconceptions propagated by several positivists themselves. For decades, most people acquainted with jurisprudential schools of thought have presumed that the pith of legal positivism resides in an insistence on the separability of law and morality. In recent years, however, some notable legal positivists—Raz, Coleman, John Gardner, Leslie Green—have rejected or otherwise denigrated that insistence. In particular, they have characterized it as much less far-reaching than it is. My discussion of the matter will seek to vindicate the received understanding of legal positivism by bringing out the versatility and power of the positivist emphasis on the disjoinability of morality and law. Although the chapter's immediate tussles are with other legal positivists, its cardinal objective is to strengthen the case for positivism's jousting with natural-law theories. Such jousting is not worth the candle unless it has impelled the jurisprudential positivists to advance theses that are ambitious and sophisticated. I aspire to show that the positivist insistence on the separability of law and morality comprehends an array of just such theses.

To grasp fully where law and morality meet, one must also grasp where they remain divergent. Whereas Part I concentrates on the meeting points between the domain of law and the domain of morality, Part II concentrates on the divergences. By championing Inclusivism and Incorporationism, Part I lays stress on some conspicuous ways in which law and morality become intertwined; by impeaching a host of ostensibly ineluctable connections between morality and law, Part II has laid stress on some major ways in which the legal domain and the moral domain continue to be distinct. Together, those two portions of the book present the 'positive' and 'negative' sides of legal positivism. The 'positive' side consists in pinning down the general nature of processes of law-ascertainment and law-application. Of greatest interest in that theoretical endeavor, of course, is the matter of pinning down whether and how moral principles can enter into those processes. Only by adequately addressing themselves to that matter can positivists come up with satisfactorily precise analyses of the workings of legal systems. This 'positive' stream of their enterprise runs alongside their 'negative' efforts to confute moralized accounts of law. Those 'negative' efforts constitute the more familiar face of legal positivism in the wider jurisprudential world, but—as has already been suggested—they are closely linked to positivism's 'positive' aspect. In each case, the prime purpose is to establish the separability of law and morality. To establish as much is to oppugn not only natural-law theories but also Exclusive Legal Positivism; separability is contrary to necessary disjoinedness as well as to necessary connectedness. Different though Part I and Part II of this book are in their specific orientations, they are components of an overarching endeavor.

III. From Legal Philosophy to Moral Philosophy

The first seven chapters of this volume, especially the first four chapters, break new ground in a number of respects. They go well beyond the arguments of my previous book on legal positivism—where, for example, I said little about the ways in which moral principles can enter into the law as validative criteria or as substantive norms. Going even further beyond those arguments, however, is the present book's final chapter, which ponders some elements of the law-morality relationship that have heretofore received virtually no attention in my writings on that relationship.

Chapter 8 investigates the widespread view—articulated by Hart and countless others—that morality differs from law in being invariably under the sway of the 'ought'-implies-'can' principle. As will be contended, theorists such as Hart have gone astray in thinking that there is no counterpart of strict legal liability (that is, legal liability irrespective of fault) within the domain of morality. Indeed, in the moral realm, the impeccable reasonableness of a person's intentions and actions is never sufficient to excuse the person from the charge of having committed a wrong. If such reasonableness does not justify the person's actions—that is, if it does not render them fully permissible—then it only mitigates their wrongness without excusing the person altogether from a moral obligation to remedy the situation that has been brought about by those actions. As will be argued, departures from the 'ought'-implies-'can' principle are even more common in morality than in law. Still, those two domains prove to resemble each other in that each of them involves numerous situations that clearly call for strict liability. Notwithstanding the separability of law and morality, then, the affinities between them are more extensive than has generally been presumed.

Stemming from an initial analysis of the concepts of moral rights and moral obligations, my arguments in Chapter 8 lead through issues such as the distinction between excuses and justifications and the overlapping distinction between exoneration and extenuation. We shall also consider how the fulfillment of some moral obligations is morally impermissible, and we shall probe the dichotomy between prima-facie moral duties and all-things-considered moral duties. Not only do my arguments disclose some oft-obscured homologies between law and morality, but they also unearth some surprising dissimilarities. Most notably, whereas legal rights are frequently thought to be integrally connected to remedies ('No right without a remedy'), we shall find that an ineluctable connection lies instead between remedies and moral rights. An alertness to this point will enable us to perceive that law and morality are fundamentally alike in being resistant to the comprehensive sweep of the 'ought'-implies-'can' principle.

IV. Where Things Stand: A Brief Conclusion

Chapter 8, then, consummates the fluctuating trajectory of this book. Part I draws attention to the potential interaction between morality and law; Part II focuses chiefly on the potential disconnectedness of law and morality; and Part III returns to highlighting the affinities between those two normative domains (while also pointing out some divergences). This sinuous trajectory is in keeping with the message expressed by the volume's title. Although a staunchly legal-positivist outlook pervades the first seven chapters of this book, and although legal positivism is distinctively preoccupied with assailing any number of claims about necessary connections between law and morality, the contestation of those claims is not indiscriminate. Any minimally sensible proponent of positivism will have grasped that, in some obvious ways and in some more subtle ways, law and morality do intersect. To concede as much readily is to evince a correct under-standing of the implications of legal positivism's insistence on the disseverability of law and morality. What makes that disseverability so noteworthy is that it pertains to two normative realms which do share some salient features and which can become interwoven in complex patterns.

In its general emphasis on the separability of law and morality, the present volume stands in some evident respects as a sequel to my *In Defense of Legal Positivism*. In much of the present volume, however, the specific paths pursued are markedly different from those pursued by the earlier book. For one thing, *In Defense of Legal Positivism* contains hardly any discussions of the problems tackled in Parts I and III below. In that previous study, I said nothing about the 'ought'-implies-'can' principle or about the power of legal officials to depart from criteria in their Rule of Recognition through their commission of mistakes, and I said virtually nothing about the controversies between Inclusivists/Incor-porationists and Exclusivists. By contrast, those topics loom large here. Even Part II of this book, which more closely resembles my earlier study than do the other two main parts, will investigate several matters (such as the distinction between actual motivations and reasons-for-action) which I have not hitherto explored in depth. Likewise, while a few of the theorists whose work is critically examined here are people whose ideas I have lengthily challenged in the past—above all, Raz and Dworkin—most of the philosophers whose writings come under scru-tiny in this book, such as Shapiro, Coleman, Simmonds, Soper, Dyzenhaus, Marmor, Gardner, and Himma, are people with whose ideas I have heretofore engaged only fleetingly if at all. Thus, although the present volume and my previous book on legal positivism are unquestionably related, the distinctness of each of them is equally manifest. Together, the two of them aim to provide robust defenses of a multifaceted jurisprudential position that has too often been subject to distortion and incomprehension.

PART I

WHERE LAW AND MORALITY MEET

Legal Positivism and the Identification of Legal Norms

for legal validity in that overarching rule are not content-focused). Precisely on account of this lack of predetermination, each legal norm constitutes a partly independent reason for an official to arrive at the rulings which the norm requires. Were the norm different in content from what it is—as it easily could have been, even within the confines of a single Rule of Recognition—the results for which the norm calls would be different. Hence, the fact that any given law does have some particular content is a basis for decisions that goes beyond any basis contained in the Rule of Recognition itself. Because that content is not preordained by the Rule of Recognition, it plays a genuinely determinative role rather than a merely encapsulatory role. Whereas the outcomes required by an Incorporationist Rule of Recognition *R1* on its own are always the same as those required by the moral principles that are validated as laws by *R1*, the outcomes required by a non-Incorporationist Rule of Recognition *R2* will hinge crucially on the norms that are validated as laws (on content-independent grounds) under *R2*. Unlike the moral principles validated as laws by an Incorporationist Rule of Recognition, then, the laws validated under a non-Incorporationist Rule of Recognition make a real difference by dint of their interposition between the ultimate criteria of law-ascertainment and the concrete decisions of adjudicators and administrators. The substance of those laws will weigh against some outcomes and in favor of others.

What is the importance of this distinction between the Incorporationist and non-Incorporationist Rules of Recognition? Shapiro contends that the distinction is of the utmost importance because of the basic role that is ascribed to law by H.L.A. Hart and most other legal positivists: the role of presenting people with norms that can guide and direct their conduct. Moral principles validated as laws under an Incorporationist Rule of Recognition cannot supply the requisite guidance. Legal norms that do not constitute any independent reasons for or against specific decisions are thereby devoid of any capacity to affect the balance of reasons that will confront the officials who might invoke the norms. Such norms in this context are empty shells, rather than considerations that should enter into a rational weighing of the factors which favor or disfavor particular outcomes. Under an Incorporationist Rule of Recognition *R1*, *R1* alone is what decisively affects the balance of reasons for the officials. It alone poses veritable reasons-for-action. Moral principles validated as laws under *R1* might serve as heuristic aids for the task of finding out exactly what *R1* requires, but they do not themselves require anything else. Officials whose reasons-for-action derive from *R1* do not gain any further reasons-for-action from the correct moral principles which they apply thereunder. Their deliberations, if rational, therefore assign no weight to those principles—which means that the principles in themselves do not guide and direct the officials' decision-making processes at all. And because those principles do not perform any directive role in connection with the officials' reaching of outcomes, they likewise cannot perform any such role in connection with the behavior of ordinary citizens. Whether the citizens are directly familiar with the nature of the officials' law-ascertaining endeavors, or whether they obtain their familiarity (if any) through intermediaries such as lawyers and the press, the moral principles validated as laws under *R1* will present the citizens with no reasons-for-action that have not already been presented to them by *R1* itself. As reason-giving guides to conduct, then, those principles/laws are utterly redundant.

Such is the gist of Shapiro's critique of Incorporationism. Now, although the second half of this chapter will raise significant doubts about the devastatingness of his critique, the basic correctness of his arguments against Incorporationism is not in question here. On the contrary, the soundness of those arguments is one principal factor underlying my wary attitude toward certain varieties of Incorporationism. Strikingly in contrast with those impressive arguments, however, is his effort to wield his critique against Inclusive Legal Positivism after having wielded it against the Incorporationist doctrine. When his target shifts to the Inclusivist thesis that conformity with a moral principle can be a necessary condition (as opposed to a sufficient condition) for the status of a norm as a legal norm, his critique becomes otiose. His attack on Inclusive Legal Positivism appears to broach two chief objections, neither of which succeeds.

Shapiro first submits or appears to submit that Inclusive Legal Positivism runs afoul of the same general difficulties that beset Incorporationism. Asking whether Hart could legitimately have adopted the Inclusivist position—as opposed to the Incorporationist position—Shapiro declares that 'he could not and for much... the same reasons that felled [Incorporationism]' (Shapiro, 'Way', 501). He goes on to affirm: 'Because someone who is guided by a rule of recognition that makes morality a necessary condition of legal validity can be neither epistemically nor motivationally guided by a rule supposedly validated by it, we must conclude that Hart cannot coherently embrace... inclusive legal positivism'. Shapiro then straightaway remarks that 'this argument is similar, but not identical, to the objection that was made against [Incorporationism]. The claim made here is not that a rule supposedly validated by an inclusive rule of recognition that made morality a necessary condition on legality cannot make a practical difference. The problem is that such a rule cannot make a practical difference *in the way that* rules are supposed to make practical differences' (Shapiro, 'Way', 502, emphasis in original). We shall shortly explore the claim advanced in this last quotation. Before turning to that claim, however, this chapter should counter any lingering suggestion that Inclusive Legal Positivism and Incorporationism are essentially on a par in the face of Shapiro's arguments.

Shapiro's key insight in his critique of Incorporationism is that an Incorporationist Rule of Recognition will preordain any concrete decisions that are properly reached thereunder. Such a Rule of Recognition will therefore render superfluous (except as heuristic aids) any intermediate moral principles which it validates as legal norms. Those norms and those concrete decisions cannot be other than what they are, inasmuch as they emerge under the sway of a Rule of

Recognition that calls for the application of correct moral principles. Everything is fixed from the outset, so long as that Rule of Recognition endures. And precisely because the contents and implications of the legally incorporated moral principles are fixed from the outset, those principles themselves do not furnish any additional reasons for officials to arrive at certain decisions. Nor do they furnish any additional reasons for citizens to adjust their behavior in certain ways. Both for officials and for citizens, the reasons-for-action created by the law in an Incorporationist regime are created entirely by the regime's Rule of Recognition. Intermediate legal norms play no independently determinative role whatsoever.

As Shapiro contends, an Incorporationist legal system is static in that its Rule of Recognition settles everything in advance. As he appositely states, there is no 'elbow room' in such a system (Shapiro, 'Way', 498). That is, insofar as judges strictly adhere to an Incorporationist Rule of Recognition, there is no room for them to adopt intermediate legal norms or to reach concrete legal decisions other than those norms and decisions that are morally requisite. Very different indeed is any Inclusivist Rule of Recognition. Far from preordaining all laws and decisions *ab initio*, such a Rule of Recognition leaves an abundance of 'elbow room'. Although it demands that laws and decisions be consistent with specified moral precepts, the congruence between the laws/decisions and the precepts is merely a threshold condition rather than a content-settling feature. Because that congruence can be adequately achieved through any of a myriad of diverse measures, the Inclusivist Rule of Recognition does not in itself select among those measures. That selection comes about through statutes or judicial doctrines or other legal norms, which consequently do provide reasons for officials to arrive at certain decisions and to eschew alternative decisions.

Let us ponder, for example, the Inclusivist Rule of Recognition depicted by Shapiro. Suppose that judges are empowered and obligated to apply any Congressional enactment unless it is grossly unfair (Shapiro, 'Way', 501). Suppose further that a minimum wage of one dollar per hour in the present-day United States would be grossly unfair to workers, and that a minimum wage of fifteen dollars per hour (for menial work) would be grossly unfair to employers. Minimum-wage levels between those two figures will not be grossly unfair. Against this background, Congress enacts a law requiring every employer to pay at least *eight* dollars per hour to every employee. In the aftermath of that enactment, the decisions of adjudicative and executive officials and their effects on citizens' behavior will diverge quite notably from the corresponding decisions and effects that would be taking place if Congress had instead enacted a law requiring every employer to pay at least *four* dollars per hour. Because of the statute requiring at least eight dollars, and only because of that statute, the officials are empowered and obligated to treat the eight-dollar level as the minimum acceptable hourly wage. Their Inclusivist Rule of Recognition in itself does not single out that level at all. Rather, the only relevant inference derivable from their Rule of Recognition is that the minimum wage in the current American economy has to lie somewhere between one dollar and fifteen dollars per hour. The eight-dollar level is in no way preordained. Had Congress passed a statute specifying six dollars, the minimum hourly wage would accordingly have been at the six-dollar level; and it would have been at the nine-dollar level if a statute specifying nine dollars had been passed. Precisely because the Inclusivist Rule of Recognition allows these and numerous other significant variations in the level of the statutory requirement, it does not predetermine specific outcomes. Those outcomes ensue instead from the changeable legislation which Congress enacts. Hence, unlike a legal system with a thoroughly Incorporationist Rule of Recognition, a legal system with an Inclusivist Rule of Recognition is not static. Legal norms validated under the latter Rule of Recognition can play a guiding and directing role. This point applies, of course, not only to the particular example of minimum-wage laws but also to the whole range of matters that might be regulated by statutes or other legal norms.

Although Shapiro does not explicitly acknowledge the point made in my preceding paragraph, and although he puts forth a few pronouncements that seem to bespeak a contrary view, he might not disagree with anything that has just been said. As was intimated four paragraphs ago, the gravamen of his argument against Inclusive Legal Positivism is quite different from his critique of Incorporationism. Here his complaint is not that legal norms validated under an Inclusivist Rule of Recognition will fail to constitute any independent reasons for officials' concrete decisions. His complaint, rather, is that the reasons constituted by those norms do not partake of the exclusionary or peremptory force that is characteristic of genuinely authoritative directives. He states his accusation forthrightly, with reference to the example of the minimum-wage statute:

Can the minimum-wage rule...motivationally guide a judge? The answer to this question is...'no.' Recall that a rule motivationally guides conduct when it is taken as a peremptory reason for action; it follows that a rule cannot motivationally guide if the agent is required to deliberate about the merits of applying the rule. As the application of the minimum-wage rule depends, pursuant to the inclusive rule of recognition, on the employer first assessing whether the rule is grossly unfair, he cannot treat the rule as a peremptory reason for action and hence cannot be motivationally guided by it. (Shapiro, 'Way', 501)

Shapiro recapitulates his argument in a passage that has already been partly quoted herein: 'The problem is that [a norm validated as a law under an Inclusivist Rule of Recognition] cannot make a practical difference *in the way that* rules are supposed to make practical differences: if the agent is required to determine whether the rule ought to be followed on the merits, then it can count neither as an epistemic tool for authoritative designation nor as a peremptory reason for action' (Shapiro, 'Way', 502).

Shapiro presumes that, if ascertaining the existence of a legal norm will perforce involve some moral judgments, then the norm cannot amount to a peremptory reason for action. Such a position, based on Geoffrey Warnock's and Joseph Raz's conception of mandatory norms as exclusionary reasons (a conception which Hart appropriated in his discussion of laws as peremptory reasons for action[3]), has disregarded Raz's observations concerning possible restrictions on the scope of any particular reason's exclusionary or peremptory force. On the one hand, by virtue of being an exclusionary reason, a legal mandate disallows certain considerations as legitimate bases for decisions or actions. The excluded considerations no longer properly count as factors that should be deemed to weigh against or for the mode of conduct which the mandate requires or forbids. On the other hand, an exclusionary reason will almost never be of such overriding importance that it disallows *all* countervailing factors as legitimate bases for decisions and actions. In almost every instance, the peremptory sway of a norm is limited. As Raz writes: 'It should be remembered that exclusionary reasons may vary in scope; they may exclude all or only some of the reasons which apply to certain practical problems. There may, for example, be some scope-affecting considerations to the effect that though Colin's promise [to act only in furtherance of the well-being of his son] apparently purports to exclude all the reasons not affecting his son's interests it does not in fact validly exclude consideration of justice to other people.'[4] So long as an exclusionary reason removes *some* factors from a balance of considerations that can be legitimately acted upon, it need not remove *all* such factors. Restrictions on the scope of a peremptory reason are fully compatible with its nature as such a reason, as Leslie Green has remarked:

Such reasons may be both prima facie, in the sense that they are not conclusive about what ought to be done, and at the same time categorical. The fact that they exclude and not merely outweigh reasons for not-ϕ-ing makes them categorical; the fact that they may not exclude all contrary reasons makes them prima facie. Thus the force of such commitments depends... [on] the scope of the reasons against ϕ-ing which they exclude.[5]

A legal norm can partake of peremptoriness even if it disqualifies only some countervailing concerns, rather than all countervailing concerns, as reasons for legitimately acting at variance with the norm's demands. Its peremptoriness consists in the fact that it does disqualify certain counterbalancing considerations. The fact that the norm does not disqualify certain other counterbalancing considerations is a matter that affects only the *scope*, and not the *existence*, of its peremptoriness.

Let us now re-examine the scenario which Shapiro discusses. The non-exclusion of gross unfairness—the non-exclusion of it as a factor that will militate against the status of a norm as a legal norm—is perfectly consistent with the

---

[3] H.L.A. Hart, *Essays on Bentham* (Oxford: Oxford University Press, 1982), chap. 10.
[4] Joseph Raz, *Practical Reason and Norms* (Princeton: Princeton University Press, 1990) (2nd edn), 40.
[5] Leslie Green, *The Authority of the State* (Oxford: Clarendon Press, 1988), 39.

exclusion of numerous other factors. For instance, a judge will be neither authorized nor obligated to depart from the terms of a minimum-wage statute simply because he thinks those terms are unfair (as opposed to grossly unfair). Though the gross unfairness of the statute is an operative consideration that must be taken into account by the judge as he gauges the statute's legal force, the mere unfairness of the statute is not such a consideration. It is excluded by the Rule of Recognition which instead makes gross unfairness the pertinent touchstone. Even more plainly excluded as a basis for the judge's decisions is the mere unwisdom of the statute. A judge who regards the minimum-wage statute as inadvisable but not as grossly unfair is forbidden to nullify the statute on the basis of his opinion about the legislature's unwisdom. (Indeed, even if he does view the statute as grossly unfair, his invalidation of it must be premised solely on that ground and not on the ground of the legislature's unwisdom.) His Rule of Recognition, which obligates him to give effect to duly enacted statutes unless they are grossly unfair, will have disallowed him from acting upon his view of the statute's sheer imprudence. Insofar as he adheres to that Rule of Recognition, he does not let statutory imprudence count as a factor that will incline him to strike down statutory requirements. He does not permit his views about the unwisdom of an enactment to inflect his official decisions about the enactment's jural status.

Hence, Shapiro errs when he submits that the legal mandates validated under an Inclusivist Rule of Recognition cannot guide people's behavior in a peremptory fashion. Those mandates do exclude a range of factors as legitimate reasons for failing to abide by the mandates' requirements. To be sure, they do not exclude *all* such factors; for example, within the Rule of Recognition portrayed by Shapiro, gross unfairness is not excluded as a reason for nullifying legislative enactments. However, as we have seen, the peremptory force of a legal norm is fully compatible with the fact that not all concerns and considerations have been ruled out as bases for invalidating the norm. The noncomprehensiveness of a law's exclusionary sway is a restriction on the *scope* of that sway rather than a negation of its very *existence* and *nature* as such.

Shapiro's critique is warranted in application to Incorporationism, but not in application to Inclusive Legal Positivism. Although a legal norm's capacity to provide reasons-for-action (beyond those provided by the prevailing Rule of Recognition) is stymied when the norm's correctness as a moral precept is a *sufficient* condition for its status as a law, that capacity is not thwarted at all when a norm's conformity with moral precepts is a *necessary* condition for its status as a law. Shapiro's challenges have left Inclusive Legal Positivism unscathed.

II. Incorporationism Revisited

Given that Incorporationism is subject to Shapiro's deft critique, we might wonder why anyone has been led to adopt the Incorporationist position. Why have Coleman and Philip Soper been prepared to affirm that a legal system can be structured by a Rule of Recognition which effectively establishes that correctness as a moral precept is sufficient to render a norm binding as a law? Why have they been prepared to accept that such a test for legal bindingness can even be the only such test in a particular legal regime? This book's Introduction has suggested the answer. Both Coleman and Soper are replying to the anti-positivist strictures of Ronald Dworkin, who has maintained that positivists cannot adequately account for the salience of moral principles in adjudication. Although some of Dworkin's objections have been aimed at Inclusive Legal Positivism, his most famous criticisms are those to which Incorporationism is a riposte.

According to Dworkin, positivism is belied by the fact that judges sometimes apply moral principles as binding laws even though the principles lack any clear-cut origins in statutes or administrative decisions or judicial opinions. Now, a natural response for somebody confronted with such a line of criticism is to contend that the positivist model of law can perfectly well accommodate the tendency of judges in some regimes to treat moral principles as legal norms. What Coleman and others have argued is that the sheer conventionality of a Rule of Recognition does not perforce impose any constraints on the substance of that complex rule's criteria. 'There is nothing in [the general notion of the Rule of Recognition] that imposes any constraints on the conditions of validity. The Incorporationist sees no reason for assuming that these conditions cannot in principle include criteria making moral value or merit a condition of legality, at least for some norms. For the Incorporationist, what matters in the rule of recognition is not the criteria of validity set forth, but its existence conditions.'[6] As Coleman reiterates: 'The key move for the Incorporationist is the claim that positivism imposes no constraint on the criteria of validity. Whether a particular rule of recognition does so depends on the practice of officials' (Coleman, 'Incorporationism', 407). A robust Incorporationist, then, is keen to stress that the processes of law-ascertainment in any given regime might render moral worthiness the lone sufficient condition for legal validity.

Before we probe the Incorporationist rejoinder to Dworkin any further, we should note two preliminary points. First, none of my arguments in support of Inclusive Legal Positivism has implied that any moral criterion in this or that Rule of Recognition must be expressed in some explicit form such as a statute or a constitutional provision or a judicial opinion. Whether officials apply moral principles as necessary conditions for legal validity is entirely a matter of the officials' law-ascertaining behavior; furthermore, whether the relevant patterns of their behavior derive from written sources of law, or whether instead they derive from largely unarticulated (and perhaps subconscious) preconceptions that inform the officials' activities, is a contingent matter that can vary from one

---

[6] Jules Coleman, 'Incorporationism, Conventionality, and the Practical Difference Thesis', 4 *Legal Theory* 381, 406–7 (1998) [hereinafter cited as Coleman, 'Incorporationism'].

Inclusivist legal system to the next. Thus, there is no warrant at all for presuming that the law-ascertaining criteria in the Inclusivist model of a jural system must be rooted in overt sources. An Inclusive Legal Positivist should readily allow that moral principles can figure in adjudication without being rooted in such sources. (Of course, Dworkin's early critiques of positivism are focused chiefly on source-less moral principles that are validated as laws by dint of their content, rather than on sourceless moral principles that are applied as necessary conditions for legal validity. However, this paragraph's discussion of moral principles in their latter role is transferable, *mutatis mutandis*, to such principles in their former role.)

A second preliminary point relates to Coleman's unduly broad formulations of his central Incorporationist thesis. Coleman writes too sweepingly when he maintains that legal positivism does not presuppose any limits on the substance of the criteria that can make up a Rule of Recognition.[7] Let us think, for example, about a fanciful society that is under the sway of officials who settle disputes by applying norms that are selected through the throwing of dice. Each official justifies his selection of norms by reference to the numbers on the dice, and each expects his fellow officials to do the same. The officials perceive themselves as adhering to a Rule of Recognition that empowers and obligates them to resolve disputes through norms that emerge from their dice-throwing efforts rather than from any other sources of law. Now, because the throwing of fair dice over time will generate numbers randomly, and because the officials' regime does not contain any other law-ascertaining criteria that might foster uniformity, the directives of the officials will be a bewilderingly higgledy-piggledy welter of conflicting signals. Unless legal positivists are comfortable with designating such a regime as a legal system, they ought to insist that there are in fact some constraints on the sorts of criteria that can form a Rule of Recognition. No such rule can consist solely of criteria that fail to secure the minimum of regularity which is prerequisite to the existence of a legal system.

In sum, Coleman's pronouncements on the elasticity of the criteria in any Rule of Recognition are excessively far-reaching statements of a thesis that should more confinedly be about the potential focus of such criteria on moral correct-ness. We therefore have to ask whether a thoroughly Incorporationist Rule of Recognition can generate enough regularity to enable the existence of a legal system. This question is a key component of our broader enquiry into the adequacy of the Incorporationist reply to Dworkin. Let us straightaway note that this question concerning regularity does indeed pertain to the *existence* of legal systems and not merely to their *efficiency*. Coleman sometimes draws too sharp a distinction between effectiveness and existence, as in the following passage:

---

[7] For similar pronouncements, see David Lyons, 'Principles, Positivism, and Legal Theory', 87 *Yale Law Journal* 415, 423–6 (1977).

We need to distinguish between law's possibility and its efficacy. Positivists insist on law's conventionality as essential to our understanding its possibility. The claim that law is made possible by a rule of recognition that supervenes on a practice accepted from an internal point of view is a conceptual claim; it states possibility or existence conditions. It does not matter, for these purposes, whether the rule of recognition is controversial and, if so, how controversial it is.

On the other hand, a rule of recognition's efficiency varies with its controversiality. No positivist believes that it does not matter whether the rule of recognition is controversial. It is just that if controversy matters, it matters from the point of view of law's efficacy, not from the point of view of law's possibility. (Coleman, 'Incorporationism', 412)

Unquestionably, the concepts of efficiency and existence are neither intensionally nor extensionally equivalent—which is why we can correctly talk about inefficient legal systems. Instead of having to hold that such institutions are not legal systems at all, we can rightly hold that they are legal systems which do not operate very well. Nevertheless, although the states of efficiency and existence are plainly not identical, they are not as straightforwardly separable as Coleman implies in the passage above.

A fairly substantial degree of regularity is essential not just for the efficiency of a legal regime, but also for its very existence as such. Severe disaccord among the countless decisions of officials will not only disrupt the smoothness of their regime's workings, but will also deprive those workings of the minimum of cohesion that is necessary for any scheme of legal governance. A jural system in its operations will have obtained as a jural system only by partaking of consistency in considerable measure. For an expression of this point, we can resort to a comment made by Coleman just a couple of pages before the passage quoted above: 'Judges may agree about what the [Rule of Recognition] is but disagree with one another over what the rule requires—especially in controversial cases. They could not disagree in every case or even in most cases, as such broad and widespread disagreement would render unintelligible their claim to be applying or following the same rule' (Coleman, 'Incorporationism', 410). Hart advanced a basically similar observation, with reference to the need for officials to uphold the various norms of their legal regime:

Individual courts of the system though they may, on occasion, deviate from [its] rules must, in general, be critically concerned with such deviations as lapses from standards, which are essentially common or public. This is not merely a matter of the efficiency or health of the legal system, but is logically a necessary condition of our ability to speak of the existence of a single legal system. If only some judges acted 'for their part only' on the footing that what the Queen in Parliament enacts is law, and made no criticisms of those who did not respect this rule of recognition, the characteristic unity and continuity of a legal system would have disappeared. For this depends on the acceptance, at this crucial point, of common standards of legal validity. In the interval between these vagaries of judicial behaviour and the chaos which would ultimately ensue when the ordinary man was faced with contrary judicial orders, we would be at a loss to describe the situation. We would be in the presence of a *lusus naturae* worth thinking about only because it sharpens our awareness of what is often too obvious to be noticed.[8]

In short, a legal system must pass a certain threshold of regularity in its workings if it is to exist as a legal system at all.[9] Above that threshold, the system will be functional and efficient to a greater or a lesser extent. Below that threshold, however, it will be nonexistent—that is, nonexistent as a legal system—rather than merely inefficient. Lon Fuller was quite correct to insist as much. (Of course, if we attempt to specify the threshold of functionality precisely, we shall encounter the difficulties faced by anyone who tackles a sorites problem. Still, our inability to pinpoint the threshold does not detract at all from my current line of argument about the qualitative difference between a legal system characterized by a significant measure of regularity and a putative legal system characterized by very extensive irregularity. Though night and day shade into each other through dawn and dusk, they remain as different as night and day.)

Let us now return to the question that is our principal concern at this stage of my overall enquiry. Will an Incorporationist Rule of Recognition yield enough cohesion and uniformity to render possible the existence of a legal system? Clearly, any answer to this question must rely on one or two general empirical premises, however uncontroversial they might be. Unlike Shapiro's critique of Incorporationism—a critique with which this chapter has not yet entirely finished—my discussion of the operational regularity or irregularity of Incorporationist law-ascertaining criteria is not purely conceptual, even though it can aptly proceed at a high level of abstraction. (Specifically, my discussion will rest on an empirical premise relating to the ineliminability of widespread disagreement about the appropriateness of various ways of dealing with moral problems.) Moreover, the question posed here will oblige us to clarify the contours of an Incorporationist Rule of Recognition. We should first consider an uncompromisingly robust version which establishes that moral worthiness is the *lone* sufficient condition for the status of any norm as a legal norm; in a jural system that is oriented toward such a criterion, every legal judgment is a moral judgment through and through. Then we should consider a milder Incorporationist Rule of Recognition which establishes that moral worthiness is a sufficient condition for the status of norms as legal norms in hard cases that cannot be resolved by reference to legal norms from other sources. As will be seen, Incorporationism of this milder variety should be wholeheartedly embraced.

In a regime where judges and other officials adhere to the robust version of the Incorporationist Rule of Recognition, their ostensible law-ascertaining activities

---

[8] H. L. A. Hart, *The Concept of Law* (Oxford: Clarendon Press, 1961), 112–13 [hereinafter cited as Hart, *Concept*].

[9] I have emphasized this point in several of my previous writings. See especially my *In Defense of Legal Positivism* (Oxford: Oxford University Press, 1999) [hereinafter cited as *IDLP*], 140–6.

will very likely partake of too little regularity to be properly classifiable as law-ascertainment. Such a Rule of Recognition instructs officials to handle every case by applying the moral norms that produce the optimal result in the circumstances. Although a system along these lines will leave some room for officials to pursue a certain degree of consistency among their decisions, there are ample reasons for thinking that the consistency in practice will be meager.[10] Let us ponder two main aspects of the situation.

First, because a thoroughly Incorporationist regime encompasses no sources of law other than the realm of moral principles, any potential touchstones for official decision-making that stem from alternative sources are not systematically treated by such a regime as authoritative. In other words, those potential touchstones are not systematically deemed to be reasons-for-action which can be dispositive independently of their substantive worthiness. If the regime's officials were systematically to ascribe content-independent dispositiveness to standards from some source(s), then they would not be adhering to a robustly Incorporationist Rule of Recognition. They would instead be adhering to ordinary law-ascertaining criteria—that is, non-Incorporationist criteria—and would simply be upholding those criteria on the basis of the moral precepts that are validated and applied directly as laws by a truly Incorporationist regime. If a robustly Incorporationist Rule of Recognition is at all distinctive, and if it is therefore more than a misleadingly labeled justificatory platform for an ordinary Rule of Recognition, it will involve nothing else than the systematic invocation and application of moral principles on content-dependent grounds. Officials in a robustly Incorporationist regime focus exclusively on the appropriate substantive resolutions of cases, rather than on formal or procedural earmarks. To be sure, as has been avouched above, many of the officials in such a regime will still undoubtedly endeavor to attain at least a modicum of consistency in their rulings, in the way of typical moral agents. Expectations that might be bred by past decisions will form part of the context in which any present decisions are made. Nevertheless, if the officials' Rule of Recognition is genuinely and comprehensively Incorporationist, any consistency among their judgments cannot derive from systematic attentiveness to the manner in which the norms applied by those judgments have been established. Precisely on account of this aspect of any uncompromisingly Incorporationist regime, the consentaneity among the multifarious determinations of the officials therein will almost certainly be low.

A second main point to be contemplated here has been emphasized not only by Hart but also by the great early modern philosophers who depicted a 'state of nature' that antecedes the political institutions of full-fledged societies. Although one key feature of centrally governed societies that distinguishes them from acephalous groupings is the existence of mechanisms for authoritative dispute-resolution, another such feature is the existence of publicly ascertainable legal

---

[10] My view here is largely similar to that presented in Joseph Raz, *supra* note 4, at 137–41.

norms by reference to which the dispute-resolution can proceed. A robustly Incorporationist regime will possess the former of these features but not the latter. As a result, it will suffer from the severe problems of uncertainty and irregularity that have been highlighted by Hart and others in relation to primitive societies. Perhaps those problems can remain within manageable limits in a very small and static and highly homogeneous social unit, where moral attitudes are widely shared. However, in any large and dynamic and heterogeneous society, the problems of moral disunity are bound to be grave indeed unless they are overmastered through the erection of a publicly ascertainable set of norms to regulate conduct. Thus, since a comprehensively Incorporationist Rule of Recognition renders every legal judgment a moral judgment, and since a regime structured by such a Rule of Recognition will therefore not subordinate any moral dissension to publicly ascertainable legal norms, it almost inevitably will be a shuddersomely fractionated regime in which the officials reach numerous clashing decisions and send out numerous clashing signals. To be sure, as has already been granted, the officials will very likely make some efforts to coordinate their decisions. However, they will not be adhering to a fully Incorporationist Rule of Recognition unless they focus persistently on substantive moral issues. In connection with those issues, the need for coordination is just one ancillary consideration among many. Consequently, the officials' adherence to a thoroughly Incorporationist Rule of Recognition will virtually ensure that their mode of governance lacks the regularity essential for the existence of a legal system.

A natural retort to the points made in the last couple of paragraphs is that the moral injunctions which constitute a robustly Incorporationist Rule of Recognition will direct the relevant legal officials to promote stability by assigning content-independent dispositiveness to their past decisions and pronouncements. A rejoinder along these lines may well be correct, but it simply highlights the unsustainability (indeed, the self-subverting unsustainability) of such a Rule of Recognition. After all, if the rejoinder is correct, it implies that the officials in a thoroughly Incorporationist regime will be morally obligated to effect a transition to a regime that is not thoroughly Incorporationist. That is, the officials are obligated under their robustly Incorporationist Rule of Recognition—a highly ephemeral Rule of Recognition—to embrace non-Incorporationist criteria for law-ascertainment, which direct them to treat their own past decisions and pronouncements as binding sources of law. The officials achieve smoothly coordinated operations of decision-making in accordance with their Incorporationist Rule of Recognition, but only by transforming and abandoning it. Exactly this respect in which an unremittingly Incorporationist standard for law-ascertainment may quickly lead to its own demise is what my penultimate paragraph above has sought to convey by indicating that such a standard can serve as a justificatory platform for the adoption of a non-Incorporationist Rule of Recognition. The state of affairs that arises from such a platform is of course not a thoroughly Incorporationist regime that is stable. Rather, although the resultant regime may very well be stable, it is not thoroughly Incorporationist at all. Instabilities have been curbed precisely because a partly or wholly non-Incorporationist Rule of Recognition has supplanted the unrelievedly Incorporationist Rule of Recognition that gave birth to it. The former has superseded the latter, on the basis of the very moral concerns that are central to the latter.

In sum, either the absence of formal sources of law in a robustly Incorporationist regime will give rise to severe irregularity that negates the very character of the regime as a system of law, or else it will lead to the replacement of the regime by a partly or wholly non-Incorporationist system that does encompass formal sources such as past decisions and pronouncements. In either case, a thoroughly Incorporationist system of law will have proved untenable. Its only way of averting the onset of crippling irregularity is to empower and obligate its officials to transform their system of law into something that is not thoroughly Incorporationist.[11]

Now, before going on to examine the milder version of the Incorporationist Rule of Recognition, we should briefly consider a couple of points that strengthen my arguments concerning the thoroughgoing version. In the first place, nothing in the last several paragraphs has presupposed the indeterminacy of answers to moral questions. Everything said here can tally with the view that each moral problem addressed by Incorporationist officials is a problem to which there is a uniquely correct solution. Although such a view is of course not entailed by the arguments in my last several paragraphs, it can perfectly well square with them. What has been presupposed by those arguments is not the *indeterminacy* of moral truth-values, but the frequent *indemonstrability* and attendant *controversiality* thereof.[12] That is, although each moral problem tackled by Incorporationist officials may lend itself to a uniquely correct solution, the unique correctness frequently cannot be demonstrated in a way that will elicit widespread agreement. Regardless of the existence of objectively right answers, controversy will

---

[11] The past four paragraphs have been aimed principally against Philip Soper, 'Legal Theory and the Obligation of a Judge: The Hart/Dworkin Dispute', 75 *Michigan Law Review* 473, 512 n.129 (1977) [hereinafter cited as Soper, 'Legal Theory']. For a perceptive rejoinder to the first two of the four paragraphs, see Philip Soper, *The Ethics of Deference* (Cambridge: Cambridge University Press, 2002), 93–4. Soper and I agree that any viable legal system will attach great importance to content-independent considerations of consistency. We arrive at divergent conclusions, however. I conclude that no thoroughly Incorporationist legal system will be viable, since any such system would attach only ancillary importance to considerations of consistency. By contrast, Soper denies that a thoroughly Incorporationist legal regime will attach only ancillary importance to considerations of consistency, and he therefore concludes that such a regime can be quite viable. My expanded argument here against his view is amplified below when I discuss the role of citizens' expectations. My position is indirectly borne out by the discussion of the similarities and dissimilarities between legal reasoning and moral reasoning in Peter Cane, *Responsibility in Law and Morality* (Oxford: Hart Publishing, 2002), 16–21.

[12] This distinction has long been emphasized by Dworkin. For one of his best and most recent discussions of the matter, see his 'Objectivity and Truth: You'd Better Believe It', 25 *Philosophy & Public Affairs* 87, 129–39 (1996).

abound irrepressibly. My arguments about the robust version of Incorporation-ism do presume that very significant moral disagreements ensuing from people's diverse perspectives are ineliminable; however, my discussion does not have to affirm (or deny) that those disagreements are matched by the indeterminacy of any moral propositions' truth-values.

The potential role of citizens' expectations is a further point to be mulled over here. As was noted above, those expectations are some of the background circumstances that form the settings for Incorporationist officials' choices of moral principles. A defender of thoroughgoing Incorporationism might accordingly submit that the moral significance of protecting people's legitimate expectations is sufficient to induce conscientious Incorporationist officials to strive for considerable regularity in their law-ascertaining activities. Neverthe-less, any such rejoinder to my arguments would run afoul of three principal snags.

First, one of the very inquiries that will occasion moral controversy in an Incorporationist scheme of things is whether the particular expectations harbored by citizens are indeed legitimate. Answers to any such inquiry concerning particular expectations will vie with one another amid the general moral disunity (and thus the general legal disunity) of an Incorporationist regime. Far from standing outside the moral fractiousness of such a regime, questions about the legitimacy of specific expectations will be a source and an object of that fractiousness.

Second, and perhaps even more important, expectations are epiphenomenal rather than foundational. If they are reasonable at all and therefore legitimate at all, they have emerged only in contexts that warrant them; once they have so emerged, they prima facie deserve to be satisfied.[13] However, if some context does not provide any grounds for their formation, the nonexistent or unwar-ranted expectations therein cannot play any constrainingly justificatory role. Exactly such a state of affairs is overwhelmingly likely under a comprehensively Incorporationist Rule of Recognition. Insofar as officials adhere to such a Rule of Recognition, they focus assiduously on matters of substantive justice, and they regard content-independent matters of consistency as secondary considerations.

---

[13] My reference here to the warrantedness of the expectations is focused on their epistemic well-foundedness, which I take to be a necessary though insufficient condition for their legitimacy. If their legitimacy did not hinge on their epistemic well-foundedness at all—if it hinged solely on the moral bearings of the things that are expected—then the expectations would drop out from playing any operative justificatory role whatsoever. Saying that John in certain circumstances can legitimately expect Mary to perform some action X would be a circumlocutory way of saying that Mary is morally required to perform X in those circumstances. All the justificatory force would derive from the expectation-independent moral principles that require the performance of X; the expectations themselves would contribute nothing. See Jules Coleman, *Risks and Wrongs* (Cambridge: Cambridge University Press, 1992), 280–1. Hence, since the argument under critical scrutiny here has maintained that legitimate expectations themselves (in combination with moral principles) are sources of moral requirements, it presupposes that any such expectations are epistemically warranted.

Thus, if the citizens ruled by such a regime are directly or indirectly acquainted with the nature of the officials' law-ascertaining criteria, they will not be inclined to form any confident expectations of consistent treatment. On the contrary, they will expect a high degree of irregularity in the patterns of adjudicative and administrative decisions. Consequently, the expectations held by citizens will not weigh in favor of the achievement of settledness and predictability in the aforementioned decisional patterns.

Third and most important is an extension of a point made above. Although the proponent of extreme Incorporationism is most likely correct in contending that the moral importance of protecting people's legitimate expectations will militate in favor of officials' striving for regularity in their invocations of legal norms, he thereby reveals the dubiousness of his extreme Incorporationist doctrine. What he is in effect contending is that an unalloyedly Incorporationist Rule of Recognition will obligate its fashioners to replace its criteria with some partly or wholly non-Incorporationist criteria. Officials' efforts to achieve regularity in their law-ascertaining endeavors will involve their systematic ascription of content-independent dispositiveness to norms that have been introduced by their past decisions and pronouncements. This systematic ascription of such dispositiveness to those norms is focused precisely on the fact that they have been so introduced. Factually identifiable matters of provenance are crucial, since the systematic training of attention on such matters is what enables the securing of ample regularity in law-ascertainment. Things are very different under a robustly Incorporationist Rule of Recognition. As has already been maintained, the distinctiveness of such a Rule of Recognition lies in the fact that the officials abiding by it are concerned overridingly with the identification and application of moral principles on content-dependent grounds. Content-independent concerns are ancillary. If officials uphold content-independent considerations of consistency and regularity as cardinal objectives, they are not in fact abiding by a robustly Incorporationist Rule of Recognition at all. Instead, as my discussion has already indicated, they are abiding by an ordinary Rule of Recognition—though, of course, they may very well be doing so in furtherance of moral ideals such as the protection of legitimate expectations. If in such circumstances a thoroughly Incorporationist Rule of Recognition has ever existed, it has occasioned a transition to a partly or wholly non-Incorporationist Rule of Recognition. Its own moral instructions have led to the supersession of itself by non-Incorporationist criteria that can properly give effect to those instructions. That is, the thoroughly Incorporationist Rule of Recognition has served as the justificatory underpinning for a non-Incorporationist Rule of Recognition that has succeeded it. Thus, although the champion of extreme Incorporationism would doubtless be correct in claiming that one of the chief moral responsibilities incumbent on legal officials is the protection of people's legitimate expectations through the attainment of substantial consistency in law-application, he would thereby underscore the failure of his own theory to recount a legal system that can durably exist. If a robustly Incorporationist regime were to arise, it would usher in its own demise posthaste by calling for the adoption of non-Incorporationist criteria. Only such criteria can yield the moral desideratum of predictable regularity which (*ex hypothesi*) is rendered obligatory by a robustly Incorporationist Rule of Recognition.

In short, at least within a large and complex society, a comprehensively Incorporationist Rule of Recognition cannot endure as more than an ersatz Rule of Recognition. Either it will bring about its own quick displacement, or—if it somehow persists—it will very likely fail to provide the degree of regularity that is prerequisite to the functionality of a legal system. Though it might conceivably structure a legal system that is woefully inefficient, it will much more probably structure nothing at all that can qualify as the rule of law. Precisely because such a Rule of Recognition is so unsuitable for sustaining the existence of a legal regime, the adoption of it by officials is exceedingly unlikely. If Incorporationist criteria for law-ascertainment play any part in the Rule of Recognition that prevails in some society, they will almost certainly play a confined part. Although we can perhaps imagine a number of intermediate variants of the Incorporationist Rule of Recognition,[14] the lone plausibly stable variant is that in which the Incorporationist criteria apply peculiarly to hard cases. If there are gaps in the source-based law that need to be filled, or if there are clashes or serious ambiguities in the source-based law that need to be resolved, then judges and other officials may well invoke moral principles in order to deal with such circumstances.

---

[14] For example, some theorists have suggested that the common law proceeds in a roughly Incorporationist vein. See, e.g., Soper, 'Legal Theory', 512 n.129; Brian Bix, 'Patrolling the Boundaries: Inclusive Legal Positivism and the Nature of Jurisprudential Debate', 12 *Canadian Journal of Law & Jurisprudence* 17, 21 (1999). Cf. Stephen Perry, 'The Varieties of Legal Positivism', 9 *Canadian Journal of Law & Jurisprudence* 361, 375–80 (1996); A.W.B. Simpson, 'The Common Law and Legal Theory', in A.W.B. Simpson (ed.), *Oxford Essays in Jurisprudence: Second Series* (Oxford: Clarendon Press, 1973), 77, 79, 80–7. Though I cannot pursue the matter here, my own view of the common law is much closer to that in Joseph Raz, *supra* note 4, at 140–1. A depiction of common-law decisions as products of an Incorporationist Rule of Recognition does not do justice to the frequently overriding salience of content-independent considerations of consistency within the various areas of the common law. To be sure, the ascription of great importance to those content-independent considerations by officials in common-law liberal democracies is undoubtedly grounded on moral reasons, to which the officials sometimes advert explicitly. Their recourse to non-Incorporationist criteria for ascertaining the common law is based on some of the moral principles that would be validated as legal norms by an Incorporationist Rule of Recognition. Nevertheless, as has been argued, the status of moral principles as a justificatory platform for the adoption of non-Incorporationist criteria is very different from their status as laws that are validated as such because of their contents. Insofar as moral principles occupy the former status (as they do in common-law processes of decision-making), they preclude their occupation of the latter status. Of course, to say as much is not to say that the common law contains no elements of Incorporationism. Hard cases in the common law, like hard cases in other domains of American or English law, are probably decided by reference to Incorporationist criteria. However, most easy cases relating to common-law matters—including most of the multitudinous potential common-law cases that never come before any courts, because they are so straightforwardly resolvable— are easy because of well-settled rules and doctrines that are ascertainable under non-Incorporationist criteria.

This mild variant of Incorporationism is particularly pertinent in the context of my overall discussion, where we are pondering ways of replying to Dworkin. As has been mentioned in the Introduction to this book, Dworkin focused entirely on hard cases in his early attacks on legal positivists for their alleged failure to acknowledge the salience of moral principles in the law. Even in his more recent work, where he expresses some doubts about the distinction between hard cases and easy cases, his whole dissection of positivism's ostensible short-comings is informed crucially by his accounts of several difficult cases.[15] Hence, a version of Incorporationism attuned to the occurrence of such cases is apt indeed for fending off Dworkin's challenges. After all, the paramount merit of those challenges is to highlight the knotty legal cruxes which judges handle by recourse to moral principles. If legal positivism is to be worthy of commendation as a jurisprudential theory, it must be able to supply an adequate account of the judges' reliance on outright moral principles for adjudicative purposes. Incorporationism in its moderate form is an endeavor to furnish just such an account.

Exclusive Legal Positivism also offers such an account, however. Notwithstanding that the Exclusive Legal Positivists deny the legal status of the moral principles which judges invoke in hard cases, they unhesitatingly grant that judges in many legal systems do indeed invoke those principles. What the Exclusivist theorists maintain is that the moral principles are binding (in difficult cases) without being legal. Although such principles constitute standards which judges in many legal systems are obligated to apply in hard cases, they do not belong to any system of legal norms in which they are invoked. They are drawn upon as touchstones external to any particular jural system, in much the same way in which the laws or procedures of a foreign country are drawn upon in a conflict-of-laws case. When a jurisdiction's existing legal norms fail to generate any answer to some dispute that has come before a court, the court can close the gap by resorting to non-legal moral precepts. Those precepts do not thereby amount to legal norms; rather, they have filled in where the law has run out. So the Exclusive Legal Positivists assert.

In a moment, this chapter will present some reasons for favoring the moderate variant of Incorporationism over Exclusive Legal Positivism. Straightaway, however, we should note a few pitfalls that can easily be circumvented by Incorporationism in its moderate form. First, unlike the robust version of an Incorporationist Rule of Recognition, the milder version does not raise the specter of cripplingly pervasive disagreements among officials in the process of ascertaining the law. On the one hand, given that officials will have to make moral judgments when tackling hard cases that are not resolvable under the existing source-based law, there is a very high likelihood of conflicts of opinion

---

[15] I of course especially have in mind Ronald Dworkin, *Law's Empire* (London: Fontana, 1986), 15–30. For Dworkin's queries about the distinction between easy cases and hard cases, see ibid., at 265–6, 350–4. For my responses to his queries, see *IDLP*, 135–40, 174–6.

among the officials in regard to those hard cases. On the other hand, so what? We scarcely should be surprised that, when judges are faced with difficult situations that are not subsumable under the prevailing source-based legal norms, the judges will frequently differ with one another as they arrive at their decisions. Such discord is a fact of judicial life—more precisely, a fact of life on appellate courts—that is wearisomely familiar to anyone who has read an English or American casebook replete with swarms of dissenting opinions. However, much more important than the prominence of judicial disunity in hard cases is the general uniformity of judgments in the large majority of cases, which are resolvable by reference to source-based legal norms without any need for supplementary moral principles. Whereas a comprehensively Incorporationist Rule of Recognition will mean that every legal decision is a moral decision through and through, a mildly Incorporationist Rule of Recognition will mean that most legal decisions (to wit, the decisions in easy cases) involve the application of authoritative norms that are perceptible as such via content-independent earmarks. As a consequence, a mildly Incorporationist regime of law can secure a healthy level of regularity in its workings that is not attainable by a robustly Incorporationist regime.

A second problem that gets defused by the moderate variant of Incorporationism is the problem on which Shapiro dwells. That problem does indeed arise here afresh. Just as the moral principles that regulate the conduct of people under a comprehensively Incorporationist scheme of governance cannot provide them with reasons-for-action (beyond those engendered by the Rule of Recognition that structures the scheme), the moral principles that regulate the conduct of people in hard cases under a moderately Incorporationist scheme of governance cannot provide them with reasons-for-action in the circumstances that give rise to the hard cases. Once again, however, so what? We ought not to be surprised that the moral principles invoked to fill the gaps in the source-based law are different from any ordinary legal norm, in that they are incapable of serving as reason-creating guides for people's conduct. Those principles cannot serve as such guides, because they do not add any reasons-for-action to the reasons that already exist by dint of the criteria in the Rule of Recognition which obligate and empower judges to rely on moral principles in difficult cases. Although the moral precepts when formulated might fulfill a heuristic function, they do not constitute any decision-determining reasons (beyond those constituted by the instruction in the Rule of Recognition requiring judges to dispose of hard cases on the basis of moral requirements). Still, the judges draw on such precepts not for the purpose of receiving or furnishing any reason-creating guidance, but for the purpose of terminating disputes. Very much because the situations that bring about hard cases are situations in which there does not exist any adequate source-based legal guidance on some or all of the relevant points of contention, the top priority of judges when handling such cases is to resolve the points at issue. Instead of somehow generating reasons-for-action where none beyond those generated by the Rule of Recognition is available, the moral principles that enable the resolution of the disputes are simply means of achieving closure. Rather than *providing* guidance, their dispute-terminating effects *substitute for* guidance. We cannot expect any more in connection with hard cases, which are hard precisely because their facts are not subsumable under the ordinary legal norms that supply guidance by amounting to partly independent reasons for specific adjudicative decisions. Though an absence of reason-engendering guidance would be deeply problematic if it obtained in a legal system across the board, it is unavoidable and untroubling when confined to the norms that are invoked in knotty cases which lie outside the ambits of the existing source-based laws. (The observations in this paragraph will be developed further in my next chapter.)

Presupposed by what has just been said is the moderate Incorporationist's way of surmounting a third problem—a problem that has been broached by Dworkin and others. When difficult cases emerge within a mildly Incorporationist legal system, and when the officials in the system therefore have to resort to moral principles to fill gaps in the source-based law, they are legally obligated by their Rule of Recognition to proceed in exactly such a manner. They do not enjoy discretion to fill the gaps as they please. If any official in a moderately Incorporationist legal regime were to decide difficult cases by adverting to factors other than credible moral precepts, he would be criticized and disciplined by his fellow officials for failing to comply with his adjudicative duties. Hence, his reliance on such precepts when tackling hard cases is not something which he is legally at liberty to eschew.

Of course, the likelihood of intractable disagreements among the officials about the appropriate outcomes in hard cases is overwhelmingly high. Their shared adherence to a mildly Incorporationist Rule of Recognition does not prevent them from diverging markedly in their selection and application of moral principles for dispatching difficult disputes. While concurring with one another about the *in*tension of their Rule of Recognition, they persistently differ with one another (in hard cases) about its *ex*tension. Nevertheless, in hard cases with no uniquely correct solutions, all the moderately Incorporationist officials will be acting in accordance with their Rule of Recognition so long as the moral principles which they invoke and the outcomes which they favor are within the range of acceptable principles and outcomes. In any hard case where a uniquely correct solution is available, by contrast, only those officials who opt for the correct solution are acting strictly in accordance with the criteria in their Rule of Recognition. However, given that all the officials are credibly endeavoring in good faith to abide by those criteria (if indeed they are so endeavoring), and given that the unique correctness of the optimal solution is indemonstrable, the fact that some officials plump for suboptimal outcomes does not mean that they have committed any punishable breaches of duties. Although those officials are not in strict compliance with the mildly Incorporationist instruction in their Rule of

Recognition, they are not punishably in violation of that instruction, either. Between strict conformity and punishable transgression is the space occupied by their bona fide efforts.[16]

In the foregoing respects, then, a moderate version of Incorporationism can remain unscathed by various difficulties—some of which would bedevil a robust version of Incorporationism. A mildly Incorporationist Rule of Recognition will not lead to disruptive levels of irregularity in the ascertainment of laws by officials; nor in most circumstances will it bring forth legal norms that fail to provide officials and citizens with independent reasons-for-action; nor will it leave officials legally free to decide hard cases in whatever manner they please. Having glanced at these important strengths of the moderate Incorporationist stance, we should now seek to choose between it and Exclusive Legal Positivism.

Considerable circumspection is advisable here. An effort to choose between an Exclusivist theory and a mild Incorporationist theory is always prone to degenerate into an exercise in arid terminological stipulations. Both the Exclusivist theorist and the mild Incorporationist theorist readily maintain that judges within some legal systems invoke moral precepts to resolve the points of contention in hard cases, which cannot be resolved on the basis of legal norms that derive from ordinary legislative/judicial/administrative sources. Theorists from both camps likewise readily accept that, within legal systems of the sort just mentioned, the resort to moral principles by judges in difficult cases is legally obligatory rather than discretionary. What is at issue, then, is neither the role of moral precepts in hard cases nor the legal mandatoriness of that role within some jural systems. What is at issue, rather, is the status of the precepts which perform that role. Are those precepts legal norms when they are applied by judges to the facts of hard cases for the purpose of resolving the disputes at hand? Or are they non-legal norms that stop up gaps in the law without having become components thereof? Are they laws that belong to the system S in which they are applied, or are they similar to the rules of sporting associations and the laws of foreign jurisdictions which might be invoked by S's judges in certain unusual cases?

Plainly, we cannot settle this matter by reference to the most obvious aspect of the applied moral principles that renders those principles akin to laws: their status within a legal system as binding standards which judges bring to bear when assessing people's conduct in order to resolve disputes. After all, as has just been remarked, the Exclusive Legal Positivists are wholly willing to endorse such a characterization of the moral principles' status. We therefore have to shift our focus to some other aspect of the moral principles—an aspect that pertinently

---

[16] Because Shapiro has responded to this paragraph—in his rejoinders which I examine in my next chapter—my editing of it has been light. The points advanced in this paragraph undergo considerable amplification and refinement in Chapters 2 and 4.

distinguishes them from the rules of clubs and sporting associations and the laws of foreign jurisdictions. If we can indeed single out some such feature of the principles, we shall have grounds for favoring a modest Incorporationist theory over an Exclusivist theory.

Consider, then, the significance of the fact that the moral precepts invoked in hard cases do not owe their correctness to anyone's deliberate acts and are not susceptible to alteration through deliberate acts. Shapiro himself emphasizes this characteristic of morality in the course of his critique of Incorporationism. Of key importance here is that the tenor of correct moral principles does not lie within the deliberate control of anyone who is outside the legal system in which the principles are applied as binding standards of conduct. In this respect, those principles are notably different from the rules of clubs or sporting associations and the laws of foreign jurisdictions. In their substance, such rules and foreign laws do indeed lie entirely within the deliberate control of people other than the officials in the legal system L where the rules and foreign laws are invoked. People who run the clubs and sporting associations determine which rules are operative therein, and they can modify those rules deliberately through amendments and amplifications and repeals. Much the same can be said *mutatis mutandis* about the officials in foreign legal regimes, who determine which laws are operative therein and who can modify those laws through such techniques as repealing, amending, enacting, invalidating, and overruling. Exactly because the foreign laws and the rules of the clubs and associations are subject to the authoritative control of people outside L, the occasional application of those rules and laws within L should not be regarded as the incorporation of them into L's matrix of legal norms. Instead, the application of them is a way of showing due respect for the norms that have been chosen and formulated in systems of authority that exist alongside L. As a means of showing such respect, the effectuation of those norms within L tends to highlight their separateness from L's own norms. Given that the ground for resorting to foreign laws or associations' rules is their origin in external structures of authority that merit some recognition as such, the process of resorting to those rules or laws will have rested on a justification which underscores the fact that they belong to systems other than L. (Of course, some of the people in charge of clubs and sporting associations might also be legal officials. Nonetheless, each such person in his public capacity as an official is distinct from himself in his private capacity as a leader of a club or an association. The public and private roles remain separate, even if they are both occupied by a single person.)

Before contrasting the properties of foreign laws and clubs' rules with the properties of moral principles in hard cases, we should look at a further potential source of binding norms: custom. Few if any legal theories deny that customary norms have the status of full-fledged laws when they are invoked as such by judges. Indeed, one of the most prominent charges leveled by Hart against John Austin was that the latter theorist could not come up with any adequate explanation of the legal status of some customary norms.[17] Now, to a limited extent, the reasons for officials' ascriptions of binding force to customary norms are similar to the reasons for their ascriptions of binding force to the rules of clubs and the laws of foreign jurisdictions. That is, the officials in L who draw upon customary norms are thereby exhibiting due regard for the practices from which those norms are distilled. Nevertheless, the dissimilarities between customary norms and foreign laws (or associations' rules) are more significant than the resemblances. Those dissimilarities warrant the difference between one's readiness to classify certain customary precepts as legal-norms-belonging-to-L and one's reluctance so to classify any foreign laws or associations' rules. In the first place, the statutory/judicial/administrative laws of foreign jurisdictions and the codified rules of sporting associations derive from the decisions of people who occupy positions of authority. Likewise, those laws and rules are subject to deliberate alteration through standard procedures undertaken by the people in the authoritative positions. By contrast, the precepts of custom emerge and develop gradually instead of being brought into existence through discrete and authoritative acts. Moreover, unlike the laws of foreign countries and the formal rules of sporting associations, customary precepts are not subject to deliberate and abrupt modification through set procedures. Nor do they issue from clear-cut channels of authority; rather, they are immanent in diffuse practices that are typically carried on in the absence of any formal hierarchies or authoritative pronouncements.

In these key respects, the norms generated by custom diverge strikingly from foreign laws and sporting associations' rules. Those laws and rules are highly malleable products of institutions that are counterparts (at least rough counterparts) of the legal system L in which the rules and laws are applied as binding external norms. By contrast, customary precepts are not highly malleable and are not attributable to any authoritative decisions handed down and ratified through institutional mechanisms broadly akin to those in L. Hence, whereas the substance of the foreign laws and associations' rules is controlled by the directives of authorities outside L, the substance of customary precepts is not really within anyone's effective control. Since the content of the customary precepts is due to diffuse patterns of behavior rather than to centrally organized decisions, and since the practices in which the precepts unfold are not authoritative institutions that are formal counterparts of L, the application of those precepts within L should be seen as the incorporation of them into L's assemblage of legal norms. Though the customary precepts are immanent in practices, they do not belong to any authoritative institutions outside L. Thus, when they receive formal recognition within L as binding norms, they are not some borrowings from another system in

---

[17] Hart, *Concept*, 44–8. I have argued elsewhere that Austin's theory can accommodate the role of custom much more resourcefully than Hart suggests. See my *Legal Theory, Political Theory, and Deconstruction: Against Rhadamanthus* (Bloomington: Indiana University Press, 1991), 106–7.

which they have an authoritatively established status. Until that point of formal recognition, they are free-floating—that is, free of any institutional affiliation which has been authoritatively set. They are consequently available for incorporation into L. Plainly, that free-floating condition and that consequent availability for incorporation will not be characteristic of foreign laws or associations' rules. (Of course, a free-floating condition is hardly in itself sufficient to confer the status of a law on each norm that informs the authoritative utterances of officials. For instance, the fact that judges rely on the free-floating rules of grammar and diction does not mean that those rules are legal norms. Unlike statutes and judicial doctrines and administrative regulations and certain customary and moral norms, grammatical rules do not serve as justificatory bases for official decisions. When judges have to explain why they are deciding a case one way as opposed to another, they do not invoke grammatical rules such as the rule against split infinitives.[18] Instead, they have to invoke some statute(s), judicial doctrine(s), administrative regulation(s), customary norm(s), moral norm(s), or other decision-justifying standard(s). As has already been fleetingly remarked about the moral principles that are applied in hard cases, the most obvious feature of those principles that weighs in favor of our classifying them as laws is that they are indeed decision-justifying standards.)

Along lines that are relevant here, principles of positive morality and principles of critical morality are much closer to customary precepts than to foreign laws or associations' rules. Indeed, moral principles of both types—especially the principles of critical morality—diverge more sharply from the aforementioned laws and rules than do customary precepts. Let us first ponder the status of positive moral standards. Positive morality consists in a mixture of customary beliefs/practices and widespread convictions. With regard to the component of positive morality that comprises a large array of customary precepts, the status of moral principles is manifestly at one with the status of norms that are grounded in custom. Therefore, given that customary norms are available for incorporation into L's laws, the same will obviously be true of positive moral precepts. Within the component of positive morality that comprises people's widely shared convictions about right and wrong, the standing of moral principles is even more clearly detached from any authoritative institutional origins. Individual convictions, no matter how pervasively they may be harbored, are not the products of formal enactments or authoritative decrees. The patterns or networks of those convictions do not belong to any system, regardless of how widespread the convictions are. People's staunchest beliefs about right and wrong are free-floating in the sense defined above. Ergo, the moral principles encapsulating those beliefs are available for incorporation into L's matrix of laws.

---

[18] In highly unusual circumstances, to be sure, rules of grammar or pronunciation could indeed serve as the justificatory bases for official decisions. A situation broadly along these lines is discussed in my *IDLP*, 35. In such circumstances, the aforementioned rules are indeed legal norms.

If the principles of positive morality can become subsumed into the overall array of *L*'s legal norms—as has just been argued—then *a fortiori* much the same is true in connection with the principles of critical morality. By definition, they are principles that possess their morally binding force independently of their having been upheld by anyone. Their soundness as moral principles does not depend at all on their having gained acceptance within any set of institutions; their status as precepts of critical morality derives from their intrinsic contents and not from their influence or roles (if any) in some formal system of authority. Their status as critical precepts certainly cannot be terminated by anybody's decisions or enactments. It is not within anyone's control. Hence, if the officials in *L* draw upon the principles of critical morality for the purpose of resolving hard cases, they are not doing so out of any perceived need to show regard for some coexistent system of formal authority. Instead, the officials are drawing on those principles as norms whose validity transcends any recognition of them in other systems. A condition of free-floatingness, in the sense defined above, is inherent in the posture of critical moral precepts as such. When those precepts are invoked and applied in *L*, they are not some borrowings from another institutional structure to which they really belong. Even more straightforwardly than customary standards, they have been available to enter *L*'s miscellany of legal norms as full-fledged elements thereof.

Should we conclude, then, that any correct recourse to moral principles by the judges in a mildly Incorporationist regime is an application of pre-existent law? Such an inference would be precipitate, for it would elide the difference between the following two types of hard cases: those in which there are uniquely correct ways of ranking the applicable moral principles, and those in which there are no uniquely correct rankings. In hard cases of the former sort, a mildly Incorporationist Rule of Recognition will have fixed the content of the prevailing law.[19] Because that Rule of Recognition empowers and obligates officials to resort to moral principles in hard cases, and because *ex hypothesi* any questions about the bearing of those principles on the facts of certain hard cases can be answered in uniquely correct ways, the officials dealing with those particular cases have to pursue the uniquely correct routes if they are to decide the cases in strict accordance with their Rule of Recognition.

In any hard case *H* where the applicable moral principles can be ranked acceptably in more than one way, a mildly Incorporationist Rule of Recognition will not have fixed the content of the prevailing law. An irreducible and significant quantum of leeway will remain. In any such hard case, then, the balance of moral principles does not preordain the apposite resolution. Although the officials' recourse to moral precepts will narrow the range of acceptable outcomes,

---

[19] On this point, though not on one or two other points, I agree with the discussion in David Lyons, 'Moral Aspects of Legal Theory', in *Moral Aspects of Legal Theory* (Cambridge: Cambridge University Press, 1993), 64, 80–2.

it will still leave key matters open—because the ranking of those precepts is open, to some extent. Accordingly, while the balance of moral norms invoked by judges to settle the points at issue in *H* may become the prevailing law that governs those points, it cannot accurately be presented as the pre-existent law thereon. Notwithstanding that the repertory of laws for hard cases under a mildly Incorporationist Rule of Recognition will encompass moral precepts, the pre-existent law for the controversy in *H* is indeterminate.

At any rate, what the second half of this chapter has sought to establish is that a moderate version of Incorporationism is preferable both to Exclusive Legal Positivism and to a thoroughgoing version of Incorporationism. Unlike the last-mentioned doctrine, the moderate variant of Incorporationism duly acknowledges the indispensability of uniformity and regularity in anything that counts as a legal system. Unlike Exclusive Legal Positivism, moreover, the position advocated in this chapter can distinguish pertinently between the status of customary norms and the status of sporting associations' rules (and of foreign laws) when those norms and rules are given effect within any particular legal system. The basis for such a distinction leads to the conclusion that the moral principles drawn upon by mildly Incorporationist judges in hard cases are sometimes laws of the system in which they are invoked and applied. In insisting on that very point, a mild version of Incorporationism is superior to Exclusive Legal Positivism. When Incorporationism is confined within appropriate limits, it proves to be a redoubtable doctrine indeed.

III. Conclusion

In the first half of this chapter, I have defended Inclusive Legal Positivism by dissociating it from Incorporationism. In the second half, I have defended a moderate version of Incorporationism by dissociating it from an unmitigated version. What ties together the two portions of the chapter is my distancing of myself from both Exclusive Legal Positivism and extreme Incorporationism. Exclusive Legal Positivism envisages undue constraints on the possible contents of law-ascertaining criteria, whereas the robust version of Incorporationism envisages insufficient constraints on those contents.

Of central importance in this matter is the fundamental degree of regularity or uniformity that must obtain if a legal system is to exist as a legal system. At least in the context of any credible society more sizeable than a handful of families, a robustly Incorporationist Rule of Recognition will not secure the requisite degree of regularity or uniformity; hence, robust Incorporationism as a general jurisprudential position is misleading and unilluminating. Exclusive Legal Positivists err in the opposite direction. They limit the range of possible law-ascertaining criteria much more severely than is necessary to ensure the functionality of a legal system. (Indeed, given their ready acknowledgment that some judges do and should invoke moral principles when adjudicating in hard cases, the Exclusive Legal Positivists could hardly claim that the limits delineated by their theory are essential prerequisites of a legal system's existence. Far from indicating any restrictions on the kinds of standards that can and should serve as adjudicative touchstones in a viable legal system, the Exclusivist limits are purely classificatory.) An Exclusivist theory suffers from some disconcerting weaknesses, such as its slighting of the similarities between customary norms and moral precepts. Weaknesses of that sort are avoided by a mildly Incorporationist theory. Like Inclusive Legal Positivism, the moderate version of Incorporationism maintains that the only constraints on the possible contents of law-ascertaining criteria are those constraints that yield the regularity which enables the basic functioning and existence of a legal system as such.

2

Throwing Light on the Role of Moral Principles in the Law: Further Reflections

In Chapter 1, I defended Inclusive Legal Positivism and a modest version of Incorporationism against some powerful objections leveled at them by Scott Shapiro. Shapiro has replied to my arguments, as has Jules Coleman from the camp of Incorporationism.[1] The present chapter will endeavor to parry their ripostes in order to clarify my wholehearted defense of Inclusive Legal Positivism and my slightly warier defense of Incorporationism. At the center of the discussion here are far-reaching matters that pertain to the fundamental nature of law and normativity.

I. Hart and Inclusive Legal Positivism

The first and foremost aim of Chapter 1 has been to rebut Shapiro's claim that the norms validated as laws under an Inclusive Rule of Recognition cannot constitute peremptory reasons for decisions by officials and citizens. Shapiro contends that, whereas any genuinely authoritative legal directives exclude their addressees from acting legitimately on considerations that run athwart the directives' terms, a mandate validated under an Inclusive Rule of Recognition requires its addressees to deliberate about the merits of giving effect to the mandate. 'The problem is that [any norm validated under an Inclusive Rule of Recognition] cannot make a practical difference *in the way that* rules are supposed to make practical differences: if the agent is required to determine whether the rule ought to be followed on the merits, then it can count neither as an epistemic tool for authoritative designation nor as a peremptory reason for action.'[2] In response to this line of argument, I have maintained that a legal norm validated under an Inclusive Rule of Recognition can perfectly well partake

---

[1] Scott Shapiro, 'Law, Morality, and the Guidance of Conduct', 6 *Legal Theory* 127 (2000) [hereinafter cited as Shapiro, 'Law']; Jules Coleman, 'Constraints on the Criteria of Legality', 6 *Legal Theory* 171 (2000) [hereinafter cited as Coleman, 'Constraints'].

[2] Scott Shapiro, 'On Hart's Way Out', 4 *Legal Theory* 469, 502 (1998) [hereinafter cited as Shapiro, 'Way'], emphasis in original.

of peremptoriness. What cannot be true, of course, is that the scope of the peremptory sway of such a norm is all-encompassing. However, restrictions on the scope of a norm's peremptoriness are familiar and straightforward, and are not in any way at odds with the character and existence of that peremptoriness.

Thus, for example, if a legal norm N is validated under an Inclusive Rule of Recognition that withholds validation from any norm that is grossly unfair, the scope of N's peremptory sway does not encompass gross unfairness but does encompass many other considerations such as unwisdom and ordinary unfairness. No factors covered by the peremptory reach of N are permissible bases for decisions or actions that are contrary to N's requirements. Some other factors such as gross unfairness fall outside that reach and can thus warrant decisions or actions contrary to N's demands. However, the upshot of such a state of affairs is not the inexistence of N's peremptoriness, but merely its limitedness in scope. Hence, despite Shapiro's arguments, a norm validated as a law under an Inclusive Rule of Recognition can make a practical difference in exactly the way in which any authoritative rule is supposed to make a practical difference.

A. Peremptoriness and Applicability

Shapiro in his rejoinder does not contest the general correctness of my defense of Inclusive Legal Positivism, but he declares that H.L.A. Hart could not have availed himself of my defense. When seeking to vindicate Inclusive Legal Positivism, I have taken for granted (*arguendo*) a conception of authoritative norms as exclusionary reasons-for-action—a conception associated originally with Geoffrey Warnock and Joseph Raz, and subsequently drawn upon by Hart. I have hitherto presumed that Shapiro implicitly attributes just such a conception to Hart. However, he now submits that Hart's account of normativity differs from the Warnockian/Razian account in ways that leave Hart unshielded by my defense of Inclusive Legal Positivism.

Under the Warnockian/Razian analysis of authoritative normativity, there is ample room for restrictions on the scope of a norm's peremptoriness. Shapiro argues that Hart's analysis, by contrast, has ruled out such restrictions. He contends that Hart viewed authoritative norms as directives that 'put an end to *all* questions about whether conformity is advisable' (Shapiro, 'Law', 165, emphasis added). Cleaving to that view of norms—so Shapiro alleges—Hart could not fall back upon the notion of scope-restrictions in order to maintain that the mandates validated under an Inclusive Rule of Recognition are genuinely peremptory. Hence, Shapiro concludes, my vindication of the Inclusivist stance does not redound to Hart's benefit at all.

Shapiro is alert to the principal difficulty that stands in the way of his renewed critique of Hart: the wholesale implausibility of a conception of legal mandates as directives whose peremptoriness is always unlimited in scope. 'Surely, it would be argued, no rule has absolute force, that is, must be followed no matter what the reason' (Shapiro, 'Law', 165). One should certainly shrink from imputing to Hart the outlandish view that legal norms are invariably endowed with absolute force. Shapiro affirms that the appropriate tack here is to distinguish carefully between limitations on a norm's peremptoriness and limitations on a norm's applicability. He suggests that, although Hart believed in the unrestricted scope of any authoritative norm's peremptoriness, such a belief was accompanied by an awareness that the conditions for the applicability of a norm are typically subject to a number of restrictions. Shapiro expresses this point as follows, by indicating how Hart would analyze a situation in which a commander has ordered some troops to complete a ten-mile training hike: 'The defeasibility of an order's requirements can be explained in terms of the order's applicability conditions. The commander's order carries with it a set of implicit exceptions, e.g., the troops are required to complete the 10 mile hike unless they, or their commander, are in serious danger... There is, thus, no need to explain the defeasibility of [norms] by making reference to the technical concept of a "partially exclusionary scope." Such cases can easily be explained in terms of the familiar notion of "applicability conditions." '[3] Having drawn this distinction between limits on peremptoriness and limits on applicability, Shapiro concludes that Hart did not posit any limits of the former sort. Consequently, Shapiro's original critique does tell against Hart, its specific target: '[S]ince peremptory reasons [in Hart's analysis as described by Shapiro] have universal scopes, no one can deliberate about the merits of following a rule and still treat the rule as a peremptory reason for action' (Shapiro, 'Law', 166).

Now, although the paramount purpose of my first chapter has been to uphold Inclusive Legal Positivism rather than to defend Hart, a few queries about Shapiro's argument ought to be raised here. First, the only passage which Shapiro cites in order to substantiate his claim about Hart's reliance on the notion of applicability-conditions is from *The Concept of Law*. That is, the passage comes from Hart's early work rather than from his later work. What makes this citation problematic is that Shapiro himself has emphasized that the conception of normativity in the earlier work of Hart is significantly divergent from the conception that is to be found in Hart's later work (Shapiro, 'Way', 492–4; Shapiro, 'Law', 162). Given the marked shift in Hart's position on the matter over time, an extract from his early writings is not a trusty indicator of his views at the much later juncture when his conception of norms as peremptory reasons-for-action gained expression. To know that Hart was still attached to the notion of limited applicability-conditions in distinction from limited peremptoriness, we would have to be presented with a germane passage from his later writings—a

---

[3] Shapiro, 'Law', 165–6. Decidedly odd, in my view, is the suggestion that the notion of 'applicability conditions' is any less clearly a technical concept than is the notion of a 'partially exclusionary scope'.

passage in which he gave voice to that abiding attachment. Shapiro offers no such passage, and (so far as I am aware) there is none.

Second, even if we leave aside the point just made, the examples on which Shapiro trades are not really apposite. He discusses Hart's view of circumstances in which a commander's order should not be followed or in which a person's promise should not be kept. In other words, he discusses situations that clearly involve the *inapplicability* of certain peremptory reasons-for-action rather than the *inexistence* thereof. Under an Inclusive Rule of Recognition, however, the very existence of legal norms as legal norms is exactly what is at stake. A mandate that does not satisfy the moral test(s) laid down by such a Rule of Recognition in some particular legal system is nonexistent within that system as a legally valid norm. Thus, if we are to flesh out Hart's understanding of authoritative norms in a way that is relevant to the debate over the tenability of Inclusive Legal Positivism, we have to focus on circumstances where the very existence of such norms is in question. (We might, for instance, ponder a situation in which someone promises to commit a murder. What is in serious doubt is whether the promise has any morally binding force at all, rather than merely whether it will fail to be applicable and determinative in some settings.[4]) When we concentrate specifically on the matter of the existence of legal norms as such, we find that Hart time and again observed that an Inclusive Rule of Recognition deals with precisely that matter. He did not discuss any such Rule of Recognition by reference to applicability-conditions at all. In his early work, for example, he wrote that '[i]n some systems, as in the United States, the ultimate criteria of legal validity explicitly incorporate principles of justice or substantive moral values', and he added that any enactment passed by American legislatures in violation of constitutional moral tests 'is liable to be treated as *ultra vires*, and declared legally invalid by the courts to the extent that it conflicts with the constitutional provisions'.[5] In his later writing, he chose virtually the same words to reiterate his view: '[I]n some systems of law, as in the United States, the ultimate criteria of legal validity... explicitly incorporate besides pedigree, principles of justice or

---

[4] Hart himself, in the essay where he analyzed legal norms as content-independent peremptory reasons-for-action, referred to the kind of situation that I am envisaging. His remarks quite plainly tally with my interpretation of his mature conception of authoritative norms: '[T]he giving of a promise is intended to be a reason not merely for the promisor doing the action when the time comes but for excluding normal free deliberation about the merits of doing it. . . . This is true even though the range of possible actions which one may validly promise to do is not unlimited and does not include grossly immoral actions or those intended to be harmful to the promisee.' H.L.A. Hart, 'Commands and Authoritative Reasons', in *Essays on Bentham* (Oxford: Clarendon Press, 1982), 243, 255.

[5] H.L.A. Hart, *The Concept of Law* (Oxford: Clarendon Press, 1961) [hereinafter cited as *Concept*], 199, 70. See also H.L.A. Hart, 'Positivism and the Separation of Law and Morals', in *Essays in Jurisprudence and Philosophy* (Oxford: Clarendon Press, 1983), 49, 54–5. (The essay just cited was originally published in 71 *Harvard Law Review* 593 (1958).) I am of course aware that laws in the United States are sometimes found to be unconstitutional as applied, rather than unconstitutional *tout court*. While highlighting the latter type of unconstitutionality—the type usually under consideration in the debates over Inclusive Legal Positivism—I am in no way denying the former.

substantive moral values, and these may form the content of legal constitutional restraints'.[6] Whenever Hart adverted to the central issue addressed by Inclusive Legal Positivism, he treated it not as an issue pertaining to limitations on norms' applicability but as an issue pertaining to limitations on the sheer existence of norms and their peremptoriness. Shapiro's exposition of Hart's account of authoritative normativity, with examples involving an unfollowed command and an unkept promise, has tended to obscure this point.

Third, and perhaps most important, even if we grant that Hart in his later work distinguished sharply between limits on peremptoriness and limits on applicability, and even if we grant that he took the peremptoriness of legal norms to be all-embracing, we shall have no grounds for accepting Shapiro's conclusion—his conclusion, quoted above, that 'since peremptory reasons [in Hart's analysis] have universal scopes, no one can deliberate about the merits of following a rule and still treat the rule as a peremptory reason for action' (Shapiro, 'Law', 166). The very distinction which Shapiro highlights, the distinction between limits on applicability and limits on peremptoriness, is what blocks his inference. Within a model of legal mandates as norms endowed with all-encompassing peremptoriness and restricted applicability, any deliberation about the merits of complying with a legal mandate will be characterized as deliberation about the applicability of the mandate in some or all sets of circumstances. Moral tests laid down by an Inclusive Rule of Recognition will be characterized as giving rise to deliberation of exactly this sort. To be sure, such a characterization is far from cogent and illuminating, because the model of authoritative normativity attributed to Hart by Shapiro is itself far from cogent and illuminating. Nevertheless, even within the unsatisfactory confines of that model, there is abundant room for denying any entailment between 'deliberating on the merits of following a mandate M' and 'failing to treat M as a peremptory reason for action'. According to the aforementioned model, M is to be treated as a peremptory reason-for-action whenever it is deemed to be applicable. According to that model, the question to be answered by deliberation about the merits of following M is whether the conditions for its applicability are indeed present. Such deliberation, then, does not constitute any incursion into M's peremptoriness. Ergo, even if we were to concede that Shapiro's recountal of Hart's mature conception of authoritative normativity is accurate, we should grasp that Hart could quite coherently leave open the possibility of Inclusivist constraints on the bindingness of legal norms.

B. A Coda to the Critique

Having submitted that Hart in his later work perceived the peremptoriness of laws as unrestricted in scope, Shapiro proceeds to consider whether Hart could

---

[6] H.L.A. Hart, 'Postscript', to *The Concept of Law* (Oxford: Clarendon Press, 1994) (2nd edn), 238, 247.

fruitfully have modified his position. Shapiro contends that such a move would have been problematic:

According to Hart, the identity of a legal system is fixed by its rule of recognition. Because the rule of recognition is a duty-imposing rule, it follows that a rule is a member of a certain legal system only if a judge is under a duty to apply such a rule in a case that comes before her. However, if legal rules were permitted to have partially exclusionary scopes, a judge might be under a duty to apply a rule in some cases, but have discretion to apply the same rule in other cases. The latter would obtain whenever the rule, even though applicable, is defeated by reasons that fell outside its (partially) exclusionary scope. The duty of a judge to apply applicable rules would thus be indeterminate—it would obtain in some cases and not in others. Accordingly, the identity of any legal system would be indeterminate. (Shapiro, 'Law', 166)

Though Shapiro goes on to avow that the problem broached in this paragraph is not insurmountable, we ought to query whether it is in fact a problem at all. Let us note two dubious aspects of his argument.

First, when a putative legal norm contravenes some moral test(s) imposed by an Inclusive Rule of Recognition, it is not true that a judge has discretion to choose between applying and not applying the norm. Instead, he is under an obligation to invalidate the norm or at least to abstain from applying it. Hence, the requisite result in such circumstances is not in any way indeterminate. Admittedly, things are different when there is no determinate answer to the question whether the ostensible legal mandate satisfies the relevant moral test(s). When that question does not lend itself to a uniquely correct answer, a judge in the Inclusivist legal system will have genuine discretion to opt between applying and not applying the ostensible mandate. However, that discretion does not stem from anything peculiarly problematic about limits on the peremptoriness of legal norms; rather, it stems from the occurrence of a hard case in which a key point of contention is not univocally resolvable. When any other difficult case hinges on an issue that is not univocally resolvable under the existing law even through the introduction of non-source-based standards, it will similarly engender a need for the exercise of genuine discretion—regardless of whether the refractory issue is connected with Inclusivist constraints. Contrariwise, when the question of the fulfillment or nonfulfillment of an Inclusivist moral test does lend itself to a uniquely correct answer, a judge in the regime which imposes the test does not enjoy any discretion of the sort described by Shapiro.

Second, also doubtful is Shapiro's claim that the identity of a legal system would be indeterminate as a consequence of the indeterminacy that might exist in some hard cases. On the one hand, it is generally true that a legal system will witness some hard cases for which no uniquely correct resolutions are available even in principle. As a result, the law to be ascertained in any particular legal system (Inclusivist or non-Inclusivist) is not fully determinate. On the other hand, the indeterminacy that obtains is present in respect of only a small proportion of the interactions among people that might engender legal proceedings. Most such interactions never lead to lawsuits at all, because the legal implications of the various modes of conduct are so clear-cut. Even among the disputes that do eventuate in legal proceedings, most are straightforwardly resolvable. The difficult cases studied by law students and legal scholars constitute only a small percentage of the lawsuits that actually materialize, and a still smaller percentage of the lawsuits that could have materialized if people had been foolishly obstinate enough to engage in them. Even some difficult cases lend themselves to uniquely correct resolutions. Thus, the instances of genuine indeterminacy and strong discretion within a legal system are marginal. Although the hard cases involving full-blown indeterminacy will of course be manifold in an enormous legal system (as will wrongly decided cases), and although some of those hard cases may well be prominent and important, the large majority of issues addressed by a legal system's workings are routine rather than vexing. Numerous though the truly knotty cases may be in an immense legal system, they are vastly outnumbered by cases that can be handled readily. Outright indeterminacy is peripheral rather than central.

Therefore, when confronted with Shapiro's claim about the indeterminacy of the identity of any legal system, we should wonder why the indeterminacy of the law in a small proportion of circumstances would undo the determinacy of the overarching legal system within which those circumstances arise. Plainly, much depends here on the purpose of the analysis or enquiry in connection with which the identity of some legal system has become a matter of interest. If our investigations require us to specify a legal system's doctrinal details with considerable precision when we are elaborating the nature of the overall system, we might have grounds for affirming that the absence of uniquely correct answers in some hard cases is sufficient to warrant our pronouncing the identity of the system to be indeterminate. Much more often, however, an enquiry into the bearings of an overall legal regime will not necessitate such detailed precision. Marginal indeterminacy can be ignored or at least can be perceived as falling well short of undermining the determinacy of the whole regime. For most theoretical and practical purposes, we are justified in concluding that the identity of a legal system is not imperiled by the open-endedness of some portions of its frontiers.

Let us ponder an analogy. Suppose that somebody needs to carry out a highly accurate census of the American population. If the guidelines that inform the census have not unequivocally answered certain questions about membership in the American population, and if there are no supplementary bases for unequivocal answers to those questions, then some degree of indeterminacy will be involved in the conducting of the census. For example, suppose that neither the guidelines nor any other relevant decisional bases have ordained an answer to the question whether American citizens living permanently abroad (in Cambridge, England, for example) are to be classified as members of the American population. Even though the people occupying that indeterminate status are far fewer in number than the people who unequivocally belong to the population, somebody assigned to produce an extremely accurate census might have to conclude that the existence of the citizens living in foreign lands has rendered the American population indeterminate. For most purposes, however, the existence of those several hundred thousand American citizens—whose status is not settled by the census guidelines, *ex hypothesi*—is hardly sufficient to warrant an ascription of indeterminacy to the American population as a whole. For most purposes, an ascription of determinacy to the overall population can withstand some peripheral unsettledness.

Shapiro might reply that, in the long passage quoted above, he does not have in mind difficult cases; instead, he is talking about indeterminacy of a much more wide-ranging kind. Such a retort would deflect the objection presented in my last few paragraphs, but it would trigger again my previous objection. That is, it would seem to posit indeterminacy where in fact there is none. When the moral tests imposed by an Inclusivist Rule of Recognition are either determinately satisfied or determinately violated by some apparent legal norm *N*, the officials in the Inclusivist regime will not enjoy any strong discretion in regard to the validation and application of *N*. As has been indicated, they are under an obligation to recognize *N* as a legal norm when the moral tests (along with tests of provenance) are determinately met, and they are under an obligation to decline to recognize *N* as a legal norm when those tests are determinately unmet. Unless Shapiro is talking about difficult cases in which neither of these unequivocal obligations is present, his references to indeterminacy are quite puzzling.

II. Incorporationism and Illumination

Although one chief purpose of this book's opening chapter has been to vindicate Inclusive Legal Positivism in response to Shapiro's critique, an additional aim has been to commend a limited version of Incorporationism while largely disapproving of an extreme version. We shall now look more searchingly at the doctrine of extreme Incorporationism. First articulated prominently by Philip Soper, the basic idea underlying that doctrine has undergone considerable development at the hands of Coleman.[7] While my opening chapter has queried a salient aspect of Coleman's theory, his work and mine are in full agreement on most issues surrounding Incorporationism. Indeed, as will be observed, both Shapiro and Coleman have overestimated the extent to which I have sought to distance myself from Coleman's robust Incorporationist stance.

---

[7] For citations to relevant works by Coleman and Soper, see note 7 of the Introduction to this volume.

A. Unchallenged Truth

The modest version of Incorporationism which this book espouses is marked by a curtailment of the range of circumstances to which the general Incorporationist thesis pertains. Like anyone who upholds some variant of that thesis, I accept that a norm's correctness as a moral principle can be a sufficient condition for its status as a legal norm in this or that system of law. However—unlike Coleman's thoroughgoing Incorporationist doctrine—my moderate Incorporationist theory submits that, in credible legal systems where moral correctness does amount to a sufficient condition for legal validity, it does not amount to such a condition in most cases. Only in hard cases do any Incorporationist criteria in a Rule of Recognition become activated. Only for such cases are moral precepts incorporated into a legal regime as some of its norms. If a scheme of governance were instead to treat moral correctness as the sufficient condition for legal validity in all circumstances (rather than only in the circumstances that breed hard cases), it would lack the regularity and coordination that are essential features of anything rightly classifiable as a regime of law. In a society where every legal judgment by judicial and executive officials is a moral judgment through and through, the congruence among the motley determinations of the officials will be too low to enable the emergence or continuation of a genuine system of legal norms. If the operations of a regime are characterized by a welter of discordant decisions and clashing rationales not only at its margins but throughout its core, then it will lack the regularity that is indispensable for its very existence as a legal regime.

As has repeatedly been acknowledged in Chapter 1, my doubts about a thoroughgoing Incorporationist position are based not purely on conceptual analyses but also on an empirical assumption. Though my empirical premise is general and uncontroversial, it is indeed empirical rather than strictly philosophical. What I assume is that, except in static and highly homogeneous societies not much larger than a handful of families, there will be widespread disagreement among people over the answers to innumerable moral questions; in any large and complex society, extensive divergences among people's moral outlooks are bound to be present. Now, this empirical assumption is scarcely novel or controversial. It is accepted by both Shapiro and Coleman, and has often figured conspicuously in legal and political philosophy. Hart, for example, relied on such a premise when discussing the disadvantages of a network of duty-imposing rules without power-conferring rules (*Concept*, 89–90). Some strands of Ronald Dworkin's critiques of legal positivism in *Taking Rights Seriously* depend on basically the same empirical assumption about the ineliminability of moral controversy.[8] Hence, although my

---

[8] See especially Ronald Dworkin, *Taking Rights Seriously* (Cambridge, MA: Harvard University Press, 1978), 65, 66–7. See also ibid. at 39–44, 54–5, 59–68. I am here looking askance at Coleman's repeated contention that Dworkin's critique of a proto-Incorporationist version of legal positivism is purely conceptual (Coleman, 'Constraints', 179–80, 181). Quite plainly empirical as well as conceptual is the Dworkinian claim that 'any reference to morality among the criteria of legality would entail controversy

wariness of any robust Incorporationist stance is partly empirical (at a very abstract level) and is not purely a matter of conceptual analysis, the general drift of the belief which underpins my reservations is certainly not unfamiliar in the domain of legal philosophy. As a consequence, the orientation and limits of Chapter 1's misgivings about extreme Incorporationism should be quite apparent.

What has become clear, however, is that Chapter 1's arguments are liable to be misconstrued. Both Shapiro and Coleman have taken me to be denying the truth of the central thesis of robust Incorporationism. Each of them retorts to my arguments in part by claiming that my challenges to the aforementioned thesis have tended to reveal that it is true. Let us first look briefly at this claim by Shapiro and Coleman, and then at a bolder affirmation of the truth of the robust Incorporationist tenet. As will be seen, I endorse that bolder affirmation without retracting my animadversions on the thoroughgoing Incorporationist tenet itself. The truth of that tenet is not in dispute, whereas its jurisprudential valuableness is.

---

sufficient to preclude the rule of recognition from generating the convergence necessary to establish its existence as a regulative social rule' (Coleman, 'Constraints', 179). Dworkin is trading on the same basic empirical assumption on which I rely; no purely conceptual analysis can tell us whether the degree of convergence stemming from the use of moral criteria will or will not be insufficient to sustain the existence of a Rule of Recognition that encompasses such criteria. Both Dworkin's argument and my own doubts about thoroughgoing Incorporationism are partly empirical—though I am more explicit than Dworkin in drawing attention to that characteristic.

I should note a further and partly related point on which I disagree with Coleman about certain aspects of Dworkin's early work. Along the following lines, Coleman takes exception to Dworkin's claim that the availability of moral principles as touchstones for adjudication will eliminate or virtually eliminate judicial discretion: 'Of course, even as discretion owing to the availability of legally binding resources decreases (as the set of available resources increases), the possibility of discretion owing to vagueness increases (as the set of controversial moral predicates legally binding on officials increases). The same predicates that reduce discretion on one front increase it on another: a consequence of Dworkin's own view that moral predicates are essentially controversial. To defeat the positivist view of discretion, Dworkin has to do more than show that the set of available legal resources on which a judge can draw goes beyond rules' (Coleman, 'Constraints', 172 n.5; Jules Coleman, 'Incorporationism, Conventionality, and the Practical Difference Thesis', 4 *Legal Theory* 381, 406 n.42 [1998] [hereinafter cited as Coleman, 'Incorporationism']). Coleman's retort tends to blur the distinction between weak and strong discretion—that is, between discretion in the application of a dispositive standard and discretion in the absence of any dispositive standard. Dworkin ascribes to legal positivism the view that judges enjoy strong discretion in hard cases. He seeks to rebut that view by pointing out that judges are obligated and empowered to resort to moral principles as determinative standards for their decisions in such cases. He can readily acknowledge that the application of those principles will always involve *weak* discretion because the correctness or incorrectness of any application is not strictly demonstrable. He can therefore readily acknowledge that a greater reliance on moral principles will entail an increase in the exercise of weak discretion. However, such an acknowledgment does not at all impair or belie his thesis that the availability of moral principles as adjudicative touchstones will significantly reduce the need for judges to exercise *strong* discretion. In short, Dworkin could endorse the first two sentences in the latest quotation from Coleman, so long as we recognize that the augmented discretion and the diminished discretion are of different types. Once we do recognize that point, however, we can see that the third sentence in the quotation is unsustainable—at least if the phrase 'positivist view of discretion' refers to the positivist view of discretion as characterized by Dworkin.

Shapiro and Coleman both contend that the thoroughgoing Incorporationist thesis is a conditional proposition. As Shapiro writes: '[T]he thesis of robust incorporationism is conditional in nature. The robust incorporationist claims that *if* a judicial convention arises that treats moral appropriateness as the sole condition of legality, *then* such a conventional rule counts as a rule of recognition' (Shapiro, 'Law', 156, emphases in original). Coleman similarly submits that his version of Incorporationism 'is properly understood as a conditional claim: If there are moral criteria of legality that are accepted by officials from an internal point of view and practiced by a sufficient number of them, and if the bulk of the population complies with the rules valid under those criteria, then there is a legal system in which morality is a condition of legality' (Coleman, 'Constraints', 182). Having formulated the robust Incorporationist position as a conditional proposition, Shapiro and Coleman can then easily demonstrate that my severe doubts about the sustainability of a robustly Incorporationist Rule of Recognition tend to underscore the truth of the position which I am assailing. After all, the antecedent in the conditional proposition is almost always false—which means that the overall proposition is almost always true regardless of the truth-value of its consequent. Moreover, since there are no grounds for thinking that the consequent will be false when the antecedent is true, we can safely conclude that the conditional claim of thoroughgoing Incorporationism is invariably true.

Now, there is absolutely no reason for me to object to the notion that the central thesis of robust Incorporationism presented as a conditional proposition is invariably true. On the contrary, I shall presently argue that a slightly bolder rendering of that thesis is likewise true. Before turning to that alternative rendering, however, we should glance at two aspects of the Shapiro/Coleman ripostes that may elicit some dissatisfaction in the reader. First, the ripostes have delineated the thoroughgoing version of Incorporationism in a manner that seems somewhat ad-hoc. Heretofore, the central tenet of Incorporationism has sometimes been expressed in other than a conditional form. It has quite frequently been expressed as an existentially quantified indicative proposition, which is precisely the form in which Shapiro articulates it at the outset of his latest article: 'There is some possible legal system where the legality of a norm does depend on some of its moral properties'.[9] Second, when the robust

---

[9] Shapiro, 'Law', 129. For further non-conditional indicative renderings of the central thesis of Incorporationism, see, e.g., Jules Coleman, 'Authority and Reason', in Robert George (ed.), *The Autonomy of Law* (Oxford: Clarendon Press, 1996) [hereinafter cited as Coleman, 'Authority'], 287, 305–6; Coleman, 'Incorporationism', 382. For some conditional formulations, see Brian Leiter, 'Realism, Hard Positivism, and Conceptual Analysis', 4 *Legal Theory* 533, 535 (1998); Scott Shapiro, 'The Difference that Rules Make', in Brian Bix (ed.), *Analyzing Law* (Oxford: Clarendon Press, 1998), 33, 57. Slightly more oblique in its conditionality is Coleman, 'Authority', 287–8, and considerably more oblique is Jules Coleman and Brian Leiter, 'Legal Positivism', in Dennis Patterson (ed.), *A Companion to Philosophy of Law and Legal Theory* (Oxford: Blackwell, 1996), 241, 251.

Incorporationist position is formulated as a conditional proposition, it becomes gratuitously unadventurous. The truth of such a proposition is consistent with the necessary falsehood of both its antecedent and its consequent.

Let us, then, concentrate on a version of thoroughgoing Incorporationism that is presented as an existentially quantified indicative claim—namely, the claim that there is at least one possible legal system in which the correctness of norms as moral principles is in all circumstances the sufficient condition for their status as legal norms. If an indicative proposition along these lines is true, then neither the antecedent nor the consequent of the conditional variant of robust Incorporationism is necessarily false. That is, the non-conditional indicative variant of robust Incorporationism is bolder and thus more interesting than its conditional counterpart. Furthermore, it is true. Contrary to what Shapiro and Coleman have supposed, I have always believed that the robust Incorporationist thesis in its ordinary indicative form (as well as in its conditional form, of course) is true.

Why, therefore, has Chapter 1 frowned upon the doctrine of thoroughgoing Incorporationism? The answer to this question lies not in a mistaken perception of that doctrine as false, but in a perception of it as highly misleading and unilluminating. For a clarification of this point, we should recall another argument by Hart in which he resorted to some elementary empirical claims. In his famous discussion of the minimum content of natural law (*Concept*, 189–95), he adverted to some basic characteristics of human beings and the world in which they live, and he concluded that the legal system in any viable society larger than a handful of families must include fundamental interdictory mandates that coincide in content with cardinal precepts of morality.[10] Now, suppose that an opponent were to point out that Hart's empirical premises do not strictly necessitate his conclusion. Such an opponent would accurately maintain that, even if we grant Hart's premises (as any sensible person should), we ought not to regard as logically incoherent the idea that a large-scale society can endure without basic legal prohibitions on murder, unprovoked assault, extensive vandalism, and other serious misdeeds. Though the sustainability of a society without those prohibitions is staggeringly unlikely, it is not logically impossible. Our imaginary opponent would thus counter Hart's position with the following thesis: there is at least one possible large-scale society that can endure in the absence of any fundamental legal proscriptions. Would such a rejoinder expose some significant shortcomings in Hart's discussion of the minimum content of natural law? Quite the contrary. We can briskly dismiss the opponent's position—not because it is false, but because (though true) it is trivial and

---

[10] I have argued elsewhere that Hart's discussion of the minimum content of natural law is fully consistent with legal positivism's insistence on the separability of law and morality. See my *In Defense of Legal Positivism* (Oxford: Oxford University Press, 1999) [hereinafter cited as *IDLP*], chap. 9.

profoundly misleading. It aridly describes a bare logical possibility that never has been actualized and never will be actualized.[11] Though the imaginary opponent would be correct in submitting that there is not any logical or conceptual incoherence in the notion of a durable large-scale society where no legal restraints whatsoever are placed on serious misdeeds, the likelihood of the emergence of such a society is so formidably remote that it should be disregarded by anyone who is constructing a theory of law or government. While the opponent's thesis is not strictly wrong, it is wholly misguided in what it emphasizes. It highlights a fanciful state of affairs that never has arisen and never will arise, and it consequently tends to obscure the fact that that state of affairs will not obtain under any minimally plausible set of circumstances.

Now, admittedly, the robust version of Incorporationism is not as outlandishly misleading as the imaginary opponent's riposte to Hart. Although the sustainability of an unalloyedly Incorporationist regime of law in any society larger than a handful of families is prodigiously unlikely—not least because the task of law-ascertainment is carried out by a government's myriad executive officials as well as by judicial officials[12]—it is not as close to being unimaginable as is the sustainability of a large-scale society without any legal curbs on serious wrongs. Hence, a doctrine that asserts the possibility of an unalloyedly Incorporationist legal regime within a large-scale society is not quite as misdirected in its emphasis as is the thesis described in my last paragraph. All the same, the proponents of robust Incorporationism highlight the prospect of a state of affairs that never has obtained and never will obtain in any sizeable society. They consequently tend to obscure the important fact that such a state of affairs will not emerge (in a sizeable society) under any credible set of circumstances.

Thus, while the extreme Incorporationist thesis is true,[13] it is unhelpfully distracting and unilluminating and needlessly problematic. Its virtues are fully shared and its shortcomings avoided by a moderate version of Incorporationism.

---

[11] As G.A. Cohen observes in a different context: '[W]hat is nearly true (though false) may be more important than what is strictly true, since what is strictly true may be only barely true'. G.A. Cohen, *History, Labour, and Freedom* (Oxford: Clarendon Press, 1988), 285.

[12] At one juncture, Shapiro points out that a robustly Incorporationist Rule of Recognition could prevail in a legal system with only two judges, 'both of whom are twin sisters, attend the same church, and are like-minded on ethical issues' (Shapiro, 'Law', 156). As is attested by my first chapter's several references to the possibility of a robustly Incorporationist Rule of Recognition in the legal system of an extremely small and homogeneous society, I have no wish whatsoever to dispute the truth of Shapiro's observation. All the same, his observation is irrelevant to the sorts of societies on which I am concentrating. With reference to medium-scale and large-scale societies, where multitudes of executive/administrative officials as well as judicial officials are obligated and empowered to engage in the activity of law-ascertainment, a scenario of a two-judge legal regime (with no executive/administrative officials, apparently) is perilously close to the Austinian depiction of each legal sovereign as a single person. Hart aptly labeled the latter depiction as 'a disastrously confusing piece of mythology' (*Concept*, 110).

[13] As is evident in Matthew H. Kramer, *Legal Theory, Political Theory, and Deconstruction* (Bloomington: Indiana University Press, 1991), 128–30, I differ from Hart in allowing that a robustly Incorporationist primitive regime of law is indeed a regime of law.

To be sure, Coleman has managed to develop a number of insights by defending the robust Incorporationist thesis against various conceptual challenges. Nevertheless, those challenges must also be parried by an advocate of moderate Incorporationism, and indeed the latter doctrine can handle them more smoothly (as will be further argued presently).

Moreover, as has been noted in Chapter 1, a modest Incorporationist thesis is peculiarly suitable for the accomplishment of the purpose which Incorporationism was devised to fulfill: that is, the purpose of fending off some of Dworkin's early attacks against legal positivism, which were focused on the role of moral principles as adjudicative touchstones in hard cases. Coleman expresses bemusement over my distinction between robust and moderate Incorporationism, alleging that it 'generate[s] more smoke than light'. He contends that 'distinguishing among kinds or categories of cases in which [Incorporationist] criteria might apply...is...not a particularly helpful dimension on which various rules of recognition can be arrayed', and he asserts that my position 'would still fail to answer the objection that motivates [Incorporationism] in the first place' (Coleman, 'Constraints', 178 n.17, 183). Yet, since the motivating objection to which Coleman adverts is Dworkin's observation that moral principles are invoked by Anglo-American judges to resolve some hard cases—a fact of Anglo-American adjudication which Dworkin believes to be incompatible with the positivist model of law—my singling out of modest Incorporationism in contradistinction to thoroughgoing Incorporationism is entirely apposite.

To grasp fully the aptness of the moderate Incorporationist thesis in this context, we should reflect briefly on what it claims. That thesis does not deny anything affirmed by the robust Incorporationist doctrine. It maintains that there is at least one credible large-scale legal system in which the moral correctness of norms is sufficient for their status as legal norms in some or all hard cases. Because this moderate thesis does not in any way deny the bolder claim of thoroughgoing Incorporationism, it does not make the mistake of suggesting that that bolder claim is false. At the same time, it draws attention to the precise point of contention between Dworkin and legal positivists; it asserts no more and no less than what is necessary to rebut Dworkin's criticism. In other words, it asserts what is necessary to respond effectively to the crux that gave rise to Incorporationist theories. A thesis focused on hard cases is singularly appropriate for overcoming an objection that is focused on hard cases. A more sweeping thesis is superfluous. (Furthermore, with regard to my highlighting of the distinction between easy cases and hard cases—though not with regard to certain other features—my espousal of modest Incorporationism manifestly runs parallel to Hart's discussion of linguistic and normative determinacy in the seventh chapter of *The Concept of Law*. Hart took the view that the existence of a legal system is consistent with pervasive disagreement in the system's penumbra but is inconsistent with such disagreement in the system's core. I correspondingly take the view that the existence of any large-scale regime of law is consistent with officials' reliance on moral correctness as the sufficient condition for legal validity throughout the regime's penumbra, but that it is inconsistent with any comparable reliance throughout the regime's core. My view follows from a combination of the Hartian view and the general empirical assumption that underlies my championing of modest Incorporationism.)

In short, because the Dworkinian attack that impelled the development of Incorporationism was concerned with the role of moral precepts in hard cases, it can most pertinently be repelled by a thesis oriented toward that role in exactly such cases. Of course, to maintain as much is not per se to establish that a modest variant of Incorporationism can surmount all the conceptual hurdles that confront it. Shapiro's challenge must be met by a modest version of the doctrine version. The rest of this chapter will seek to show that a moderate Incorporationist position changes—not by refuting them, but by defusing

Before we move on a quick caveat should be entered. Nothing i way to depreciate the importance and value o When such argumentation is illuminating an rable to philosophical argumentation that relic Indeed, Chapter 1's defense of Inclusive Leg My complaint here is only about conceptua that do not shed light on any past, present, or future states of affairs (in societies that are not tiny and highly homogeneous). Such theses are more obfuscatory than instructive.

B. What Happens in Hard Cases

In my first chapter, I unreservedly acknowledged the correctness of Shapiro's observation that the moral principles validated by an Incorporationist Rule of Recognition do not constitute any reasons-for-action beyond those constituted by the Incorporationist criteria themselves. His observation plainly applies to a moderately Incorporationist Rule of Recognition as much as to a robust version. My tack in Chapter 1 has not been to gainsay the soundness of Shapiro's arguments on this point, but to remove their sting when they are invoked against modest Incorporationism. Specifically I have contended that, although incorporated moral precepts cannot furnish judges or citizens with any independent reasons-for-action (that is, reasons beyond those furnished by an Incorporationist Rule of Recognition itself), such an inability is untroubling in hard cases because those precepts are called upon to play an altogether different role therein. Given that the hard cases lie outside the determinate ambits of the source-based legal norms, and given that a mildly Incorporationist Rule of Recognition predetermines the correct ways of resolving any disputes that do lie outside those ambits, the hard cases will not be decided by reference to legal norms that serve as partly independent reasons-for-action. Moral precepts appropriately invoked to handle those cases are obviously not such reasons, then, but are means of specifying the requirements ordained by the Incorporationist strand in the Rule of Recognition. Though the precepts do not add to what the Rule of Recognition demands, they enable its demands to be spelled out.

In Chapter 1, I have described the function of moral precepts in hard cases as that of 'terminating disputes' and 'achieving closure' and 'resolv[ing] the points at issue'. The last-mentioned phrase in particular has led Shapiro to misconstrue my argument. He writes: 'When a rule is used to resolve a dispute, the rule is treated as a reason to decide the dispute in accordance with the rule. To resolve disputes, therefore, is to guide evaluative behavior. If my argument is correct, then moral rules that lack pedigrees cannot resolve disputes because these rules cannot motivate a judge to resolve a dispute in a manner differently than he might have, had he not appealed to the rule' (Shapiro, 'Law', 159). Though Shapiro's misreading of my remarks is pardonable, it is indeed a misreading that impels his rejoinder. My account of the invocation of apposite moral principles in hard cases does not attribute to them the role of independent bases for reaching certain decisions in those cases and for eschewing contrary decisions. Rather, the principles as properly formulated by judges are simply the vehicles through which the dispute-terminating effects of the Incorporationist strand in the Rule of Recognition become discernible and gain expression.

When moral precepts are adduced appropriately in hard cases within a modestly Incorporationist legal system, they operate in two chief ways. First, they enable or facilitate the endeavors of judges to figure out what their Rule of Recognition requires. As Shapiro states, 'a judge might appeal to moral principles themselves to aid him in applying the rule of recognition' (Shapiro, 'Law', 159 n.65). Of course, this heuristic function does not consist in providing some new reasons for any particular decisions; all decision-determining reasons in properly decided hard cases are provided by the mildly Incorporationist criterion in the Rule of Recognition. The moral principles' heuristic function consists instead in clarifying and distilling the demands of that criterion. While crystallizing or concretizing those demands, the moral principles do not add thereto (or subtract therefrom). They encapsulate at an intermediate level the implications of the Incorporationist instruction in the Rule of Recognition, and they accordingly supply judges with a cognitive handle on that abstract instruction.

In addition, the moral precepts correctly cited by the moderately Incorporationist judges are the means by which they express to citizens and their fellow officials the requirements of their Rule of Recognition. Although that Rule of Recognition has already settled the proper resolution of each hard case to which there is a uniquely correct moral answer, the invocation of a moral principle enables the judges in such a case to indicate persuasively what the already-settled resolution is. By adducing a moral principle to specify quite concretely the demands of morality in the context of a knotty dispute that is not resolvable through recourse to source-based laws, the judges signal the moral soundness of their decision and its consequent conformity with the prevailing standards of law-ascertainment. They reaffirm to citizens the moral appropriateness and requisiteness of their verdict. They reaffirm to their fellow officials their compliance with the moderately Incorporationist Rule of Recognition which makes moral requisiteness the touchstone for selecting norms to deal with hard cases.

Thus, when moral precepts are applied to the facts of hard cases within a mildly Incorporationist regime, they perform both a heuristic function and a confirmatory function. Moreover, they are fully genuine mandates in that they require certain outcomes and disallow contrary outcomes. What they cannot do, of course—if they have been chosen correctly—is to require anything other than what is required by the mildly Incorporationist Rule of Recognition itself. In the eyes of Shapiro, that inability is sufficient to disqualify those sourceless moral precepts from being classified as legal norms. He adheres to a tenet designated as the 'Practical Difference Thesis', which he states as follows: 'Legal rules must in principle be capable of securing compliance by making a difference to an agent's practical reasoning' (Shapiro, 'Law', 129). Because moral principles incorporated into the law will never lead to conclusions other than those dictated by the Rule of Recognition under which the principles have been incorporated, they do not satisfy the Practical Difference Thesis. They are therefore only ersatz legal norms, in Shapiro's view.

Let us note a key ambiguity in the Practical Difference Thesis. Is its implicit quantifier universal or plurative? That is, does the thesis assert something about *all* legal norms or only about *most* legal norms? Shapiro obviously intends the thesis to be taken as a conceptual claim containing a universal quantifier, whereas I subscribe to it as a partly conceptual and partly empirical claim containing a plurative quantifier. Let us probe his argument in favor of the thesis as he construes it.

Shapiro connects the Practical Difference Thesis to a broader conception of law, which he labels as 'functionalist' (Shapiro, 'Law', 167–9). He correctly remarks that Hartian legal positivism attributes to law the function of guiding conduct by means of the norms which a legal system sets forth as authoritative standards of behavior. Shapiro presumes that law's fulfillment of this function entails the capacity of every legal mandate to guide conduct. '[A]ll legal rules have, as their function, the guidance of conduct.' And since a norm's guidance of conduct involves its making a difference to people's practical reasoning—by requiring patterns of behavior that are not already required by the Rule of Recognition in the legal system where the norm is located—Shapiro can conclude that 'no rule that is in principle incapable of making a practical difference can be a legal rule' (Shapiro, 'Law', 168).

The suspect link in this chain of reasoning is the premise that the accomplishment of law's function entails the capacity of *every* legal mandate to guide conduct. We need to be told why a legal system's performance of that function excludes the possibility that *most* of the system's mandates, as opposed to *all* of its mandates, are endowed with a guiding capacity. Responding to some criticisms largely along these lines from Wilfrid Waluchow and Kenneth Himma, Shapiro offers the following argument in support of his premise: '[I]n the case of legal rules and legal institutions[,] such an inference [an inference that a part has the function F just because the whole has the function F] is sound. For legal rules are *the means by which* legal systems guide conduct. We can say that the function of legal rules is to guide conduct because they have been produced by legal institutions in order to guide conduct' (Shapiro, 'Law', 169, emphasis in original). The argument in this quotation does not clinch the matter, for the quotation's final two sentences are just as ambiguous as the initial formulation of the Practical Difference Thesis. Each of those sentences can stand up perfectly well even if the phrase 'legal rules' in each of them is taken to denote *most* legal mandates rather than *all* such mandates. A legal system can admirably carry out its function of laying down authoritative directives to steer human conduct into prescribed channels, even if some of its mandates do not contribute to that function but instead play only heuristic and confirmatory roles. Shapiro cannot settle the choice between a universal quantifier and a plurative quantifier for his Practical Difference Thesis by adverting to the role which Hart attributed to law. An ascription of that role to law is consistent with the Practical Difference Thesis under either interpretation.

Indeed, the overall guiding function of law can hardly avail Exclusive Legal Positivists such as Shapiro, since the difficult cases in which moral principles get invoked as decisive standards are cases in which the source-based legal norms do not provide determinate guidance. Gaps or contradictions or ambiguities in the array of source-based norms give rise to lacunae in the guiding sway of law that are filled (in some regimes) by officials' resorting to moral principles. For the Exclusive Legal Positivist, the overcoming of those lacunae does not in any way mean that the invoked moral principles are legal norms. As substitutes for legal norms, the principles fill in where the law has run out. Hence, an Exclusive Legal Positivist such as Shapiro, who accepts Hart's characterization of law's function, must also accept that any particular legal system can and does perform that function notwithstanding the occurrence of lacunae in the system's matrix of source-based norms. Most disputes that arise in the jurisdiction of each system are covered by such a matrix, but some of the disputes fall within the lacunae. In other words, when Exclusive Legal Positivists and moderate Incorporationists endorse Hart's functionalist conception of law, they are at one in thinking that a legal regime's guiding role is performed across most circumstances but not across all circumstances. Neither the Exclusive Legal Positivists nor the modest Incorporationists believe that the guidance offered by a legal system through its source-based norms is seamless or comprehensive. Everyone believes that at any given juncture the source-based norms omit from their coverage a number of possible sets of circumstances. All the same, everyone believes that the guiding function of law can be fulfilled and is fulfilled. Hence, the Exclusivists and the moderate Incorporationists differ only over the question how the moral precepts correctly invoked in hard cases should be classified. Exclusivists will perceive those precepts as non-legal norms to which judges appeal when the guidance of legal norms (source-based norms) has run out. Modest Incorporationists will perceive those precepts as non-guiding legal norms that are adduced by judges for heuristic and confirmatory purposes when the guidance of source-based legal norms has run out. That is, the sole issue in controversy is whether the moral principles are non-legal norms or non-guiding legal norms. Such an issue cannot be resolved by reference to the role of law as an institution that establishes source-based standards for the purpose of steering conduct. After all, the Exclusive Legal Positivists and the moderate Incorporationists can agree not only in attributing such a role to law, but also on the following points: the source-based standards do not provide determinate guidance in hard cases; the role of law can be achieved and is achieved despite the inability of the source-based standards to yield determinate guidance in certain circumstances; the moral principles correctly relied upon by mildly Incorporationist judges in hard cases perform no more than heuristic and confirmatory roles. The only area of disagreement, then, is the question whether the non-guiding principles invoked in hard cases are legal or non-legal. Any dispute over that question cannot be put to an end by recourse to the role of law mentioned just above, since neither side to the dispute has contested that role.

If we are to break out of the deadlock just described, we shall have to marshal arguments that go beyond a focus on law's basic function. Chapter 1 has sought to present just such an argument, by maintaining that the considerations which lead us to acknowledge the status of some customary norms as legal mandates should lead us also to acknowledge the status of incorporated moral principles as legal norms. That line of reasoning will not be recapitulated here, because Shapiro does not address it at all. (We shall return to it in Chapter 3.) Nonetheless, what should be noted in the present context is that the specified line of reasoning has been put forward in an effort to keep the debate between Exclusive Legal Positivists and modest Incorporationists from amounting to no more than an exchange of rival stipulations. My argument tries to offer a route for moving beyond the frustrating stand-off that would ensue from such an exchange.

Let us close this subsection by pondering the nature of Shapiro's Practical Difference Thesis, as understood by a proponent of moderate Incorporationism. Construed as a purely conceptual claim, that thesis should be rejected—regardless of whether we deem its implicit quantifier to be universal or plurative.[14] Coleman is quite correct to maintain as much. If the scheme of governance in a

---

[14] In fairness to Shapiro, I should note that he acknowledges the possibility of one's coherently rejecting his version of the Practical Difference Thesis. See, e.g., Shapiro, 'Law', 129–30.

very small and stable and homogeneous community achieves considerable regularity in its operations on the basis of a robustly Incorporationist Rule of Recognition, then the conditions for the existence of a legal system are satisfied even though the Practical Difference Thesis is not.

By contrast, when the Practical Difference Thesis is construed as a partly empirical claim—which is how a modest Incorporationist will generally choose to construe it—it is fully acceptable as long as its implicit quantifier is plurative rather than universal. So understood, that thesis submits that most legal norms constitute partly independent reasons for officials and citizens to behave in certain prescribed ways. Left open is the possibility that some legal norms in this or that system are incapable of constituting such reasons (though they are capable of performing heuristic and confirmatory functions); moral precepts are just such norms, when invoked under a mildly Incorporationist Rule of Recognition in hard cases where the source-based legal standards do not yield determinate guidance. Now, we can know—to some degree as an empirical matter— that most of the norms in any large-scale system of law will be partly independent reasons-for-action that are ascertainable as such. Where most of the norms applied by a large-scale scheme of governance do not form such reasons, the scheme will lack the regularity and coordination that are indispensable for the existence of a legal regime. Ergo, in a large-scale society where a legal system prevails (that is, in any realistic large-scale society that is tenable at all), most of the authoritative norms applied by officials for the assessment of conduct will amount to reasons-for-action that are not wholly derivative of the reasons furnished by the society's Rule of Recognition itself. Such is the message of a plurative and partly empirical version of the Practical Difference Thesis, which effectively encapsulates the conceptual and empirical claims of modest Incorporationism. That thesis reserves a place for non-source-based legal norms, but the place is correctly characterized as the domain of exceptionality rather than the domain of typicality.

C. Regularity in Irregular Circumstances

Coleman suggests that I have contended that the officials who run a mildly Incorporationist legal system will arrive at decisions in hard cases in a coordinated fashion as if they were applying straightforward source-based legal norms. He writes: 'I am unpersuaded by Kramer's view that modest Incorporationism can sustain a legal practice in hard cases, but not more generally. Surely if there are lots of hard cases, then on Kramer's view the controversiality of morality ought to undermine the efforts of officials to resolve disputes in a coordinated fashion. Controversy is controversy regardless of the scope of application' (Coleman, 'Constraints', 183 n.24). Had my first chapter put forward the view which Coleman here derides, it would indeed have been vulnerable to his strictures. In fact, however, Chapter 1 has sought to emphasize that the likelihood of intractable disagreements among legal officials about the appropriate outcomes in hard cases is overwhelmingly high. The shared adherence by the officials to a mildly Incorporationist Rule of Recognition does not prevent them from diverging markedly in their selection and application of moral principles for dispatching difficult disputes.

Shapiro acknowledges that I have taken account of the high probability of judicial disunity, but he maintains that my effort to deal with it is unsuccessful. He queries whether officials can abide by the Incorporationist criterion in a moderately Incorporationist Rule of Recognition, given that the officials will persistently disagree with one another in hard cases, and given that uniquely correct answers will be available in some hard cases under the Incorporationist criterion. In a hard case where a uniquely correct answer is available and where only some officials arrive at that answer, there is no relevant convergence of the officials' behavior to the extent that is necessary for the existence of a conventional norm. Since this pattern of non-convergence will obtain in a large majority of hard cases, the Incorporationist criterion in a moderately Incorporationist Rule of Recognition cannot exist as such. After all, if that criterion has materialized, it has materialized as a conventional norm that underlies and presupposes the convergent behavior of officials in hard cases. Since that convergent behavior is missing, however, the Incorporationist criterion must itself be nonexistent. Shapiro presses this point forcefully:

> Rules of recognition are conventional rules, and conventional rules must be practiced. It is not enough that people try to conform to such rules—what matters is that they do as they are required to do. If most people who entered churches neglected to take off their hats, but instead mistakenly removed their shoes, then there would be no convention in that community requiring the removal of hats in church. Hence, if Kramer lacks confidence that judges will normally conform to the rule of recognition in hard cases, then it cannot be said that a rule of recognition exists that regulates these hard cases. (Shapiro, 'Law', 160)

Though Shapiro's argument is powerful, it is not irrebuttable. One consideration which partly defuses his argument is that in some hard cases there will not be any uniquely correct answers. In each hard case for which no determination is uniquely correct, all the officials who operate a mildly Incorporationist regime will be acting in accordance with the Incorporationist criterion in their Rule of Recognition so long as their favored decisions and justifications are within a range of acceptable decisions and justifications. Within that range there will be ample room for clashing verdicts. Hence, in hard cases that lack uniquely correct solutions, the intractability of the disagreements among officials is fully consistent with the adherence by every official to an Incorporationist criterion for handling such cases. Manifold divergences among officials concerning the *ex*tension of such a criterion are compatible with a general consensus among them on the criterion's *in*tension.

More significant in the present context is a way of coping with the crux posed when a uniquely correct resolution of a difficult case is available under a moderately Incorporationist Rule of Recognition. In any such set of circumstances, only those officials who arrive at the uniquely correct verdict are acting in strict conformity with the Incorporationist criterion in their Rule of Recognition. Should we accordingly conclude that there is no convergence on that criterion by the other officials? And should we thus conclude (with Shapiro) that there is no sufficiently convergent behavior to ground the existence of the Incorporationist criterion as a conventional norm?

In reply to these questions, we should have recourse to a distinction that has been highlighted by Coleman in virtually all of his writings on legal positivism: the distinction between disagreements over content and disagreements over application.[15] In a hard case where some outcome is uniquely correct under a moderately Incorporationist Rule of Recognition, the officials who plump in good faith for other outcomes are engaged in a controversy over the *application* (rather than the basic *nature*) of the Incorporationist criterion in their Rule of Recognition. Even though they are wrong and their fellow officials are correct about the application of that criterion, they are indeed differing with their fellow officials over matters of application rather than over the matter of the criterion's basic tenor. Their misguided beliefs about the implementation of that criterion do not amount to a rejection of it and to an embrace of some other law-ascertaining benchmark. They are at one with their fellow officials in upholding an Incorporationist criterion in their Rule of Recognition, though they are less astute than their fellow officials in understanding what that criterion requires in particular settings.

Two potential rejoinders to the argument in the last paragraph must be deflected. First, in line with some of the remarks in Dworkin's early assaults on legal positivism,[16] a critic might object that my argument presupposes a consensus among mildly Incorporationist officials on some formulation of the Incorporationist criterion in their Rule of Recognition. Yet, the critic would retort, a construal of the officials' interaction along these lines would implausibly portray their differences over the Incorporationist criterion as disputes over borderline applications of terms. Second, a critic might simply point out that some of the officials in the envisaged legal system are misapplying the Incorporationist criterion, perhaps even in every hard case where a uniquely correct answer is available. How, then, can we rightly say that those officials are adhering to that criterion?

---

[15] Coleman's work in this area has been valuable, but it does not squarely address the precise question which I shall be pondering: the question whether, in a hard case where one outcome is uniquely correct, the officials in a mildly Incorporationist regime who opt in good faith for other outcomes are conforming to the Incorporationist criterion in their Rule of Recognition.

[16] Ronald Dworkin, *supra* note 8, at 56, 62–3.

These two objections can be parried by way of the same general observation. On the one hand, the objections should hardly be dismissed summarily. As the first of them rightly suggests, a depiction of the officials' disharmony as a set of quarrels over borderline uses of words is far from compelling. Although a widely accepted formulation of the Incorporationist criterion in the officials' Rule of Recognition may well crystallize within the highly reflective and deliberative processes of jural decision-making, one cannot often credibly maintain that the clashing verdicts of the officials in hard cases are products of divergent definitions of the words in any such formulation. Likewise, the second of the posited ripostes is warranted in submitting that, if strict compliance in the form of correct implementation is an essential earmark of adherence to a conventional norm, then the officials who misapply an Incorporationist criterion in some hard cases are not adhering to that criterion. If there were no alternative basis for deeming them to be in compliance with that criterion—that is, if the only sort of compliance were strict compliance involving correct applications—then the second of the posited rejoinders above would be quite telling, in regard to hard cases with uniquely correct outcomes.

On the other hand, fortunately, both of the aforementioned rejoinders can be countered by a focus on the patterns of officials' arguments and justifications. Contrary to what the first objection maintains, the existence of an Incorporationist criterion in a modestly Incorporationist Rule of Recognition does not depend on the emergence of a formulation to which all the officials subscribe. Instead, it depends on a practice of justification in which the Incorporationist criterion is immanent as a shared presupposition (and also as an effect). When the officials in a moderately Incorporationist regime present their decisions in hard cases, they seek to explain and justify those decisions by reference to considerations that are identifiably moral. Underlying this practice of moral justification is the Incorporationist criterion in their Rule of Recognition. Though the officials might give expression to that criterion in a formulation on which they concur, they might cleave to it simply as a tacit preconception that informs their decisions and their articulated rationales. In either event, we can usually best understand the disaccord in hard cases (within a mildly Incorporationist legal system) as disagreements over the implications and rankings of moral values rather than over the meanings of words.

Contrary to what is contended by the second of the potential objections, strict compliance with the Incorporationist criterion in a Rule of Recognition— namely, compliance that involves correct applications of the concepts in that criterion—is not the only species of compliance. In hard cases with uniquely correct outcomes, officials who arrive at the wrong decisions can nonetheless be upholding their Incorporationist criterion for dealing with such cases, so long as they endeavor plausibly to explain those decisions by reference to pertinent reasons. In this context, the phrase 'pertinent reasons' denotes any considerations that are identifiable as ethically significant factors which should be taken into account by someone who is passing moral judgment on the problems which the officials have to address. Insofar as the officials credibly tie their verdicts to such factors, they are engaging in the process of moral assessment and moral justification which their Incorporationist criterion requires of them. Although they are advocating erroneous outcomes, they are thereby misapplying their Incorporationist criterion rather than shifting to some other touchstone for law-ascertainment. Their upholding of that criterion is evidenced by the fact that they appeal to germane reasons for their decisions. In other words, they acknowledge the general tenor of the Incorporationist strand in their Rule of Recognition by commending their determinations on grounds of the very sort which that strand makes relevant. The fact that they get the balance of reasons wrong is merely indicative of a failure to apply the Incorporationist criterion correctly; it does not at all consist in a rejection of that criterion or in a failure to grasp the nature of the rationales which the officials are obligated thereunder to advance. Once we concentrate on the patterns and categories of official justifications, we can see that the mistaken judgments of some officials are errors of application rather than errors in identifying the basic law-ascertaining standard to be applied. (Of course, nothing said here is meant to suggest that officials in hard cases cannot be disagreeing with one another about the substance of the criteria in their Rule of Recognition. Some hard cases undoubtedly do involve disputes over the nature of those criteria, and do not extend solely to the applications thereof. My purpose has been merely to argue that not all hard cases are of that kind; some such cases involve disputes solely at the level of criterial *applications*. In so arguing, I have been seeking to overcome Shapiro's attempt to demonstrate the impossibility of a mildly Incorporationist Rule of Recognition. That is, I have been seeking to establish that the existence of an Incorporationist criterion for dealing with hard cases is not belied by the sheer fact that, in just about any hard case with a uniquely correct outcome, there will be a number of officials who champion erroneous conclusions.)

In light of these remarks, let us probe afresh Shapiro's example of a conventional norm requiring people to doff their hats when entering churches. Shapiro unimpeachably asserts that no such norm exists if many people in fact keep their hats on and remove their shoes when they enter churches. Because conventional norms are immanent in certain patterns of convergent behavior, no conventional hat-doffing norm obtains if many people seldom or never take their hats off. Suppose, however, that the norm in question does not specifically require the removing of hats but instead requires each person to show proper respect and courtesy when entering a church. Or perhaps, slightly more concretely, the norm requires each person to show proper respect and courtesy by doffing some item of apparel when entering a church. In either event, disagreements among people over the removal of shoes versus the removal of hats are disagreements about the correct application of a norm whose content is not in dispute. Divergence at the level of application does not preclude convergence at the level of the norm's existence and general tenor.

Now suppose that, under the norm requiring displays of proper respect and courtesy (norm *N*), there is a uniquely correct answer to the question concerning the removal of hats versus the removal of shoes. If a correct application of *N* would yield the conclusion that hats are the items of attire that should be doffed, then anyone who instead takes off his shoes when entering a church has misapplied *N*. However, if his removal of his shoes is a sincere effort to comply with *N*'s requirements, then he has indeed misapplied the norm rather than flouted it. He does not thereby deny the bindingness or the nature of *N*, but simply goes astray in seeking to implement its demands. A conventional norm calling for courtesy and respect can perfectly well obtain as such even if many people commit misjudgments when bringing to bear its requirements on some particular circumstances.

How, then, do we tell which norm is the operative norm? That is, how do we tell whether the people who take off their shoes before entering churches are endeavoring to abide by *N* or are instead endeavoring to abide by a much more specifically focused norm along the lines described by Shapiro? Clearly, this question cannot be answered *in abstracto*. In order to answer it at all, we have to study the sorts of justifications that would be offered by the people whose behavior is under scrutiny. If (when asked) those people would sincerely reply that they remove their shoes in order to comply with a social norm which requires that very type of behavior from anyone who enters a church, then they falsely believe that a conventional shoe-doffing norm exists in their society. If by contrast their replies would focus on the appositeness of taking off one's shoes as a means of showing proper respect and courtesy, and if the people who doff their hats would characterize their own conduct similarly with reference to the demands of courtesy and respect, then *N* is the operative norm which the two sets of people are applying. Of course, *ex hypothesi* any people in this latter scenario who remove their shoes are misapplying *N*, but the key point is that they are disagreeing with the hat-doffers only at the level of application and not at the level of content. A situation in which some churchgoers take off their hats whereas others take off their shoes can be a situation involving a sufficient degree of convergence to constitute a conventional norm; the convergence resides not in the specific modes of conduct but in the justificatory orientation that impels those modes of conduct.

To be sure, the nature of the prevailing norm will not always be as clear-cut as has been envisaged in the preceding paragraph. Sometimes people's actual or hypothetical justifications of their behavior will not be precise enough to enable the identification of the exact norm toward which that behavior is oriented. (Perhaps there is no unequivocal fact of the matter in regard to the norm's content, or perhaps the norm's determinate content is not unequivocally ascertainable by an observer.) My aim in the last few paragraphs has not been to submit that the bearings of a social practice's normative structure will always be univocal and transparent. Rather, my aim has merely been to note that those bearings can be univocal and that the norm underlying the churchgoers' practice can consist in N. To establish as much is not to deny that in other circumstances the underlying norm might be quite unsettled; nor, plainly, am I denying the possibility of an underlying norm that is much more concretely focused than N, like the hat-doffing rule to which Shapiro adverts. The last few paragraphs have certainly not attempted to demonstrate that Shapiro's account of the church-goers' behavior is necessarily wrong. Instead, in response to Shapiro's claim that the churchgoers' nonconvergent behavior cannot be oriented toward any con-ventional norm, my discussion has sought to reveal that just such a norm—albeit a fairly abstract norm such as N—can serve as the unifying fundament of their disparate modes of conduct, which emerge as applications (and misapplications) of that norm. Much the same is true, of course, in connection with an Incorpora-tionist criterion for dealing with hard cases. Officials' disagreements at the level of specific invocations of moral principles are consistent with their shared adherence to the aforementioned criterion, which the officials apply or misapply when they take their divergent stances at the level of the specific invocations.

Has my argument in this subsection disclosed a route for the rehabilitation of thoroughgoing Incorporationism? Having given salience to Coleman's distinc-tion between disagreements over content and disagreements over application, my discussion here may seem to have undercut my previous lines of reasoning about the unsustainability of a robustly Incorporationist legal regime. My claim (a partly empirical claim) in those previous lines of reasoning has been that an unremittingly Incorporationist regime would lack the regularity and coordin-ation that are essential for the existence of a legal system as such. Contrariwise, the discussion in the present subsection has contended that a lack of congruence among the judgments of various people is compatible with their shared adher-ence to an overarching norm such as N. A proponent of thoroughgoing Incor-porationism might respond by declaring that a pervasive lack of consistency among the judgments of officials is compatible with their shared adherence to a thoroughly Incorporationist Rule of Recognition. Though the disaccord among the officials' decisions will be severe, its occurrence is not at odds with the sway of such a Rule of Recognition. So the advocate of robust Incorporationism might argue.

Any argument along those lines would founder, for it would miss the point of my challenges to robust Incorporationism. While accepting that officials' clash-ing decisions within a thoroughly Incorporationist scheme of governance can be subsumed under a conventional norm that comprehends the scheme, one should insist that any such norm is not a Rule of Recognition. It is not a Rule of Recognition, because the scheme of governance which it underpins is devoid of the operational regularity that characterizes any genuine system of law. In other words, my eschewal of robust Incorporationism is focused on the level of application. At that level, the inconsistencies among the law-ascertaining deci-sions of the officials in a large-scale robustly Incorporationist regime will run athwart law's regularized channeling of conduct, to such an extent that no legal system can be said to exist therein. Whether or not the hugger-mugger of such a regime is a set of applications and misapplications of some underlying conventional norm, it disqualifies the regime from being classified as a legal system. There cannot be any functional system of law in a society whose dispute-resolving institutions yield so little consistency among outcomes and among the rationales for those outcomes.

Naturally, a dearth of consistency among outcomes and among rationales will obtain as well in modestly Incorporationist legal systems, in regard to hard cases. When confined to such cases, however, the paucity of consistency does not preclude the existence or impair the vibrancy of a legal regime at all. Any such regime will throw up controversies involving questions to which there are no determinate answers under the applicable source-based legal norms. Although such controversies will be numerous in a huge legal system, they will not amount to more than a small proportion of the situations in which judicial officials or executive officials reach decisions (implicitly or explicitly) on people's legal entitlements. In the large majority of such decision-making situations in any veritable legal regime, the implications of the prevailing legal norms will be clear-cut and will thus not be productive of any nontrivial uncertainty. Hence, the occurrence of unpredictability and unabating disagreements in hard cases will not detract damagingly from the general functioning of a system of law. Suitably hemmed in as they are—that is, tightly hemmed in—the disagreements and the unpredictability are valuably invigorating rather than disquieting. Consequently, although some alternative ways of dealing with hard cases could yield greater predictability,[17] the modest Incorporationist approach to the matter helps to ensure both the sustainability and the dynamism of a legal system.

Finally, we should ponder a complexity which is not explicitly broached by Shapiro but which is obliquely raised by his remarks. One of the paramount aims of moderate Incorporationism has been to defend the notion that moral principles invoked by legal officials for hard cases are among the standing laws in any legal system where the invocation of such principles for such cases is a regularized practice. Yet, if courts are persistently misidentifying the moral principles that are suitable for dealing with hard cases, how can we accurately say that the mandates of morality have been incorporated into the law of the society in which the courts operate? In such circumstances, indeed, is there any fact of the matter concerning the norms which the courts are generally disposed to apply in hard cases? Whereas Shapiro has trained attention on the Incorporationist criterion within a mildly Incorporationist Rule of Recognition, these questions train attention on the moral principles that are validated as legal norms under such a criterion. One

---

[17] For some suggestive remarks on this point, see Ronald Dworkin, 'Is There Really No Right Answer in Hard Cases?' in *A Matter of Principle* (Cambridge, MA: Harvard University Press, 1985), 119, 128–30.

can rebut Shapiro's objection by adverting to the shared justificatory orientation of legal officials, but these new questions might seem insusceptible to being similarly parried. After all, even if the officials' Rule of Recognition is moderately Incorporationist in its content, the persistent misapplications of its Incorporationist criterion will amount to a failure to endow moral principles with the status of legal norms that are regularly invoked and applied in a proper ranking. Far from becoming incorporated into the law—so it might be argued—the correct moral principles get shunted aside in favor of other principles. Given as much, the questions above have recast Shapiro's objection in a stronger form. My own arguments have highlighted the likelihood of widespread disagreements among legal officials about the appropriate touchstones for addressing hard cases within a moderately Incorporationist regime. In light of the pervasiveness of those disagreements, and in light of the consequent irregularity in the patterns of officials' selections of the aforementioned touchstones, we might be inclined to infer that the officials' Rule of Recognition is Incorporationist only in its content and not in its effects. That is, we might be inclined to infer that their Rule of Recognition does not result in the entry of correct moral principles into the law.

Although the questions in the last paragraph do raise problems that are more formidable than Shapiro's query, they do not pose any fatal difficulties for modest Incorporationism. Let us consider a few responses, in an ascending order of importance. In the first place, the prime objective of this closing subsection has been to refute Shapiro's view that the existence of a moderately Incorporationist Rule of Recognition is impossible. Even if there were no way of defusing the questions advanced in my last paragraph, we would have no reason to conclude that a modestly Incorporationist Rule of Recognition is impossible. We would instead have to conclude that the existence of a legal system with a modestly Incorporationist Rule of Recognition is highly improbable. As a conceptual matter, nothing rules out the possibility that the officials in some legal regime will correctly identify moral principles with sufficient frequency (in hard cases) to incorporate those principles into the law as regularly invoked legal mandates. Especially when we note that regularity can fall quite far short of unerringness, we can see that the chances of the realization of the possibility just mentioned are very slim rather than nil. Accordingly, the chances of the emergence of a mildly Incorporationist legal system would at worst be very slim rather than nil. At worst, then, my refutation of Shapiro's stance remains intact.

A second point worth remarking here, in reply to the latter of the penultimate paragraph's two questions, is that legal officials who persistently choose the wrong moral principles when coming to grips with hard cases might nonetheless be invoking some set of principles with substantial regularity. Most likely, of course, is that they are invoking many of the principles that constitute the conventional morality of their society or their class. In any event, so long as the courts achieve a significant measure of uniformity in their invocations of norms for hard cases, there will be a fact of the matter concerning the norms which the sundry courts

are generally disposed to apply in such cases. Admittedly, because of the considerable likelihood of intractable divergences among officials on many of the points
of contention that are thrown up by hard cases, the chances of a substantial
degree of uniformity in the dispatching of such cases are slim; nevertheless, the
chances of such uniformity centered on *some or another* set of norms are higher
than the chances of such uniformity centered distinctively on the set of correct
moral principles in their proper ranking. Thus, the possible presence of some
fact of the matter concerning the norms which the courts are generally disposed
to apply in hard cases is something that especially clearly survives Shapiro's
challenges.

Third, and far more important, moral principles can get incorporated into the
law even if they are not correctly invoked on most occasions when they are
applicable. If a Rule of Recognition is indeed moderately Incorporationist in its
content, then it brings moral principles into the law regardless of how often they
are drawn upon correctly. In other words, the implications of the Incorporationist criterion in the specified Rule of Recognition are not determined by what
the officials think when they adhere to that criterion. Its extension is fixed not by
their beliefs about its extension, but by the facts of morality.[18] Whether or not the
officials make any correct judgments of application when they resort to their
moderately Incorporationist criterion, their acceptance of it has endowed the true
principles of morality with the status of laws that are to be brought to bear on the
controversies in hard cases. Perhaps those laws seldom get activated suitably, but
they are the applicable laws all the same.

In connection with this third response to the questions posed several paragraphs ago, a problem immediately arises. If the officials within a modestly
Incorporationist legal regime very seldom apply the Incorporationist criterion
in their Rule of Recognition correctly, then in what sense are they upholding that
criterion at all? How do we know what the content of their Rule of Recognition

---

[18] Obviously, I am presupposing that some moral propositions are determinately correct and that the
determinate correctness or incorrectness of such propositions is independent of what anyone thinks
about them. My conception of moral objectivity is very close to that in Ronald Dworkin, 'Objectivity
and Truth: You'd Better Believe It', 25 *Philosophy & Public Affairs* 87 (1996). In *IDLP*, 154–7, I have
discussed Dworkin's reflections on moral truth. A slightly more distant source of inspiration for my
remarks here is the work of Hilary Putnam and Saul Kripke (and others) on natural-kind terms. See, e.g.,
Hilary Putnam, 'The Meaning of "Meaning"', in *Mind, Language, and Reality* (Cambridge: Cambridge
University Press, 1975), 215; Saul Kripke, *Naming and Necessity* (Princeton: Princeton University Press,
1980), Lecture III.

However, I should make clear that my present discussion is perfectly consistent with the truth of almost
any variety of moral relativism (excluding only extreme subjectivism). If some variety of moral relativism is
true, then people's convictions pertaining to moral categories and to the implications thereof are determinative of the categories' actual implications. Yet there is a fact of the matter in respect of those
convictions themselves, a fact of the matter that is independent of anyone's second-order beliefs about
the first-order convictions. What those convictions are is independent of what anyone thinks that they are.
Thus, there is ample room for judicial error under an Incorporationist Rule of Recognition if moral
relativism is true, just as there is if moral objectivism is true. The truth of moral relativism would not make
my present discussion any less germane.

is, if we take them to be misapplying it frequently? The answers to these questions can be gathered from my discussion of Shapiro's scenario of the people who remove their shoes. That is, the key to the content of the moderately Incorporationist Rule of Recognition lies in the justificatory orientation of the officials who ascertain the law by reference to that Rule of Recognition. Let us suppose that, when actually or hypothetically called upon to justify their choices of authoritative precepts for resolving hard cases, the officials do maintain or would maintain that those choices fulfill the demands of morality. Let us suppose further that the officials do indeed sincerely adduce basic moral considerations and invoke basic moral categories when they come up with norms to handle the hard cases. If so, then their Rule of Recognition is moderately Incorporationist notwithstanding that its Incorporationist component is (*ex hypothesi*) often implemented wrongly. If contrariwise the conditions just mentioned do not obtain, then the officials' Rule of Recognition is not genuinely Incorporationist. For example, if the officials orient their law-ascertaining efforts toward specific moral precepts that are erroneous—rather than toward general moral concerns whose implications the officials misunderstand—then their Rule of Recognition is not genuinely Incorporationist. Its ostensibly Incorporationist element is not really focused on the demands of morality, but is instead focused directly on some misconceived renderings of those demands. (It is analogous to a rule requiring the removal of shoes, as opposed to a more general rule requiring apposite displays of courtesy, in the scenario adduced by Shapiro.) In such circumstances, the officials' endeavors to handle hard cases do not amount to misapplications of a criterion that requires invocations of correct moral principles; instead, their endeavors amount to accurate applications of ill-advised criteria. Those misguided law-ascertaining criteria that govern the handling of the hard cases are not veritably Incorporationist at all.

Of course, what has been said earlier in this subsection about the possible opacity of the content of a legal system's Rule of Recognition is pertinent here as well. We shall not always be able to tell, in the manner delineated by the preceding paragraph, whether a Rule of Recognition is genuinely Incorporationist or only ostensibly so. In such a situation, any apt characterization of a Rule of Recognition as Incorporationist or non-Incorporationist has to be overtly probabilistic. To acknowledge as much, however, is hardly to deny the reality and importance of the distinction between Incorporationist and non-Incorporationist regimes. That distinction is like any other major dichotomy in giving rise (quite harmlessly) to gray areas in its extension.

Thus, my strengthened version of Shapiro's objection—which raises its queries at the level of the moral principles that are incorporated into the law, rather than at the level of the law-ascertaining criteria under which those principles are incorporated—does not expose any weaknesses in modest Incorporationism. The existence of modestly Incorporationist legal systems is not only conceptually possible, but also eminently credible. To be sure, a legal system where officials correctly invoke moral principles with substantial uniformity in hard cases is fanciful. However, a legal system where the officials converge in their acceptance of a mildly Incorporationist Rule of Recognition while disagreeing with one another about the extension of its Incorporationist criterion is fully believable. So long as the officials earnestly essay to tailor their law-ascertaining determinations in hard cases entirely to the general demands of morality, their Rule of Recognition is moderately Incorporationist; that those determinations clash with one another among the different officials is neither here nor there. The existence of a mildly Incorporationist Rule of Recognition leaves plenty of room for disaccord at the level of concrete law-ascertaining choices. Such disaccord does not alter the fact that the norms incorporated into the law for hard cases by the mildly Incorporationist Rule of Recognition are the veritable principles of morality. Whether those principles are correctly identified in hard cases often or seldom, they have been made the dispositive touchstones for such cases by the tenor of the prevailing standards for law-ascertainment. Insofar as the officials appeal to those standards, they have committed themselves to the proposition that the true principles of morality are the laws that govern hard cases—even though the officials may typically go astray in hard cases by invoking and applying alternative norms (in a higgledy-piggledy fashion) which they mistakenly believe to be the true principles of morality. Precisely because a modestly Incorporationist regime can obtain as such even when errors of that sort are persistently occurring, we do not have any reason to think that the existence of such a regime is outlandishly rare. On the contrary, moderately Incorporationist legal systems are probably quite common.

3

On Morality as a Necessary or Sufficient Condition for Legality

Each of the last two chapters has defended Inclusive Legal Positivism and a modest variety of Incorporationism against Exclusive Legal Positivism and an extreme version of Incorporationism. The present chapter continues that enterprise by parrying some further lines of argument which the votaries of Exclusive Legal Positivism have marshaled, and by amplifying some aspects of the positions that have been staked out heretofore in this book. As has been true so far, the points of contention addressed by this chapter are topics that in recent years have been debated mainly among legal positivists rather than between legal positivists and their opponents. Hence, what is under consideration at this stage is not the general correctness of jurisprudential positivism, but some of its more specific implications. To say as much, of course, is hardly to say that the matters pondered herein are of minor significance. On the contrary, they pertain to central features of law and to the ways in which those features can most illuminatingly be explicated within a legal-positivist theory. We have seen as much in the last two chapters' encounters with Scott Shapiro, who submits that an Inclusivist or Incorporationist Rule of Recognition would preclude the fulfillment of law's guiding function. In the present chapter, we shall confront arguments which purport to show that an Inclusivist or Incorporationist Rule of Recognition would be incompatible with some of law's other fundamental properties: its conventionality, its regularity, its capacity to limit official discretion. In defense of Inclusive Legal Positivism and a modest Incorporationist position, this chapter will impugn each of those Exclusivist arguments. It will then move from a 'defensive' to an 'offensive' posture, as it expands on lines of reasoning from the previous two chapters. It explores further why the role of some customary norms as laws is a key to the superiority of Incorporationism over Exclusivism, and it likewise ponders afresh why the moderate version of Incorporationism is markedly preferable to the extreme version. With these defensive and offensive tacks, the current chapter significantly widens the scope of my efforts to uphold Inclusive Legal Positivism and modest Incorporationism against some rival conceptions of law put forward by other jurisprudential positivists.

I. Ripostes to Exclusive Legal Positivism

A. Andrei Marmor and the Conventionality of Law

Andrei Marmor has recently published a thought-provoking and philosophically sophisticated book in which he mounts a novel attack against Incorporationism.[1] Although some strands of his Exclusivist arguments are taken directly from his mentor Joseph Raz, his freshest and most interesting line of reasoning is based on his endeavor to reconceive the conventional foundations of law. That proposed reconception emerges in the opening chapter of his book, where he probes the character of the Rule of Recognition under which the officials in each legal system ascertain their system's laws. Like some other legal positivists in recent years, Marmor has concluded that the modeling of a Rule of Recognition as a set of solutions to game-theoretical coordination problems is far too confining. (A coordination problem of that sort is a situation in which people face alternative possible ways of acting, and in which the importance of acting concertedly is greater for each person than the importance of acting in the way which he or she independently prefers.) Marmor maintains that any Rule of Recognition is best understood not as a coordination convention but instead as a constitutive convention. That is, the law-ascertaining criteria in a Rule of Recognition are not a solution to some pre-existing problem of getting certain people to align their patterns of behavior; rather, those criteria constitute a social practice within which any number of distinctive values and objectives and problems develop. In this respect, a Rule of Recognition is similar to the rules of chess and other games. Its criteria establish the point or purpose of the enterprise which they constitute, instead of being impelled entirely by some antecedent point or purpose which they tend to serve. 'It is a typical feature of conventions constituting such practices as the game of chess, that they partly constitute the point or value of the activity itself, and it is in this sense that we can talk about autonomous practices: namely, that the point of engaging in them is not fully determined by any particular purpose or value which is external to the conventions constituting the practice' (Marmor, *Law*, 14). Although a social practice established by constitutive conventions is never fully autonomous from the broader concerns of human life that press upon it from the outside, it is autonomous to quite a perceptible degree. It invests each participant with some aims and values and preoccupations which are distinctively associated with that particular practice and which are therefore not simply derivative of the aforementioned broader concerns.

Though Marmor's account of law-ascertaining criteria is piquant and illuminating, it is scarcely unproblematic. For example, Marmor maintains that constitutive conventions are prone to change, whereas coordination conventions tend

---

[1] Andrei Marmor, *Positive Law and Objective Values* (Oxford: Oxford University Press, 2001) [hereinafter cited as Marmor, *Law*].

to be much more stable. He points to the rapid and manifold changes in the visual arts as 'a dramatic example of this process' (Marmor, *Law*, 16). The snag for an analysis along these lines is that some other constitutive conventions such as the rules of chess are generally very stable, whereas some coordination conventions such as ordinary language are susceptible to numerous mutations. Of course, one should not put forward such an observation as a knockdown objection to Marmor's approach, by any means; but it does indicate that the constitution/coordination demarcation is more complicated than his discussion sometimes suggests.

At any rate, the foregoing query and other queries that could be raised about the distinction drawn by Marmor between two broad types of conventions are beside the point. What is of interest here is not per se his account of law-ascertaining criteria as constitutive conventions, but the uses to which he puts that account in his attempt to vindicate Exclusive Legal Positivism. In the third chapter of his book, he argues squarely against the Incorporationist thesis that the correctness of a norm as a moral principle can be a sufficient condition for the norm's status as a law within any legal system whose officials treat such correctness as a hallmark of legal validity. His sheer oppugning of that thesis is not novel, of course, but his effort to ground his stance on his analysis of constitutive conventions is indeed a new twist on the Exclusivist credo. His basic line of reasoning, which appeals to the constitutive character of the criteria in any Rule of Recognition, is as follows: '[A]n essential element of such a social practice like law is that it is founded on *constitutive conventions*, namely, on a set of conventions which determine what the practice is and how one goes about engaging in it. . . . [C]onstitutive conventions have no role to play in determining that we should act according to moral reasons. Moral and other practical reasons are there to be acted upon, regardless of conventions. Conventions . . . cannot constitute reasons for acting according to reasons' (Marmor, *Law*, 51, emphasis in original).

According to Marmor, constitutive conventions are necessary if people are to have reasons to carry out the various steps that amount to participation in the activities which those conventions have shaped. In the absence of such conventions, people would have no reasons to perform those steps (such as the moving of chess pieces in certain ways). Yet, Marmor maintains, any Incorporationist criteria for the ascertainment of law cannot play such a reason-engendering role. Those criteria direct officials to arrive at decisions by reference to moral principles on which the officials already have reasons to rely. Instead of creating reasons where none has existed before, the Incorporationist conventions simply recapitulate the existing reasons. Hence, Marmor concludes, any norms classified as laws by Incorporationist criteria will not be products of constitutive conventions. Those norms obtain independently of all such conventions, as obligatory foci for the handling of the sundry controversies that are to be resolved by legal officials. They therefore cannot be genuinely legal standards, since constitutive conventions are essential for the existence of law.

This line of reasoning by Marmor is question-begging at best, and is thus wholly inconclusive. After all, as he himself emphasizes, the law-ascertaining determinations required by the Incorporationist criteria in a Rule of Recognition are crucially different from chess-playing moves; there are sufficient convention-independent reasons for arriving at the former, whereas there are no such reasons for engaging in the latter. An Incorporationist theorist should consequently reject the premise that, if there are sufficient reasons for orienting oneself toward the content of any law, they must comprise the intra-conventional reasons created by constitutive conventions. Marmor would retort that the law-ascertaining determinations reached by reference to Incorporationist criteria are not legal determinations at all, precisely because officials have sufficient reasons to arrive at those determinations even without any constitutive conventions that form a practice of law-ascertainment. However, he would thereby beg the question on the key point at issue. An Incorporationist theorist should reply that the norms singled out by Incorporationist criteria can be laws even if officials have sufficient convention-independent reasons to resort to those norms. Marmor would in turn contend that his opponents are abandoning their adherence to the notion that law is essentially conventional. Here we have come to the gist of the dispute. Two main rejoinders are pertinent.

First, even if it were true that *law* is essentially conventional in Marmor's sense, it would not necessarily be true that *every law* is a norm which officials have no sufficient convention-independent reasons to invoke. One could accept that every legal system is a product of constitutive conventions, while also affirming that any such system can contain some laws that would be binding as outcome-determining mandates even in the absence of the conventions that form the system in which they exist as laws. In other words, the situation concerning the legal norms validated by constitutive law-ascertaining criteria is broadly similar to the situation concerning the capacity of legal norms to make a difference in the practical reasoning of people. My questioning of Shapiro's Practical Difference Thesis in Chapter 2 is transferable, *mutatis mutandis*, to Marmor's account of the constitutive conventions that make up legal systems. Let us suppose for a moment that Marmor had come up with a Convention-Dependent Thesis: 'Legal norms must be such that, in the absence of a Rule of Recognition under which they gain their status as laws, there would not be sufficient reasons for anyone to resort to them when dealing with the sorts of disputes and problems that are handled by a legal system'. Just as my second chapter has asked about the implicit quantifier in Shapiro's Practical Difference Thesis, so too my present discussion should pose such a query about this imagined Convention-Dependent Thesis. Is its quantifier universal or plurative? That is, does the thesis purport to encompass *all* legal norms or only *most* such norms? Nothing in Marmor's analysis of constitutive conventions will have warranted the bolder version of the thesis rather than the milder version—which means that his analysis does not impugn my modest variant of Incorporationism.

Second, and perhaps even more important, one need not grant that every possible legal system is indeed a product of constitutive conventions. To insist on the conventionality of law is not perforce to concede that the conventionality must invariably be as Marmor describes it. Even a thoroughly Incorporationist legal regime is conventional in that it consists in sundry convergent modes of behavior (on the part of officials), which sustain a Rule of Recognition with a content that would have been different if the officials' convergent modes of behavior had been different. In other words, that content is determined by the patterns of behavior—including, of course, the attitudes which the behavior expresses—and is not preordained by the sheer nature of law. Albeit the principles validated as laws by an Incorporationist Rule of Recognition are not themselves conventional qua precepts of critical morality, their status *as laws* is indeed conventional through and through in the sense just delineated. That status would cease to obtain if the Rule of Recognition were to change in certain ways because of alterations in the behavior and attitudes of the relevant officials.

Furthermore, the prevailing Incorporationist criteria for the ascertainment of legal norms are likewise conventional in that an important reason why each official should adhere to those criteria is that other officials adhere to them and arrive at decisions based on them. To be sure, that reason is not the lone reason for each official to rely on the norms that are validated as laws by those criteria; as has been stated, each official also has sufficient convention-independent reasons for resorting to such norms. Moreover, admittedly, any particular official might in fact be motivated only by those convention-independent reasons. That is, he might base his law-ascertaining determinations solely on those convention-independent considerations notwithstanding that he also has convention-dependent reasons for the very same determinations. Nevertheless, in regard to each official, the concertedness of the behavior of other officials is indeed a factor that militates in favor of his going along with them by employing Incorporationist standards for the ascertainment of laws. The concertedness of their behavior in a legitimate enterprise that requires concertedness is a sufficient reason for him to do as they do.

In sum, Marmor's defense of Exclusive Legal Positivism is at best inconclusive. His analysis of constitutive conventions is stimulating, but it does not clinch his attack on Incorporationism. Even the boldest variety of Incorporationism does not fall prey to his strictures, for even such a variety is consistent with the premise of law's conventionality—so long as the conventionality is understood somewhat differently from the way in which Marmor understands it. He has failed to demonstrate any tension between Incorporationism and the central tenets of legal positivism, and he has likewise failed to expose any other weaknesses in the Incorporationist account of law.

B. On Uncertainty

In an important recent book,[2] Jules Coleman submits that some champions of Inclusive Legal Positivism and Incorporationism have misconstrued the tenor of the challenges to their positions that have been mounted by Exclusive Legal Positivists. Specifically, he contends, some proponents of Inclusivism have mistakenly thought that Exclusive Legal Positivists are concerned about the controversy and consequent uncertainty that would be engendered by Incorporationist criteria in a Rule of Recognition. In reply to this misguided conception of the debates between Exclusivists and Incorporationists, Coleman repeatedly maintains that '[c]ontroversy is *not* the issue for the exclusive legal positivist' (Coleman, *Practice*, 114, emphasis in original).

Exactly whose misconceptions are being dispelled by Coleman's broadsides is quite unclear. Coleman does not identify any Incorporationists or Inclusive Legal Positivists who have committed the error which he denounces. Although that error was perpetrated by Coleman himself in a 1996 essay,[3] it has not been perpetrated by other opponents of Exclusive Legal Positivism. Some of the wording in the relevant portion of his book suggests that he is attributing such an error to me. However, as should be evident from my opening two chapters, I have focused on the controversial character of moral principles not in order to combat Exclusive Legal Positivism but in order to explain why Coleman's version of Incorporationism is needlessly unilluminating. My contestation of Exclusivism (as opposed to robust Incorporationism) has not been focused on controversy and uncertainty at all. Thus, one should seriously doubt whether Coleman's animadversions will have found any genuine target; the blundering Inclusivist theorists whom he describes are imaginary.

All the same, whether or not any Inclusive Legal Positivists have ever stood in need of correction from Coleman on this matter, he is certainly justified in affirming that Exclusive Legal Positivists such as Raz and Shapiro are not preoccupied with the uncertainties of moral deliberation when they reject the doctrines of Inclusivism and Incorporationism. As Coleman aptly observes, Raz and Shapiro concentrate on 'the *conceptual possibility* of legal authority, not the *de facto* possibility of legality'.[4] However, because Coleman confines his attention to those two theorists, he apparently does not realize that some Exclusive Legal

---

[2] Jules Coleman, *The Practice of Principle* (Oxford: Oxford University Press, 2001) [hereinafter cited as Coleman, *Practice*], 111–14.

[3] Jules Coleman, 'Authority and Reason', in Robert George (ed.), *The Autonomy of Law* (Oxford: Clarendon Press, 1996), 287, 307–8. For a retraction, see Jules Coleman, 'Incorporationism, Conventionality, and the Practical Difference Thesis', 4 *Legal Theory* 381, 386 n.10 (1998).

[4] Coleman, *Practice*, 114. Cf. Joseph Raz, 'Postema on Law's Autonomy and Public Practical Reasons: A Critical Comment', 4 *Legal Theory* 1, 13, 16 (1998) [hereinafter cited as Raz, 'Postema']. Coleman, however, characteristically overstates the distinction between the conceptual issue and the factual issue, as is apparent from the following remark by Raz: 'The sources thesis [the essence of Raz's Exclusive Legal Positivism] is based on the mediating role of the law. It is true that the law fails in that role if

Positivists have indeed assailed Inclusivism and Incorporationism partly on the ground that law as modeled by each of those doctrines would be marked by inordinate uncertainty.

For example, Eleni Mitrophanous, a steadfast supporter of Raz, has adopted just such a tack (though, revealingly, she does not cite Raz's work at all in the relevant portion of her article).[5] Her remarks on this topic will enable us to see why Raz and Shapiro have been wise to shy away from raising any general concerns about controversy and uncertainty in their critiques of Inclusivism and Incorporationism. Such concerns are misplaced—for reasons indicated by Coleman and for reasons that go beyond what he has argued—and an attack that stems from those concerns can easily be turned against the Exclusivist camp.

Mitrophanous observes that a crucial function of a legal system is to reduce sharply the uncertainty that would prevail in the absence of such a system. She infers that the criteria in any Rule of Recognition must 'secure certainty in the identification of laws' (Mitrophanous, 'Positivism', 627), and she contends that those criteria as understood by Inclusivists or Incorporationists would not be capable of achieving adequate certainty. While acknowledging that not all moral matters are controversial and that not all factual matters are uncontroversial, she submits that the inclusion of morality in the law would very likely generate an unacceptable level of uncertainty that would thwart the fulfillment of law's function. She allows that '[t]he question is one of degree', and she asks '[w]hat degree of uncertainty in the identification of law can be tolerated by a consistent [Incorporationist or Inclusive Legal Positivist]' (Mitrophanous, 'Positivism', 628). Proceeding on the assumption that a thoroughly Incorporationist Rule of Recognition would give rise to intolerable uncertainty, she complains that Incorporationists do not have any principled way of drawing a line between thoroughgoing Incorporationism and some more modest variant thereof. If an Incorporationist regime is to be sustainable as a system of law, she declares, it must be 'characterized not by its allowing moral criteria to figure in the determination of the existence of valid law, but by its allowing *some* such criteria to do so. It needs to place a restriction on the number and type of such criteria.' She asserts that Incorporationism 'offers no argument for a screening process to avoid uncertainty' (Mitrophanous, 'Positivism', 629). According to her, in other words, the Incorporationists are doomed to arbitrariness when they seek to place limits on the role of moral principles in the law. They need to impose such limits if the role of those principles is to be compatible with the existence of a legal system, but they cannot meaningfully specify where the limits are to be set.

---

it is not, in general, easier to establish and less controversial than the underlying considerations it reflects.' Joseph Raz, *Ethics in the Public Domain* (Oxford: Clarendon Press, 1994) [hereinafter cited as Raz, *Ethics*], 218.

[5] Eleni Mitrophanous, 'Soft Positivism', 17 *Oxford Journal of Legal Studies* 621, 627–9 (1997) [hereinafter cited as Mitrophanous, 'Positivism'].

Mitrophanous's analysis is unquestionably vulnerable to some of the objections raised by Coleman against the putative Inclusive Legal Positivists from whom he distances himself. For example, Mitrophanous does not suitably distinguish between the role of *law* in overcoming dissensus among *citizens* and the role of the *Rule of Recognition* in overcoming dissensus among *officials*. She moves too hastily from a thesis about the former to a thesis about the latter. A very closely related point is that she fails to discriminate adequately between the role of the Rule of Recognition in endowing norms with legal validity and the role of the Rule of Recognition in enabling the identification of legal norms by citizens. Unlike the former role, the latter can be highly indirect. Accordingly, given that the focus by Mitrophanous on uncertainty is connected with the latter role, she moves too quickly in drawing inferences about the nature of the Rule of Recognition in its former role. She gives voice to her precipitate inferential leap in the following passage: 'The law promotes certainty by offering a test by which to identify valid law. The rule of recognition is that test and therefore it is right to attribute the law's function of providing certainty to it' (Mitrophanous, 'Positivism', 634).

Criticisms along the lines just recounted, which have only been mentioned rather than fully developed here, are undoubtedly justified and telling. Let us put those strictures aside, however, and consider two principal ripostes to Mitrophanous that go beyond anything suggested by Coleman. First, her claim about the absence of a specifiable cut-off point for the prevalence of moral principles in the law is impelled by a misunderstanding of the aims and character of philosophical analysis. The appropriate response to her claim is not to deny it, but to express puzzlement at the thought that she could regard it as damaging. No philosophical analysis proceeding at an abstract level can specify a particular stage where the uncertainties introduced by controversial moral principles will have undermined the status of a legal system as such. Two difficulties stand in the way of such a specification. Even if we confine our attention to a single legal system, there is no talismanic point at which the regularity of the system's functioning as a regime of law abruptly switches to the irregularity of lawlessness. Just as there is no precisely specifiable point where cumulative grains of sand become a heap, so too there is no precisely specifiable point where greater and greater degrees of uncertainty in a structure of legal governance undo its classifiability as such a structure. Furthermore, the inappositeness of trying to identify such a point is compounded when one realizes that a philosophical theory of law is seeking to expound the essential features of every legal system rather than of one particular system. The extent to which moral principles can figure in a community's law without creating inordinate uncertainty will hinge on the degree of cohesion among the relevant officials in their grasp of moral issues. That degree of moral cohesion will vary from one society to the next. Consequently, not only are we unable to specify a precise point at which the level of controversy and uncertainty in a scheme of governance will have transformed it from a system of law to a situation of lawlessness; in addition, in an enterprise of philosophical analysis applicable to all legal systems, we cannot say when some level of controversy and uncertainty will have been produced through the presence of moral principles in the law. The tendency of those principles to generate such an effect is determined by the greater or lesser uniformity among the moral outlooks of officials—a factor that is itself hardly uniform across all legal systems. Accordingly, Mitrophanous goes astray if she believes that Inclusive Legal Positivists and Incorporationists should be dismayed over the fact that they have not concretely indicated exactly how far moral principles can enter into the law. Any effort to pin down that matter, at a philosophical level of abstraction, would be futile and misconceived. It is perfectly respectable (and eminently sensible) for Incorporationists and Inclusive Legal Positivists to reply to Mitrophanous simply as follows: the norms of a legal system can include moral principles so long as any uncertainty engendered by officials' reliance on those principles is not so severe and persistent as to deprive the system of the regularity that is essential for the rule of law.

Maybe even more important is a second rejoinder to Mitrophanous. An air of unreality hangs over any Exclusivist criticism of Inclusivism or Incorporationism for fostering excessive levels of uncertainty. What Ronald Dworkin has described as the 'heroic artificiality' of the Exclusivist position is evident here.[6] After all, controversy and uncertainty detract from the regularity of a legal system when they affect the ways in which legal norms are brought to bear on citizens' conduct. If people cannot know with any confidence whether their activities will be deemed by legal officials to have been permissible or impermissible, and if people cannot know with any confidence whether legal officials will discipline others for behaving in various ways, then the regularized guidance and the behavior-channeling effects of the rule of law are missing. At the level of law-application, that is, the presence of severe and sustained uncertainty imperils the very existence of the rule of law in a society. Yet at that very level there is no difference that makes a difference between the guidance provided by a regime to citizens of an Exclusivist bent and the guidance provided by a regime to citizens of an Incorporationist or Inclusivist bent.

Raz and his disciples do not deny that moral principles figure in adjudication and in other processes of law-application. They endeavor to reconcile their Exclusivism with their acknowledgment of the role of such principles, by distinguishing between reasoning about the law and reasoning according to the law.[7] Understood by reference to that distinction, officials' decisions at the level of law-application involve reasoning-according-to-the-law when those decisions are

---

[6] Ronald Dworkin, 'Thirty Years On', 115 *Harvard Law Review* 1655, 1675 (2002). I should note that a number of Dworkin's other comments on Exclusive Legal Positivism are misconceived.

[7] See, e.g., Raz, *Ethics*, 316–17. Cf. Joseph Raz, 'On the Nature of Law', 82 *Archiv für Rechts- und Sozialphilosophie* 1, 19 (1996). For the same distinction expressed in somewhat different terms—'reasoning to the content of the law' versus 'reasoning from the content of the law'—see Raz, 'Postema', 5–6.

informed by moral principles. By contrast, when the decisions are not inflected by moral principles in any way, they only involve reasoning about the law. Thus, whenever a judge or some other legal official arrives at a determination that includes some element of moral judgment, the Razian view is that his determination consists of two components: the portion in which the official has reasoned about the law, and the portion in which he has reasoned according to the law. For example, if a judge decides that a certain legal norm applied in a certain manner would violate some constitutional moral test, and if he therefore decides not to deem somebody punishable under that norm, he has reasoned about the law in order to ascertain the existence and content of the norm and has reasoned according to the law in order to determine whether the norm satisfies the constitutional moral test. Because the first component ('reasoning about the law') does not involve any moral judgment, and because only that component consists in ascertaining the existence and content of a legal norm, the uncertainties attendant on moral deliberations are not generated by the process of law-ascertainment as analyzed by Exclusivists. To avoid the specter of inordinate uncertainty in the law, then, we should opt for Exclusivism in preference to Inclusivism or Incorporationism. So runs Mitrophanous's line of reasoning.

Such a line of reasoning, however, is misguided. To be sure, Mitrophanous's position would make sense if it were a proposal for institutional reform, whereby judges and other officials would cease to resort to moral tests when deciding whether and how laws are to be implemented. Just such a stance has been adopted by Tom Campbell and other so-called prescriptive positivists,[8] whose views are based partly on the perceived desirability of avoiding the uncertainty that ensues from the introduction of moral tests at the level of law-application. Whatever may be the merits of their position—a position that can remain strictly neutral in the debates between Exclusivists and Inclusivists/Incorporationists—it is quite intelligible as a proposal for delimiting the range of the factors that are to be taken into account by judges and other officials when resolving disputes. Mitrophanous, however, is not putting forward any suggestion concerning how officials should behave or the range of factors which their decisions should take into account. Rather, she is putting forward a suggestion concerning how we ought to analyze what officials do in legal systems where moral considerations plainly affect the processes of law-application.

Mitrophanous wants to separate the officials' deliberations into the two components mentioned above, in order to guard against inordinate uncertainty in the law. Yet the presence of serious uncertainty is problematic not just in relation to one of those components, but in relation to the two of them together. Officials' reasoning-about-the-law and their reasoning-according-to-the-law together make up the processes by which legal norms are brought to bear on people's

---

[8] See, e.g., Tom Campbell, *The Legal Theory of Ethical Positivism* (Aldershot: Dartmouth Publishing, 1996). I discuss prescriptive positivism at greater length in Chapter 5.

doings. If those overall processes comprising the two types of reasoning are racked by uncertainty, then the regularized guidance and the behavior-channeling effects of the rule of law will be gravely jeopardized in the manner outlined above. By highlighting the fact that morally fraught reasoning-*according-to*-the-law will foster considerable uncertainty, Mitrophanous effectively emphasizes that just such uncertainty will afflict the overall processes of law-application. Whether or not the officials' reasoning-*about*-the-law will give rise to uncertainty is neither here nor there. Insofar as the two components of any determination by the officials impinge on citizens' conduct, they do so in combination rather than as strands that can be isolated in practice. When citizens seek to adjust their conduct in light of the requirements laid upon them by legal norms, they are not inquiring about officials' reasoning-about-the-law in isolation from the officials' reasoning-according-to-the-law; instead, they are inquiring about the ways in which the two aforementioned types of reasoning will *together* lead the officials to bring legal norms to bear on the countless modes of conduct that might be adopted by citizens. If those ways of enforcement are highly unpredictable— because the upshot of the officials' reasoning according to the law is highly unpredictable—then the problem of uncertainty at the practical level of law-application is every bit as severe for citizens who adhere to Exclusivism as for citizens who adhere to Inclusivism/Incorporationism. Admittedly, the citizens in the former camp might describe the problem somewhat differently from the citizens in the latter camp. The former might say that the functioning of their community's legal system is shot through with uncertainty, whereas the latter might say that their community's law is shot through with uncertainty (though they could equally well opt for the other description). Regardless of how the problem is labeled, it will confront Exclusivist citizens just as much as Inclusivist/ Incorporationist citizens. If the problem is sufficiently acute to undermine the rule of law in some society, it will undermine the rule of law for Exclusivist citizens just as much as for their Inclusivist/Incorporationist counterparts. Though Mitrophanous may have pointed to a troublesome factor that threatens the sustainability of a legal system,[9] she has certainly not identified anything that is peculiarly problematic for Inclusivism and Incorporationism.

In short, if a wide-ranging role for moral criteria in the adjudicative and administrative activities of officials will tend to bring about severe uncertainty that can devastate the operations of a legal system as such, an apt solution lies not in Exclusive Legal Positivism but in prescriptive positivism. What is needed, in other words, is not a reclassification of the adjudicative and administrative endeavors that are guided by moral criteria—a reclassification of them as 'reasoning according to the law' rather than as 'reasoning about the law'. Instead,

---

[9] Of course, as should be apparent from the preceding two chapters, my view is that her fears about controversy and uncertainty are exaggerated. She would be correct in most circumstances to worry about the viability of a thoroughly Incorporationist regime, but her concerns are generally misplaced in connection with Inclusivist or modestly Incorporationist legal systems.

what is needed is the removal or lessening of the role of moral criteria in those endeavors. Unlike the Razian reclassification mentioned just above, such a step would be practical rather than purely theoretical. It would reduce undesirable uncertainties, instead of merely relabeling them. Mitrophanous with her warnings about crippling uncertainty and controversy has not done anything to vindicate Exclusive Legal Positivism, but she has gone some way toward vindicating prescriptive positivism. (Of course, nothing said in this paragraph should be taken as an endorsement of any thoroughgoing variety of prescriptive positivism. Unsustainable though a *sweepingly* Incorporationist regime would be in nearly every society, a regime of law that is Inclusivist and *modestly* Incorporationist should normally be able to operate well. A thoroughgoing version of prescriptive positivism would throw the baby out with the bathwater.)

C. The Razian Challenge

Neither in the previous chapters nor in this chapter have my rejoinders to Exclusive Legal Positivism concentrated sustainedly on the work of Raz, from whose writings the debates between Exclusivists and Inclusivists/Incorporationists have developed. Though his writings have been seminal in that respect, there are two principal reasons for my leaving them largely unexplored in my ripostes to Exclusivism. First, Raz's analyses have already elicited a large number of suitably deft responses, not least from Coleman. Second, and more important, is a consideration broached in the Introduction to this book. Raz's most interesting arguments in support of Exclusive Legal Positivism are based squarely on his thesis that the law-applying pronouncements of officials invariably profess to be endowed with moral authority. Because I have elsewhere maintained at length that that thesis is false, my issuance of a retort to some arguments which presuppose the truth of that thesis would be largely redundant.

One point raised by Raz should be probed briefly here, however. In an early defense of Exclusivism, he throws down the following challenge to Inclusivists and Incorporationists: 'Supporters of [Inclusivism or Incorporationism] have to provide an adequate criterion for separating legal references to morality, which make its application a case of applying pre-existing legal rules from cases of judicial discretion in which the judge, by resorting to moral consideration[s], is changing the law'.[10] Two replies to this challenge are appropriate. First, suppose for a moment that there is not any generally applicable basis for the distinction which Raz specifies, beyond the form of the distinction itself. So what? At more concrete levels we can find serviceable indicators. For example, we can pay attention to officials' own descriptions of their adjudicative and administrative activities. To be sure, officials' expressed understandings of their own endeavors

---

[10] Joseph Raz, *The Authority of Law* (Oxford: Clarendon Press, 1979) [hereinafter cited as Raz, *Authority*], 47 n.8.

are not always determinative. However, given the self-reflective character of the authoritative discourses and argumentation in most systems of law, those expressed understandings are typically useful points of departure and are often dispositive. Whereas officials sometimes indicate that they are modifying or tempering the law through recourse to moral principles, they at other times indicate that they are applying moral principles as norms immanent in the law (though not explicitly and specifically laid down therein). Dworkin is quite correct to highlight the latter pattern of official behavior, even though he ignores the former pattern. Unless there are clear reasons for declining to accept the pronouncements of judges and other officials at face value, we can take those pronouncements as a key signpost for drawing the distinction to which Raz adverts.

A second reply to the Razian challenge can serve as an anticipation of the most obvious way in which a defender of Raz might seek to counter the first reply. Such a defender might point to the fact that officials' characterizations of their own activities and decisions are not always veracious, and he might maintain that some further test is consequently essential if we are to differentiate between the veracious and the unreliable. Furthermore, the defender of Raz might argue, legal officials do not always state explicitly how they understand their own actions. In a case where the precise character of their recourse to moral principles is left implicit, we shall not be able to discover what they are doing from what they say. That is, their statements will not inform us (reliably or unreliably) whether they are modifying or instead articulating the law's requirements when they fall back upon moral principles. Once again, then, some broader criterion is necessary if we are to be able to distinguish between modifications and articulations.

Fortunately, a broader standard of the sort required is indeed available. Let us initially consider the circumstances in which a resort by officials to moral principles will amount to a departure from the existing law. When a perspicuous source-based legal position (such as a requirement or a permission) is altered by officials' explicit or implicit reliance on some moral principle(s), and when the operations of their legal system do not include any regular practice of subordinating perspicuous source-based legal positions to the demands of morality, the alteration amounts to a modification of the existing law. Likewise, when the explicit or implicit reliance by officials on some moral principle(s) establishes a legal position that has theretofore been neither clearly upheld nor clearly denied within the formal sources of the law in their regime, and when the operations of their regime do not include any regular practice of establishing legal positions in such a manner, the introduction of the new position amounts to a modification—an amplification—of the existing law. By contrast, an explicit or implicit reliance by officials on some moral principle(s) will amount to an *articulation* of the existing law when it occurs in the context of a regular practice of either type just mentioned. That is, when the operations of the officials' system include a regular practice of adjusting source-based norms in light of the requirements of morality, then adjustments along those lines will be *applications* of existing legal requirements rather than *transformations* thereof. Any such adjustment will consist in the prioritization of one kind of legal norm over another, a prioritization ordained by the officials' Rule of Recognition. Similarly, when the operations of their system include a regular practice of settling previously unclarified points of law by reference to moral principles, any instance of settling such a point of law in that fashion is an application of some existing legal norm(s). In sum, a focus on the regularity of the Inclusivist/Incorporationist practices within a legal system will enable us to meet the challenge thrown down by Raz.

Of course, the concept of regularity is vague. There will inevitably be a gray area of situations to which the distinction outlined in the preceding paragraph is neither clearly applicable nor clearly inapplicable. An Incorporationist practice at its inception will generate effects that are plainly changes in the existing law, and such a practice when long standing and regularized will generate effects that are plainly applications of the existing law; but the effects produced at intermediate stages will be less straightforwardly classifiable. Equally problematic are the effects generated by an Incorporationist practice that is followed by officials on only some of the occasions when their adherence to it would be appropriate. Though such a practice might be of long standing, its effects are perhaps too sporadic to be straightforwardly classifiable as applications of existing legal norms. Some degree of equivocality in respect of certain circumstances is inevitable, then, when we draw upon the distinction outlined in my preceding paragraph. In this or that society, there might not be a discernible fact of the matter. So what? Any dichotomy in legal or political philosophy is bound to be associated with a gray area of problematically classifiable cases. The existence of such a gray area does not deprive a dichotomy of its reality or importance. As Chapter 1 has remarked, day and night remain as starkly different from each other as day and night even though they shade into each other through dawn and dusk.

Now, as presented so far, my riposte to Raz may seem to presuppose that the presence of moral principles in the law will yield a uniquely correct answer to every legal problem on which the principles are brought to bear. Such a presupposition is by no means wildly outlandish, so long as we take account of the division between determinacy and demonstrability—that is, the division between (1) the unique correctness of an answer as an objective matter of fact and (2) the possibility of proving an answer's unique correctness to the satisfaction of every rational person who ruminates competently upon the matter. The determinate truth of a judgment hardly entails its demonstrable truth. Nevertheless, though not preposterous, the presupposition mentioned above is too bold. We need not and should not presume that the domain of morality will yield a uniquely correct answer to *every* problem that falls outside the determinate ambits of source-based legal norms. Some indeterminacy and gaps in the implications of moral requirements will undoubtedly abide. To that extent, then, the reliance of officials on

moral principles in their handling of legal controversies will involve changes in
the law rather than mere applications or articulations of its mandates. In such
circumstances, some points of contention that have been left unsettled by the
source-based norms are also left unsettled by the moral considerations to which
the officials have supplementary recourse. To settle those points is therefore to
expand the law rather than simply to express its already-existing requirements.
Thus, even if a practice of falling back upon moral considerations in hard cases is
well established, it leaves room for openness in the law.

Let us note a further respect in which my rejoinder to Raz as presented so
far is perhaps somewhat misleadingly stated. Hitherto, my remarks may have
conveyed the impression that officials' reliance on moral principles for the
resolution of legal controversies in hard cases will always eventuate in correct
invocations of those principles. Manifestly, any such suggestion would be
needlessly and unsustainably bold. Especially when grappling with tricky
questions in hard cases, officials will be prone to go astray when they resort
to moral principles. I have underscored this point in the closing pages of
Chapter 2. Insofar as officials do go astray by misidentifying the principles that
should ground their decisions in hard cases, and insofar as their misidentifica-
tions have precedential force, they alter the law instead of genuinely giving
effect to it—just as they alter it when they misidentify source-based legal
norms. Still, as has been argued near the end of Chapter 2, the officials can
be adhering to a moderately Incorporationist Rule of Recognition even if they
frequently do go astray in the fashion just indicated. So long as their law-
ascertaining determinations in hard cases are oriented toward the general
requirements of morality, the officials are upholding an Incorporationist criterion for selecting legal norms in such cases. The fact that they often misapply
that criterion is consistent with their acceptance of it, since its extension as an
objective standard which they endorse is not fixed by their beliefs about its
extension. Consequently, the misapplications of the criterion do not undermine
the maintenance by the officials of a well-established practice of relying on
moral norms for hard cases. Within that practice, any precedent-setting misapplications of the mildly Incorporationist criterion modify the law instead of
activating it; but those misapplications do not alter the fact that the practice of
law-ascertainment structured by such a criterion has absorbed the true principles of morality into the law of the system in which the aforesaid practice
prevails. Indeed, only because those principles have been absorbed into the law
are the misapplications of the Incorporationist criterion classifiable as misapplications in a process of law-ascertainment. Likewise, only because those principles have been so absorbed are any precedent-setting effects of the
misapplications classifiable as changes in the law. Thus, my rejoinder to Raz,
which does presuppose the credible possibility of a well-established practice of
resolving contentious issues in hard cases by reference to moral principles, does
not implausibly presuppose that the officials who operate such a practice will

typically identify the applicable moral principles correctly. Because persistent errors by the officials in identifying those principles will not undo the nature of their mildly Incorporationist practice as such, and because those errors will therefore not deprive the true moral principles of their status as legal norms within the system which encompasses the Incorporationist practice, there is no reason to deny the likelihood of the occurrence of such errors. Any imputation of virtual infallibility to Incorporationist officials would not only be utterly unrealistic but would also be wholly gratuitous.

In sum, if one is seeking to operationalize my response to Raz, one should not be inquiring about the regularity with which the officials in a legal system correctly identify the moral principles that are applicable to the hard cases which the officials must resolve. Rather, one should be inquiring about the regularity with which the officials take the basic demands of morality as the reference point for their selections of the norms (sourceless norms) with which they dispatch the hard cases. If the fundamental requirements of morality do regularly serve as such a reference point, then—whether or not the officials understand and implement those requirements correctly—the true principles of morality have become endowed with the status of legal mandates for hard cases. Correct invocations of those principles effectuate the law instead of enlarging or altering it. By contrast, incorrect choices of principles modify the law if they acquire the force of precedents. They modify the law precisely because they are incorrect as selections of legal norms, and they are incorrect as selections of legal norms precisely because they take place within a regularized practice of law-ascertainment that requires the invocation of properly ranked moral principles for dealing with hard cases. Insofar as there does obtain a regularized practice of that sort—a practice which can exist even if officials seldom identify moral principles appropriately—any correct invocations of moral principles in hard cases are articulations of the law rather than discretionary alterations or amplifications of it. Contrariwise, if no regularized Incorporationist practice of law-ascertainment prevails, any invocations of moral principles in hard cases are discretionary amplifications of the law rather than expressions of it. And so this discussion has answered Raz's challenge.

II. Clarifications and Elaborations

Having sought to supplement the first two chapters by warding off some additional onslaughts against Inclusive Legal Positivism and Incorporationism, this chapter will now endeavor to refine some of the central lines of reasoning that have been presented in the earlier portions of this book. Let us start by pondering afresh Chapter 1's argument concerning the role of custom in many legal systems.

A. Norms that Float Freely

Chapter 1 has observed that, when customary norms are officially treated as binding bases for dispute-resolution within some legal system, they are correctly classifiable as legal norms of that system.[11] Our ascription of such a status to them militates in favor of our ascribing a similar status to moral precepts that are likewise officially treated as binding within some legal system. Despite the many disanalogies between the norms of custom and the norms of morality, there are homologies between them that bear directly on their respective statuses as laws. Most notably, the norms of either sort are free-floating in the sense defined by Chapter 1. That is, they are not the products of formally authoritative institutions such as sporting associations or foreign legal systems. They are consequently available for incorporation into this or that legal system as some of its laws.

Underlying my discussion of this matter in Chapter 1 is the following disjunctive test for the status of a norm as a law within any particular legal system. Each norm officially treated as a binding basis for dispute-resolution within some legal system is a law of the system if and only if it satisfies one of the following two conditions: either it is a product of one or more of the authoritative law-generating organs of the system, such as a legislature or an administrative agency or a court or a constitutional assembly; or it is free-floating. In combination with the fact that some norm N is officially treated as a binding basis for judgments within some legal system S, the overall disjunction of the two conditions just specified will have set forth a necessary and sufficient grounding for the status of N as a law of S, while each of the two disjuncts will have set forth a sufficient grounding for that status. When we apply this disjunctive test to customary norms that are officially treated as binding bases for dispute-resolution, we can easily see that those norms owe their status as laws to the second disjunct rather than to the first. Although they are not engendered by authoritative law-creating organs of the legal system within which they are operative, they are free-floating and are thus available for incorporation into that system. In this pregnant respect they are distinguishable from foreign laws and from the rules of sporting associations, which are neither free-floating nor brought into existence by authoritative organs of the legal system within which they are invoked.

Now, nobody on any side of the debates between Exclusive Legal Positivists and their Inclusivist/Incorporationist opponents has denied that customary norms regarded by officials as binding bases for judgments are full-blown laws of the system in which they are operative. Raz indeed explicitly construes custom as a source of law on a par with legislation and adjudi-

---

[11] I arrived at some of the lines of thought in this subsection when replying to queries about Chapter 1 from Mark McBride, to whom I am grateful for his perceptive challenges.

cation.[12] As much as Inclusivists and Incorporationists, then, the members of the Exclusivist camp take as given that the norms of custom are crucially distinguishable from foreign laws and the rules of sporting associations. Only because of their distinguishability from those laws and those rules, can the norms of custom be endowed with a status which everyone in the controversy between Exclusivists and Incorporationists has ascribed to them: namely, the status of laws that belong as such to the system in which they abide as bases for adjudicative or administrative judgments.

Any adequate account of this matter must therefore pin down the germane point of dissimilarity between customary norms and foreign laws or sporting associations' rules. Plainly, the dissimilarity does not reside in anything pertaining to the first disjunct of the test that has been delineated above. Customary norms and foreign laws and the rules of sporting associations are all alike in failing to satisfy the condition laid down by that first disjunct. Nor will we apprehend any relevant difference if we focus on the need for moral deliberations in our ascertainment of the aforementioned norms or laws or rules. Although the existence and contents of customary norms can be ascertained empirically without recourse to such deliberations, exactly the same is true of foreign laws and sporting associations' rules. We have to look elsewhere for a feature that renders customary norms distinctive. The only feature that can pertinently be singled out is the free-floatingness of such norms—a quality that cannot correctly be predicated of foreign laws and sporting associations' rules. For reasons indicated in my first chapter, the quality of free-floatingness does bear directly on the appositeness of classifying customary norms as laws of the system in which they are perceived by officials as justificatory bases for adjudicative and administrative determinations. Whereas any foreign law or any rule of a sporting association is a product of some contemporaneous system of authority to which it distinctively belongs, a customary norm is not. When legal officials treat such a norm as a binding standard within their regime, they are not doing so in order to give due acknowledgment to a co-existent institutional scheme within which the norm has emerged through some process of formal enactment. Instead, the officials are incorporating the norm into their own matrix of laws as something that can belong integrally thereto precisely because it does not owe its applicability and existence to its having been formally adopted by some alternative jurisdiction or organization.

Thus, since everyone in the debates between Exclusivism and Incorporationism accepts that customary norms are laws of the legal system *S* in which they are operative, and since everyone accepts that foreign laws and sporting

---

[12] Raz, *Ethics*, 205; Raz, *Authority*, 46 n.7; Raz, 'Postema,' 13. See also Joseph Raz, 'Legal Principles and the Limits of Law', in Marshall Cohen (ed.), *Ronald Dworkin and Contemporary Jurisprudence* (London: Duckworth, 1984) 73, 77, 80. This point is neglected in Kenneth Einar Himma, 'Inclusive Legal Positivism', in Jules Coleman and Scott Shapiro (eds), *The Oxford Handbook of Jurisprudence and Philosophy of Law* (Oxford: Oxford University Press, 2002), 125, 163–4.

associations' rules cannot similarly belong to *S* as some of its legal mandates, everyone is implicitly or explicitly committed to the view that free-floatingness is a sufficient condition for a norm's membership of *S* if the norm is treated by officials in *S* as a binding basis for their judgments. Everyone, in other words, is committed to the view that the second disjunct in my test for the status of any judgment-justifying norm as a law does indeed set forth a sufficient condition for that status. Given as much, however, everyone is implicitly or explicitly committed to the thesis that moral principles are laws of any jural system in which they are treated by officials as touchstones for the authoritative resolution of disputes. After all, any such moral principles—the norms of critical morality—satisfy the second disjunct of my test as surely as do customary norms. Whereas the laws of foreign nations and the rules of sporting associations are precluded from becoming laws of *S* because they already belong to alternative systems of authority, the norms of morality are aligned with the norms of custom in not being so precluded. Morality and custom are strictly homologous in this key respect, which bears decisively on the question whether the principles of morality can ever belong to any legal system as some of its laws. Any disanalogies between morality and custom in other respects do not affect the answer to that question.

Let us consider the most prominent of those disanalogies. Principles of critical morality obtain as such irrespective of whether they are widely recognized and followed, whereas customary norms obtain as such only by dint of being widely accepted. However important this dissimilarity between these two sets of norms might be for other purposes, it is of no importance for our present purpose. Unlike the property of free-floatingness, the property of acceptance-independence is not something on which we can usefully focus in order to answer the question broached at the end of the preceding paragraph. Whereas we can nicely distinguish between customary norms and foreign laws (or sporting associations' rules) by looking for the presence or absence of the former property, we cannot comparably distinguish between them by looking for the presence or absence of the latter property. Neither customary norms nor foreign laws are acceptance-independent. Hence, a lack of acceptance-independence is not the feature of customary norms that renders them susceptible to being incorporated into any legal system where they are treated as binding. If that lack were the key feature, then foreign laws and sporting associations' rules would be susceptible to incorporation as well; yet everyone agrees that they are not.

To be sure, a denial of the acceptance-independence of foreign laws has to be advanced with due care. (Much the same can be said in connection with the rules of clubs and sporting associations. However, to avoid unwieldy prose, I shall concentrate here on foreign laws.) It is not the case that every single foreign law must be widely accepted—either in the sense of being generally obeyed by citizens or in the sense of being generally upheld by officials as a binding standard of conduct—within the domestic jurisdiction to which each such law belongs.

Some valid laws such as jaywalking ordinances are very frequently flouted and are very seldom enforced, yet they remain valid laws. However, what must be true in any functional legal system is that most of the system's directives are obeyed by most citizens and upheld by most officials in most circumstances to which the directives are applicable.[13] Even though this or that particular law can exist despite being ignored by everyone, any foreign nation's laws as a total array are not acceptance-independent. Within their own domestic jurisdiction, those laws as an overall array must be generally heeded if they are to exist at all as the jurisdiction's legal framework. In that respect they differ fundamentally from the norms of critical morality, which obtain as such even if all or most of them are persistently disregarded. Acceptance-independence is an earmark of the norms of critical morality as a total array (and also individually), whereas acceptance-independence is no such earmark of foreign laws as a total array.

Now, since *every* foreign law is susceptible to being incorporated into one's legal system if *any* such law is so susceptible, the appropriate level when we look for the presence or the absence of acceptance-independence is that of foreign laws as an overall matrix. At that level, as has just been observed, foreign laws are like customary norms in lacking acceptance-independence. A focus on the property of acceptance-independence is therefore misdirected when we are seeking to understand why customary norms are available for incorporation into one's legal system and why foreign laws are not. If we hope to differentiate between those norms and those laws in a germane fashion, we shall have to focus instead on the property of free-floatingness. Attentiveness to that property will then enable us to break out of the Exclusivist-versus-Incorporationist deadlock, by prompting us to see that moral principles are indeed available for incorporation into any legal systems where they are treated by officials as touchstones for adjudicative and administrative judgments.

Before we leave the topic of customary norms, we should consider a remark by Raz on Incorporationism: 'The main thrust of the incorporation thesis is that all that is derivable from the [source-based] law (with the help of other true premises) is law. It makes the law include standards which are inconsistent with its mediating role, for they were never endorsed by the law-making institutions on whose authority they are supposed to rest' (Raz, *Ethics*, 213). This remark is to be understood against the background of the central thesis which Raz attributes to Incorporationism: 'All law is either source-based or entailed by source-based law' (Raz, *Ethics*, 194). Let us initially note that the first sentence in the first of these quotations does not follow at all from the thesis formulated in the second quotation, and that it is far too strong in any event. Raz has plainly stumbled in suggesting that that first sentence conveys the 'main thrust' of the thesis which he ascribes to Incorporationists, for the proposition that every *X* is *Y*

---

[13] This point, of course, is famously emphasized in H.L.A. Hart, *The Concept of Law* (Oxford: Clarendon Press, 1961), 112–14.

or Z does not in any way entail the proposition that every Z is X. From the claim that every legal norm is either source-based or entailed by source-based law, it does not follow that everything entailed by source-based law is a legal norm. Ergo, Raz is guilty of a paralogism when he asserts that 'the incorporation thesis...insists that the law includes all the logical consequences of source-based law'.[14] Moreover, the first of the quoted sentences recounts a position which no sensible theorist would ever affirm. Because any proposition entails itself, every true proposition P will be derivable from the source-based law with the help of any additional true premises that encompass P. Accordingly, if everything derivable from the source-based law with the help of any additional true premises is to count as a legal norm, propositions such as 'Abraham Lincoln was assassinated in 1865' and 'Paris is the capital of France' will count as legal norms. Such a ludicrous view has never been espoused by anyone, and should consequently not be attributed to the proponents of Incorporationism.

Even more important in the present context is the second sentence in the first of the quotations above. There Raz states his chief objection to the doctrine of Incorporationists, who classify moral principles as laws of any jural system in which those principles are treated by officials as fulcra for adjudicative and administrative decisions. Incorporationists adopt this classification even though the moral principles in their origins 'were never endorsed by the law-making institutions on whose authority they are supposed to rest'. Raz is here complaining that a necessary condition for the authoritativeness of moral principles as laws is unfulfilled, and that such principles therefore cannot genuinely count as laws. Uncomfortably for Raz, however, his objection would also rule out custom as a source of law. Like moral principles, customary norms in their origins are not endorsed or created by the law-making institutions of the society within which they emerge. Raz himself indeed freely acknowledges that customary norms are 'not normally generated by people intending to make law' (Raz, *Ethics*, 205). Hence, his complaint about the lack of any original endorsement from law-making institutions is as applicable to the norms of custom as to the principles of morality. Yet he unequivocally believes that customary norms are laws of any jural system in which they are treated by officials as bases for adjudicative determinations. Given that he believes as much, he ought to believe the same about moral principles. If the absence of any original endorsement is no bar to the status of customary norms as laws, it should be no bar to such a status for moral principles.

Of course, Raz's reference to endorsements by law-making institutions might conceivably have been meant to cover not the *provenance* of moral principles but the *application* of them to various disputes. If so, then once again the norms of custom and the principles of morality are on a par. Customary norms are not

---

[14] Raz, *Ethics*, 213–14. This paralogism is not a minor slip. Rather, it informs Raz's whole critique of Incorporationism in the essay from which I have here quoted.

laws unless they are treated by officials as touchstones for adjudicative and administrative judgments. Those norms are so treated when the officials adhere to a Rule of Recognition under which they are required to invoke such norms as touchstones in the event of any circumstances that activate the norms' applicability. Exactly the same is true of moral principles. They are not laws unless they are treated by officials in the manner just specified. Both with regard to the norms of custom and with regard to the principles of critical morality, then, the fact that officials are required under their Rule of Recognition to invoke and apply certain mandates in the event of any triggering circumstances is a necessary condition for the status of those mandates as laws. In other words, when Raz's remark is construed as referring to the level of law-application rather than to the level of law-creation, it is no more successful in ferreting out any point of dissimilarity between custom and critical morality. If Raz wisely thinks that customary norms are laws of any jural system in which they are perceived by officials as binding, then he should plump for the same position in respect of moral principles.

B. On Prodigious Unlikelihood

Coleman, in his recent book, has intimated that my repudiation of his thoroughgoing version of Incorporationism is based on the view that a Rule of Recognition which comprises only Incorporationist criteria is impossible (Coleman, *Practice*, 112–13). In fact, as should be evident from my preceding two chapters —especially Chapter 2—my disapproval of his position does not involve any such conceptual claim. Rather, trading on some elementary empirical assumptions about the diversity of moral-political outlooks among people in any realistic society larger than a handful of families, my arguments have maintained that the sustainability of a sizeable legal system with a sweepingly Incorporationist Rule of Recognition is overwhelmingly unlikely. Though the existence of such a legal system is not starkly impossible as a conceptual matter, the prospect of it is so extravagantly far-fetched that it can safely be disregarded for virtually all purposes. To center one's theory of law on that prospect is to offer a regrettably skewed and misleading account which is not strictly wrong but which is unilluminatingly distortive.

The problem with centering one's theory of law on a bare logical possibility— such as the possibility of a thoroughly Incorporationist legal system in a sizeable society—is that just about anything can serve as the focal point of such an approach. Imagine, for example, a legal system in which every official unremittingly believes that he is performing the role of Hamlet as he carries out his sundry adjudicative or administrative responsibilities. Despite this weird belief on the part of every official, each of them manages to interact with his fellow officials in ways that are somehow sufficiently responsive and regularized to constitute the workings of a legal system. A regime of law in those circumstances is operated by people who each act on the basis of delusions about playing the role of Hamlet. Such a situation is outlandish and is overwhelmingly unlikely ever to arise, but it is not logically impossible. There could be a world—a truly bizarre world, but not a self-contradictory world—in which it would obtain. Still, for virtually any purpose, we can and should pretermit the possibility of such a world. We have no reason to take account of it when we ponder the range of motivations and outlooks that might underlie the behavior of legal officials in their performance of their authoritative functions.

A legal philosopher would be very foolish indeed if he centered his theory of law on the possibility of the state of affairs that has just been sketched. He might label his anserine theory as 'Hamletism' and might formulate its cardinal thesis as follows: 'There is at least one possible legal system in which every official who participates in running the system is motivated to do so by the delusion that he is thereby acting out the part of Hamlet'. Although the situation recounted in this Hamletist thesis is wildly preposterous, it is not utterly incoherent. Formidably improbable though it is, its emergence is not strictly ruled out by the constraints of the Law of Noncontradiction. A Hamletist philosopher of law would seize upon this small gap between what is overwhelmingly unlikely and what is starkly impossible, and would insist that his theory enhances our understanding of law by highlighting one of the conceptually possible ways in which the institutions of law can operate. Bent on showing that Hamletism is quite coherent, he would defend it against challengers who might contend that no Hamletist legal system can ever exist. In fending off such challengers, the proponent of Hamletism would be confident that he is shedding important light on the nature of law.

To be sure, the robust version of Incorporationism is not amusingly ridiculous in the manner of Hamletism. It draws attention to an extreme situation, but not to a situation that is comically fanciful. Indeed, as has been readily acknowledged in my previous two chapters, a robustly Incorporationist legal regime is undoubtedly quite a live possibility in a tiny and static and highly homogeneous society. Moreover, whereas moderately Incorporationist legal systems are very likely present in some large-scale societies, a moderately Hamletist legal system—in which certain officials (as opposed to all officials) are motivated on certain occasions (as opposed to all occasions) by the delusion of performing the role of Hamlet—has never existed and will never exist. Legal officials often deal with hard cases by recourse to moral principles, but neither in easy cases nor in hard cases will a legal official be prone to believe that his authoritative functions constitute a portrayal of a moody prince of Denmark.

Nevertheless, although Hamletism as a jurisprudential doctrine is risible whereas extreme Incorporationism is not, the paramount vice of each of those theories is the same. That is, each of them is preoccupied with legal systems of an exceedingly improbable and anomalous kind. Each tends to obfuscate the normal workings of legal institutions by training undue attention on the extreme periphery of the range of things that count as such institutions at all. Each theory, in other words, inverts the jurisprudential method that was pursued so incisively by H.L.A. Hart. Hart sought to expound the necessary and sufficient conditions for the existence of any paradigmatic legal system, so that he could then proceed in an informed manner to mull over the status of marginal instances of legal systems such as the institutions of international law. By distilling the essential features of clear-cut legal regimes, he was in a position to ponder discerningly whether the absence of one or more of those features from a less straightforward regime should lead us to deny its very status as a system of law.[15] Hart's approach gets inverted by the proponent of robust Hamletism or of robust Incorporationism. A champion of extreme Incorporationism devotes his scrutiny not principally to legal systems that are unproblematically classifiable as such, but instead to some legal systems whose status as such is fiendishly problematic and murky. In societies that are not tiny and homogeneous, legal systems of a thoroughly Incorporationist tenor have never existed and will never exist. That important fact, which reveals to us a lot about the functioning and import of ordinary legal systems, is obscured when a theorist preoccupies himself with the possibility of a robustly Incorporationist Rule of Recognition. Although that possibility should not be gainsaid as a bare possibility, and although the central thesis of extreme Incorporationism is therefore true, a focus on the state of affairs described in that thesis is far more misleading than enlightening. We learn virtually nothing about the distinctiveness of law when we are alerted to the possibility of a robustly Hamletist legal regime, and we learn not very much more when we are alerted to the possibility of a thoroughly Incorporationist Rule of Recognition. In each case, the typical operations and effects of a full-blown legal system are altogether overshadowed as a result of a theorist's fixation on establishing the possibility of some operations and effects that never have occurred and never will occur. Any genuinely valuable insights gained through the elaboration of a robustly Incorporationist theory of law can also be gained through the elaboration of a moderate variant of such a theory—a variant that will keep a proper focus on the workings of ordinary legal systems.

---

[15] To be sure, the usefulness of Hart's method is somewhat limited when a theoretical controversy involves significant disagreement over the extension of the category of paradigmatic legal systems. Such disagreement is present, to a certain degree, in the debates between legal positivists and natural-law theorists. However, as has been observed, the battles over Incorporationism and Exclusivism have been waged among legal positivists rather than between legal positivists and their opponents. Among positivists, there is a very large measure of agreement on the extension of the category of paradigmatic legal systems. In the context of these intrapositivist battles, then, Hart's method is eminently suitable.

Incidentally, as should be evident from the text, I dissent to some degree from the exposition of Hart's method presented in Timothy Endicott, 'Herbert Hart and the Semantic Sting', 4 *Legal Theory* 283, 289–90 (1998). With his interesting but excessively Wittgensteinian interpretation of Hart, Endicott obliges himself to explain away far too many of Hart's pronouncements. On the one hand, as has recently been loudly re-emphasized in Jules Coleman and Ori Simchen, ' "Law," ' 9 *Legal Theory* 1, 41 (2003), Hart was certainly not attempting to lay down necessary and sufficient conditions for correct uses of the term 'law'. On the other hand, he did explicitly aim to set forth necessary and sufficient conditions for the existence of any paradigmatic legal system. (For a quite different but overlapping account of Hart's methodology, see Michael Moore, 'Hart's Concluding Scientific Postscript', 4 *Legal Theory* 301, 310–15 (1998).)

Demonstrating a bare logical possibility, such as the possibility of a thoroughly Hamletist legal system or the possibility of a comprehensively Incorporationist Rule of Recognition that structures the legal system of a sizeable community, is too easy and is thus pointlessly uninformative. Because the constraint of non-contradictoriness is so unconfining, it will leave open any number of potential states of affairs that are overwhelmingly unlikely—for example, a legal system in which every official believes that he is performing the role of Othello as he carries out his authoritative functions. When one accurately insists on the possibility of such a state of affairs as a conceptual matter, one advances our understanding of law hardly at all. If we want to apprehend some important and distinctive characteristics of law, we shall have to go beyond a search for bare logical possibilities. We shall have to search for credible possibilities such as that of a moderately Incorporationist legal system. When a theorist defends a moderately Incorporationist jurisprudential stance against the criticisms of Exclusivists, she will have to make all the valuable points that are made by extreme Incorporationists; but she will do so without losing sight of the peculiar properties of law that are earmarks of its normal functioning. Having given a satisfactory account of that normal functioning, she will then be in a strong position to come to grips with peripheral instances of legal systems such as those on which the extreme Incorporationists dwell.

The needless vulnerability of Coleman's extreme Incorporationist position becomes apparent in his rejoinders to Shapiro in *The Practice of Principle*. Coleman concentrates on showing that moral principles validated as laws by an Incorporationist Rule of Recognition can provide epistemic guidance to everybody who is subject to them. On the one hand, his reasoning in support of his stance on that issue is agilely resourceful; indeed, as has been contended by Wilfrid Waluchow,[16] Coleman's arguments are more sturdy than Coleman himself seems to recognize. On the other hand, however, those arguments are largely immaterial, since the truly formidable crux posed by Shapiro is something that pertains not to epistemic guidance but to reasons-for-action. What Shapiro maintains is that anyone provided with reasons-for-action by the Incorporationist criteria in a Rule of Recognition cannot be provided with any further reasons-for-action by the principles that are validated as laws under those criteria. Coleman's ingenious arguments relating to epistemic guidance do nothing to rebut Shapiro's critique relating to reasons-for-action.

Coleman eventually resorts to a line of argument that would constitute a suitable rebuttal if he had not disqualified himself from making use of it. Opting for a tack that has previously been adopted by Waluchow, Kenneth Himma, and me, he writes: 'Instead of abandoning the claim that law must be capable of making a practical difference, all we need give up is the claim that this is a

---

[16] Wil Waluchow, 'In Pursuit of Pragmatic Legal Theory', 15 *Canadian Journal of Law and Jurisprudence* 125, 148–9 (2002).

conceptual constraint on *each* law. Surely it does not follow logically that because *law* must be capable of [providing reasons-for-action], no norm can count as *a law* unless it is capable of [providing reasons-for-action] in the requisite way' (Coleman, *Practice*, 143, emphases in original). Effective though this retort may be against Shapiro when wielded by moderate Incorporationists, it is not really available to Coleman. After all, his extreme Incorporationism not merely allows but highlights the possibility of a legal system in which the *only* criteria for legal validity are Incorporationist criteria. In other words, he preoccupies himself with a legal system in which *no* law is capable of providing reasons-for-action to anyone who has been provided with such reasons by the system's Rule of Recognition. By centering his theory on the possibility of such a situation, Coleman largely disables himself from falling back upon the riposte that has just been quoted. Unlike the modest Incorporationist, the robust Incorporationist has few if any routes of escape from Shapiro's critique.

Note that the points made in the preceding two paragraphs are applicable not only to officials who directly orient their actions and decisions toward the Incorporationist criteria in their Rule of Recognition, but also to citizens who are subject to the norms that are validated as laws by those criteria. Coleman himself lays great stress on the distinction between a person's reasons-for-action and the reasons on which a person acts; somebody's reasons-for-action exist independently of her awareness of them, whereas the reasons on which somebody acts are the considerations that motivate her through her awareness of them (Coleman, *Practice*, 71–2). With this distinction in hand, we can see that the Incorporationist criteria in a Rule of Recognition provide citizens with reasons-for-action even if some or all of the citizens remain unaware of those reasons (because the citizens are not directly guided by the criteria). Whether or not each citizen knows as much, the Incorporationist Rule of Recognition in her society has supplied her with fresh reasons to adjust her behavior to the precepts of morality, which are endowed with the status of laws under that Rule of Recognition. Shapiro's critique of Incorporationism, which focuses on reasons-for-action, will thus bear on the situation of citizens as much as on the situation of officials. Hence, when Coleman dwells on a sweepingly Incorporationist legal system in which no law at all is capable of providing reasons-for-action to anyone who has been provided with such reasons by the system's Rule of Recognition, he is concentrating on a regime in which every law furnishes no reasons-for-action whatsoever to officials or to citizens.

We should avoid Coleman's unhappy predicament not by denying the truth of his extreme Incorporationist thesis—which, as my second chapter has emphasized, is indeed true—but by approaching that thesis from the opposite direction. Instead of beginning with Coleman's thesis and building a theory around it, we should start with a moderate Incorporationist thesis which affirms what can be true of a paradigmatic legal system. (Specifically, it affirms that the moral principles treated by judges and other officials as binding standards for determinations in hard cases are laws of any jural system in which they are so treated.) Any satisfactory defense of the moderate Incorporationist position will have to parry the challenges mounted by Exclusivists. In that respect, moderate Incorporationism and extreme Incorporationism are aligned with each other. However, unlike the extreme Incorporationists, the moderate Incorporationist theorist will fend off Exclusivist objections in order to uphold a claim about the workings of ordinary legal systems. Such a theorist will then be in a strong position to say whether the strikingly far-fetched mode of governance high-lighted by extreme Incorporationists is properly classifiable as a regime of law. She can ponder whether that mode of governance exhibits enough of the essential properties of a standard legal system to qualify as a legal system itself. In other words, she can ponder whether an extreme Incorporationist regime partakes of the essential features of everything that will count as a legal system at all. In so doing, she will be applying the same method that was fruitfully put to use by Hart. That is, she will be moving from paradigmatic instances of the rule of law to problematically aberrant instances, rather than the other way around. If Incorporationism is to be suitably elaborated as a jurisprudential doctrine that illuminates rather than obscures the central workings of legal institutions, the theorizing in support of it should indeed flow in this direction. Extreme Incor-porationism should not be rejected outright, but it should certainly be relegated to a subordinate role.

4

Of Final Things: Morality as one of the Ultimate Determinants of Legal Validity

In the course of investigating the ultimate standards by reference to which the officials in each legal system ascertain the norms which they are empowered and obligated to uphold as laws, this chapter returns to some issues that were discussed in the closing pages of Chapter 2. We shall explore both the ultimacy of the criteria that make up a legal system's Rule of Recognition, and the ultimacy of the highest tribunal in such a system. As will be seen, these matters have a special bearing on the question whether the criteria in a Rule of Recognition can encompass moral standards. From a distinctive angle, that is, we shall once again be pondering the sustainability of Incorporationism and Inclusive Legal Positivism.

This chapter will first consider some basic properties of any Rule of Recognition, and will in particular take account of two levels at which a Rule of Recognition can exist. Although those opening discussions go somewhat beyond H.L.A. Hart's seminal work, they will be broadly in line with his accounts of the Rule of Recognition and will develop some of the implications of his remarks. In the second major section of the chapter, my focus will shift to some arguments recently put forward by Kenneth Himma. Himma has forcefully maintained that, although the existence of a Rule of Recognition which includes moral directives among its criteria is a bare possibility, it is not a minimally credible possibility in just about any human society. Only under far-fetched circumstances, which will hardly ever be present, can such a Rule of Recognition obtain. Or so Himma contends. In undertaking his critique of Inclusive Legal Positivism and Incorporationism (a critique that extends to moderate Incorporationism as well as to the extreme version), he trains his attention on the role of the highest adjudicative body in any believable regime of law. We shall therefore have to scrutinize that role. As will become apparent, Himma goes astray by neglecting the multiplicity and hierarchical ordering of the criteria in virtually any Rule of Recognition. When the multiplicity and rankings of the criteria are kept in view, we can perceive that his strictures against Incorporationism and Inclusivism lose their force. The ultimacy of a highest court's decision-making power is fully consistent with the ultimacy of moral directives as criteria in a Rule of Recognition.

The present chapter will complete my advocacy of Inclusive Legal Positivism and modest Incorporationism. Having defended those doctrines against barrages of objections from other legal positivists, this book will then move on (in the next three chapters) to the task of upholding the basic claims of positivism against various criticisms leveled by its detractors.

I. Basic Reflections

One of Hart's greatest contributions to the philosophy of law was his insistence that the foundation of any legal system resides in an array of normative presuppositions that underlie the efforts of officials to ascertain the existence and contents of the norms that belong to their system as laws. Hart's label for that array of presuppositions, 'the Rule of Recognition', has become one of the most familiar phrases in contemporary legal philosophy. I have used that phrase throughout this book, and will presently justify my employment of it. Nonetheless, it is quite a misleading designation, since it suggests that the fundament of the law-ascertaining process in each legal system is a single norm. In fact, as has been indicated already, any typical Rule of Recognition consists in a complicated bundle of standards that are largely or fully ranked vis-à-vis one another. Some of those standards are power-conferring, and some are duty-imposing. They both obligate and empower officials to ascertain the law authoritatively by reference to the multiple touchstones which the standards specify.

Hart himself once or twice wrote as if the criteria in each Rule of Recognition were solely power-conferring, and some of his exponents have declared that those criteria are solely duty-imposing.[1] For the most part, however, Hart's discussions make quite clear that any Rule of Recognition is both power-conferring and duty-imposing. Its duty-imposing character indeed ties in directly with its power-conferring character. A Rule of Recognition lays obligations on officials to recognize certain sources of laws as binding, and it bestows powers on them to engage in authoritative acts of law-identification that can fulfill those obligations. Whereas norms of adjudication empower officials to ascertain authoritatively whether any violations of the prevailing laws have occurred, the Rule of Recognition empowers them to ascertain authoritatively the existence and contents of the laws themselves. (Of course, a law-ascertaining determination is essential for

---

[1] For a somewhat misleading passage by Hart, see his *The Concept of Law* (Oxford: Clarendon Press, 1961) [hereinafter cited as Hart, *Concept*], 109–10. For an example of a critic who was led badly astray by some of Hart's remarks, see Lon Fuller, *The Morality of Law* (New Haven, CT: Yale University Press, 1969) (rev. edn), 137. For the view that the Rule of Recognition is exclusively duty-imposing, see Joseph Raz, *The Authority of Law* (Oxford: Clarendon Press, 1979) [hereinafter cited as Raz, *Authority*], 93; Joseph Raz, *The Concept of a Legal System* (Oxford: Clarendon Press, 1980) (2nd edn) [hereinafter cited as Raz, *System*], 199; Neil MacCormick, *H.L.A. Hart* (Stanford: Stanford University Press, 1981) [hereinafter cited as MacCormick, *Hart*], 21, chap. 9.

any violation-detecting determination. Consequently, when the former takes place, it often is an element of the latter. Nonetheless, the two types of determinations can be distinguished analytically. Admittedly, distinguishing them in practice will in some contexts be much more difficult.) Precisely because the law-ascertaining endeavors of the officials are dispositive—precisely because the officials legally bind citizens and other officials with their findings, and because they thereby alter people's legal positions—their engaging in those endeavors will amount to their exercising of legal powers vested in them by their Rule of Recognition.

Were the Rule of Recognition not duty-imposing, the officials in each legal regime would be at liberty to identify any norms at all as the laws of their system. Were the Rule of Recognition not power-conferring, the officials would be unable to identify the law in a legally binding fashion and would thus be unable to carry out their duties as officials. They would not be able to undertake definitively the process of law-ascertainment which they are duty-bound to perform in accordance with the requirements which their Rule of Recognition establishes. In short, only the hybrid bearings of each Rule of Recognition provide both the structured constrainingness and the dynamic operability of a legal system.

A. On the Encompassing Unity of a Rule of Recognition

In an important respect, there need not and typically will not be a wholly uniform Rule of Recognition in this or that particular regime of law. As Ronald Dworkin has argued in opposition to Hart's model of law-ascertainment, the officials in a legal system need not and typically will not adhere to exactly the same set of criteria for ascertaining the law. Some degree of variation among officials is common—which is why in certain difficult cases they disagree with one another at the level of the criteria in their Rule of Recognition rather than exclusively at the level where some shared criteria are brought to bear on problematic matters of classification.[2] As I have argued elsewhere (*IDLP*, 142–6), the divergences among officials are fully compatible with the regularity of a legal regime, so long as the points of contention among them concern the less important layers of their Rule of Recognition. If officials converge on the chief layers of the criteria for law-ascertainment, they can differ with one another about the remaining layers while still operating a mode of governance that is endowed with the regularity and stability of a full-blown legal system. On the one hand, persistent disagreements about the paramount criteria in a Rule of Recognition would lead to civil war or revolution or governmental chaos that would

---

[2] I have discussed at length Dworkin's critique of the Hartian model of law-ascertainment in my *In Defense of Legal Positivism* (Oxford: Oxford University Press, 1999) [hereinafter cited as *IDLP*], 130–61.

interrupt the rule of law. On the other hand, a lack of unanimity on some of the lesser criteria in a Rule of Recognition is quite consistent with the regularized functioning of a legal regime as such. Given as much, we have no reason to believe that there will always or typically be unanimity on those lesser criteria. More likely is that the officials in any particular system will indeed diverge from one another in their understandings of the details of their Rule of Recognition. They can do so while arriving at convergent determinations in the vast majority of circumstances to which the laws of their system apply.

Thus, if the notion of a single overarching Rule of Recognition somehow required full agreement among all the relevant officials on the details of their law-ascertaining criteria, hardly any legal system would contain such a Rule of Recognition. In fact, of course, we should realize that no such consentaneity among the officials is necessary. We can correctly maintain that a single Rule of Recognition exists in this or that legal system even though the officials therein do not all subscribe to exactly the same set of criteria, just as we can correctly maintain that the people in some community speak a single language even though they do not all adhere to precisely the same set of semantic and syntactic criteria. Exhaustive uniformity is not prerequisite to the unity that is a hallmark of a legal system.

In other respects as well, the Rule of Recognition in each legal system is a single overarching array. Joseph Raz has submitted that a legal system can comprise multiple Rules of Recognition, each of which specifies an ultimate source of law. Either those multiple rules will be unranked, or else each of them will independently indicate how it is to be ranked vis-à-vis any other bases for legal validity. So Raz argues (Raz, *Authority*, 95–6). Yet, with reference to a legal system that has been operating as such for more than an extremely short period, one cannot plausibly suggest that its criteria for legal validity will remain largely or entirely unranked. In any realistic setting, those criteria will have come into conflict and will thus have given rise to the need for some prioritization. Whether explicitly through what the officials say or implicitly through what they do, their prioritization of the sources of law within their legal regime will be evinced to any careful observer of the regime. To be sure, the rankings will frequently remain unsettled in some of their details—either because the officials take disparate views of those details or because the questions to be answered by the intricacies of the scheme of prioritization have not yet had to be addressed. Nevertheless, the unsettledness of the Rule of Recognition in such matters of detail is something that any legal positivist can and should readily acknowledge. Hart himself famously insisted that any Rule of Recognition will partake of an open texture at its fringes (Hart, *Concept*, 144–50). Admittedly, he perhaps did not sufficiently emphasize that the openness of a Rule of Recognition at its margins is typically due not only to divergences among officials in their handling of problematic borderline phenomena, but also to their disagreements about the regnant law-validating criteria themselves. All the same, he was correct in thinking that the structuring of a legal system by a Rule of Recognition does not necessitate the unequivocality of that complex rule in every one of its myriad involutions. Subtle questions relating to the rankings of criteria, as well as subtle questions relating to the contents of those criteria, might lack determinate answers at any given juncture. To allow as much is to allow nothing at odds with the view that a single Rule of Recognition exists in the society where the determinate answers to those minor questions are missing.

Let us turn, then, to the other possibility delineated by Raz: his suggestion that each of the multiple Rules of Recognition in some legal system might independently indicate its own superiority or subordination to each of the other such rules in the system. One of the foremost difficulties with such a suggestion is that we would be hard-pressed indeed to tell whether any particular scheme of prioritization exemplifies what Raz has posited or not. That is, we would be hard-pressed to tell whether any such scheme derives from specifications of rankings that are internal to the various law-validating criteria, or whether it instead derives from a set of priority rules that complement those criteria. If the officials in a regime are sufficiently self-aware to make explicit whether the rankings in their Rule of Recognition are criteria-internal or criteria-complementing, then we will be able to tell. Otherwise, however, we shall be reduced to uninformative conjectures about a point concerning which there might be no fact of the matter. If a Rule of Recognition can be equally well formulated through either of the two main ways of encapsulating its rankings—namely, through an encapsulation that locates the rankings in the law-validating criteria themselves, or through an encapsulation that locates the rankings in a concomitant set of priority rules—why should we feel any need to choose speculatively between them? If a difference does not make a difference, we need not attend very closely to it. Moreover, even when we can be sure that the scheme of prioritization in a Rule of Recognition is internal to the law-validating criteria, we should not follow Raz's terminological recommendation. What that recommendation obscures is Hart's reason for speaking of a single Rule of Recognition in each legal system. As has already been intimated, the misleadingness of Hart's phraseology is offset by a potent countervailing consideration. Writing about a Rule of Recognition with multiple criteria, Hart explained that '[t]he reason for still speaking of "a rule" at this point is that, notwithstanding their multiplicity, these distinct criteria are unified by their hierarchical arrangement'.[3] Whether a scheme of prioritization ensues from prescriptions within the law-validating criteria or from the ordering introduced by supplementary rules of ranking, it ties the criteria together as a coherently interrelated set of standards. The integratedness which it bestows upon them is what justifies our designating those criteria and their rankings as an overarching Rule of Recognition. Although Hart's label is misleading in respects already

---

[3] H.L.A. Hart, 'Lon L. Fuller: *The Morality of Law*', in *Essays in Jurisprudence and Philosophy* (Oxford: Clarendon Press, 1983), 343, 360.

noted, it well captures the unity of a throng of law-ascertaining touchstones that stand in quite clear relationships of superiority and subordination to one another.

Raz has elsewhere posed another objection to the idea of a single Rule of Recognition in each legal system. He raises *en passant* the possibility that 'there are various rules of recognition, each addressed to a different kind of officials' (Raz, *System*, 200). This fleeting suggestion has been subjected to scrutiny illuminatingly by Kent Greenawalt, who considers it against the background of the institutional stratification that prevails in virtually every legal system.[4] Any typical legal regime will involve multiple levels of officials. At each tier in the hierarchy, the officials have to bow to the determinations reached by officials in any of the levels above them. We might be inclined to think that officials in different tiers of a legal system are adhering to different versions of a Rule of Recognition. After all, the officials in the topmost level will not have to defer to anyone else in the system. They will therefore always be addressing themselves to the law-ascertaining criteria that directly guide the other officials only when any relevant issues have not yet been decided by the officials in the uppermost tier of the hierarchy. On many occasions, the lower-level officials will be guided not by the aforementioned criteria, but by a criterion which instructs them to uphold whatever the topmost officials have determined. For those topmost officials, by contrast, that latter criterion is beside the point. They do not have to heed a directive that is applicable only to lower-level officials. Accordingly, we might be tempted to endorse the view expressed in the quotation from Raz.

That view might seem to find further support in another fact pointed out by Greenawalt (Greenawalt, 'Rule', 634–36). On a key issue relating to the Rule of Recognition in the United States—the issue whether a constitutional amendment has been properly adopted—the courts defer unreservedly to congressional determinations. Those determinations are themselves guided by the prescriptions laid down in the amending clause of the American Constitution. Hence, Congress abides directly by the prescriptions of the amending clause, whereas the courts abide directly by the determinations of Congress concerning those prescriptions and their fulfillment or nonfulfillment. Once again, then, we might be tempted toward Raz's view. It may seem that the members of Congress are following one Rule of Recognition while the members of the judiciary are following another.

Greenawalt wisely rejects the Razian view, but his alternative position is not entirely satisfactory. He contends that the best approach to ferreting out a single Rule of Recognition is to 'understand the rule of recognition as the ultimate standards of law used by officials who are not simply accepting the judgments of other officials' (Greenawalt, 'Rule', 636). Under this approach, the officials in the uppermost stratum of the hierarchy of a legal system are always guided by their

---

[4] Kent Greenawalt, 'The Rule of Recognition and the Constitution', 85 *Michigan Law Review* 621, 635–6 (1987) [hereinafter cited as Greenawalt, 'Rule'].

Rule of Recognition when they ascertain the law, whereas the officials in the lower strata are frequently instead guided exclusively by the law-ascertaining judgments of their superiors. Much the same can be said—under Greenawalt's approach—about the members of Congress and the members of the judiciary in the United States. Members of Congress orient themselves toward the American Rule of Recognition when handling matters of constitutional amendments, whereas judges instead orient themselves toward the decisions of Congress on such matters.

Although Greenawalt's stance is preferable to Raz's position, it still presents too fragmented a portrayal of the processes of law-ascertainment. Even more important, it obfuscates the respects in which lower-tier officials (or the members of the American judiciary) are guided by their Rule of Recognition when they acquiesce unreservedly in the conclusions reached by upper-tier officials (or by the members of the American Congress). Rather than opting for Greenawalt's solution to the problem addressed by his valuable discussion, we should conclude that—subject to the qualifications already mentioned, concerning divergences on matters of detail—the sundry officials in each legal system adhere to a single Rule of Recognition. Their Rule of Recognition includes criteria directing lower-level officials to treat the law-ascertaining determinations of upper-level officials as binding. The lower-tier officials manifest their adherence to those criteria by indeed treating such determinations as dispositive. Of course, the officials in the uppermost tier do not manifest their acceptance of those criteria in parallel ways, since such officials are not subordinate to anyone else. Criteria calling for deference do not apply to them and do not directly guide their own ascertainment of legal norms. Nevertheless, the topmost officials do accept those criteria and will be disposed to manifest their acceptance in other ways. They are disposed to criticize any deviations from those criteria by lower-tier officials, and they will very likely go further when the deviations are not rapidly corrected. In such situations, they will arrange suitable penalties for the contumacious subordinates. Through their preparedness to engage in criticism and (when necessary) in punitive measures, the officials at the top of a legal system's hierarchy join the lower-echelon officials in upholding a single Rule of Recognition. They do not themselves seek to comply with the deference-prescribing directives in that Rule of Recognition—since those directives are not applicable to them—but they are firmly disposed to ensure that those directives are heeded by their subordinates, to whom the directives are applicable. In that crucial respect, the upper-echelon officials are adhering to the same Rule of Recognition to which the compliant subordinate officials adhere. The overarching unity of their Rule of Recognition is comparable to that of a religious code of appropriate observances which includes some provisions that apply only to men and some provisions that apply only to women; everyone in a society can be upholding that one code even though its precise bearing on each person's behavior will differ between the sexes.

In sum, so long as we keep in mind that the deference-prescribing elements of a Rule of Recognition will carry different implications for the officials in different strata of a legal system's hierarchy, we should encounter no difficulty in discerning the cohesiveness of that Rule of Recognition. Those deference-prescribing instructions directly guide some of the law-ascertaining determinations of officials in the lower strata. Pari passu, they directly guide some of the second-order determinations whereby the officials in the paramount stratum (and in the lower strata) gauge the correctness of the law-ascertaining decisions that have been reached by the lower-echelon officials. Thus, although the deference-requiring portions of a Rule of Recognition impinge on the officials' behavior in varying ways and to varying degrees, they impinge on every official's behavior to some extent. They provide a common focus or reference point for the officials' law-ascertaining endeavors—that is, they set standards toward which the officials orient themselves for varying purposes in those endeavors—just as do the other criteria in a Rule of Recognition. Hence, the inclusion of such provisions in any Rule of Recognition is no reason whatsoever for denying its role as an integrated assemblage of touchstones that are presupposed and upheld by authoritative actions of every official.

B. What is Foundational and What is Derivative

Not every standard for legal validity is a component of a Rule of Recognition, for some such standards are derivative of the criteria which make up that overarching rule (MacCormick, *Hart*, 115; Raz, *Authority*, 95). If for example there arises a question whether an administrative agency has created a binding law by issuing a regulation concerning some activity within the area of the agency's expertise, the judges who rule on the matter will typically have recourse to the terms of the legislative enactment under which the agency has been authorized to promulgate regulations. Any standards laid down by that enactment are derivative, rather than directly constitutive, of a Rule of Recognition. They obtain as determinative standards because criteria in the Rule of Recognition instruct officials to treat certain materials (statutory enactments or constitutional provisions) as binding sources of law.

Somewhat more subtle than the distinction between ultimate and derivative standards for legal validity—though clearly related to it—is the distinction between the pre-formulated and formulated versions of the Rule of Recognition. As has been stated, the Rule of Recognition in any legal system exists as a set of normative presuppositions that underlie and structure the law-ascertaining activities of the system's officials. It is an array of norms on the basis of which the officials determine what counts as legally binding and what does not. Those norms can and do operate even if they remain unarticulated by the officials who ground their determinations on them. Perhaps the officials would not be able to articulate some of the criteria in their Rule of Recognition even if they attempted to do so, or perhaps they simply do not attempt to do so. Whatever may be the reason for the fact that those criteria remain unexpressed (if they do indeed remain unexpressed), they can guide and animate the officials' law-ascertaining endeavors all the same. In this respect, the standards that make up a Rule of Recognition are similar to the rules of a natural language. Competent speakers of a language adhere to any number of syntactical and semantic and grammatical rules even if they seldom or never articulate those rules—and indeed even if they are incapable of articulating any of those rules. Such rules guide and structure the speakers' linguistic behavior notwithstanding that they never get stated explicitly by anyone (if in fact they never get stated explicitly). They exist as a set of norms that are presupposed by the multitudinous utterances and interpretations which the users of the language undertake in the course of daily communications. The efficacy of those norms as underlying presuppositions is in no way dependent on their coming to the surface as propositions whose contents are overtly expressed.

What has been described in the last paragraph is the Rule of Recognition at the foundational level of its existence. That level, at which it obtains as an array of normative preconceptions that are independent of any formulations of their contents, is the only level of the Rule of Recognition in some legal systems. In many a legal regime, however, the contents of some or all of the criteria in the Rule of Recognition come to be formulated and codified as constitutional provisions or statutory enactments. Any such formulations amount to the Rule of Recognition in its epiphenomenal guise. In that guise, the Rule of Recognition exists not as a set of presuppositions that antecede any articulations of their contents, but as the articulations themselves. Its statutory or constitutional encapsulation is the form in which it obtains at the epiphenomenal level. Of course, that epiphenomenal level never supplants the foundational level. A Rule of Recognition can exist in a foundational form without existing in an epiphenomenal form, but not vice versa. After all, any constitutional provisions or statutory enactments carry binding force only because criteria in the foundational Rule of Recognition instruct officials to treat those provisions or enactments as determinative. Hart perceptively grasped as much: 'Even if [the content of a Rule of Recognition] were enacted by statute, this would not reduce it to the level of a statute; for the legal status of such an enactment necessarily would depend on the fact that the rule existed antecedently to and independently of the enactment' (Hart, *Concept*, 108). Nonetheless, although never independent of the foundational level, the Rule of Recognition in its epiphenomenal guise is often a focus of attention for officials and citizens.

Just as a Rule of Recognition at the foundational level is analogous in some important respects to the sundry rules of a natural language, so too a Rule of Recognition at the epiphenomenal level is roughly analogous to various works that are produced as codifications of linguistic rules. On the one hand, a natural language can perfectly well function as a complex medium of communication even if no one has sought to formulate its underlying rules. On the other hand, lexicographers and linguists and grammatical experts often do compile works that systematically recount the structural or semantic features of a language. Dictionaries and grammatical manuals and other such publications distill those features, and they thereby bring to the surface the standards on which the competent users of the language rely when they communicate with one another. In that regard, those publications are broadly comparable to statutory or constitutional provisions that formulate the criteria in a legal system's Rule of Recognition.

Dictionaries and other guides to language are derivative of the patterns of usage that actually prevail in a linguistic community. Unlike works of fiction (such as J.R.R. Tolkien's invention of an elaborate parlance for Middle-earth), such publications present themselves as reflective of the rules or patterns of discourse that are actually operative in the employment of a language by competent speakers and writers. To be sure, lexicographers and grammatical experts typically do not eschew prescriptive ambitions entirely. Within the bounds of their roles, they can favor some of the prevailing patterns of usage and disfavor others. Nevertheless, their publications will not be minimally successful in the fulfillment of their assigned functions unless their accounts of linguistic features do accurately represent the workings of the language to which those features are ascribed. If those accounts are not to be fictional or antiquated, they will have to reflect the norms that are actually presupposed in the communications of the relevant language's users. Once again, then, we can perceive an analogy between the domain of language and the domain of officials' law-ascertaining activities. In a legal system where the officials aim to codify their Rule of Recognition in a constitutional or statutory form, their efforts will be unsuccessful if they fail to capture the ultimate norms that are actually presupposed by their law-ascertaining endeavors. Of course, the officials might instead be aiming to set new criteria for legal validity that will modify the pre-formulated criteria to which they have thitherto adhered. (Any such transfigurative ventures will themselves depend on other pre-formulated criteria, which direct the officials to attribute binding force to the statutory or constitutional provisions that contain the new standards for legal validity.) Still, if the officials are indeed trying to formulate rather than alter their Rule of Recognition, they will have to strive for accuracy in their recapitulation of it. The Rule of Recognition at the epiphenomenal level is derivative of the Rule of Recognition at the foundational level, not only in that the former is dependent on the latter for its binding force, but also in that the content of the former has to match the content of the latter.

Yet, notwithstanding the twofold derivativeness of any Rule of Recognition in its epiphenomenal guise, it can influence the foundational Rule of Recognition. Before considering this point in connection with law, we should glance again at the domain of language. As has been noted, dictionaries and other linguistic guides are designed to encapsulate the semantic or structural characteristics that are actually present in some language. Their role is that of recapitulation rather than invention. All the same, such works can affect the components of the very language which they aspire to chart. This influence can operate in either of two main ways. (I shall concentrate here on dictionaries, since they are especially likely to engender the sorts of effects which I envisage.) First, if the compilers of a dictionary inadvertently or deliberately depart from some prevailing patterns of usage, they might bring about certain changes in some of those patterns. It may be that the linguistic behavior of the users of the relevant language will adapt to what is specified in the dictionary. In that event, the dictionary will have transmuted some of the elements of the behavior which it purports to recount. Admittedly, such adaptations will normally be quite circumscribed in scope. Their occurrence is considerably more likely if the dictionary enjoys authoritativeness by virtue of being largely accurate. If such a publication were instead to include sweeping departures from the existent norms of the language, its ability to induce people to shift their linguistic habits would be greatly impaired if not altogether eliminated. Striking though the innovative power of a dictionary can sometimes be, its effectiveness is generally dependent on the dictionary's overall reliability as a summation of the meanings that are actually attached to words in the relevant linguistic community. Nonetheless, within limits, the potential for innovation abides.

A second respect in which a dictionary can influence a language is conservative rather than innovative. On the one hand, the prestige of a dictionary typically derives from the proficiency with which its compilers have executed their task of assembling the senses that have come to be associated with various words. On the other hand, once that prestige has been gained, the dictionary will often take on a life of its own. In addition to gauging the estimableness of a dictionary on the basis of its accuracy in tracking how myriad words are employed, people will start to gauge the semantic propriety of their utterances on the basis of their conformity to the definitions enumerated in the dictionary. Instead of being only a reflection, the dictionary becomes also a lodestar. Having captured the ways in which any number of words are used, it tends to entrench those ways by endowing them with an authoritatively certified status. To some extent, then, it retards change in the medium of communication from which it has emerged as a distillation.

Although the analogy between the discoursive behavior of the speakers of a language and the law-ascertaining activities of a legal system's officials is far from perfect, the codifying of a Rule of Recognition by officials can affect its criteria in broadly the same fashion in which a dictionary can influence the meanings of words. One of the two principal aspects of the codification's potential influence has already been briefly broached. If officials adopt some statutory or constitutional standards for legal validity that do not accurately reflect the criteria which have been presupposed theretofore by their law-ascertaining endeavors, they might effect some modifications in those criteria. Such an upshot is not inevitable—since the statutes or constitutional formulations might remain uneffectuated—but it is quite plausible. Indeed, the innovative power of constitutional or statutory provisions may well prove more far-reaching than the innovative power of a dictionary. Whereas extensive changes in the patterns of usage of a natural language over a short period are extremely unlikely, some quite sweeping changes in law-ascertaining practices could realistically be sought through the codification of new criteria. In any such circumstances, major adjustments in a legal system's foundational Rule of Recognition can come about through the elaboration of its epiphenomenal Rule of Recognition. (Of course, as has already been noted, any such process of transformation depends on criteria in the foundational Rule of Recognition which lead officials to treat the epiphenomenal Rule of Recognition as something to be heeded. The innovative influence of any formulated version of a legal regime's Rule of Recognition is always ultimately derivative of the pre-formulated norms that constitute the regime's Rule of Recognition at the foundational level.)

Like a dictionary, the codification of a Rule of Recognition can play a conservative role at least as robustly as an innovative role. Let us suppose that the officials in some legal system accurately formulate some or all of the criteria in their Rule of Recognition as constitutional provisions. Those provisions are derivative of the system's foundational Rule of Recognition in the two respects already mentioned: the binding force of the provisions is due to the fact that that Rule of Recognition attributes binding force to them, and their contents reflect the contents of its criteria. In turn, the provisions can serve to reinforce the normative presuppositions on which they are dependent. Like a dictionary, a Rule of Recognition in its epiphenomenal guise can take on a life of its own. The constitutional formulations can become the focal point of the law-ascertaining enterprise undertaken by the system's officials, as they justify their determinations (to themselves and to their fellow officials) by reference to those formulations. Since the foundational criteria that ascribe binding force to the constitutional provisions might be much more resistant to change than the foundational criteria that are given expression in those provisions, the codification of the latter set of criteria can greatly strengthen their durability. In such a context, the disinclination of each official to depart from those criteria is primarily attributable not to their contents, but to the sheer fact of their having been enshrined in the articles of a constitution. In short, although the standards for legal validity in a Rule of Recognition at the epiphenomenal level are always products of standards for legal validity in a Rule of Recognition at the foundational level, the flow of influence between the two levels is by no means entirely unidirectional.

II. Moral Precepts and Legal Validity:
The Revival of Rule-Skepticism

In some incisive recent articles,[5] Himma has contended that the power of the highest court in a legal system to interpret definitively the prevailing standards of legal validity is at odds with the notion that those standards themselves determine what is legally valid and what is not. His particular target, as has been indicated, is the claim that a credible Rule of Recognition can make moral soundness a necessary condition or a sufficient condition for legal validity. Hence, while his reasoning clearly relates to my present chapter's preoccupation with the ultimacy of the criteria in any Rule of Recognition and with the ultimacy of certain construals of those criteria, it also returns us to some of the issues investigated in the first few chapters of this book. In salient respects, my rejoinders to his reasoning will amount to a defense of Inclusive Legal Positivism and Incorporationism.

A. Himma's Arguments

Himma takes a conceptual thesis and an uncontroversial empirical thesis as his points of departure. His conceptual thesis is that the criteria for legal validity in any system of law are conventional in character. That is, those criteria are norms presupposed by officials' law-ascertaining activities, and are not norms external to those activities. His uncontroversial empirical claim is that the highest court in the American legal system and in any relevantly similar legal system is legally empowered to bind all other officials with rulings concerning the existence and contents of legal norms. (Lower courts are likewise empowered to deliver binding rulings, but their determinations are subject to being overturned by higher courts.) Now, the key point arising from this empirical observation is not the identity of the institution with the final say over the existence and contents of legal norms; rather, the key point is that *some* person or body of persons must have such a final say if a legal system is to be sustainable. In the American legal system, that ultimate responsibility—in connection with matters of federal and constitutional law— rests with the Supreme Court. In virtually every other Western legal system, the highest court plays a similar role. Himma thus presents his analysis with reference

---

[5] 'Making Sense of Constitutional Disagreement: Legal Positivism, the Bill of Rights, and the Conventional Rule of Recognition in the United States,' 4 *Journal of Law in Society* 149 (2003) [hereinafter cited as Himma, 'Sense']; 'Final Authority to Bind with Moral Mistakes: On the Explanatory Potential of Inclusive Legal Positivism,' 23 *Law and Philosophy* (2004) [hereinafter cited as Himma, 'Authority']. My citations to the latter article include the page numbers of the proofs, which will not be the same as the page numbers of the article in its final published form.

to the finality of a legal system's highest court. However, his conclusions are equally applicable (*mutatis mutandis*) to a legal system in which the ultimate law-ascertaining power is vested in some legislative or executive body. As far as the solidity or weakness of the general drift of his arguments is concerned, nothing hinges on the precise location of that ultimate power. If his basic contentions were correct, they would be correct in application to any legal system.

What Himma highlights is the fact that, within a very broad compass, the US Supreme Court has the legal power to bind all other American officials with mistaken determinations. When issues relating to the existence or contents of legal norms are addressed by the Court, other officials will be legally obligated to give effect to its rulings irrespective of the objective correctness or incorrectness of each ruling. Suppose for example that the Court has to decide whether some statutes that regulate the availability of procedures for abortions are consistent with the American Constitution. In so deciding, the Court will be deeming those statutes to be legally valid or legally invalid. Yet, regardless of which outcome the Court reaches, all the other officials in the American governmental system will be legally obligated to uphold that outcome. Although some of the officials might comply with such an obligation very grudgingly in connection with the particular issue, and although a small proportion of them might decline altogether to heed the Court on that issue, the vast majority of them will acknowledge the legally binding force of the Court's ruling. Such a situation obtains as a matter of empirically verifiable fact, and *some* such situation—involving the finality of the determinations of *some* institution(s) in response to most of the questions that arise in the course of the American legal system's workings—must obtain if the American system of legal governance is to be viable.

While tracing the full implications of his conceptual and empirical premises, Himma readily avouches that in two distinct respects the power of the US Supreme Court to resolve matters definitively is hemmed in. First, although the Court's power is formidably expansive, it is not utterly unlimited. If the Court's rationale for some ruling were truly preposterous, then the ruling itself would probably not be upheld by most officials. For example, if the Court were to adduce the Constitution's specification of the minimum age of a President as the sole basis for a decision concerning the regulation of procedures for abortions, the bizarre irrationality of such a justification might deprive the decision itself of its legally binding force in the eyes of most officials. Nevertheless, although such a constraint on the Court's power is almost certainly in place, it is unconfining for nearly all practical purposes. It will leave the Court able to opt for either of two conflicting decisions in just about every case. '[T]his limit really doesn't amount to much in determining the *outcome[s]* of validity cases. . . . [The limit] operates to constrain the Court in *justifying* its decisions in hard validity cases, but it does not operate to limit the *outcomes* available to the Court' (Himma, 'Sense', 170–1, emphases in original). Himma indeed declares that this constraint on the Court's power has never or almost never been transgressed

(Himma, 'Sense', 175–6). However intensely controversial some of the Court's decisions have proved to be, they have never been based on rationales that are so outlandishly nonsensical as to occasion widespread revolts on the part of other officials.

A second trammel under which the Court operates is a duty rather than a limitation on its power. According to Himma, the Court is legally obligated to arrive at decisions about the legal validity of norms in conformity with the morally best interpretation of the American Constitution (Himma, 'Sense', 184; Himma, 'Authority', 23). Notwithstanding that the Court has the legal power to bind other officials with its determinations even if those determinations do not follow from the morally best interpretation of the Constitution, it is under a duty to reach decisions that do follow therefrom. Insofar as the Court fails to fulfill that duty, it will undergo chiding from other officials—who will nonetheless give effect to its rulings. As Himma states: 'If officials criticize judges for failing to decide cases according to some norm *N* and judges routinely strive and expect each other to decide cases according to *N*, then it follows…that officials are practicing a norm that requires judges to decide cases according to *N*. *N* thus functions as a legal constraint on the decision-making of judges—even if officials routinely enforce the court's decisions without regard to whether those decisions really do satisfy *N*' (Himma, 'Authority', 12). Himma maintains that this duty is connected with a further limitation on the Supreme Court's power. If the Court were to decide a case without making any apparent effort to ground its judgment in the morally best interpretation of the Constitution, the judgment would not be upheld by the other officials within the American legal system. If for instance the Court were ever to advert to some aleatory procedure such as the flipping of a coin as the basis for a ruling on the legal validity of enactments that regulate abortions, the ruling would not be treated as legally binding by other officials. They would refuse to act upon it and would demand that it be justified afresh. In sum, although the Court has the legal power to obligate other officials to effectuate its rulings even when those rulings do not satisfy the Court's duty to derive its decisions from the morally best interpretation of the Constitution, it does not have the legal power to obligate other officials to effectuate its rulings when those rulings and their justifications do not exhibit any genuine effort by the Court to satisfy the duty just mentioned.

Having noted the constraints that lie upon the Court, and having indicated that those constraints are only minimally confining for all practical purposes, Himma prosecutes his critique of Inclusive Legal Positivism and Incorporationism. His basic claim is that consistency with some moral principle(s) cannot be a necessary condition for a norm's legal validity and that correctness as a moral principle cannot be a sufficient condition for a norm's legal validity—except in highly unusual circumstances that almost certainly do not obtain in the American legal system—because the necessary or sufficient condition will instead reside in the judgments of the Supreme Court (or in the judgments of any other body that has the final say over matters of law-ascertainment). What the Court thinks about the aforesaid consistency or correctness, rather than the consistency or correctness itself, is determinative of legal validity.

Suppose that, under an Inclusivist understanding of the American legal system, consistency with some moral principle *P* is a necessary condition for the legal validity of any enactment. The snag for this Inclusivist analysis of the situation, Himma contends, is that the Supreme Court has the legal power to deem enactments legally valid even if they are at odds with *P.* (It also has the legal power to deem enactments legally invalid even if they are compatible with *P.*) Within the very broad limits described above, the Court has the legal power to bind other officials with its erroneous judgments as well as with its correct judgments. Thus, the Court's incorrect validation of any norm that violates *P* would be determinative of that norm's legal status. Consequently—and pace the Inclusive Legal Positivists—consistency with *P* is not a necessary condition for legal validity. Even if the Court in fact invalidates every enactment that runs athwart *P,* it could have upheld the validity of any such enactment and could thereby have obligated all other American legal officials to recognize such an enactment as a law. Congruity with *P,* then, is not essential for the standing of any particular norm *Q* as a law. Essential instead is the Court's preparedness to hold that *Q* is congruent with *P.*

Suppose now that, under a moderately Incorporationist understanding of the American legal system, the correctness of a norm *N* as a moral principle is a sufficient condition for the status of that norm as a law in hard cases. Irreconcilable with this Incorporationist analysis, according to Himma, is that the Supreme Court has the legal power to reject *N* as a law in hard cases and to invoke and apply some contrary norm(s). Within very broad limits, the Court has the legal power to bind other officials with its mistaken holdings as well as with its appropriate holdings. Hence, the Court's inappropriate invalidation of *N* as a legal norm would be determinative of *N*'s legal status—its status as something that does not belong to the American legal system as one of the laws thereof. Consequently, and pace the Incorporationists, the correctness of a norm as a moral principle is not sufficient for the norm's legal validity. Even if the Court in fact treats *N* as legally valid, it could have declined to do so and could thereby have obligated all other American legal officials to treat *N* as lacking the status of a law. Not sufficient for such a status, then, is *N*'s correctness as a moral principle. Sufficient instead (in hard cases) is the Court's affirmation that *N* is correct as a moral principle.

Because Inclusive Legal Positivists and Incorporationists adhere to the positivist view that the criteria for legal validity in any system of law are thoroughly conventional, they cannot aptly respond to Himma's challenge by adverting to standards for legal validity that are external to those which American officials accept. If American officials do in fact treat the rulings of the Supreme Court as the decisive touchstones for the legal validity of enactments, then positivists of every stripe have to concede that the Court's rulings are indeed such touchstones. There accordingly seems to be no route of escape for Inclusivists and Incorporationists from Himma's critique.

His critique appears to establish the falsity of Inclusivism and Incorporationism not only in application to the contemporary United States, but also in application to virtually any legal system—since, as has already been observed, virtually any functional legal system will have to entrust some institution(s) with ultimate responsibility over matters of legal validity. Any such institution(s) in an Inclusivist regime will stand ready to reach binding judgments concerning the consistency of ostensible laws with some moral standards for legal validity. As a result, the approval bestowed by those judgments will have displaced that consistency itself as a necessary condition for the status of any norm as a law. Likewise, the institution(s) with ultimate responsibility in an Incorporationist regime will stand ready to reach binding judgments concerning the correctness of norms as moral principles that are to be applied as laws in hard cases. As a consequence, the approval bestowed by those judgments will have displaced that correctness itself as a sufficient condition for the status of a norm as a law that is to be applied in hard cases. In the aftermath of Himma's trenchant critique, then, Inclusivism and Incorporationism appear to be in desperate straits. If proponents of those theories hope to sustain their positions, they will have to come up with suitable rejoinders.

B. Rejoinders to Himma: Some Preliminary Queries

Though Himma's discussions prescind from a host of complexities that would be involved in any attempt to specify the content of the Rule of Recognition within an advanced legal system such as that of the United States, they also contain a number of insights and subtleties that have not been recounted here. (They additionally contain a few oddities that have likewise not been recounted here.[6]) For my purposes, the general lines of reasoning summarized above are what must be contested. If those lines of reasoning were sound, they would be devastating for the varieties of legal positivism which I have championed in the preceding three chapters of this book. Moreover, even theorists who look askance at Inclusivism and Incorporationism should recoil from Himma's analyses. After all, his arguments can very easily be extended into an audacious form of rule-skepticism. Of course, to maintain as much is not per se to maintain that his arguments are wrong. A line of reasoning can generate unpalatable conclusions and still be sound. Nonetheless, the fact that Himma has logically committed himself to a sweeping doctrine of rule-skepticism—*malgré lui*—is a strong reason

---

[6] I shall mention only one of these. Himma persistently uses the word 'criteria' to refer not to the standards for legal validity that are followed by judges, but to descriptive encapsulations of those standards. I do not join him in this idiosyncratic pattern of usage.

for resisting his contentions. That reason helps to motivate my ripostes. Hence, before we turn to those ripostes, we should briefly consider why his arguments lead to rule-skepticism.

If Himma's critique of Inclusivist and Incorporationist accounts of law-*ascertainment* were correct, then a parallel critique would apply to every process of law-*application*. Let us suppose that, under ordinary ways of thinking, the consistency of a course of action with various legal norms—such as statutes and administrative decrees and judicial doctrines—is necessary for the permissibility of that course of action. Let us suppose further that, under ordinary ways of thinking, the existence of some legal mandate(s) is sufficient for the forbiddenness of any course of action that runs counter to the terms of the mandate(s). An advocate of Himma's challenge to Inclusivism and Incorporationism can now reason as follows. Neither the aforementioned permissibility nor the aforementioned forbiddenness is ever genuinely determined by any legal norm(s), except in highly unusual circumstances that do not obtain in the American legal system or in other legal systems that are known to us. Rather, what determines the permissibility or forbiddenness within the American legal system is the Supreme Court's decisions concerning the legal norm(s) in question. After all, within a very wide scope, the Supreme Court has the legal power to bind lower courts and administrators with this or that application of any legal norm, even if the application is objectively incorrect in its understanding of the norm's true implications. Hence, the actual consistency between any legal norms and some course of action cannot ever genuinely be necessary for the permissibility of that course of action. If the Court were to decide incorrectly that a mode of conduct is permissible under the terms of the applicable laws, its erroneous verdict would bind the other officials in the American legal system to treat that mode of conduct as unprohibited. Similarly, the existence of any legal mandate cannot ever genuinely be sufficient for the forbiddenness of some course of action. If the Court were to decide incorrectly that a mode of conduct is permissible notwithstanding the existence of some law that objectively forbids it, the mistaken determination would bind the other officials in the American legal system to treat that mode of conduct as unproscribed. In sum, a boldly rule-skeptical conclusion beckons. Legal norms in the United States are never determinative of the legal permissibility or legal impermissibility of people's behavior; always determinative instead are the Supreme Court's discrete holdings.

Even the precedential force of each of the Court's holdings will be swallowed up by the potential occurrence of future mistaken decisions. Within very expansive limits, the Court has the legal power to bind lower courts and administrators with erroneous decisions—as well as with correct decisions, of course—concerning the precedential implications of any of its past judgments. Ergo, those implications are determined not by the past judgments but by the Court's subsequent decisions (be they decisions which the Court actually reaches or decisions which the Court would reach if suitable cases were to come before it). Naturally, any precedential implications of each of those subsequent decisions are in turn to be settled by the potential occurrence of still further judgments in the future. Because the Court has the legal power to bind other officials with either of two conflicting answers to any question relating to the precedential scope of any of its past holdings, that scope is never determined by a past holding itself. No more than a statute or an administrative regulation can the Court's previous rulings bear on the present permissibility of anyone's conduct. What instead bears on that present permissibility is the Court's current thinking about those previous rulings. In other words, when Himma's critique is transferred from the context of law-ascertainment to the context of law-application, it yields a rule-skeptical account of every source of law. It generates the conclusion that any legal consequence—the legal permissibility or impermissibility of any course of action—is a product not of statutes or administrative regulations or judicial doctrines, but of case-by-case decisions that are actually or potentially rendered by the Supreme Court.

Himma might seek to defend himself against a charge of thoroughgoing rule-skepticism by contending that the Supreme Court's legal power to bind other officials with mistaken determinations is less extensive in connection with law-application than in connection with law-ascertainment. Specifically, he might maintain that the Court's power is especially ample in connection with Inclusivist or Incorporationist processes of law-ascertainment, which require moral judgments. Because of the inherently controversial character of such judgments, officials might be particularly inclined to acquiesce in law-ascertaining decisions by the Court with which they disagree. By contrast, the officials would not be so firmly disposed to give effect to the Court's mistaken *applications* of the law, which (insofar as they have not involved moral judgments) are demonstrably incorrect. Consequently, although the Court does have the legal power to bind other officials with erroneous law-applying decisions, its power in that respect is relatively cabined. Thus, any rule-skeptical conclusions arising from an acknowledgment of that power will themselves be quite modest. Or so a defender of Himma might submit.

Such a response to my analysis would be problematic partly because it would hinge on highly speculative empirical assertions rather than solely on the uncontroversial empirical assertions advanced by Himma. More important, the posited response adverts to what is at most a fairly minor difference of degree rather than a difference of kind. On the one hand, it may well be that the moral judgments necessitated by the presence of Inclusivist criteria in a legal system's Rule of Recognition will give rise to greater and more persistent disputation than will the judgments involved in the application of ordinary legal mandates. It might therefore be that the preparedness of American officials to uphold misguided rulings by the Supreme Court is more robust in Inclusivist contexts of law-ascertainment than in ordinary contexts of law-application. Perceiving that intractable disagreements are more common in the former set of contexts, those officials might be more apt to go along there with rulings by the Court that strike them as erroneous. On the other hand, such a difference does not alter the fact that most issues (of law-ascertainment) resolved by reference to Inclusivist criteria are straightforward, just like most issues (of law-application) resolved by reference to typical legal mandates. Himma himself unhesitatingly affirms that most of the problems addressed by an Inclusivist criterion will lend themselves to demonstrably correct answers: '[S]ince hard cases represent a very small percentage of cases that arise under [a moral criterion *N*], unmediated recourse to *N* by officials is sufficient to dispose of the vast majority of cases that might arise under *N*' (Himma, 'Authority', 26). Thus, even if the empirical conjectures that underlie the defense of Himma outlined in my last paragraph are correct, they should not impel us to presume that the Supreme Court's legal power to bind other officials with its mistaken holdings is substantially more tenuous in matters of law-application than in matters of Inclusivist law-ascertainment. Even if the straightforwardness of the issues to be decided has a bearing on the likelihood that officials will put up with the Court's missteps, that bearing will not markedly differ between processes of law-application and Inclusivist processes of law-ascertainment. Hence, if the limitations on the Court's power in regard to the latter processes are meager indeed, the limitations on its power in regard to the former processes are likewise meager. Were Himma on solid ground in arriving at strongly rule-skeptical conclusions about Inclusivist criteria for ascertaining the law, we would be on solid ground in reaching some similar conclusions about the legal norms that get applied to people's conduct. (My remarks in this paragraph have been confined to Inclusivism and have not made any mention of Incorporationism, because the first few chapters of this book have argued that Incorporationist criteria in a Rule of Recognition are sustainable only when restricted to cases that are not straightforwardly resolvable by reference to the prevailing source-based laws. Accordingly, there is no occasion for pondering the extent to which the Supreme Court has the legal power to bind other American officials with erroneous Incorporationist law-ascertaining decisions in easy cases.)

Before we move on, we should note that Himma himself appears to believe that the Supreme Court lacks the legal power to bind other American officials with mistaken Inclusivist law-ascertaining determinations in easy cases. He suggests that 'officials decline, as a general rule, to treat the court's incorrect decisions in easy cases regarding [an Inclusivist criterion *N*] as establishing the law', and he declares that 'in many developed legal systems, the officials practice a norm granting a court final authority to decide whether a proposition counts as law in virtue of satisfying *N* in only hard cases' (Himma, 'Authority', 29, 26). To be sure, his position on this topic is not entirely perspicuous, for he later states that 'the other officials in a system allow the court an appreciable degree of freedom to make mistakes under some putatively inclusive recognition norm' (Himma, 'Authority', 35 n.36). Nonetheless, he presents quite a long discussion that is premised—at least for the sake of argument—on the notion that American officials will not uphold mistaken rulings by the Supreme Court if those rulings pertain to clear-cut matters.[7] His tactic is to concede such a notion at least *arguendo* and then to explain why that concession is not sufficient to rescue Inclusive Legal Positivism. Both the concession and the explanation are ill-advised.

Let us first probe the concession. If it is true that the officials in the American legal system would not regard themselves as legally bound by a mistaken judgment of the Supreme Court in any easy case, then the rule-skeptical upshot of Himma's argumentation is greatly diminished in its reach and import—even if we pretermit the other shortcomings in his argumentation that will be explored shortly. However, such a surmise about the dispositions of American officials is very likely false. On the one hand, it is doubtless true that the officials would cease to treat the mistaken rulings of the Court as binding if those rulings occurred in a large number of easy cases. In such circumstances, the Court would effectively have forfeited its legal power to obligate the other officials to abide by its decisions. A host of truly outlandish judgments would quite predictably produce such an effect. On the other hand, if we examine each easy case on its own rather than together with other easy cases, and if we inquire whether the Court has the legal power to bind other officials with a mistaken determination in that particular easy case, the answer to our inquiry is almost certainly affirmative. A blunder by the Court in any one easy case would not trigger a rebellion on the part of most officials in the American legal system. All or most of the officials would grit their teeth and acquiesce in the Court's misguided decision. Yet, since this point is applicable to every easy case or virtually every easy case, Himma's rule-skeptical conclusions—if otherwise correct—will apply to every such case. In connection with any straightforward matter to be decided under an Inclusivist criterion for law-ascertainment, the Supreme Court has the legal power to bind other officials with an erroneous ruling. Once we distinguish between what is true of *each* easy case (considered individually) and what is true of *all* or *many* easy cases (considered collectively), we can discern that Himma has very likely erred by suggesting that the Court lacks the power just mentioned. That power is present in every easy case.

Let us now look at Himma's attempt to explain why his critique of Inclusive Legal Positivism would retain its force even when accompanied by his concession concerning easy cases. Given his concession, an apparently Inclusivist criterion would govern the validity of norms as laws in clear-cut cases, whereas the Supreme Court's decisions about that criterion would govern the validity of norms as laws in difficult cases. Himma submits that a defender of Inclusivism

---

[7] That discussion occurs in Himma, 'Authority', 26–32. The discussion actually focuses on advanced legal systems generally, rather than specifically on the American legal system. However, Himma explicitly and repeatedly classifies the American legal system as one of the advanced legal systems which he has in mind.

'might argue that the easy, uncontroversial content of [a moral norm *N*] defines a moral criterion of legality in such circumstances'. He elaborates:

> On this line of reasoning, the characteristic authority of the courts to bind officials in hard cases with either of two conflicting decisions precludes incorporation of the hard, controversial content of *N*, but does not preclude incorporation of *N*'s easy, uncontroversial content. If officials decline, as a general rule, to treat the court's incorrect decisions in easy cases regarding *N* as establishing the law, they are practicing a rule that makes the uncontroversial content of *N* a legality criterion. In such cases, it is reasonable to conclude that the easy content of *N* functions as a moral criterion of legality. (Himma, 'Authority', 29)

Himma seeks to rebut the posited defense of Inclusivism by challenging the inference broached in the final sentence of this quotation. He contends that the partitioning of the content of *N* into a straightforward component and a knotty component will not yield two moral principles. Neither of those components will itself be a genuine moral principle, any more than the components of a moral prohibition on murder if we partition it into a norm that prohibits only the murder of Caucasian people and a norm that prohibits only the murder of non-Caucasian people. Thus, although the straightforward component of *N* does function as a criterion for legal validity within the envisaged legal system, that component is not a moral principle and is therefore not a genuinely Inclusivist criterion. So Himma maintains, as he presumes to have stymied Inclusivism once again.

Both the defense which Himma constructs for Inclusivism and his rebuttal of that defense are irredeemably objectionable. The posited defense overlooks the distinction between the intension and the extension of any norm—a distinction to which Himma is elsewhere aptly attentive (Himma, 'Authority', 33 n.34). In the legal system which he envisions, where the officials reach their law-ascertaining decisions in easy cases by reference to *N* and in hard cases by reference to the Supreme Court's rulings about *N*, the content of the Inclusivist criterion on which they rely in easy cases is *N* rather than some portion of *N*. The difference between a reliance on *N* for easy cases only and a reliance on *N* for all cases does not reside in the meaning or content of *N*, but in the range of situations to which that Inclusivist criterion gets applied. When officials implicitly or explicitly invoke *N* in easy cases only, that criterion means exactly the same as when it is invoked in all cases. Suppose, for example, that *N* is a moral principle which invalidates any enactments that are grossly unfair. When officials in easy cases have recourse to *N* in order to uphold enactments that are not grossly unfair and in order to reject enactments that are grossly unfair, the content of the basis for their assessments is exactly the same as it would be if the officials also had recourse to *N* in difficult cases. In any case of either type, the officials would be gauging whether some law has imposed hugely inordinate burdens on certain people, and whether it has conferred hugely inordinate benefits on certain people, and whether it differentiates among people in a markedly invidious fashion. Those inquiries will be asked (implicitly or explicitly) in easy cases, and those very same inquiries would be asked in hard cases if the officials resorted to N in such cases. The questions do not differ between easy cases and hard cases; what differs is the range of the problems to which affirmative and negative answers get applied. That is, the difference is purely extensional rather than intensional.

At any rate, even if Himma were right in thinking that the content of N would have to be partitioned if N were to be invoked only in easy cases, his discussion of partitioning would be unsupportable. As has been mentioned, he adverts to a moral prohibition on murder in order to substantiate his claim that the partitioning of a moral principle can yield a pair of more specific standards that are not themselves moral norms. He states that a race-based partitioning of the moral prohibition on murder would yield a norm that forbids the murder of Caucasian people only and a norm that forbids the murder of non-Caucasian people only, and he contends that neither of those norms is a credible moral precept. In fact, however, the sole tenable rendering of each of those two norms will have belied his contention that neither of them is a genuine moral precept.

Let us designate the norm forbidding only the murder of Caucasian people as 'M_1', and let us designate the norm forbidding only the murder of non-Caucasian people as 'M_2'. Now, clearly, M_1 and M_2 will be inconsistent with each other if either of them permits what the other proscribes. Hence, we have to construe M_1 as a prohibition on the murder of Caucasian people that simply does not address the murder of other people. We cannot construe it as a prohibition on the murder of Caucasian people that permits the murder of other people. If we construed M_1 in the latter fashion, we would render it inconsistent with M_2. In that event, of course, M_1 and M_2 would not be the products of a partitioning of the general prohibition on murder. After all, that general prohibition is hardly an incoherent combination of two inconsistent norms. Accordingly, if we are to accept Himma's claim that the general prohibition on murder divides into M_1 and M_2, we have to conclude that M_1 simply does not address the murder of non-Caucasian people. In other words, we have to reject the notion that M_1 permits the murder of such people. We have to draw cognate conclusions about M_2, of course. That is, we have to infer that M_2 simply does not address the murder of Caucasian people. If M_2 is to be compatible with M_1—as it must be if M_1 and M_2 together make up the general prohibition on murder—it cannot permit the murder of Caucasian people.

Once we have construed M_1 and M_2 along the lines indicated in the preceding paragraph, however, we should repudiate Himma's view that neither of those norms is a credible moral standard. Let us concentrate here on M_1. Although there is certainly no valid moral precept that forbids the murder of Caucasian people and permits the murder of other people, there is a valid moral precept that forbids the murder of Caucasian people without addressing the murder of other people. Such a precept is on a par with a moral norm that prohibits the murder of children without addressing the murder of adults, or a moral norm that prohibits the murder of mentally retarded people without addressing the murder of mentally sound people. One can easily imagine circumstances in which the moral precept forbidding the murder of Caucasian people could appropriately be invoked. Suppose, for example, that the members of a black inner-city gang are targeting Caucasians for murder. A black clergyman or urban leader meets with the members of the gang in order to remonstrate with them. He urges them to recognize that the murder of Caucasian people is wrong. In so doing, he is certainly not implying that the murder of non-Caucasian people is permissible. Rather, he is implicitly or explicitly contending that the wrongness of murdering non-Caucasians is paralleled by the wrongness of murdering Caucasians. His invocation of M_1 is the invocation of a genuine moral precept.

While dismissing the status of M_1 as a moral standard, Himma himself trades on the non-equivalence of 'does not prohibit' and 'permits'. He writes: 'While there is no moral standard that prohibits killing white people but does not prohibit killing people of color, there is a moral norm that prohibits murder but does not prohibit theft' (Himma, 'Authority', 31). The second half of this quoted statement is true only if 'does not prohibit' is not equivalent to 'permits', since there is no sound moral norm that permits theft. However, once we perceive the non-equivalence of 'does not prohibit' and 'permits' in the second half of the statement, we should perceive it also in regard to the first half. Although M_1 does not prohibit murders of non-Caucasians, it does not permit them, either. It simply does not address the issue one way or the other. In that respect it is similar to the general prohibition on murder, which does not address the issue of theft one way or the other. Now, neither Himma nor anyone else doubts that that general prohibition on murder is a moral norm; likewise, no one should doubt that M_1 is a moral norm. In sum, even were Himma correct in declaring that an Inclusivist criterion will be intensionally partitioned if it is operative only in easy cases, he would be incorrect in claiming that the products of the partitioning are not moral precepts. To renounce that false claim, he should begin by retracting his unwise supposition that American officials in any easy case are not disposed to uphold a mistaken ruling by the Supreme Court. He can then renounce the false conclusions toward which that supposition has impelled him.

C. Rejoinders to Himma: Duties and Justifications

Himma repeatedly refers to the Supreme Court's discretion and to its authority to bind other officials with its law-ascertaining determinations. His references to the Court's authority and discretion are largely inapposite, for what he really has in mind is the Court's legal *power* to bind other officials with its erroneous law-ascertaining determinations. Here and elsewhere, I use the term 'power' in its Hohfeldian sense to denote an ability to effect changes in other people's legal positions and in one's own legal positions. In precisely that sense, the Supreme Court has the legal power to obligate other officials to uphold its mistaken rulings (as well as its correct rulings). Terms such as 'authority' and 'discretion' are at best misleading in this context, since they denote legal powers combined with legal liberties. If someone is legally empowered to accomplish a certain alteration in legal relations but is not legally at liberty to do so, then she does not have the discretion or authority to do so. She *can* accomplish the alteration, but she *may* not; that is, she cannot *permissibly* accomplish it. Yet, according to Himma, the Supreme Court is in precisely such a position in connection with its erroneous law-ascertaining judgments. As has been indicated in my terse synopsis of his arguments, he maintains that the Court operates under a legal duty to arrive at its law-ascertaining decisions in conformity with the morally best interpretation of the Constitution. When the Court mistakenly reaches a law-ascertaining decision that does not tally with the morally best interpretation of the Constitution, it breaches that legal duty. With its breach of duty, nonetheless, the Court has bound other officials to give effect to what it has decided. It has the legal power to bind them with a mistaken ruling, even though it is not legally at liberty to exercise that power. In other words, it has the legal power but not the legal authority to obligate the other officials to treat its mistakes as legally determinative.

We should now investigate more closely the nature of the duty that is incumbent on the Court. In the first place, we should take account of the distinction between duties and disabilities. A legal disability is the absence of a legal power; if Joe is legally disabled from altering someone else's entitlements in a certain fashion, he lacks the legal power to alter those entitlements in that fashion. A legal duty, by contrast, is a requirement for someone to act (or to abstain from acting) in a certain manner. Now, as my last paragraph has observed, someone can have a legal power to change some entitlements of another person while being under a legal duty to abstain from effecting such a change. The Supreme Court has the power to alter the legal positions of American officials with its incorrect judgments, but is under a legal duty not to exercise that power. What we should now additionally notice is that someone who is legally disabled from achieving a certain result might not be under any legal duty to forbear from seeking to achieve that result. Himma misses this latter point, and in the process confuses a disability with a duty, when he writes as follows: '[T]he First Amendment [to the American Constitution] seems to define second-order legislative duties by restricting the lawmaking activity of the Congress and is, for this reason, ostensibly treated by the courts as defining a validity criterion in the following sense: any legislative enactment that violates the First Amendment is legally invalid' (Himma, 'Sense', 159). Instead of imposing duties on Congress, the First Amendment disables Congress from achieving any binding legislative results that are at odds with the First Amendment's terms. If a congressional enactment fails to satisfy those terms, neither Congress as a body nor any members of Congress will be penalized. Instead, their efforts to produce a valid enactment will simply have come to nought. By misdescribing the situation, Himma has elided the distinction between nullity and sanctions—an elision aptly criticized by Hart many years ago (Hart, *Concept*, 33–5).

More important and problematic are the attempts by Himma to pin down the conditions for the existence of the Supreme Court's legal duty to ascertain the law in accordance with the morally best interpretation of the Constitution. He does not adequately distinguish between two specifications of those conditions, which are crucially different from each other. At some junctures, he strongly suggests that the key condition for the existence of the Court's duty is that the Court undergoes criticism when and only when its law-ascertaining judgments are not reconcilable with the morally best interpretation of the Constitution. Let us look again, for example, at a sentence quoted earlier: 'If officials criticize judges for failing to decide cases according to some moral norm N and judges routinely strive and expect each other to decide cases according to N, then it follows . . . that officials are practicing a norm that requires judges to decide cases according to N' (Himma, 'Authority', 12). A similar theme is sounded in the following statement: 'On the assumption that the officials of the system take the internal point of view towards [the legal requirements imposed on the Court's law-ascertaining deter-minations by the standards laid down in the Constitution], they view decisions that deviate from these standards as legally incorrect and hence as justifiably criticized' (Himma, 'Authority', 16). These quoted assertions appear to indicate a bifurcated condition for the existence of the Court's legal duty. That duty obtains because (1) officials criticize the Court whenever its interpretations of the Consti-tution are unsound, *and* (2) officials abstain from criticizing the Court whenever its interpretations of the Constitution are sound. Of course, the quotations do not give voice to the second of these two conjuncts. They mention only the fact that the officials denounce departures from the morally best understanding of the Constitution. Nonetheless, the second conjunct is crucial if the first conjunct is to play the role which Himma assigns to it. If the Court undergoes censure regardless of whether its law-ascertaining decisions tally with the morally best interpretation of the Constitution, then the occurrence of the censure is scarcely an earmark of a duty incumbent on the Court to reach those decisions in accordance with that interpretation. If the occurrence of censure were such an earmark in those circumstances, then it would also be an earmark of a duty incumbent on the Court to refrain from basing any law-ascertaining judgments on a morally optimal interpretation of the Constitution—since, *ex hypothesi*, censure descends upon the Court whenever its judgments are based on such an interpretation. Thus, if the Court's legal duty is to be as Himma maintains, and if the Court is to be free of any conflicting obligation,[8] then both of the conjuncts

---

[8] To be sure, although a conflict between duties is almost always undesirable, it is entirely possible as a matter of logic. See Matthew H. Kramer, 'Rights without Trimmings', in Matthew H. Kramer,

in the bifurcated condition for the duty's existence (as delineated above) are essential.

The difficulty for Himma is that that bifurcated condition will hardly ever be realized. To perceive as much, we should first note that the relevant duty lies on the Court in hard cases as much as in easy cases. Indeed, Himma's whole discussion of the behavior which undergirds that duty is focused on the criticism leveled against the Court for its decisions in hard cases (Himma, 'Sense', 178–85). Hence, if the bifurcated condition above is to be satisfied, the Court in hard cases will be undergoing rebukes from other officials—and from the Court's Justices themselves—when *and only when* its judgments about the legal validity of norms are at odds with the morally best interpretation of the Constitution. In fact, however, there is no reason to believe that the 'and only when' restriction will ever be fulfilled in hard cases. Not only will the Court in such cases undergo censure when its interpretations of the Constitution are objectively wrong, but in addition it will undergo censure when its interpretations are objectively correct. On the latter occasions, many officials (including some of the Court's Justices) will mistakenly think that the Court's interpretations are suboptimal, and they will consequently chastise the Court for what they deem to be its errors. Of course, the provenance and extent of the criticism will vary from case to case. Some officials will view this or that objectively erroneous decision by the Court as correct, and some officials will view this or that objectively correct decision by the Court as erroneous. Nonetheless, what will abide is the fact that the Court elicits reprimands from quite a few officials—whoever they may be—in virtually every hard case. Accordingly, the 'and only when' restriction that is imposed by the second conjunct in Himma's dyadic condition for the existence of the Court's law-ascertaining duty will not be fulfilled. If Himma were correct in specifying that condition, we would have to conclude that no such duty obtains.

Fortunately, there is an alternative condition for the existence of that duty, which Himma himself descries (though he fails to differentiate it sufficiently from the unsatisfiable condition which we have just been considering). The defining element of this alternative condition is not the sheer incidence of criticism from officials, but the justificatory orientation of such criticism. If officials converge in taking the abstract moral categories of the Constitution as their points of reference for applauding or deploring the law-ascertaining determinations of the Supreme Court, the Court is under a duty to apply those categories correctly when it passes judgment on the legal validity of norms. Irrespective of how often in hard cases the Supreme Court Justices and other officials misapply the basic moral concepts that guide their law-ascertaining

---

N.E. Simmonds, and Hillel Steiner, *A Debate over Rights* (Oxford: Oxford University Press, 1998), 7, 17–19; see also my discussion of the Permissibility Theorem in Chapter 8 of the present volume. However, Himma would plainly not wish to maintain that the US Supreme Court is under a legal duty to eschew the morally best interpretation of the American Constitution when ascertaining the law.

endeavors, their shared justificatory focus on those concepts is enough to settle the content of the duty to which those endeavors are subject. Because officials' sundry criticisms of the Court's law-ascertaining decisions in hard cases are all made with reference to those basic concepts, the criticisms sustain a state of affairs in which the Court is under a legal duty to give effect to those concepts when validating or invalidating norms as laws. Of course, what counts as genuinely giving effect to those concepts is not determined by the beliefs of the Justices or of the other officials. As has been remarked in Chapter 2 in a slightly different context, the extensions of the basic moral categories invoked by officials as their touchstones for law-ascertainment are fixed not by the officials' specific applications of those categories, but by the objective facts of morality. Precisely because of the mind-independence of those extensions, the manifold misapplications of the moral categories by American officials do not detract from the fact that the officials are upholding those categories as the standards to which the Supreme Court's decisions must conform. Given the shared justificatory orientation of the officials toward the Constitution's fundamental moral precepts, their frequently incorrect understandings of those precepts are indeed misunderstandings rather than manifestations of an allegiance to alternative principles. Their missteps are errors of application rather than errors of selection concerning the precepts which they are inclined to invoke as binding upon the Court.

In most of his pronouncements on this topic, Himma seems to have in mind the position just outlined. While concentrating especially on the role of the Supreme Court Justices themselves, for example, he writes that '[t]he most coherent explanation for the fact that Justices criticize each other for failing to produce the best interpretation of the Constitution is that they regard themselves as *bound* by the best interpretation in making validity decisions'. He adds that 'Justices attempt to: (1) conform their behavior to a norm that obligates them to decide cases according to the morally best interpretation of the Constitution; and (2) take the internal point of view towards that standard as governing their behavior as officials. The other officials also seem to take the internal point of view towards [that standard]' (Himma, 'Sense', 179, 184, emphasis in original). What these quoted statements highlight is not the sheer occurrence of criticism by the Justices and by other officials, but the justificatory orientation of that criticism. There is no suggestion that officials reprove the Court only when it has genuinely gone astray in its judgments as an objective matter. Instead, the emphasis in these statements is on the fact that the Justices and other officials commend their stands and denounce contrary stands by reference to the same fundamental lodestar—the notion of the morally best interpretation of the Constitution. They differ markedly of course in their specific conceptions of that notion, but they are at one in taking it as their guiding principle when they offer their assessments of the Court's decisions about the legal validity of norms. Because the officials' denunciations and commendations of the Court's rulings share an underlying orientation toward that guiding principle, they sustain the existence of a duty on the Court to ascertain the law in accordance with that principle's requirements. Even when the denunciations and commendations are inapposite in their specific bearings, their justificatory foundations establish the standard which the Court is obligated to meet.

Insofar as Himma does subscribe to the position that has been sketched in the last couple of paragraphs—in line with most of his comments on this topic—his analysis of the chief condition for the existence of the Supreme Court's law-ascertaining duty is unexceptionable. Nevertheless, we are well advised to take careful heed of that analysis, since its focus on the justificatory orientation of officials' exchanges and remonstrations will be paralleled in my principal riposte to Himma in the next subsection. As will be seen, an alertness to that justificatory orientation can enable us to discern why his critique of Inclusivism and Incorporationism founders. Given that he here exhibits such alertness himself when seeking to account for the foremost duty that lies upon the Court, he should more broadly recognize the central importance of the justifications that underpin officials' ascertainment of the law. Partly on the basis of such a broader recognition, however, we shall be able to detect the untenability of his revival of rule-skepticism.

Before moving on to my main set of rejoinders to his rule-skepticism, we should notice three anomalous properties of the duty to which the Supreme Court's law-ascertaining enterprise is subject. Each of these features has surfaced already, but we should briefly examine them together. Though Himma does not himself draw attention to them (save for the first of them, in rather misleading terms), he deserves credit for coming up with analyses that prompt reflections on them.

Perhaps least strange is the fact that the Court has the legal power to bind other American officials with its mistaken law-ascertaining determinations even though it is legally obligated not to arrive at such determinations. It is legally empowered to produce results which it is legally duty-bound to eschew. Still, the combination of empoweredness and prohibitedness is present in many other areas of life as well, in varying manifestations and for varying purposes. As Nigel Simmonds has observed: 'Situations where persons possess legal powers that they are under a duty not to exercise are, in fact, not at all unfamiliar'.[9] For instance, somebody who steals some valuable item can under certain circumstances transfer ownership of the item to a bona fide purchaser. In such circumstances, the thief has the legal power to transfer title even though he is under a legal obligation to abstain from doing so. Though strikingly different in its details, this legal situation is structurally homologous with the legal situation of the Supreme Court as it passes judgment on the validity of norms as laws.

---

[9] N.E. Simmonds, 'Rights at the Cutting Edge', in Matthew H. Kramer, N.E. Simmonds, and Hillel Steiner, *A Debate over Rights* (Oxford: Oxford University Press, 1998), 113, 220.

More unusual is the nature of the means by which the legal duty of the Court is undergirded. We can best approach this matter by pondering first a different legal duty, the duty of each lower-level official to abide by what the Court has decided. Himma describes the position of such an official as follows: 'An official who refused to enforce some holding of the court with final authority on the ground that it was mistaken and hence not law would surely bring upon herself a cascade of criticism and a court order to enforce the holding or face sanctions for contempt' (Himma, 'Authority', 11). Here we encounter a legal duty that is given effect not only through the leveling of criticism but also through force or the threat of force. In that respect, the obligation of each lower-echelon official is typical of the general species of legal obligations. Indeed, as Hart and countless other theorists have affirmed (Hart, *Concept*, 175–6), one of the major points of dissimilarity between legal obligations and moral obligations is that the former are characteristically backed up not only by expostulations but also by forcible sanctions. Atypical, then, is the legal duty of the Supreme Court to ascertain the law in accordance with the morally best interpretation of the Constitution. Though the chiding heaped upon the Court is sometimes excoriating, it is never or almost never combined with any forcible sanctions. While the removal of Justices through impeachment proceedings is possible in reaction to very serious misconduct, it is not available as a sanction for mere mistakes in law-ascertainment. When there has been no serious misconduct, that is, the only means of enforcing the Court's paramount legal duty is the voicing of reprimands.

Thus, the Court's obligation to be guided in its law-ascertaining endeavors by the morally best interpretation of the Constitution is what I have elsewhere designated as a nominal obligation.[10] It resides in what people say—specifically in the justificatory orientation of what American officials say as they assess the Court's law-ascertaining determinations—and it does not receive any backing beyond what they say. It is like other nominal legal duties, which are imposed by the terms of legislative or judicial or administrative utterances but which carry no penalties for violations. Of course, the reprehension directed at the Court by officials might sometimes be effective in inducing the Justices to modify their stances. However, when the reprehension is indeed effective, it operates in the manner of moral adjuration rather than through the direct infliction or threat of force. There is no provision for coercive sanctions. (Note that such sanctions would not be strictly inconsistent with the finality of the Court's rulings. Just as a thief who transfers ownership of some pilfered item to a bona fide purchaser can be punished even while the transfer of title is authoritatively recognized as binding, so the Court could be penalized for erroneous determinations even while those determinations are upheld by officials as binding. Nonetheless, given

---

[10] See Matthew H. Kramer, 'Getting Rights Right', in Matthew H. Kramer (ed.), *Rights, Wrongs, and Responsibilities* (Basingstoke: Palgrave, 2001), 28, 65–78.

the second-guessing of the Court's decisions that would inevitably be involved in the application of forcible sanctions, any provision for such sanctions would engender some formidably huge practical problems.)

Even more striking than the nominal status of the Court's legal duty to decide matters of legal validity on the basis of the morally best interpretation of the Constitution is the fact that the sole apparent means of backing up such a duty— namely, the upbraiding of the Court by officials—is brought to bear not only on the Court's botched decisions but also on its appropriate decisions. As has been remarked, animadversions will descend upon the Court in the aftermath of hard cases irrespective of the outcomes that are reached. Those outcomes will of course determine which of the officials engage in the animadversions, and will also naturally affect the specific tenor of their complaints; however, the sheer fact that numerous complaints will be voiced is not something that hinges on the specific way in which any hard case is resolved. Thus, not only is it true that the Court's breaches of its principal legal duty elicit no coercive remedies, but it is additionally true that the non-coercive remedies triggered by those breaches are also triggered by rulings that fulfill the Court's duty.

Notwithstanding the three odd features of the Supreme Court's foremost legal obligation that have just been recounted, the Court is undoubtedly under that obligation whenever it validates or invalidates norms as laws. Himma is certainly correct to contend as much, and in particular is correct to contend that that obligation bears on the Court's decision-making in hard cases as much as in easy cases. Of chief importance here is that the three peculiar aspects of the Court's obligation serve to underscore the significance of the justificatory orientation of officials' dealings with one another. When we join Himma in perceiving that the Court is indeed under a legal duty to ground its ascertainment of the law in the morally best interpretation of the Constitution, we need to figure out the basis for that duty. What reasons do we have for agreeing with him that such a duty exists? We cannot point to any limit on the Court's legal powers that marks the duty's existence and scope, since we know that the Court has the legal power to bind other officials with rulings which breach its duty. (Moreover, we should not follow Himma in conflating disabilities and duties.) Likewise, we cannot point to any coercive penalties that signal the existence of a legal obligation incumbent on the Court, nor can we point to any negative reactions that are evoked when *and only when* the Court has failed to fulfill its obligation. In the absence of any of those factors, we are led with Himma to concentrate on the fundamental moral categories to which the American officials advert when they gauge the soundness of the Court's law-ascertaining decisions. Whether condemning or admiring the decisions, the officials concur in taking those categories as their frame of reference. In so doing, they collectively establish the Court's duty and fix the content thereof.

In short, as we have seen, an exploration of the duty-bound character of the Court's law-ascertaining enterprise impels us to apprehend the importance of

the basic concepts that form the shared justificatory structure of officials' interactions with one another. It therefore harbingers my responses to Himma in the
closing portions of this chapter, to which we shall now turn. There we shall once
again discover that the common justificatory matrix of officials' pronouncements
is the key to understanding the full ramifications of those pronouncements. It is
also the key to countering Himma's attack on Inclusive Legal Positivism and
Incorporationism.

D. Rejoinders to Himma: Multiplicity and Rankings

In assailing the view that a norm's consistency with some moral principle(s) can
be a necessary condition for its legal validity and that a norm's correctness as a
moral principle can be a sufficient condition for its legal validity, Himma submits
that the finality of the Supreme Court's rulings on such matters is incompatible
with any determinative role that might be performed by the moral criteria in a
Rule of Recognition. Having heretofore examined his arguments in application
to Inclusivism, we shall henceforth examine them in application to Incorporationism (specifically, the moderate variety of Incorporationism). My shift of
attention to the latter doctrine stems largely from stylistic considerations of
concision and clarity, but is also warranted because the present discussion will
tie in nicely with the discussion of the tenability of modest Incorporationism in
the concluding pages of Chapter 2. I shall here draw upon that chapter's account
of the way in which moral principles can get incorporated into the law for hard
cases despite the intractable disagreements among officials concerning the identification of those principles. Still, notwithstanding that my focus in the rest of
this chapter will lie on modest Incorporationism rather than on Inclusivism, the
replies to Himma presented here could quite easily be adapted for a defense of
Inclusivism as well. The basic points advanced in this subsection are all serviceable for such a defense, *mutatis mutandis*.

   Himma persistently goes amiss by overlooking the multiplicity and rankings
of the criteria within any complex Rule of Recognition such as that in the
American legal system. On the one hand, he is of course correct in maintaining
that American officials adhere to criteria which obligate and empower them to
treat the Supreme Court's law-ascertaining determinations as binding. Whenever
the Court pronounces on the validity or invalidity of some norm as a law, its
ruling settles the status of that norm (as a law or not) and also settles the status of
any other norm which is relevantly similar and which is thus within the precedential ambit of the ruling. No minimally credible exposition of the Rule of
Recognition in the United States could fail to acknowledge as much. On the
other hand, Himma errs in thinking that the Supreme Court's legal power to
settle the status of norms as valid laws is incompatible with the emergence of
norms as laws through other means. In particular, he errs by contending that any
Incorporationist criterion in a Rule of Recognition cannot have a genuine

bearing on the legal validity or invalidity of norms. (Throughout this discussion, I shall assume that the American Rule of Recognition is moderately Incorporationist. Such an assumption cannot be confirmed or disconfirmed except through a careful empirical investigation of the justificatory concepts to which the officials in the American legal system advert when they select norms as laws for the resolution of hard cases. However plausible is the notion that those concepts are basic moral categories, it is something that can only be verified or disproved empirically. At any rate, nothing apart from stylistic convenience hinges on this empirical premise. Even if an empirical study were to disclose that American officials do not generally resort to fundamental moral categories as the bases for selecting laws to deal with hard cases, we could easily imagine some other credible legal regime in which the officials regularly resort to those categories for that purpose. Himma's critique and my rebuttal of his critique should then be understood as applying to that regime rather than to the American legal system. Nevertheless, no such complications need be introduced here. For the sake of convenience, and also because of the plausibility of the idea that the American legal system is indeed moderately Incorporationist, I shall join Himma in taking as given that American officials do have recourse to basic moral precepts when coming up with dispositive norms in hard cases.)

Although the validating and invalidating effects of the Incorporationist criteria in the American Rule of Recognition are indeed superseded by any Supreme Court decisions that run contrary to those effects, they are superseded only within the precedential purviews of the decisions. Beyond the precedential scope of each of those decisions, the moral principles absorbed into the law by the Incorporationist criteria will have retained their force as legal standards to which the conduct of everyone within the jurisdiction is subject. Pace Himma, those criteria do directly determine the content of the law, even though their content-determining effects are subordinate to those of the Court's rulings. The subordination of any such effects consists in their susceptibility to being displaced by the Court's judgments, but that susceptibility is activated only within the confines of the judgments themselves and of their precedential impacts. There is no across-the-board displacement; there are only piecemeal displacements. In a situation of multiple law-validating criteria that are ranked, the priority of one criterion over another does not result in the wholesale elimination of the latter. Instead, the priority simply negates any implications of the latter criterion that are inconsistent with the implications of the former.

As has been explained in the closing portion of Chapter 2, the officials in a legal system can be adhering to a moderately Incorporationist Rule of Recognition even if they frequently misidentify the moral principles that should be applied to hard cases. So long as the officials sustain a regular practice of appealing to the general requirements of morality as the basis for choosing the norms with which they resolve hard cases, they are abiding by a Rule of Recognition which incorporates the true principles of morality into the law for

such cases. Their justificatory orientation is the crucial fundament of the modestly Incorporationist criteria in their Rule of Recognition, just as a related facet
of the justificatory orientation of American officials is the crucial fundament of
the Supreme Court's duty to ascertain the law in accordance with the morally best
interpretation of the Constitution. Consequently, the officials' misapplications of
the Incorporationist criteria in hard cases do not alter the general fact that those
criteria endow the correct principles of morality with the status of laws for such
cases. Yet, insofar as the misapplications have precedential force, they effect
specific alterations in the law. Any such misapplication displaces some moral
precept that is optimal for addressing hard cases of some type, and substitutes for
it an inferior precept which has thereby gained the status of a law for addressing
the cases of that type. These specific displacements occur because the Incorporationist criteria in the American Rule of Recognition are subordinate to criteria
which obligate and empower officials to treat precedent-setting decisions (most
notably those of the Supreme Court) as binding. On any points in regard to
which the subordinate criteria and the superior criteria conflict, the former give
way. However, what is of greatest importance here is that they give way only on
those points of conflict. In all other respects, the subordinate criteria continue to
function as such. Even while any number of precedent-setting misapplications of
the Incorporationist criteria bring about specific changes in the law—that is, in
the law as it would be if those criteria were always correctly implemented—the
justificatory orientation of American officials preserves those criteria as such. It
therefore sustains their effect of absorbing the true principles of morality into the
law. Insofar (albeit only insofar) as that effect does not clash with anything
ordained by superior criteria in the American Rule of Recognition, it abides.
Though each of the true principles of morality is subject to being superseded as a
law by a precedent-setting invocation of some alternative touchstone, each of
those principles remains a law until it is so superseded.

Himma systematically obscures the multiplicity and rankings of the criteria in
the American Rule of Recognition, by concentrating unduly on the power of the
Supreme Court to bind other officials with mistaken decisions. His blinkered
preoccupation with that power becomes especially manifest when his descriptive
distillation of the American officials' law-ascertaining practice is formulated as a
biconditional: 'A duly enacted norm is legally valid if and only if it conforms to
what the Supreme Court takes to be the morally best interpretation of the
substantive protections of the Constitution'.[11] The biconditionality of this
formulation—the inclusion of the words 'and only if'—conveys the message
that legal validity derives exclusively from the specific rulings of the Supreme
Court. Imparting such a message, Himma has flatly ruled out the possibility of

---

[11] Himma, 'Sense', 187. The words 'duly enacted' should not lead us to infer that the quoted
formulation pertains only to statutes. It pertains equally to judicial doctrines and administrative regulations.

subordinate criteria which establish alternative bases for the endowment of norms with legal validity (bases such as the objective correctness of norms as moral principles). Only the case-by-case holdings of the Supreme Court are genuinely determinative, under Himma's formulation.

To be sure, Himma in his more recent article has unobtrusively abandoned the biconditional formulation in favor of a merely conditional statement: 'A proposition is a law if the court with final authority holds that it represents the best interpretation of the relevant legal materials that comports with the existing institutional history' (Himma, 'Authority', 13). Nonetheless, in his more recent essay just as persistently as in his earlier piece, he obfuscates the multiplicity and rankings of the criteria in the American Rule of Recognition. He insists, for example, that 'an official cannot consistently take the internal point of view towards [an Incorporationist criterion N] as establishing the content of the law and take the internal point of view towards the court's holdings regarding N as establishing the content of the law' (Himma, 'Authority', 28). On the contrary, the two points of view which Himma broaches are perfectly compatible. We can readily discern as much, provided that we recognize the subordination of the Incorporationist criterion N to the Supreme Court's rulings about the implications of N. Officials adopt the internal point of view toward the Court's rulings by being firmly disposed to give effect to them as binding determinations irrespective of their objective correctness as construals of N. At the same time, the officials adopt the internal point of view toward N in that they resort to it when selecting norms for the resolution of hard cases. They might frequently misapply N, but they regularly have recourse to it as the justificatory foundation for their selections of norms in hard cases. Their selections are indeed applications and misapplications of N, rather than applications of some alternative law-validating criterion. Because of their acceptance of N as the lodestar for their ascertainment of legal requirements in hard cases, the veritable principles of morality have been incorporated into the law for such cases. That result is fully reconcilable with the officials' preparedness to uphold the Court's judgments, since each of the veritable principles of morality retains its status as a legal norm for hard cases if *and only if* that status has not been removed by any of those judgments (or by any other precedent-setting judgments). Once we grasp the relationship of priority between the criteria that call for officials to effectuate the Court's holdings and the criteria that call for officials to rely on appropriate moral principles in their disposition of hard cases, we can see that there is no inconsistency between those sets of criteria. They can coexist smoothly. Though the priority of the former criteria does negate some of the particular entailments of the latter criteria, those latter criteria themselves are not negated. They remain operative, and they bestow legal validity on every moral principle that has not been set aside as a legal norm by any rulings of the Supreme Court or by any other authoritative rulings.

E. Rejoinders to Himma: Conclusion

Although Himma displays a curious blindness to the multiplicity and rankings of the criteria in the American Rule of Recognition, and although he consequently does not perceive that those rankings resolve inconsistencies among the criteria, he perceptively adumbrates a couple of the ideas that inform my riposte to his critique. We have already considered how the importance of the justificatory orientation of officials is underscored by his treatment of the Supreme Court's legal duty to ascertain the law in accordance with the morally best interpretation of the American Constitution. He more conspicuously draws attention to that justificatory orientation in a remarkable footnote (Himma, 'Sense', 156 n.11), where he acknowledges that legal officials might 'misidentify certain norms as being valid under the recognition norms they... accept'. He elaborates as follows:

> Suppose, for example, that officials all agree in accepting the norm 'officials are required to treat as law all and only those norms that have property P' but also treat as law norms that have property Q under the mistaken belief that anything that has property Q also has property P. On these suppositions, the attitudes and behaviors of the officials diverge on the issue of whether property Q is sufficient for legal validity.
>
> This is a problem case for Hart [or any other legal positivist] because he takes the position that a conventional rule R exists when persons in the relevant social group accept R and the behavior of such persons converges on satisfying the requirements of R. In the case above, however, the officials take the internal point of view towards a rule that validates only norms having property P but they converge in their behavior on satisfying the requirements of a different rule—namely, one that validates norms that have property P and norms that have property Q.

Himma avouches that 'there is a legal system in the United States regardless of whether officials make these sorts of mistakes about the rule of recognition and what it requires of them'. Thus, although he raises this matter only in order to indicate that he is not sure how to come to grips with it, he has here aptly highlighted the potential divergence between the justificatory focal point of officials' law-ascertaining endeavors and the specific identifications of norms that are reached by reference to that focal point. Exactly such a divergence is highly probable within a modestly Incorporationist legal system—where the officials in hard cases rely on basic moral categories as their touchstones for selecting dispositive norms, even while they frequently misapply those categories. Under their Rule of Recognition, which they shape through their justificatory orientation, the officials are obligated and empowered to handle hard cases by bringing apposite moral precepts to bear on the facts of those cases. What the officials are required to do under the Incorporationist criteria in their Rule of Recognition is determined not by their beliefs about the extensions of those criteria, but by the objective extensions themselves. The officials are required to fall back upon the true principles of morality as laws for hard cases, even though they cannot manage to identify those principles correctly much of the time. In short, there is quite a strong likelihood that the officials in any particular hard case will fail to apply the Incorporationist criteria in their Rule of Recognition appropriately; in other words, there is quite a strong likelihood of a discrepancy between their underlying justificatory orientation and their specific law-ascertaining decision in any such case. An awareness of the likelihood of that discrepancy is crucial if we are to understand how an Incorporationist Rule of Recognition absorbs the veritable precepts of morality into the law. Those precepts are so absorbed notwithstanding the probability that they will get drawn upon only erratically.

In addition to glimpsing the significance of the justificatory focus of officials, Himma in his more recent essay on the finality of adjudicative rulings has repeatedly pointed out that norms duly adopted through legislative or judicial or administrative procedures are legally valid before any subsequent adjudicative pronouncements on their validity. Until those norms are challenged in the courts—if in fact they ever are challenged—they are routinely treated by officials as laws and are therefore properly classifiable as laws. Himma writes, for example, that 'a duly enacted norm might be treated by officials as law for an extended period without any sort of explicit affirmation by the court. Indeed, if citizens are very diligent in obeying the norm (or behaving in a manner that conforms to its requirements), then the relevant propositional content constituting the norm is fairly characterized as law even without an official affirmation by the court with final authority' (Himma, 'Authority', 13). He goes on to maintain that the American Rule of Recognition includes a criterion which legally obligates American officials 'to treat any federal norm that satisfies the clear meanings of the procedural provisions of the Constitution as law until some appropriate court holds that it violates the substantive norms of the Constitution' (Himma, 'Authority', 19). In these passages and at some other junctures in his recent essay, Himma rightly contends that the status of a norm as a law in the United States need not derive from the fact that the norm has been or would be deemed a law by the Supreme Court Justices in the event of a challenge to its constitutionality. A duly adopted norm's status as a law antecedes any such ruling by the Court, and continues until the norm is deemed unconstitutional by the Court or by an unappealed lower-court judgment—or until the norm is rescinded, of course.

This second of Himma's two key insights is in need of some amplification, in the context of my discussion of a moderately Incorporationist legal system. (His analyses concentrate chiefly on Inclusivism, and his principal theses are formulated accordingly.) For one thing, Himma's references to officials' treatment of norms as laws should be construed as pertaining not only to the officials' decisions about specifically designated norms, but also to their sustainment of a general pattern of justification that incorporates moral principles into the law. By regularly adverting to the fundamental requirements of morality as the foundation for their choices of dispositive norms in hard cases, the officials engage in an Incorporationist practice that absorbs all genuine precepts of morality into the law regardless of whether those precepts have been discretely identified and designated as such.[12] That blanket absorption through the justificatory orientation of the officials is the cardinal way in which they treat moral principles as laws. Furthermore, Himma's references to constitutional challenges should be supplemented here with a reference to hard cases in which the courts have to make precedent-setting selections of norms. Whenever the Justices or judges choose correctly in such cases, they preserve the legal validity of moral mandates which their justificatory focus has already incorporated into the law. If the Justices or judges instead choose incorrectly, then—in application to the types of facts that are covered by the precedential scopes of their rulings—they have removed the legal validity of some of those incorporated moral mandates. They thereby change the law instead of giving effect to it as it has stood. They are legally empowered to change the law in that fashion, because of the ranking of the criteria in their Rule of Recognition. Insofar as the criterion which obligates the other officials to uphold the Justices' or judges' mistaken selections of norms is in conflict with the criterion which obligates the Justices and judges and other officials to rely on veritable moral precepts for the disposition of hard cases, the clash is resolved in favor of the former criterion. Still, that resolution of any such clash leaves the latter criterion intact. That latter criterion continues to confer legal validity on the principles of morality, each of which retains that validity unless stripped of it by some precedent-setting misjudgment.

In sum, Himma goes quite a distance toward supplying the lines of thought with which his critique of Inclusivism and Incorporationism can be parried. Having mooted some issues of great importance, he ferrets out many of their subtleties; in the process, to some extent, he counteracts his own angle on them. At any rate, despite his piquant arguments, he has not managed to refute the notion that law and morality can credibly meet in the ways envisaged by Inclusivists and Incorporationists.

---

[12] Many Exclusive Legal Positivists miss this point. See, e.g., Michael Giudice, 'Unconstitutionality, Invalidity, and Charter Challenges', 15 *Canadian Journal of Law & Jurisprudence* 69 (2002).

PART II

WHERE LAW AND MORALITY DIVERGE

Legal Positivism Reaffirmed

5

Legal Positivism Defended

David Dyzenhaus has recently sought to counter my defense of legal positivism, and in so doing has made a few interesting observations.[1] However, most of Dyzenhaus's discussion does not adequately shed light on the ideas advanced and the problems addressed by legal positivists. This chapter will concentrate on two main sets of misconceptions that are propagated in Dyzenhaus's article: misconceptions pertaining to the positivists' treatment of adjudication, and misconceptions pertaining to the positivists' view of the law/morality relationship more generally. Given that those sets of issues cannot be neatly compartmentalized, however, a certain amount of interweaving will be inevitable.

I. Adjudicative Matters

Dyzenhaus submits that present-day legal positivists have become preoccupied with matters relating to adjudication, and that this new focus derives from the critiques of their theories by Ronald Dworkin: 'Dworkin's critique of positivism is so powerful that it forced positivism to shift debate in legal theory to his terrain—the terrain of adjudication' (p. 719). This pronouncement by Dyzenhaus is somewhat odd in a number of respects. First, insofar as we accept his claim that positivists have come to train their attention on issues of adjudication, we should note that a lot of the influential positivists in recent decades have been Americans and that the preoccupation of American legal theorists with adjudication long antedates Dworkin's work. As H.L.A. Hart pointed out many years ago,[2] American jurisprudence during much of the past century has been predominantly a succession of theories of the adjudicative enterprise (no doubt largely because of the overwhelming prominence of federal constitutional

---

[1] David Dyzenhaus, 'Positivism's Stagnant Research Programme', 20 *Oxford Journal of Legal Studies* 703 (2000) (reviewing Matthew Kramer, *In Defense of Legal Positivism: Law Without Trimmings* [Oxford University Press, 1999] [hereinafter cited as *IDLP*]). All citations to Dyzenhaus's review article will be by page number alone.

[2] H.L.A. Hart, 'American Jurisprudence through English Eyes: The Nightmare and the Noble Dream' [hereinafter cited as Hart, 'American Jurisprudence'], in *Essays in Jurisprudence and Philosophy* (Oxford: Oxford University Press, 1983), 123.

adjudication in American life). Second, while it is certainly true that issues of adjudication are at the heart of the debates between the Exclusivist and Inclusivist/Incorporationist camps of legal positivism, the central role of Dworkin in galvanizing those debates has been fully acknowledged and indeed emphasized by the participants therein.[3] The Introduction and the first few chapters of the present book, for example, have repeatedly referred to Dworkin. Dyzenhaus, in short, is trumpeting some rather old news.

Third, the claims by Dyzenhaus about legal positivists' fixation on matters of adjudication are unsustainable in application to Hart and to me, the two positivists whom he discusses at greatest length. In connection with Hart, suffice it here to juxtapose two of Dyzenhaus's assertions. On the one hand, Dyzenhaus contends that legal positivists with their obsessive focus on adjudication believe that '[s]tatutes are ... pre-legal, political acts whose only interest for legal philosophy is the way in which they disturb judicial deliberations' (p. 719). On the other hand, near the outset of his article, he recognizes that Hart vigorously criticized John Austin's command model of law for 'put[ting] the sovereign outside the law which does not account for the fact that "nothing which legislators do makes law unless they comply with fundamental accepted rules specifying the essential law-making procedures" '.[4]

In connection with me, Dyzenhaus's complaints about a preoccupation with adjudication are equally inapposite. For one thing, some large parts of my previous volume on legal positivism—such as its long final chapter on the obligation of each citizen to obey the law—do not have anything to do with questions of adjudication. Likewise, the Inclusivist/Exclusivist controversy is discussed only briefly in that earlier book. Moreover, even in the portions of that book which do clearly bear on adjudicative matters, I draw no sharp distinction between adjudication and administration but instead regard them as different facets of the enterprise of law-application. Thus, for example (by no means the only example), I warn against thinking that easy cases are only those cases that are readily resolved by courts; also to be classified as easy cases are the countless situations which are perceived by regulatory and policing officials as wholly unproblematic and which consequently never give rise to judicial proceedings at all.[5] Particularly odd is Dyzenhaus's contention that my treatment of

---

[3] See, e.g., Jules Coleman, 'Constraints on the Criteria of Legality', 6 *Legal Theory* 171 (2000): 'The [key issue disputed between Exclusivists and Inclusivists/Incorporationists] was brought into contemporary prominence by Ronald Dworkin'.

[4] Dyzenhaus, p 704, quoting H.L.A. Hart, 'Positivism and the Separation of Law and Morals' [hereinafter cited as Hart, 'Positivism'], in *Essays in Jurisprudence and Philosophy, supra* note 2, at 49, 59. I have silently corrected a minor inaccuracy in Dyzenhaus's quotation of Hart's words.

[5] See, e.g., *IDLP*, 174: 'Both in the untold multitude of ordinary situations where people's interaction does not generate lawsuits, and in the numerous easy cases that do come before trial courts (perhaps only to be settled), the supplementary criterion of moral appealingness is wholly superfluous .... [J]udicial and executive officials seldom have to make moral judgments when giving effect to the law.' See also ibid., at 141, 175.

Lon Fuller's work 'operates within the margins which exclude the phenomena of legislation and administration with which Fuller was as much concerned as he was with adjudication' (p. 721). My chapter-long discussion of Fuller in *In Defense of Legal Positivism* deals chiefly with his best-known text *The Morality of Law*—a text which, as has often been remarked,[6] is concerned primarily with legislation.

Still, although most legal positivists have not been obsessed with adjudication in the manner suggested by Dyzenhaus, they have of course written extensively on the topic. We should therefore now turn to his animadversions on the positivists' efforts to come to grips with the activities of judges.

A. A Matter of General Discretion?

Early in his article, Dyzenhaus declares that Hart perceived adjudication as 'for the most part highly discretionary' (p. 707). Surprisingly, Dyzenhaus does not seek to substantiate this assertion through any citations to Hart's writings. Numerous passages in those writings in fact reveal that, although Hart certainly believed that judges exercise quasi-legislative discretion in difficult cases, he felt that most situations in most areas of law are highly determinate in their implications. For example, in the essay which Dyzenhaus has principally in mind at this juncture, Hart clearly distinguished between the core of settledness and the penumbra of unsettledness in any legal system (as Dyzenhaus acknowledges), and he wrote that a 'preoccupation with the penumbra [of indeterminacy] is, if I may say so, as rich a source of confusion in the American legal tradition as formalism [that is, a wholesale denial of indeterminacy] in the English' (Hart, 'Positivism', 72). Precisely how Hart saw the balance between the core and the penumbra is evident in a later essay, where he commended Oliver Wendell Holmes for eschewing a skeptical view of law: 'Though [Holmes] proclaimed that judges do and must legislate at certain points, he conceded that a vast area of statutory law and many firmly established doctrines of the common law, such as the requirement of consideration for contracts, and the demands of even the comparatively loose American theory of binding precedent, were sufficiently determinate to make it absurd to represent the judge as primarily a law-maker' (Hart, 'American Jurisprudence', 128). To exactly the same effect is the position taken by Hart in *The Concept of Law*. On the one hand, to be sure, he was no formalist. In opposition to formalism, he maintained that '[i]n every legal system a large and important field is left open for the exercise of discretion by courts and other officials in rendering initially vague standards determinate, in resolving the uncertainties of statutes, or in developing and qualifying rules only broadly

---

[6] See, e.g., Kenneth Winston, 'Three Models for the Study of Law', in Willem Witteveen and Wibren van der Burg (eds), *Rediscovering Fuller* (Amsterdam: Amsterdam University Press, 1999), 51, 69.

communicated by authoritative precedents'.[7] On the other hand, we would be misunderstanding Hart if we were to endorse the notion that he regarded adjudication as for the most part highly discretionary (in Dyzenhaus's words). Immediately after the statement just quoted, he added that 'these activities, important and insufficiently studied though they are, must not disguise the fact that both the framework within which they take place and their chief end-product is one of general rules. These are rules the application of which individuals can see for themselves in case after case, without further recourse to official direction or discretion' (Hart, *Concept*, 132–3). Likewise, at the close of his famous chapter on adjudication, when discussing the elaboration of fundamental constitutional norms by judges, Hart submitted that 'at the fringe of these very fundamental things, we should welcome the rule-sceptic, as long as he does not forget that it is at the fringe that he is welcome; and does not blind us to the fact that what makes possible these striking developments by courts of the most fundamental rules is, in great measure, the prestige gathered by courts from their unquestionably rule-governed operations over the vast, central areas of the law' (Hart, *Concept*, 150).

Dyzenhaus, when purporting to describe Hart's view of adjudication, does not make reference to any of the statements quoted above or to any other passages from Hart's work. Instead, he relies on two main points. First, he observes that Hart unhesitatingly acknowledged the existence of legal systems 'where judges are given the authority to test the validity of law by reference to constitutionally entrenched, broadly stated, moral standards, which makes large parts of the core potentially subject to judicial overrule' (p. 707). Insofar as this statement by Dyzenhaus is sustainable, it does not tell in favor of his thesis that Hart regarded adjudication as highly discretionary in most circumstances. Perhaps the closing words—'which makes large parts [indeed, all parts] of the core potentially subject to judicial overrule'—are simply meant to indicate that every enactment in a legal system such as the American system is subject to moral tests laid down in constitutional provisions. If so, then that wording is wholly unobjectionable. Hart certainly recognized the role of constitutional moral tests in some legal regimes. So construed, however, the words in question do not lend any support to Dyzenhaus's claim that Hart viewed adjudication as highly discretionary in most circumstances.

In any viable legal system that includes constitutional moral tests for the legal validity of enactments, it cannot be the case that under those tests there are no uniquely acceptable answers to questions about the validity or invalidity of most enactments. Although a fairly small proportion of enactments in any system will be neither clearly valid nor clearly invalid, such a condition cannot be true of most of the system's norms. If there were serious uncertainty in regard to most

---

[7] H.L.A. Hart, *The Concept of Law* (Oxford: Oxford University Press, 1961) [hereinafter cited as Hart, *Concept*], 132.

enactments, the system comprising those enactments would not be performing the conduct-guiding function that is a hallmark of any veritable legal regime. Most questions of legal validity or invalidity will be straightforwardly resolvable, even though a minority of such questions will be genuinely difficult and controversial. If a judge were to adopt a maverick position on the question of legal validity in any of the countless cases where that question is straightforwardly answerable, his fellow judges would begin to doubt his fitness for office. In any readily resolvable case of that sort, a particular answer to the question of legal validity is generally perceived as uniquely correct, and any contrary answer is generally perceived as wrong. Thus, one's acknowledgment of the role of constitutional moral tests in some legal systems does not in any way commit one to the view that such tests give rise to a pervasively discretionary mode of legal decision-making. As officials apply such tests, their latitude in most situations will be tightly restricted by the perceptions of their fellow officials concerning the unique correctness of certain outcomes as opposed to others. In most circumstances, the latitude of the officials in the application of such tests will be no less tightly restricted than their latitude in most circumstances when they are applying other legal norms.[8]

In short, Hart's recognition of the salience of constitutional moral tests for enactments in some legal systems is fully compatible with his frequently stated belief that most areas of the law within any sustainable society will in most respects (though not all respects) be highly determinate at any given juncture. Let us, then, look at Dyzenhaus's other attempt to substantiate his claim about Hart's view of adjudication as pervasively discretionary. With a citation to Joseph Raz rather than to Hart, Dyzenhaus contends that '[t]he upshot [of Hart's theorizing] seemed to be that adjudication is so shot through with discretion that [the process of law-ascertainment] does little more than identify the law, and then only perhaps the sources of law, relevant to the decision' (pp. 707–8). In other words, according to Dyzenhaus, the positivist model of law-ascertainment presumes that judges are legally required to identify certain norms as laws but are legally at liberty to interpret those norms as they please. Now, even if we overlook

---

[8] In this paragraph I have deliberately forborne from speaking of various decisions under constitutional moral tests as objectively correct: that is, correct independently of their being generally perceived as such. On the one hand, as should be clear from *IDLP*, 152–7, I believe that characterizing many moral decisions as objectively correct is wholly unproblematic and appropriate. On the other hand, at least at the time of writing *The Concept of Law*, Hart probably held a different view (largely, as I argue in *IDLP*, because he mistakenly took the matter of objective correctness to be metaphysical rather than moral). At any rate, appeals to objective correctness are wholly superfluous here because the key point at issue is whether certain decisions are pervasively perceived—by judges and other officials—as uniquely correct. If so, then the discretion of any official to opt for contrary decisions is sharply limited, even in the unlikely event that he would be inclined to opt for such aberrant decisions. The discretion of each official is confined by the consensus among his fellow officials concerning what counts as professionally competent or professionally incompetent determinations. Thus, in the present context, we can leave aside the question whether the discretion of each official is also confined independently of anyone's thoughts and convictions.

the strangeness of referring to Raz's conception of adjudication in order to substantiate a proposition about Hart's conception of adjudication, we should here reject Dyzenhaus's line of argument—since it is based on a misrepresentation of Raz's position.

In the essay which Dyzenhaus cites,[9] Raz does not suggest that judges are engaged in a highly discretionary task when they interpret the legal norms which they have ascertained. On the contrary, he simply distinguishes between law-ascertainment and legal interpretation. That is, he distinguishes between determining what the applicable legal norms are and determining what they mean. He does not maintain that the process of discovering the meanings of legal norms is a free-for-all with little determinacy. Instead, his point is merely that the standards used in interpreting legal norms—not only the general assumptions and beliefs involved in making sense of any utterances, but also the 'technical rules or conventions of interpretation specific to the legal system concerned' (Raz, 'New Link', 1107)—are not among the criteria that compose a legal system's Rule of Recognition. Such a thesis, which I do not endorse with reference to the technical rules and conventions, is fully consistent with the view that the bearings of legal norms are reassuringly determinate and discernible in most circumstances. To highlight the need for general background assumptions and technical conventions in legal interpretation is not at all to indicate that such interpretation will be generally amorphous and unsettled.

To interpret the statement 'The day of the week on which the 4th of July occurred in 1999 was a Tuesday', one must rely on general background beliefs and on linguistic conventions; but, in doing so, one has not somehow caused one's construal of that statement to be 'shot through with discretion'. Except in exceedingly unusual circumstances, the meaning and the truth-value of the statement about the 4th of July will be utterly uncontroversial. Naturally, some legal norms will not be nearly as clear-cut and precise as the aforementioned statement, which is informative rather than prescriptive. Every legal norm, indeed, will sometimes engender controversy and unclarity when applied to concrete situations. Nonetheless, most legal norms in most circumstances will be determinate and uncontroversial in their implications. Of course, any such norms must be interpreted when they are invoked in adjudication; but that fact is scarcely a reason for thinking that the implications of those norms are markedly unsettled in most circumstances, any more than one's inevitable resort to interpretation in one's understanding of the proposition about the 4th of July is a reason for thinking that the meaning of such a proposition will be markedly

[9] Joseph Raz, 'Dworkin: A New Link in the Chain', 74 *California Law Review* 1103, 1107 (1986) [hereinafter cited as Raz, 'New Link']. Neither Hart nor I would accept Raz's view that technical standards for the interpretation of legal norms are not among the criteria in the Rule of Recognition. However, the lack of agreement on that point is immaterial here. For a valuable account of the place of technical interpretive standards in the American Rule of Recognition, see Kent Greenawalt, 'The Rule of Recognition and the Constitution', 85 *Michigan Law Review* 621, 654–8 (1987).

unsettled in most circumstances. Dyzenhaus commits a *non sequitur* when he adduces the Razian distinction between law-ascertainment and legal interpretation in support of his allegation that the positivists conceive of adjudication as profoundly discretionary. Though legal positivists plainly do believe that adjudication must involve interpretation, they have hardly thereby committed themselves to the view that adjudication is sweepingly discretionary in most situations.

B. Mistaken Identity

Dyzenhaus contends that legal positivists subscribe to a proposition which he designates as the 'Identification Thesis': '[A] determination of what law is does not depend on moral criteria or argument' (p. 706). Both in the formulation of this thesis and in his subsequent discussions pertaining to it, Dyzenhaus does not sufficiently disentangle three ways in which it can be understood. The differences among those ways are crucial, for each rendering of the thesis will be acceptable only to some legal positivists and not to others.

A first version of the Identification Thesis would equate 'does not' therein with 'cannot'. According to this first version of the thesis, in other words, the task of identifying the law in any society cannot ever involve moral judgments. Were moral judgments required for the carrying out of that task—so the advocates of this version of the Identification Thesis argue—law would not be capable of possessing some key characteristic(s) which it always or typically or sometimes possesses. Thus, if a legal system is to obtain and function as such, the existence and contents of its norms must be discernible without recourse to moral considerations. A rendering of the Identification Thesis along these lines would be unacceptable both to Hart and to me, of course, but it has been championed by Scott Shapiro and Raz and other proponents of Exclusive Legal Positivism.

A second version of the Identification Thesis would equate 'does not' therein with 'need not'. So construed, the thesis affirms that the enterprise of discovering the existence and contents of legal norms can involve recourse to moral considerations but can likewise be independent of such considerations. The role of moral principles as operative touchstones in such an enterprise is neither ruled out nor preordained by the nature of law. That role may well differ—in being present or absent—from one legal system to the next. Understood in this fashion, the Identification Thesis is one aspect or element of the broader legal-positivist insistence on the separability of law and morality. Comprising both Inclusive Legal Positivism and Incorporationism, this variant of the Identification Thesis (albeit not under that name) has been explored at length in this book's Introduction and first four chapters.

A third reading of the Identification Thesis would equate 'does not' with 'should not'. Explicated in this manner, the thesis is prescriptive in its tenor. It calls for a certain mode of adjudication by recommending that legal norms should be such that there is no need for adjudicators to have recourse to moral judgments when basing their decisions on those norms. Both the existence and the content of each legal norm should be ascertainable without reference to moral considerations, because only then can the law be appropriately effective in guiding people's conduct. This prescriptive version of positivism, which looks askance at constitutional moral tests, has been powerfully elaborated in recent years by theorists such as Tom Campbell and Jeffrey Goldsworthy.[10] It is a position from which I have remained distant, as has been made clear in Chapter 3's discussion of Eleni Mitrophanous.

This chapter will mull over the prescriptive variant of legal positivism shortly; for now, let us focus on the first two renderings of the Identification Thesis. When discussing that thesis as something endorsed by Hart and by me, Dyzenhaus advances a number of assertions and arguments in which he appears to have in mind the first version of the aforementioned thesis as an expression of the Exclusivist variety of legal positivism. Given that only the second (Inclusivist/ Incorporationist) version of the Identification Thesis is something endorsed by Hart and by me, Dyzenhaus's strictures on this topic are misdirected.

Consider, for example, the following passage in which Dyzenhaus remarks that Inclusive Legal Positivists 'say that it is contingent whether a legal order will incorporate moral criteria among its criteria for the validity of law. But they also allow the possibility that often the Identification Thesis does not apply. They say that in legal orders which do incorporate morality the identification of law might depend on moral criteria' (p. 706). Clearly, if the Identification Thesis is construed along Inclusivist lines—as it should be, in a discussion of Inclusive Legal Positivists—Dyzenhaus's statement that that thesis does not apply is false. Since the thesis so construed is a proposition affirming the possibility (as well as the contingency) of the inclusion of moral principles among the criteria for jural validity in this or that legal system, it is hardly inapplicable to systems in which that very possibility is realized. Of course, if the Identification Thesis is instead understood along Exclusivist lines, and if the Inclusive theorists are correct in maintaining that some legal systems include moral principles among their criteria for law-ascertainment, then the Identification Thesis is belied by such systems. But so what? Since Inclusive Legal Positivists reject the Exclusivist version of the Identification Thesis, they are scarcely apt to feel troubled by any weaknesses that may be exposed in it.

Even more puzzling is a pronouncement made by Dyzenhaus at a juncture where he is explicitly referring to the Razian (Exclusivist) variant of the Identification Thesis. He submits that Hart in a renowned 1958 *Harvard Law Review* article 'considered Bentham, Austin, and himself to hold . . . the Identification

---

[10] See, e.g., Tom Campbell, *The Legal Theory of Ethical Positivism* (Aldershot: Dartmouth, 1996); Jeffrey Goldsworthy, *The Sovereignty of Parliament* (Oxford: Oxford University Press, 1999). While upbraiding contemporary legal positivists for forsaking the prescriptive side of the positivist tradition, Dyzenhaus makes no mention of either Campbell or Goldsworthy.

Thes[i]s [in its Exclusivist form]' (p. 706). Curiously, Dyzenhaus does not cite any passages in order to substantiate his claim, and he ignores a passage which reveals that claim to be false. In direct conflict with the remark just quoted, Hart wrote in his 1958 article as follows:

[N]either Bentham nor his followers denied that by explicit legal provisions moral principles might at different points be brought into a legal system and form part of its rules, or that courts might be legally bound to decide in accordance with what they thought just or best. Bentham indeed recognized, as Austin did not, that even the supreme legislative power might be subjected to legal restraints by a constitution and would not have denied that moral principles, like those of the Fifth Amendment, might form the content of such legal constitutional restraints. (Hart, 'Positivism', 54–5, footnote omitted)

Still more regrettable is Dyzenhaus's assumption that neither Hart nor I could ever come to grips adequately with a legal system whose judges 'divide between those who adopt a positivistic account of legal authority, in which valid law is the law established in accordance with the Identification Thesis, and those who adopt a Dworkinian account, in which authority accrues only to those statements of the law which are supported by a moral theory which justifies them' (p. 712). Since Hart and I are the theorists whom Dyzenhaus is discussing at this stage, he should be writing about the Identification Thesis in its Inclusivist/Incorporationist guise. After all, that thesis in its Exclusivist guise would be rejected both by Hart and by me. Nonetheless, if we suppose that Dyzenhaus has in mind the Inclusivist/Incorporationist version of the Identification Thesis, the remark just quoted is baffling. Inclusive Legal Positivism or Incorporationism is a theory concerning what *need* not be the case, rather than a theory concerning what *can*not be the case. Inclusivism and Incorporationism are fully compatible with the existence of a regime whose judges do not regard statements of the law as authoritative unless those statements are 'supported by a moral theory which justifies them'. Of course, if (outlandishly) the judges believe that their morally laden adjudicative posture is an essential feature of everything that counts as a legal system, their underlying belief is not a tenet to which any Inclusive Legal Positivists or Incorporationists would subscribe. However, the morally laden adjudicative posture itself is something which any Inclusive Legal Positivists and Incorporationists can happily acknowledge. Contrary to what Dyzenhaus suggests—if we construe his reference to the Identification Thesis as a reference to the Inclusivist/Incorporationist version of that thesis—Inclusive Legal Positivists and Incorporationists do not adhere to a conception of authority that is somehow at odds with the conception to which the Dworkinian judges adhere. Rather, the basic claim of Inclusivist and Incorporationist theorists is that, in any particular legal system, the criteria defining legal authoritativeness or the laws validated by those criteria can encompass but need not encompass moral principles. That claim is manifestly not in tension with a Dworkinian adjudicative practice among the judges in some regime.[11] A theory which highlights the possibility of a certain state of affairs is not cast into doubt by the emergence or continuation of that state of affairs.

By contrast, if we suppose that Dyzenhaus in the quotation above is referring to the Exclusivist version of the Identification Thesis, his remark is more straightforward. Raz's conception of legal authority does indeed differ from that of Dworkin, and thus the notion of a tension or competition between the two conceptions is meaningful. However, when Dyzenhaus's remark is interpreted along these lines, two difficulties immediately present themselves. First, and less important, the competition between the Dworkinian and Razian conceptions of legal authority might make little or no difference at the practical level of adjudicative outcomes. For Raz, adjudication consists in reasoning according to the law as well as reasoning about the law; therefore, the Razian judges might decide cases in a manner indistinguishable or virtually indistinguishable from that of the Dworkinian judges. Though such a practical convergence is hardly inevitable, it is far from impossible. Second, and much more important for our present purposes, the remark quoted above is from a portion of Dyzenhaus's article that is expressly aimed at Hart and at me. One should consequently feel puzzled that Dyzenhaus is there invoking the Exclusivist version of the Identification Thesis—a version abjured both by Hart and by me.

More generally, insofar as Dworkinianism is understood as an adjudicative approach rather than as a jurisprudential theory that explicates the essence of law, the idea of an opposition between Dworkinianism and Inclusive Legal Positivism (or Incorporationism) loses its pertinence. Dyzenhaus makes the mistake of thinking otherwise. He writes, for example, that Inclusive Legal Positivists and Incorporationists take account of certain practices of adjudication 'by admitting the substance of an anti-positivist position like Dworkin's' (p. 715). Yet the only Dworkinian position for which Inclusive Legal Positivism or Incorporationism leaves room—namely, Dworkinianism as an approach to adjudication in this or that legal system—is not anti-positivist at all, because the questions to which it is addressed are crucially different from those addressed by either the Inclusivist/Incorporationist variety or the Exclusivist variety of legal positivism. Dworkinianism as an adjudicative posture is a morally charged set of principles for the resolution of legal controversies in some particular society, whereas legal positivism is a theory about the nature of law-ascertainment in every society. Exclusive Legal Positivism offers a restrictive answer to the question (about every society) which it addresses, whereas Incorporationism and Inclusive Legal Positivism offer more capacious answers. Though an Exclusive Legal Positivist will insist that Dworkinian judges are going beyond the strict ascertainment of the law in their adjudicative endeavors, the nature of those endeavors as possible adjudicative processes is not something which any Exclusive theorist would deny. Even more

---

[11] Cf. W.J. Waluchow, *Inclusive Legal Positivism* (Oxford: Clarendon Press, 1994), 186–8.

patently compatible with Dworkinianism-qua-adjudicative-stance are the Inclusivist and Incorporationist varieties of legal positivism. Incorporationists and Inclusive Legal Positivists not only explicitly recognize that the Dworkinian stance is possible, but they also accept that the invocations of moral principles by Dworkinian judges are applications of legal norms or applications of authoritative criteria for law-ascertainment. An acknowledgment of that point does not amount to an endorsement of anything that is 'anti-positivist'. On the contrary, that acknowledgment is warranted precisely because Dworkinianism as an adjudicative approach (rather than as a jurisprudential theory) does not in itself involve any claims or logical commitments that are irreconcilable with positivism.[12]

C. Prescriptive Rigidity

My last subsection has observed that the only varieties of legal positivism relevant for a riposte to Hart or to me—Incorporationism and Inclusive Legal Positivism—leave open the possibility of regimes in which the law is ascertained partly on the basis of moral principles. Understood as a fundamentally descriptive theory which analyzes the general nature of law and of law-ascertainment, legal positivism is not at all belied or undermined by the existence of such regimes. Let us now consider the prescriptive variant of positivism, on which Dyzenhaus trains much of his attention.

Although Dyzenhaus more than once characterizes Hart as a methodological positivist, that label obscures a distinction between two ways in which moral considerations might enter into positivist theorizing. First, a proponent of one of the descriptive versions of legal positivism (whether Inclusivist/Incorporationist or Exclusivist) might seek to justify his doctrine at least in part by reference to the salutary moral consequences that are likely to flow from an acceptance of it. Hart, both in his 1958 essay and in *The Concept of Law*, sought to justify his legal-positivist position in exactly this fashion.[13] By contrast, I have forsworn any such tack—partly because any justification along those lines is inconclusive and speculative, and partly because of my general sense that conceptual analyses should be based on theoretical-analytical considerations rather than on moral-political concerns. Whereas Hart cannot accurately be designated as a methodological positivist, I indeed can.

---

[12] This point seems to me overlooked in N.E. Simmonds, *Central Issues in Jurisprudence* (London: Sweet & Maxwell, 2002) (2nd edn), 249–53.

[13] Hart, 'Positivism', 72–8; Hart, *Concept*, 203–7. For my own methodological stance, which is largely unsympathetic to Hart's approach, see *IDLP*, 177–82. Still, although Hart's approach should be rejected for the reasons stated in the text, Julie Dickson goes astray in contending that such an approach—which she attributes to Frederick Schauer—is argumentatively misshapen. See her *Evaluation and Legal Theory* (Oxford: Hart Publishing, 2001), 84–93. I have criticized Dickson at some length in my 'Book Review', 62 *Cambridge Law Journal* 210, 213–14 (2003).

However, on a second point relating to the role of moral-political factors in positivist theorizing,[14] Hart's stance tallies with mine. Hart never endorsed the prescriptive version of the Identification Thesis, and I have eschewed that variant of the thesis. Neither in Hart's work nor in my own writings is there any attempt to single out a specific mode of adjudication as especially estimable. In particular, there is no recommendation that constitutional provisions and statutes and other authoritative norms in any legal system should be drafted so as to ensure that the processes of law-ascertainment in the system do not involve moral judgments. (Likewise, of course, neither in Hart's work nor in my writings is there an opposite recommendation to the effect that the processes of law-ascertainment in any particular legal system should be devised so as to ensure their reliance on moral judgments.) Though any descriptive variant of legal positivism is compatible with prescriptive positivism, neither entails the other. Both Hart's work and my writings reflect that lack of entailment.

Dyzenhaus castigates contemporary legal positivists for abandoning the prescriptive stance taken by earlier writers in the positivist tradition such as Thomas Hobbes. While never mentioning theorists such as Campbell and Goldsworthy who adopt that prescriptive stance in the present day, he submits that the earlier writers with their 'fully political positivist positions' were 'the true standard bearers of the tradition' (p. 709 n.16). In passing, let us note that Dyzenhaus wavers in his efforts to declare what lies at the heart of legal-positivist theorizing. Though he here proclaims the prescriptive version of such theorizing to be the uniquely genuine and worthwhile element of the positivist tradition, he recognizes near the outset of his article that a general insistence on the separability of law and morality—the so-called Separability Thesis—'is rightly regarded as the hallmark of a positivist legal theory' (p. 704). Since he also correctly maintains that neither the Separability Thesis nor the prescriptive version of the Identification Thesis entails the other (p. 706), his position on the true heart of the positivist legacy is not altogether clear.

At any rate, more important than the unclarity on that point is the tension between some of the reproaches which Dyzenhaus levels against the contemporary positivists who have detached themselves from the prescriptive strand of their tradition. On the one hand, he chastises these positivists for severing their ties with their predecessors by declining to advocate a mode of legal governance that would eliminate or minimize the need for moral deliberations in adjudicative decision-making. He contends that this departure from those predecessors has caused modern positivism to 'become a stagnant research programme' (p. 715). On the other hand, when describing the present-day judges whom he regards as 'the true heirs of [prescriptive] legal positivism' (p. 717), he makes quite plain that their approach to adjudication is disconcertingly unattractive. Indeed, one of

---

[14] Some commentators have failed to distinguish this second point sufficiently from the first. See, e.g., Michael Moore, 'Hart's Concluding Scientific Postscript', 4 *Legal Theory* 301, 308–10 (1998).

his criticisms of me—in an argument that will be examined presently—is that my remarks on adjudication will somehow 'encourage positivist judges' (p. 717). We can wonder, then, why contemporary positivists are being upbraided for having shunned a prescriptive approach that would have subjected them to obloquy if they had embraced it.

Even more bemusing is Dyzenhaus's assertion that my analyses will tend to encourage the prescriptive-positivist judges in their misguided endeavors. He describes their position as follows:

First, positivist judges adopt a version of a Hobbesian moral duty to obey the law, whatever its content. Second, since such a version requires that law have a content determinable in accordance with the Identification Thesis, they attempt to make their decisions correspond to the requirements of such a thesis. Put differently, they attempt to make their institution one which serves an ideal that guides the whole of legal order.

Contemporary legal positivism generally has nothing more critical to say to such judges than it has to Dworkinian judges. (p. 717)

Interpreted generously, the final sentence of this extract is true. That is, if we construe it to mean simply that neither Inclusivism/Incorporationism nor Exclusivism will have ruled out the position of the prescriptive-positivist judges as a possible adjudicative stance, then the sentence is of course true. As those judges engage in their dismayingly wooden approach to legal decision-making, they are undertaking an activity that would be classified as adjudication both by Inclusivist/Incorporationist theorists and by Exclusivist theorists. Though all or most of those theorists would undoubtedly regard that adjudicative approach as foolish and potentially harmful, they would not deny that it is an adjudicative approach. The judges involved are benighted, but they are indeed judges who are performing their roles as such.

When the final sentence in the extract above is interpreted more straightforwardly in accordance with its terms, however, it is untenable. Given that my *In Defense of Legal Positivism* argues at length against the existence of any content-independent moral obligation to obey the law, and given that Raz and Hart have years ago taken much the same position as have I, it is bewildering to be told by Dyzenhaus that we have nothing critical to say to judges who begin from the premise that just such a content-independent obligation exists.[15] On the basis of the large portions of *In Defense of Legal Positivism* which deal with the matter of

---

[15] For the relevant analyses, see *IDLP*, 204–9, 254–308. For Raz's views, see, e.g., his *Practical Reason and Norms* (Princeton: Princeton University Press, 1990), 162–9; *The Authority of Law* (Oxford: Clarendon Press, 1979), chaps 12–13; *Ethics in the Public Domain* (Oxford: Clarendon Press, 1994), chaps 14–15; 'About Morality and the Nature of Law', 48 *American Journal of Jurisprudence* 1 (2003). For Hart's view, see, e.g., his 'Comment', in Ruth Gavison (ed.), *Issues in Contemporary Legal Philosophy* (Oxford: Clarendon Press, 1987), 35, 40–2. For a strange misrepresentation of my position on this matter, see Patrick Capps, 'Being Positive about Positivism', 63 *Modern Law Review* 774, 783–4 (2000).

each citizen's obligation to obey the law, we can discern that the fundamental line of reasoning on which the prescriptive-positivist judges rely is irredeemably unsound. If I say to those judges that their reasons for adopting their adjudicative posture are grounded in a fallacy, am I not saying something critical to them?

Moreover, as should be evident from the penultimate paragraph above, legal positivists can go further than merely pointing out the intellectual errors in the arguments that underlie the judges' stance. Quite apart from the feebleness of the *foundation* of the judges' adjudicative position, that position itself is ridiculous and potentially dangerous. Whether or not one takes the view that there are uniquely correct answers to the questions raised in very difficult legal cases, one should recognize that any way of dealing with those questions must tacitly or expressly draw on normative assumptions. (Legal positivists should quickly add, however, that the normativity—the orientation of a person toward what he *ought* to do or decide—can be prudential rather than moral.) Any effort to forgo normative assumptions altogether is deluded. Furthermore, such an effort can all too easily lead to ill-advised decisions that bespeak the blinkeredness and contrivedness of the reasoning by which they are reached. Thus, in sum, legal positivists can and should denounce an adjudicative approach whose practitioners doggedly purport to uphold the prescriptive strand of the positivist tradition. Though milder forms of that approach are generally unobjectionable, an extreme form is to be discountenanced. Any Inclusive Legal Positivist or Incorporationist or Exclusive Legal Positivist should readily apprehend as much.

Since legal positivists so emphatically do have the theoretical resources for criticizing the Hobbesian judges whom Dyzenhaus describes, why does he insist otherwise? Why does he suggest that my account of adjudication will actually encourage those judges? Though his line of argument here is not entirely perspicuous, his worry seems to be a familiar one in the anti-positivist literature. He appears to think that, because of my willingness to classify the activities of the Hobbesian judges as legal decision-making even if they are motivated by purely prudential considerations, I am conveying the impression that those activities are generally irreproachable. Such a contention is reminiscent of the sorts of arguments against which Hart was reacting when he sought to underscore what he took to be the moral and political advantages of legal positivism. In other words, as far as one can tell, the contention by Dyzenhaus is that my designation of a system of governance as 'legal' will imply that that system is legitimate and perhaps even worthy; such a designation should consequently be withheld from a regime in which Hobbesian judges are acting on the basis of purely prudential concerns. If the 'legal' designation is not withheld in those circumstances, the Hobbesian judges will apparently be encouraged to persist in their misguided behavior.

In reply to this natural-law line of argument, two brief observations are appropriate. First, as has already been indicated, the analytical and conceptual choices in my writings are based on theoretical-explanatory considerations rather than on moral-political considerations. Hence, even if it were clearly true that legal positivists' analytical and conceptual choices will tend to shore up some undesirable adjudicative practices, the countervailing theoretical-explanatory advantages of those choices would outweigh the regrettable moral-political effects thereof. Second, in any event, it is certainly not clearly true and is probably untrue that legal positivism's analyses will tend to foster unfortunate attitudes on the part of officials or citizens. The ripostes by Hart to natural-law theorists on that point were at least as plausible and powerful as the arguments which he was seeking to counter, even though the debate between him and them about the moral merits of their respective theories was inconclusive and speculative. Hence, Dyzenhaus's remark about the supposedly deleterious effects of my positivist ruminations should here be put aside.

II. Officials' Reasons-for-Action

Dyzenhaus repeatedly adverts to my analyses of the reasons that can underlie the law-creating and law-applying activities of officials.[16] He misunderstands the basic point of those analyses and a number of their specific claims. Along the way, he makes some dubious comments on several prominent controversies between positivists and their opponents.

Before examining the missteps just mentioned, we should ponder a methodological problem that Dyzenhaus raises. Every jurisprudential positivist would gladly avouch that the outlooks of legal officials in most regimes are very often focused on moral reasons-for-action rather than solely or primarily on prudential reasons-for-action. That is, nobody would deny that frequently the law-creating and law-applying activities of the officials in those regimes are undertaken in furtherance of the interests of citizens rather than solely or primarily in furtherance of the interests of the officials themselves. Dyzenhaus queries whether legal positivists can acknowledge as much while remaining faithful to the methodological aspirations of their theorizing.

Dyzenhaus writes that Hart 'thought it possible to describe a moral attitude or perspective neutrally... In other words, Hart maintains that description does not entail endorsement' (pp. 711–12). Slightly later he adds that 'Hart, as we have seen, supposes that [the attitudes of Dworkinian judges] could be described in a value-neutral fashion' (p. 716). Dyzenhaus goes on to contend that Hart's methodological aims cannot be fulfilled. In a moment we shall look at his assertions to that effect. Let us, however, straightaway notice some confusion in

---

[16] Whenever I refer to reasons-for-action in this section, I am focusing not only on the considerations to which officials *do* give weight in deciding how they should behave, but also (and more importantly) on the considerations to which they *would* give weight if they grasped the serviceability of those considerations for the furtherance of their general aims. I develop this distinction in my next chapter.

his characterizations of those methodological aims. The term 'neutrally' in the first quotation above is at best misleading. On the one hand, if that term simply indicates that a moral attitude can be described without any endorsement or other moral assessment of that attitude, then it is apt and unproblematic. So construed—in line with the latter half of the first quotation—the term captures what Hart correctly believed about his analytical-descriptive project. On the other hand, the remark in the second quotation above (which refers back to the remark about describing 'neutrally') is a sign of confusion on Dyzenhaus's part. Neither Hart nor any other contemporary legal positivist would maintain that an analytical exposition of law can be value-free. As *In Defense of Legal Positivism* emphasizes at several junctures, evaluative judgments concerning the importance of various phenomena are essential for any such exposition. In the absence of such judgments, a putative theory would be a hopelessly unillumin-ating and largely unintelligible jumble of observations. It would not be a theory at all. Legal positivists fully recognize as much, and are therefore not disposed to characterize their own theoretical endeavors as value-neutral.

Nevertheless, as *In Defense of Legal Positivism* also repeatedly emphasizes, the values that inform one's judgments of importance are not perforce moral values. Because my account of law is methodologically as well as substantively positivist in its orientation, the values that inform my judgments of importance are theoretical-explanatory rather than moral. That is, those judgments proceed by reference to theoretical values such as comprehensiveness, explanatory power, subtlety, parsimony, precision, plausibility, and clarity. My assessments of importance are not moral in character, and are certainly not in themselves ascriptions of moral worthiness to the phenomena which I highlight. Hence, while robustly declaring that no theory can ever be value-free, a legal positivist can perfectly consistently affirm as well that his own theory is morally neutral in all of its analyses.[17]

Having misrepresented the exact bearings of Hart's methodological ambitions, Dyzenhaus might nonetheless be correct in thinking that those ambitions are unrealizable. Consequently, we should peruse his claim that legal positivists cannot remain morally neutral when they chart the attitudes and beliefs of officials. That is, we should peruse his claim that legal positivists 'must accept wholesale the normative attitudes [attitudes which Dyzenhaus takes to be inevit-ably moral] that travel with the conduct of the central participants in legal practice' (p. 715). His argument for this proposition is contained in the following two sentences:

To the extent that legal positivism is driven by methodological commitments which require taking into account the internal perspectives of important participants in the

---

[17] For a failure to recognize this point, see Capps, *supra* note 15, at 780–2. For a quite useful though uneven introductory-level discussion of the methodological issues that have been touched upon here, see Julie Dickson, *supra* note 13.

practice of law, the existence of Dworkinian judicial attitudes throws into question the very commitments which require that they be taken into account . . . [T]he viewpoint or perspective constituted by such attitudes presupposes a substantive understanding of the point of law, which is in direct competition with legal positivism's concept, or, perhaps better put, conceptions. (pp. 715–16)

Dyzenhaus makes no reference to some pages of *In Defense of Legal Positivism* that confront the line of reasoning which he marshals here (*IDLP,* 168–70). Indeed, the posited line of argument which I have there sought to rebut is more powerful than is his version of the argument—since it does not suggest that law-ascertaining officials necessarily or typically ground their activities on an understanding of the point of *law,* as opposed to an understanding of the point of *the law* (namely, law as it exists in their regime). Because legal positivism attributes a general function to *law* without taking any position on the point of *the law* in this or that particular regime, its theses are not usually in competition with the presuppositions of officials' endeavors. Normally the officials' presuppositions are regime-specific rather than regime-transcendent in their focus, whereas precisely the opposite is true of the positivist imputation of a general function to law.

Let us, however, put aside the foregoing objection to Dyzenhaus's anti-positivist line of reasoning. Let us suppose that the judges in some regime do ground their law-ascertaining activities on their beliefs about the nature of law generally (rather than just about the nature of the law in their society). Alternatively, let us suppose that a positivist theorist wishes to analyze and expound the workings of a legal regime operated by Dworkinian judges, regardless of whether their underlying beliefs are focused on law or on the law. We are now contemplating a situation in which some of the positivist theorist's claims will be akin in content to the Dworkinian judges' understandings of their own enterprise. After all, the positivist theorist must try to apprehend the purposes served by the judges' law-ascertaining activities, in order to be able to ascribe to the judges a set of normative preconceptions that inform those activities. Only by coming up with an understanding of the character of their regime does the theorist enable himself to fathom the perceptions and attitudes that can plausibly be said to animate the running of that regime. Yet, to arrive at an accurate understanding of a Dworkinian legal system, the positivist theorist will have to grasp the moral principles to which the judges therein adhere. Does his explicative project logically commit him to endorsing those principles?

As should be evident from the pages of *In Defense of Legal Positivism* mentioned above, the answer to this question is negative. The positivist theorist ferrets out the officials' perspective not in order to embrace it but in order to ascribe it to the officials themselves. Although he must make claims about the character of their regime, that fact goes no way toward effacing the distinction between attribution and advocacy. Instead of reiterating the arguments which I have previously mustered in order to underscore that distinction, I shall here adduce an example that can pertinently illustrate the basic conclusion of those arguments.

Consider, then, a theorist who wants to elucidate and analyze the workings of an iniquitous legal system such as the Nazi system. Striving for a rich and accurate exposition, he does his best to descry the beliefs and attitudes that impel the officials of the particular system to perform their roles in the ways in which they do. He needs to gain a sense of the various major objectives which their regime pursues, if he is to develop an awareness of the outlooks of the people who are engaged in advancing those objectives. Suppose, for example, that his study of the regime's workings—his study of its norms and decisions and of the officials' justifications for those norms and decisions—leads him to attribute to the Nazi officials a number of repugnant attitudes such as anti-Semitism, racism, intolerance, illiberality, servile deference to superiors, and so forth. Is he thereby obliged to endorse those distasteful attitudes? Must a theorist be sympathetic to Nazism if he is to produce an accurate exposition of Nazi law?

Presumably, the appropriateness of negative answers to these questions is uncontroversially plain. Someone probing the numerous unsavory aspects of a fascist legal system is not perforce committed to applauding those aspects, and is indeed probably investigating them partly in order to denounce them and to warn against the emergence of them elsewhere. Yet, if the distinction between ascribing beliefs to others and endorsing those beliefs oneself is so clear-cut in application to monstrous legal regimes, it should be equally clear-cut in application to vastly more attractive legal institutions. Whether the object of a theorist's attention is a repellent Nazi legal system or a highly appealing Dworkinian regime of law, the general tasks of interpretation and explication and analysis for the theorist are fundamentally the same. Though any decent observer is much more likely to approve of Dworkinian principles than of fascist principles, approval is not an essential element of the observer's efforts in either case. Of course, a theorist *might* seek to fathom the activities and outlooks of Dworkinian judges with the aim of lauding their regime, but he might instead simply be endeavoring to arrive at a comprehensive and accurate recountal of their regime's operations, or indeed he might even be venturing to criticize various facets of those operations. Unless his aim is purely to commend, then, he will preserve a distinction between ascribing and endorsing certain morally pregnant views.

A. Prudence and the Rule of Law

At many junctures in *In Defense of Legal Positivism*, I argue that elementary rule-of-law requirements—Fuller's eight principles of legality—are not intrinsically moral either in their effects or in the considerations that can credibly induce adherence to them. Especially pertinent here is the latter point about potential motivations, which relies centrally on a contrast between prudential reasons-for-action and moral reasons-for-action. That contrast, broached near the outset of this section, consists (roughly) in a distinction between two sorts of factors that might impel officials to behave in certain ways: factors exclusively or primarily involving the promotion of the officials' own interests, and factors exclusively or primarily involving the promotion of the interests of citizens. One of my principal theses in my arguments against the inherently moral status of rule-of-law requirements is that the factors prompting the fulfillment of those requirements by officials can credibly be purely prudential. My arguments in support of that thesis go well beyond establishing merely that there is a logical possibility of a regime in which the officials abide by the rule of law on the basis of purely prudential considerations. As has been contended in Chapters 2 and 3 of the present book and in several passages of my earlier book on positivism (*IDLP*, 65–7, 77, 205–6), a claim about a bare logical possibility would be too jejune to be worth defending. At the same time, my arguments do not attempt to establish that the existence of legal systems with officials driven solely by prudential concerns is common or likely (*IDLP*, 233). Though my sense is that the prominence of prudential motivations among officials in some legal regimes is significantly underestimated by a lot of legal philosophers, my defense of jurisprudential positivism does not in any way depend on a demonstration that such motivations are indeed prominent in any particular legal system(s). Rather, one of the chief questions addressed by my arguments in *In Defense of Legal Positivism* is as follows. If the officials who run an evil legal regime are motivated by purely prudential considerations, will they have strong reasons (prudential reasons that go beyond dissimulation) for complying with rule-of-law requirements to a substantial extent? The answer to that conditional question is affirmative, even though the state of affairs described in its antecedent clause might very seldom obtain. Because the answer to that question is affirmative, the rule-of-law requirements themselves are not intrinsically moral. Highly serviceable for the pursuit of wickedly power-hungry ends by any officials who act solely out of concern for the furtherance of their own interests, an adherence to the principles of the rule of law is not a pattern of behavior that can only plausibly be motivated by moral reasons-for-action (or by a deceitful desire to *appear* to be motivated by moral reasons-for-action).

The foregoing paragraph delineates the basic character of my arguments concerning the motivational underpinnings of the rule of law. Thus, even before we ponder a brief summation of the substance of those arguments, we can detect the inappositeness of some of Dyzenhaus's responses. At least thrice (pp. 712, 715, 717), Dyzenhaus suggests that my central thesis concerns the logical possibility of a regime in which the officials carry out their roles on the basis of thoroughly prudential reasons-for-action. Yet, as has been made clear afresh here, my challenge to the inherently moral status of the rule of law is not a proclamation or demonstration of bare logical possibilities. As Chapter 3 of the present volume has stressed, establishing the logically possible status of this or that pattern of behavior is far too easy and is therefore utterly uninteresting. My defense of legal positivism has concerned itself with the more difficult and important task of showing that evil officials bent on strengthening their own power and their exploitation of the citizenry will have solid prudential reasons for complying with rule-of-law requirements to a considerable degree.

Even more patently inapt than Dyzenhaus's remarks about logical possibilities is his suggestion that I have implied that a regime of officials driven by purely prudential concerns is the central case or paradigmatic instance of a legal system. This suggestion occurs immediately after one of his remarks about logical possibilities: '[W]hile Kramer presents his model as a logically possible one, it also seems clear that he means it to operate as a central case or paradigmatic account of judicial motivation.... [Kramer's model] of judicial motivation... must be regarded as the central case or paradigm' (p. 717). In this extract, the shift from the indefinite article 'a' to the definite article 'the' is crucial. On the one hand, if an evil regime of officials acting on the basis of thoroughly prudential considerations is a regime that complies with all of Fuller's principles of legality to a substantial degree, then I would indeed classify it as *a* central case or paradigmatic instance of a legal system (*IDLP*, 92 n.7, 236)—precisely because I take any such classification to hinge not on the presence or absence of certain types of motivations among officials, but on the presence or absence of the features encapsulated in Fuller's principles. On the other hand, however, Dyzenhaus distorts my arguments when he moves to the definite article ('the'). As my penultimate paragraph above has reaffirmed, *In Defense of Legal Positivism* explicitly disclaims the view that the existence of legal systems with all or most officials motivated exclusively by prudential reasons-for-action is common or likely. Nowhere in that book is there any intimation that a system operated by such self-serving officials is *the* central case or paradigmatic instance of a legal regime. Not only would such an intimation be ridiculous in itself, but it would also be at odds with my insistence that the underlying motivations of officials are beside the point when we are determining whether any particular scheme of governance counts as a 'central' or 'paradigmatic' legal system.

Dyzenhaus's shift from the indefinite article to the definite is not a pardonable instance of stylistic carelessness. His comments which follow the sentences quoted above are clearly premised on the notion that I regard thoroughly prudential modes of legal decision-making as typical or common. For example, Dyzenhaus writes: 'According to Kramer, when judges disapprove of deviations from a practice of positivistic authority, their manifestations of disapproval will arise because of [their purely prudential concerns]' (p. 717). By attributing to me a general view about the interaction among officials in each legal regime, this remark conveys the impression that I have portrayed such interaction as distinctively or quintessentially prudential. Consequently, the remark misrepresents my defense of legal positivism, and it runs athwart several of my express pronouncements. Let us recall that the conditional question which my defense of positivism addresses is as follows. If officials in some regime are concerned exclusively or primarily with the furtherance of their own interests in extending and strengthening their exploitative grip over their society, will they have strong prudential reasons (beyond dissimulation) for abiding by rule-of-law principles to a substantial extent? As has been stated above, my affirmative answer to that question does not commit me to any view about the frequency or likelihood of the existence of legal institutions in which all or most officials are indeed thoroughly preoccupied with their own power-hungry interests. My affirmative answer certainly does not commit me to the asinine view that legal institutions staffed by such people are typical or common.

Dyzenhaus's transmogrification of my reflections on the motivational under-pinnings of the rule of law is an offshoot of his broader tendency to suggest that legal positivists deny any possible place for moral considerations among those underpinnings. For example, when referring to Hart's apt insistence that the reasons for officials' acceptance of their Rule of Recognition need not be moral reasons, Dyzenhaus offers the following summary: 'Hart maintains that there is no need to take the extra step of supposing acceptance must be on moral grounds just because . . . judges might have many different reasons for accepting the law as authoritative. It is thus unnecessary to refer to . . . moral reasons in the set of possible reasons' (p. 711). Hart never committed the *non sequitur* which these statements foist on him. To submit that judges' reasons for accepting their Rule of Recognition are *not necessarily* moral reasons is hardly to submit that their reasons are *necessarily not* moral reasons. One should readily grant that moral considerations are among the possible reasons-for-action that can credibly under-lie officials' behavior, while one also insists that the domain of those reasons-for-action is far from exhausted by such considerations. Hart took precisely such a view whenever he discussed the range of factors that can motivate officials.

Much the same misstep by Dyzenhaus occurs when he asserts that 'Hart and Kramer want to exclude the moral component in judicial acceptance of the rule of recognition' (p. 715). Once again, a thesis concerning what is not necessarily the case has been mistaken by Dyzenhaus for a thesis concerning what is not possibly the case. Both in Hart's work and in mine, the former thesis is upheld whereas the latter thesis is rejected. While contending that certain prudential considerations can be powerful reasons for the conformity with rule-of-law requirements by evil officials, one should unhesitatingly allow that various moral considerations are powerful reasons for the conformity with rule-of-law requirements by upright officials. (As is also noted in *In Defense of Legal Positivism—IDLP*, 187—sundry reasons-for-action which are wicked but non-prudential can likewise serve as powerful underpinnings for evil officials' adher-ence to rule-of-law principles.)

At this stage, a very brief synopsis of my arguments about prudential grounds for upholding the rule of law is advisable. Those arguments focus on the efficacy of law in guiding and directing human conduct. If officials in a heinous regime wish to channel the conduct of citizens into certain paths—paths that will be

maximally promotive of the officials' own interests and their nefarious aims—
they will generally be well advised to govern in ways that satisfy Fuller's principles
of legality to a high degree. A system of legal governance provides clear-cut
indicators to citizens concerning what is demanded of them. Equally important,
it tends to create strong incentives for citizens to comply with their rulers'
dictates, because it penalizes people for non-compliance and leaves people
unpunished when they are obedient. Furthermore, it greatly enhances the effective coordination of the myriad instances of interaction among the officials
themselves, who could not carry out large-scale projects over a sustained period
of time without the regularity and the complicatedly interlocked expectations
which a functional legal system makes possible. Whether the demands imposed
and the objectives pursued by officials are products of moral concern or of
exploitative selfishness, then, the officials can usually best achieve their ends
through the operations of a legal system. They can trade on the major
direction-providing and incentive-fostering and coordination-facilitating advantages of such a system.

Although the preceding paragraph supplies no more than a terse conspectus of
some of the cardinal points for which I argue at length in *In Defense of Legal
Positivism*, it enables us to discern the untenability of many of Dyzenhaus's
assertions about the nature of prudential reasons-for-action as underpinnings
for officials' adherence to the rule of law. For example, when pondering whether
officials' acceptance of their Rule of Recognition can be grounded on factors
other than moral considerations, Dyzenhaus declares that 'to confine acceptance
to something very weak' would '"whittle down" that notion [of acceptance]
implausibly' (pp. 710–11). As *In Defense of Legal Positivism* attempts to establish
through a number of lines of argument—some principal conclusions of which
are sketched in the last paragraph above—prudential concerns as grounds for
officials' upholding of a Rule of Recognition are not 'something very weak'. On
the contrary, those concerns can be powerful promptings for the officials' behavior, since that behavior (namely, the officials' adherence to the rule of law) will
redound to the furtherance of many selfishly exploitative objectives which the
officials may be inclined to pursue. If power-hungry rulers are determined to
exert and reinforce their repressive reign over a large territory throughout a
sustained period, their efforts will be severely set back if they do not avail
themselves of the coordination and the incentive-securing regularity made possible by the rule of law. To suggest that their self-interested ambitions are 'very
weak' as reasons for them to comply with rule-of-law principles is to disregard the
serviceability of their compliance for the effectuation of those ambitions. Whatever may be the rareness of situations in which some purely prudential factors
underlie the fulfillment of rule-of-law requirements by officials, those factors can
weigh strongly indeed in favor of such a pattern of behavior.

Another ill-advised pronouncement by Dyzenhaus is his claim that, in highlighting the strength of selfishly exploitative objectives as potential grounds for

officials' adherence to the rule of law, I fail 'to see the oddness of an account of normative authority which does not explain the *normative* basis for accepting the claims of authority' (p. 711, emphasis in original). Perhaps Dyzenhaus is here using the term 'normative' as a synonym for 'moral'. If so, then his error lies in implicitly attributing to me the view that the authority of law is an inherently moral authority. Since my writings have contested that view by maintaining that starkly prudential concerns can operate as strong supports for the commitment of officials to the rule of law, I naturally do not depict the normative basis for that shared commitment as invariably or intrinsically moral.

If Dyzenhaus is instead using 'normative' more expansively to denote any orientation toward what ought to be, his comment is even more peculiar. The distinction between morality and prudence is precisely a distinction between two types of normativity. Prudential judgments are normative judgments, whereby people determine how they ought to behave or what they ought to accept. To the same extent as a first-person moral judgment (that is, an agent's moral judgment concerning how the agent himself ought to behave), a first-person prudential judgment relates to how an agent ought to conduct himself. Of course, the tenor of the 'ought' is markedly different between a first-person moral judgment and a first-person prudential judgment; the 'ought' in the former derives from a primary or sole focus on other people's interests, whereas the 'ought' in the latter derives from a primary or sole focus on one's own interests. Nevertheless, the normative character of the judgments—the sheer fact that they prescribe how the people making the judgments ought to behave—is not impaired in any way by the divisions within normativity itself. Hence, when my writings explain the potential robustness of prudential considerations as grounds for evil officials' conformity with rule-of-law principles, I am indeed recounting a *normative* basis for their acceptance of the authority of their legal system. I am doing so, moreover, while of course recognizing that moral concerns are an alternative normative basis for any such acceptance.

Even less persuasive than Dyzenhaus's statement about normative authority are his slightly earlier assertions about the outlooks of judges and other officials who uphold a Rule of Recognition. We are told that 'legal officials, represented usually by judges, will regard their rule of recognition as morally justified ... Put differently, even if the rule of recognition has a settled content, the fact that judges accept it as providing the criteria which they should apply cannot be understood other than by supposing that they regard it as legitimate' (p. 710). The assertions in this extract are indeed assertions which in themselves provide no grounds for anyone to credit what they state. Dyzenhaus attempts to substantiate the claims in this extract partly through the pronouncements and reasoning that have already been scrutinized in this section, and partly through some remarks about Raz and Hart that will be examined shortly. If those remarks prove as insolid as his analyses which we have already explored, then the proclamations just quoted will turn out to be unsupported.

Before turning to Dyzenhaus's observations on Raz versus Hart, however, we should briefly note a line of argument that emerges near the end of his article. Dyzenhaus declares that, according to me, 'the only reciprocal relationship necessary [within a legal system] is between law-creating and law-applying institutions [rather than between officials and citizens]' (p. 717). He then goes on to maintain that the contrast between Fuller's position and mine 'is between a vision of law in which the principles of reciprocity are necessary internal constraints on legal authority and one in which the relationship of reciprocity is conceived in such a way that any principled constraints are *a priori* ruled out' (p. 721). Now, even if the statement in the first of these quotations were unimpeachable, the pronouncement in the second quotation would be plainly unwarranted. Therein Dyzenhaus once again misrepresents a thesis that concerns what is not necessarily the case, by characterizing it as a thesis that concerns what is necessarily not the case. Let us, however, put aside that point for the moment. A broader correction is pertinent here.

Unless Dyzenhaus is using 'reciprocal' and 'principled' as sweepingly moral terms, his claims in these quotations are misconceived—even if we assume that each of the quoted passages is attributing to me a thesis concerning what is not necessarily the case. As should be inferable from this chapter's earlier remarks about the central function of law in channeling and directing human conduct, an element of reciprocity is essential within any operative legal system. To be operative and sustainable at all, any such system must perform the central function of law and must accordingly involve the considerable degree of regularity that is necessary for the carrying out of that very function. If human conduct is to be subjected to the governance of the guiding and controlling sway of legal norms, then there must be a general congruence between those norms and the administrative-adjudicative activities of officials. Fuller was entirely correct to affirm as much, and was correct to suggest that that general congruence engenders interlocked expectations among officials and citizens concerning the consequences of law-abidingness. That interlocking of expectations is the reciprocity that amounts to an indispensable feature of any viable legal system. Thus, since my writings explicitly ascribe to law the function of subjecting human conduct to the governance of authoritative norms, Dyzenhaus is incorrect when he attributes to me the view that a relationship of reciprocity between officials and citizens is not an essential characteristic of any legal system.

Moreover, contrary to what Dyzenhaus appears to think, I can happily accept his claim that the relationship of reciprocity 'enables [citizens] to call to account for their fidelity to law the legal officials with authority to make, interpret, and implement the law' (p. 721). The divide between Fuller and Dyzenhaus on the one hand and me on the other hand does not pertain to the sheer fact that officials in any veritable legal system are accountable for their performance of their law-applying roles. Rather, as Dyzenhaus himself observes, the divide centers on his insistence that the reciprocity and the concomitant accountability are intrinsically moral in character. Any legal positivist should reject that insistence, for at least two reasons.

First, insofar as morality is contrasted with prudence, neither the reciprocity nor the accountability at work in the relationship between officials and citizens is perforce moral in its motivational underpinnings. As has been noted in this chapter and argued at length in *In Defense of Legal Positivism*, selfishly exploitative objectives (to be pursued on a large scale over a long period) can powerfully impel officials to comply with Fuller's principles of legality in order to reap the coordination-securing and direction-imparting and incentive-stimulating benefits of a regime of law. Insofar as such objectives underlie officials' adherence to those principles, the reciprocity that informs their relationship with citizens— the interlocking of expectations concerning the consequences of law-abiding behavior—does not derive from any moral compunctions on the officials' part. That reciprocity is not a condition that bespeaks any nonprudential considerations on which the officials act. In such circumstances, any means or mechanisms for holding officials accountable will likewise be grounded in prudential concerns rather than in moral reservations (*IDLP*, 75–7). Opportunities for citizens to highlight officials' departures from the prevailing norms will in effect be opportunities for them to draw the attention of other officials to behavior that generally impairs the smooth functioning of a regime on which all the officials have pinned their fortunes. Deviant officials will be brought into line by their fellow officials on that basis. (Again, it is immaterial here whether the existence of regimes oriented entirely toward selfishly exploitative objectives is exceedingly rare or not. As has been stressed already, my enquiry into the inherently moral status of the rule of law hinges solely on the question whether purely prudential considerations—beyond dissimulation—can be strong reasons for officials to uphold rule-of-law principles to a substantial degree. Because the answer to that question is 'yes', those principles and the reciprocity which they encapsulate are not intrinsically moral. Questions about the rarity or commonness of certain types of regimes can here be put aside as irrelevant to my enquiry.)

A second reason for rejecting Fuller's and Dyzenhaus's moralized conception of the accountability of legal officials is evident when we turn from the morality/ prudence distinction to the morality/immorality distinction. The availability of opportunities for holding legal officials accountable is by no means always morally commendable. Everything depends on the moral worthiness or unworthiness of the applicable legal norms and on the circumstances of the accountability. If the applicable norms are flagitious, and if opportunities for demanding the enforcement of them are therefore promotive of gross injustices, then the legal system involved would be morally better if those opportunities were not present.

Ponder, for example, the situation of Jesus as recounted in chapter 19 of the Gospel of John. Let us suppose that his preaching of his message of otherworldly salvation was sufficient to constitute a straightforward violation of harshly repressive Roman laws against any practices that might be insurrectionary. Such a violation was punishable by crucifixion. Nonetheless, Pilate declined to convict Jesus, and he repeatedly proclaimed that 'I find no crime in him' (John 18:38, 19:4, 19:6) Taking advantage of opportunities to hold Pilate accountable for his refusal to give effect to the brutally severe laws, the members of the crowd hostile to Jesus cried out: 'If you release this man, you are not Caesar's friend; every one who makes himself a king sets himself against Caesar' (John 19:12). Faced with this threat of being reported to his superiors as insufficiently diligent in giving effect to legal restrictions on dissent, Pilate capitulated and sent Jesus to his death.

Now, although the gospel's narrative with its prettified depiction of the butcherous Pontius Pilate is preposterous as an account of any historical events, it serves our present purposes admirably. That is, it vividly portrays a situation in which the feasibility of calling officials to account is an instrument of manifest injustice. Broadly similar situations can arise in countless other contexts—for instance, in deeply racist societies where the citizens insist on the strict implementation of laws that reflect their own animosity toward people from other races. When the applicable norms in a legal system are iniquitous, and when mechanisms of accountability ensure that officials cannot get away with benign departures from the terms of the norms, those mechanisms debase the system *pro tanto*. Hence, before we can judge whether the well-enforced accountability of officials in any particular legal system is morally estimable, we have to know the precise bearings of that accountability. In other words, any moral worthiness correctly ascribable to the state of their accountability is ascribable thereto by dint of substantive factors rather than by dint of anything inherent in every such state.

B. Razian Reflections

Raz presents several sophisticated arguments in favor of his view that officials' statements of legal obligations implicitly or explicitly take as given that there are interest-independent reasons (morally binding reasons) for people to act in compliance with the obligations. The fourth chapter of my *In Defense of Legal Positivism* seeks to refute his arguments, by maintaining that some official statements of legal obligations do not implicitly or explicitly presuppose the existence of any punishment-unrelated reasons for people to act in conformity with those obligations. In the legal systems in which such statements are made, the norms laying down the obligations are stark imperatives rather than prescriptions.

Dyzenhaus embraces a version of Raz's position, in an effort to support his own claim that legal officials invariably perform their roles on the basis of nonprudential considerations. In the course of taking such a stance, he puts forward a number of inadvisable assertions. Let us begin our critical scrutiny of his remarks by looking at one of his observations concerning Hart's resistance to the arguments by Raz about officials' obligation-affirming statements. Dyzenhaus writes that 'of grave concern to Hart is that Raz's account follows Hobbes's too closely and thus cannot establish enough distance between contemporary legal positivism and Hobbes's claim that there is a prior moral obligation to obey the law' (p. 711). A few paragraphs later, Dyzenhaus again declares that Hart feared that Raz's position 'leads to the conclusion that there is a prior moral obligation to obey the law' (p. 712). Dyzenhaus cites some pages from Hart's work in order to bear out the first of these quoted statements, but his citation of those pages simply helps to make clear that Hart nowhere expressed the misgivings which Dyzenhaus imputes to him. On the one hand, to be sure, Dyzenhaus is correct in thinking that Hart 'wished to avoid at all costs the Hobbesian thesis of prior moral obligation because that idea threatens the Separability Thesis' (pp. 711–12). On the other hand, however, Dyzenhaus is mistaken in thinking that Hart's rejection of the Razian account of officials' obligation-affirming statements had anything to do with his rejection of the notion of a comprehensively applicable moral obligation-to-obey-the-law. Far from worrying that Raz's position would point to the existence of such a moral obligation, Hart explicitly disavowed any concern along those lines:

Raz, true to his general positivist account, does not stipulate as a condition of the existence of a legal system that the belief which a judge may either hold or pretend to hold that there are sound moral reasons requiring compliance with the law as such be true and in fact, as we learn from his writing on political obligation, Raz thinks it must be false. This makes the moral component in the judge's acceptance very small indeed.[18]

In sum, the unease supposedly felt by Hart is something which he in fact disclaimed. Hart rejected Raz's view of obligation-affirming statements not because he believed that that view would commit him to acknowledging the existence of a moral obligation to obey every legal norm, but instead because he regarded Raz's analysis as contrived and unnecessary. As he expressly stated: 'Small as this moral component is[,] insistence on it to my mind conveys an unrealistic picture of the way in which the judges envisage their task of identifying and applying the law, and it also rests, I think, on a mistaken cognitive account of normative propositions of law' (Hart, 'Legal Duty', 158). Though my specific reasons for looking askance at Raz's position are only partly the same as Hart's reasons, I too give no credence to the notion that the Razian position is linked to the Hobbesian doctrine repeatedly mentioned by Dyzenhaus. His persistent references to that doctrine in this context are a red herring.

Apart from misrepresenting the concerns that prompted Hart to distance himself from Raz's account of officials' statements, Dyzenhaus sometimes misrepresents the substance of that account itself. He does so by misstating the points of controversy between Hart and Raz. For example, he recounts Hart's criticism of Raz as follows: 'Hart maintains that there is no need to take the extra

---

[18] H.L.A. Hart, 'Legal Duty and Obligation', in *Essays on Bentham* (Oxford: Clarendon Press, 1982) [hereinafter cited as Hart, 'Legal Duty'], 127, 158 (footnote omitted).

step of supposing acceptance must be on moral grounds just because, at least where the "law is clearly settled and determinate", judges might have many different reasons for accepting the law as authoritative' (p. 711). Dyzenhaus here distorts the debate between Hart and Raz, since the latter theorist is no more inclined than the former to contend that judges' acceptance of legal norms 'must be on moral grounds'. Contrary to what Dyzenhaus slightly later suggests, Raz does not submit that legal officials must harbor a 'sense that there are moral reasons for obedience' (p. 712). Rather, as Dyzenhaus himself initially avouches, the claim by Raz is that judges must endorse *or appear to endorse* the proposition that the legal norms which they apply are morally obligatory. Hart fully recognized that he and Raz were disagreeing about the professed beliefs, rather than the actual beliefs, of legal officials. He wrote that a judge's estimation of the moral merits of the law 'may be favourable or unfavourable, or simply absent, or, without dereliction of his duty as a judge, he may have formed no view of the moral merits. Raz indeed seems to admit as much by conceding that pretending to believe or the avowal of belief in the merits, is enough' (Hart, 'Legal Duty', 159). Unlike Dyzenhaus, then, Hart maintained a steady grip on what was at stake in his challenge to Raz's position.

Finally, we should ask whether Dyzenhaus can correctly call upon Raz's work in order to bolster his own claims about the nature of the adherence by legal officials to any Rule of Recognition. Recall that Dyzenhaus takes for granted that, in every legal system, the officials regard their Rule of Recognition as morally justified. He believes that 'Raz has given this common-sense observation a philosophical foundation' (p. 710). Hoping to reinforce his own assertions about the inherently moral character of officials' attitudes toward the enterprise of ascertaining the law, he rehearses Raz's views: 'The law's claim to authority is always a claim then to legitimate authority, because the law claims to supply reasons for action which in any case apply to its subjects. It thus also follows that judges must at least give the appearance of accepting the law's claim to legitimate authority since they do not merely decide whether they themselves are bound by the law but also make statements which impose obligations on others' (p. 710). This passage accurately synopsizes Raz's position. However, insofar as Dyzenhaus wants to draw upon that position in order to shore up his own account of officials' outlooks, his efforts are doomed to failure. Let us consider two points.

First, precisely because this latest extract does accurately summarize Raz's contentions, it reveals an unbridgeable gap between those contentions and Dyzenhaus's assertions. Whereas Dyzenhaus declares that judges and other officials in any legal regime invariably do perceive their Rule of Recognition as morally justified, Raz claims merely that they invariably perceive *or appear to perceive* their Rule of Recognition in that light. For Raz, the *appearance* of moral commitment on the part of officials (whether the appearances are well-founded or not) is an essential feature of every legal system; for Dyzenhaus, by contrast, the *actuality* of officials' moral commitment is what is essential. When Dyzenhaus subsequently attributes his own notion to Raz—while discussing the debate between Raz and Hart—he glosses over the fact that Raz's work is not supportive of that notion.

Second, even if we pretermit the point just made, we should note that the Razian propositions invoked by Dyzenhaus have been sustainedly contested by me in *In Defense of Legal Positivism*. Unfortunately, Dyzenhaus simply restates those propositions instead of defending them against my lines of critique. Indeed, just about his only direct observation concerning my analyses of Raz's work is that 'Kramer, though he has a chapter devoted to Raz, does not deal explicitly with Raz's account of authority' (p. 711). This remark is true only in the sense that I do not challenge Raz's conception of legitimate authority at all. Such a challenge would have been wholly gratuitous, even if I had harbored any serious dissatisfaction with his conception. After all, Raz nowhere implies that every legal system is endowed with legitimate authority; nor does he imply that the officials in every legal system believe it to be endowed with legitimate authority. What he does maintain is that the law invariably *claims* legitimate authority. That thesis about the law's claim to legitimate authority plays a key role in Raz's arguments concerning the tenor and implications of officials' obligation-affirming statements, as is evident in my principal quotation from Dyzenhaus two paragraphs ago. That thesis, accordingly, is impugned at considerable length in *In Defense of Legal Positivism* (*IDLP*, 92–101). Whereas a challenge to Raz's conception of legitimate authority would have been irrelevant (and unwarranted), a critique of his thesis about the law's *claim* to legitimate authority is singularly relevant—which is exactly why I undertook such a critique. To the extent that Dyzenhaus responds to my arguments, he does so on the basis of misconceptions that have already been parried in this chapter. Hence, his invocation of Raz's position adds nothing that would buttress his own insistence on the inherently moral character of officials' attitudes toward their law-ascertaining endeavors. His pronouncements concerning those attitudes, which were quoted earlier, remain groundless.

In short, Dyzenhaus's treatment of the Razian account of officials' obligation-affirming statements is redolent of the shortcomings in his review article more generally. Far too often evincing insufficient attentiveness to the texts with which he is engaging, Dyzenhaus imputes to legal positivists a number of positions which they do not hold and a number of forebodings which they do not feel. Misconstruing both the questions addressed and the answers supplied by legal positivists, Dyzenhaus presents an overview of contemporary legal philosophy in accordance with his own anti-positivistic preoccupations. Whether or not an author should expect more from a reviewer, one can certainly hope for more.

6

On the Moral Status of the Rule of Law

As the preceding chapters in this book have sought to underline, legal positivists do not (or should not) focus on bare logical possibilities when putting forward their theses. Neither when championing a moderate version of Incorporationism in preference to an extreme version, nor in affirming the separability of law and morality in any number of respects, has this book ever endeavored to clinch its case by pointing to bare logical possibilities. If legal positivists were foolish enough to seek to win arguments in that fashion, they would render their position too arid and jejune to be of any real interest. This point about my eschewal of any reliance on bare logical possibilities will emerge again in the present chapter, which concentrates on the moral status of the rule of law.

By the phrase 'the rule of law', this book means nothing more and nothing less than the state of affairs that obtains when a legal system exists and functions. In Lon Fuller's felicitous formulation (somewhat modified and amplified), the rule of law is the subjection of human conduct to the governance of legal norms through the operations of a legal system. Indeed, the rule of law as understood throughout this book is admirably encapsulated in Fuller's eight principles of legality.[1] Under those principles, (1) a system of governance operates through general norms, and all or most of the norms partake of the following properties: (2) they are promulgated to the people who are required to comply with them; (3) they are prospective rather than retrospective; (4) they are understandable rather than hopelessly unintelligible; (5) they do not contradict one another and do not impose duties that conflict; (6) they do not impose requirements that cannot possibly be fulfilled; (7) they persist over substantial periods of time, instead of being changed with disorienting frequency; and (8) they are generally given effect in accordance with their terms, so that there is a congruence between the norms as formulated and the norms as implemented. Although these basic precepts of legality are never perfectly satisfied by any regime of law, the satisfaction of each of them to a substantial degree is essential for the existence

---

[1] For a full-scale exposition of the eight principles of legality, see Lon Fuller, *The Morality of Law* (New Haven, CT: Yale University Press, 1969) (rev. edn), chap. 2. I have examined Fuller's work at length in my *In Defense of Legal Positivism* (Oxford: Oxford University Press, 1999) [hereinafter cited as *IDLP*], chap. 3.

of any legal system. The state of affairs constituted by the substantial fulfillment of those precepts is the rule of law.

As has been recounted in Chapter 5, many of my analyses in support of legal positivism have aimed to show that the rule of law is not an inherently moral ideal. The first main section of the current chapter will attempt to elucidate this point further and to parry some objections that might be lodged against it. We shall then examine how a couple of major legal philosophers have responded to the arguments about the rule of law that were marshaled by my *In Defense of Legal Positivism*. Some powerful rejoinders by Nigel Simmonds and Philip Soper to those arguments will provide occasions for clarifying and strengthening my position. Although I shall be striving to rebut their criticisms, they have raised genuinely important issues in insightful ways. Their ripostes merit careful attention indeed from anyone who aspires to uphold the theses of legal positivism.

I. Reasons Rather than Probabilities

As Chapter 5 has sought to make clear, my challenges to the status of the rule of law as an inherently moral ideal do not commit me to any view about the frequency with which the officials in heinous legal regimes are motivated by purely prudential considerations. On the one hand, as my fifth chapter has remarked in passing, the prevalence of purely prudential considerations among the actual determinants of the conduct of officials in iniquitous regimes is almost certainly underestimated by many legal philosophers. On the other hand, any claim about the actual determinants of officials' behavior—whether in accordance or at odds with the view stated in the preceding sentence—is an empirical assertion that cannot be substantiated or disconfirmed through philosophical reasoning. To ascertain the considerations that in fact motivate evil officials, we would have to undertake a lot of social-scientific research within the legal systems of a wide range of countries. Such a project would undoubtedly involve complex questionnaires and interviews as well as careful observation of the patterns of official decisions and actions. After all, exactly what typically motivates nefarious legal officials is a matter that hinges on contingent features of human psychology and sociocultural influences. Neither any legal-positivist philosopher nor any philosophical opponent of legal positivism has ever engaged in extensive research of the sort that would be required for the adequate investigation of those psychological and sociocultural phenomena. Yet the fact that jurisprudential theorists have not pursued the complicated empirical enquiries just mentioned is hardly due to remissness on their part. Rather, any enquiries along those lines would be largely or wholly beside the point, since the controversies between the proponents and the foes of legal positivism are philosophical rather than empirical. To be sure, the arguments mustered in those controversies do often rely on some empirical premises. However, the operative premises are on a very high plane of abstraction and generality, and are therefore not the points at issue between the supporters and detractors of jurisprudential positivism; although those premises figure in controversies, they are not themselves controversial. Instead, the chief points of contention in debates over the soundness of legal-positivist theses are conceptual.

More specifically for our present purposes, the chief points of contention pertain to reasons-for-action. Here, as in Chapter 5, the phrase 'reasons-for-action' refers not only to factors that actually do motivate people, but also to factors that *would* motivate them if they understood the serviceability of those factors for the furtherance of their general objectives. Because of this counter-factual element in many reasons-for-action, my reflections on the motivational underpinnings of the rule of law are not empirical. Those reflections are focused primarily on the sundry considerations that are promotive of the ends of wickedly self-interested officials, whether or not the considerations are actually perceived by the officials as so promotive. Irrespective of whether the consider-ations get taken into account when the evil officials choose how to behave, they are among the officials' reasons-for-action if they would get taken into account by anyone who is unremittingly clear-sighted in pursuing the officials' aims.

At the same time, the conception of reasons-for-action that informs my discussions of the moral status of the rule of law does not encompass external interest-independent reasons—that is, reasons which stand as reasons for a selfish person P regardless of whether they serve any of the objectives that are actually desired by P. Although interest-independent reasons not accepted as such by P would of course have to be included in any comprehensive account of reasons-for-action, no such account is needed or envisaged here. I concentrate for most of this chapter on strictly prudential considerations,[2] simply because we are here pondering whether such considerations are sufficient to warrant a substantial level of adherence to rule-of-law principles by selfishly power-hungry officials. For the contemplation of that issue, a restrictive conception of reasons-for-action is singularly appropriate.

Let us recall, then, the paramount question—a conditional question—that is addressed by my critique of the moral status of the rule of law. If the officials who operate a morally deplorable system of governance are motivated purely by prudential considerations relating to the consolidation of their own power and the exploitation of the citizenry, will they have solid reasons for abiding by rule-of-law requirements to a significant extent? In light of what has been said in the last couple of paragraphs, we know that the solid reasons need not be grasped and heeded as such by the evil officials; but we also know that those reasons, insofar as they exist, are purely prudential. (As Chapter 5 has indicated,[3] we further know

---

[2] The only portion of the chapter in which I invoke a broader conception of reasons-for-action is my discussion of promise-keeping in Section II(C).

[3] I have made this point at greater length in *IDLP*, 66.

that the relevant prudential reasons must consist in something more than opportunities to deceive others by appearing to be acting morally. If one's only prudential reason for engaging in a certain mode of behavior *B* lies in the likelihood that one will be perceived as acting on the basis of solicitude for the interests of others, and if one carries out *B* for exactly that prudential reason, then one's devious conduct is in effect a testament to the moral significance of *B*.) What is of most importance for us to notice afresh is that the conditional question about the wicked officials' reasons-for-action is not an empirical inquiry about their actual motivations. One can answer the question perfectly well through philosophical argumentation, without speculating about the frequency with which the officials in flagitious regimes are in fact animated purely by selfish concerns. An affirmative answer to my conditional question is perfectly consistent with the empirical claim that the officials in nefarious regimes are always or almost always motivated by nonprudential considerations (morally warped nonprudential considerations, of course, such as a concern for the purity of some racial or ethnic group). Although I do not subscribe to such an empirical thesis, a denial of it here would be wholly superfluous. My legal-positivist critique of the moral tenor of the rule of law does not depend on any such denial, for it does not contend that the factors which actually drive the conduct of repressive officials are of this or that particular type. Whatever those factors may be in any given setting, there will obtain strong prudential reasons for the officials to exert their sway through the rule of law—at least if they aspire to exert their sway for a sustained period over a society larger than a handful of families.

That such strong prudential reasons-for-action will indeed obtain is a proposition which my *In Defense of Legal Positivism* has endeavored at length to substantiate—in order to bear out my positivist denial of the inherently moral character of the rule of law—with some lines of argumentation that are very tersely summarized in Chapter 5 of the present volume. Instead of rehearsing anew those lines of argumentation, which reveal the prodigious direction-imparting and incentive-building and coordination-enabling capacity of the rule of law, my discussion here will explore an ostensible problem or shortcoming that pertains to the point which has just been highlighted. By fixing upon the fact that my analysis of the moral status of the rule of law has left open the possibility that wicked legal officials are never or almost never driven purely by prudential concerns, a critic might retort by questioning whether my conclusions about that moral status are really justified. Such a critic may well accept that there are solid prudential reasons for exploitative officials to conform with rule-of-law requirements, but he will query the importance of such an observation. Given that my arguments concerning the officials' reasons-for-action do not rule out the possibility that their motivations are in fact entirely nonprudential, the critic may feel that I have not genuinely cast doubt on the inherently moral character of the rule of law. If the animating concerns of evil officials in their compliance with rule-of-law precepts are not the prudential reasons for such compliance, and if as a matter of fact those animating concerns are always nonprudential, then why should we not regard the rule of law as a morally pregnant state of affairs? Though such a state of affairs is not always associated with morally worthy effects, its actual motivational underpinnings are (*ex hypothesi*) always moral in the sense of being nonprudential. Why then, the critic may ask, should the legal-positivist assessment of the rule of law not be discounted as something that lacks any purchase on the real world?

One quite minor weakness in an objection of this sort, of course, is that it treats a possibility as if it were an established actuality. My legal-positivist approach to the rule of law—which addresses the conditional question specified at the beginning of the penultimate paragraph above—has left open the possibility seized upon by the hypothetical critic, simply because my approach does not commit me to any view whatsoever on the actual promptings that lead the officials in each repressive regime of law to operate it as a regime of law. Not dealing with that matter at all, I scarcely have to concede that the critic's supposition about the invariably moral character of those promptings is correct. Still, that weakness in the critic's challenge can be put aside here, for his retort founders in a more serious respect. The unacceptable crudeness of his challenge becomes manifest when we consider some of the conclusions that would be generated if his line of reasoning were to be applied to other patterns of behavior.

Let us ponder the example of shooting a gun at somebody else at point-blank range. Suppose that, as a matter of empirically verifiable fact, everybody or virtually everybody who deliberately engages in such a mode of conduct is motivated by nonprudential considerations (albeit often deeply misguided and iniquitous considerations). Perhaps because of the horrific consequences of shooting someone else in cold blood and because of limits on human callousness, no one or virtually no one who deliberately fires a gun at point-blank range is prompted to undertake such conduct by selfish urgings. We may suppose that only someone driven wholly or predominantly by nonprudential motives is psychologically capable of pumping a bullet into a nearby human being. Only such motives can give rise to the requisite degree of unrelenting sternness. Although I believe that such an empirical thesis is false, it might conceivably be true as a contingent matter of human psychology, and in any event its truth-value is beside the point when we gauge the moral status of the act of shooting another person. For the task of apprehending that status, we have to ask a conditional question parallel to the one which I have posed about the rule of law. If someone is motivated by unalloyedly prudential concerns, will there be strong reasons in highly credible circumstances for him to fire a gun directly at somebody else?

Especially if we ignore the prospect of a person's being punished for committing such a misdeed—a prospect that has no bearing on the moral character of the misdeed itself—the answer to this conditional question is plainly 'yes'. There will clearly be numerous credible contexts in which somebody driven solely by self-interested considerations will have strong reasons (strong prudential reasons) for shooting some other person(s), at least if there is little or no chance of his undergoing sanctions for his homicidal conduct. Perhaps no one will ever actually act upon those prudential reasons, because of the putative facts of human psychology hypothesized in my last paragraph; maybe acts of homicidal shooting will occur only on the basis of nonprudential zeal. Nevertheless, the weighty prudential reasons for many such acts will obtain as such. Precisely because those reasons will indeed obtain, the pattern of conduct that consists in firing a gun at somebody else at close range is not inherently moral. It is not a mode of behavior that can hardly ever be credibly described as strongly promotive of the selfish interests of somebody who resorts to it.

If the hypothetical critic's animadversions on my analysis of evil officials' adherence to rule-of-law principles were correct, they would apply as well to any comparable analysis of the act of shooting a person at point-blank range. If one rejects the animadversions in application to the act of firing a gun, and if one maintains that the ample serviceability of such an act for the selfish interests of any thug who undertakes it is enough to justify our denying that it is intrinsically moral, then one should adopt the same position with regard to the wicked officials' fulfillment of rule-of-law requirements. Of course, to say as much is not to say that we can safely ignore all differences between the two patterns of behavior. We manifestly have to take some such differences into account. Most notably, the tendency of an instance of homicide to further the selfish aims of an evil person who perpetrates it is immediately obvious, whereas the tendency of the rule of law to further the selfish aims of nefarious officials who operate a legal regime is not nearly as evident on first glance. Exactly because of this dissimilarity between the slaying of someone with a gun and the sustainment of the rule of law, I have felt a need to offer lengthy arguments that highlight the expediency of the latter mode of behavior for the furtherance of the power-hungry interests of repressive officials. Only through such arguments, which have been presented on a full scale in *In Defense of Legal Positivism* and summarized laconically in the fifth chapter of the present book, can we recognize that the correct answer to my conditional question about the rule of law is affirmative. Nevertheless, what those arguments enable us to grasp is that the answer to that question is indeed affirmative—just as surely (though not as obviously) as the answer to the parallel question about the act of shooting a gun at someone at point-blank range.

Note that cognate conditional questions can pertinently be posed about countless other modes of conduct that are perhaps never pursued by people except on the basis of nonprudential concerns. Let us contemplate, for example, the activity of gambling at cards. Maybe, as a contingent matter of human psychology, such an empty and degrading mode of conduct never sufficiently entices anyone who is not inspired by solicitude for others to seek a means of acquiring money rapidly. Though such an empirical claim is hardly very convincing, it could conceivably be true. Possibly, every card-playing gambler is like the grandfather portrayed in *The Old Curiosity Shop*, whose reckless attempts to win at cards were motivated entirely by his love for his granddaughter Nell. As Charles Dickens wrote, the old man 'gambl[ed] with such a savage thirst for gain as the most insatiable gambler never felt, [yet] had not one selfish thought!'[4] Even in the highly unlikely event that all card-playing gamblers are similarly motivated, we scarcely have to accept that the pursuit of gain through gambling at cards is an inherently moral endeavor. About that pursuit we should ask a conditional question similar to the ones that we have asked about adhering to rule-of-law requirements and firing a gun at a nearby person. If somebody prone to gambling were motivated exclusively by selfish promptings, and if his chances of winning at cards were as high as he himself believes, would there be strong reasons for him to follow his card-playing propensity? Like the answer to each of our other conditional questions, the answer to this latest conditional question is plainly affirmative. If someone with a decent chance of faring well at cards is driven wholly by prudential concerns, there will be many credible contexts in which he will have solid reasons for gambling at the card table. To be sure, perhaps nobody ever actually acts on the basis of those prudential reasons; perhaps every gambler instead resorts to betting on cards solely for the further-ance of nonprudential aspirations. Nonetheless, even if that exceedingly implaus-ible empirical suggestion is true, anyone with good prospects of success will still have solid prudential reasons for indulging in such betting. The existence of those reasons is independent of one's inclination or disinclination to be moved by them. Precisely because those reasons will indeed exist in many credible circumstances, the pattern of behavior that consists in the pursuit of winnings through cards is not inherently moral in its motivational underpin-nings—even if its actual motivational underpinnings are always moral as a matter of fact.

We could go through homologous lines of analysis in respect of sundry other types of conduct. The upshot would of course be the same in each case. If the hypothetical critic were correct in taking exception to my account of the rule of law, then it would also be true that firing guns at people and gambling at cards— and countless other dubious activities—are intrinsically moral. In other words, the critic's rejoinder does not tell against my account of the rule of law at all. By focusing on a question about actual motivations (or, rather, about motivations that supposedly are actual) when the germane question is about reasons-for-action, the rejoinder would lead us to classify absolutely every kind of behavior as inherently moral. It would thereby remove all significance and content from the category of 'inherently moral kinds of behavior', at least insofar as our assess-ments of behavior are oriented toward its motivational underpinnings. Far from having shown that the bearings of the rule of law are in any way distinctive, the hypothetical critic's retort would in effect be contending that officials'

---

[4] Charles Dickens, *The Old Curiosity Shop* (London: Everyman, 1995) (Paul Schlicke ed.), 231.

sustainment of the rule of law is on a par with every other way in which human beings might act.

Naturally, the hypothetical critic might respond along the following lines. With regard to acts such as homicidal shootings and activities such as gambling at cards, we would be not only wrong but plainly wrong if we were to assume that the actual underlying motivations are always nonprudential. By contrast, so the critic might maintain, such an assumption about actual motivations is not so evidently wrong when applied to the conformity by authoritarian officials with rule-of-law requirements. Although the critic might allow that the assumption is incorrect even in this last-mentioned case, he would add that it is not manifestly so. Whereas we need no detailed empirical enquiries in order to feel confident that the actual motivations for homicidal shootings and for wagers on cards are not invariably nonprudential, some detailed enquiries will be necessary if we are to feel similarly confident about the actual motivations for evil officials' adherence to rule-of-law principles. Such, at least, is what the hypothetical critic might affirm in order to redeem his rejoinder to my positivist reflections on the rule of law.

Any response of this sort by the critic would be intensely problematic. Obviousness is a scalar property which obtains in varying degrees.[5] Hence, the critic's latest retort would suggest that the difference between the moral status of wicked officials' cleaving to the rule of law and the moral status of gun-shooting or card-playing exploits is at most a matter of degree. Having conceded as much, the critic is then vulnerable to arguments which indicate that the difference of degree is quite meager. In this connection, let us mull over a couple of points.

We should first recall that, although officials' compliance with the Fullerian precepts of legality is prerequisite to the existence of a legal system, the degree of compliance will be less than unfailing perfection. Any regime of law, including a benignly liberal-democratic regime, will fall quite a way short of adhering perfectly to Fuller's precepts. There will be neither moral reasons nor prudential reasons in favor of unremitting adherence. Now, on the one hand, given that crimes of many types will be detected more readily by a stiflingly repressive and intrusive regime than by a liberal-democratic system of governance that leaves its citizens ample room for individual freedom, the satisfaction of Fuller's crucial eighth principle—calling for congruity between the law as formulated and the law as enforced—will often be realized to a greater extent within illiberal systems of law. On the other hand, a crushingly exploitative regime might typically fall further short than a liberal-democratic regime in the degree of its conformity with some of the other precepts of legality. After all, the repressive rulers will be disposed to depart from those precepts on some occasions when liberal-

---

[5] For a discussion of the difference between scalar and non-scalar properties, see Matthew H. Kramer, *The Quality of Freedom* (Oxford: Oxford University Press, 2003), 169–84.

democratic rulers would feel morally inhibited from doing so. (Contrariwise, the repressive rulers will be disposed to show gruff inflexibility in matters of enforcement that would probably elicit greater complaisance on the part of liberal-democratic rulers. Moral reasons in favor of departures from the Fullerian precepts will not count for much in the eyes of autocratic officials.) Still, although a grimly exploitative regime will not be meticulously unwavering in its fulfillment of the principles of legality, its officials will have solid prudential reasons for abiding by those principles to a substantial degree. If the officials act in accordance with those reasons, then the level of their compliance with rule-of-law requirements will be sufficient to endow their system of governance with the character of a legal system. What should be highlighted here is that the status of that system of governance as a legal system is quite compatible with the fact that the wicked officials are not punctiliously unswerving in their adherence to every one of the Fullerian principles. It is quite compatible with the occurrence of their deviations from those principles, as long as the deviations are not so wide-ranging and numerous as to plunge their regime below some threshold of regularity and coordination. Thus, when we ponder whether the actual motivations for evil officials' sustainment of the rule of law are always nonprudential, we should keep in mind that heinous incarnations of the rule of law will tend to be marked by certain types of aberrations that would not typically occur on the same scale under a liberal-democratic scheme of governance. Though officials bent on exploitation and dominance will not usually have prudential reasons (or moral reasons) for cleaving with extreme fastidiousness to the Fullerian principles,[6] the nefarious regimes that receive most attention in my discussions of the rule of law are not regimes in which the officials are generally fastidious. They adhere to the Fullerian principles to a significant extent—if their systems of governance are indeed systems of law—but their adherence is combined with ruthless deviations when their interests are thereby served. When we have in view this combination of oppressively efficient governance and unconscionable departures from norms, the evil officials' sustainment of the rule of law will no longer seem so different from homicidal shootings and betting on cards, in respect of its actual

---

[6] There will typically not be any solid reasons—either prudential or moral—for officials to cleave with extreme fastidiousness to the Fullerian precepts of legality. Fuller himself drew attention to quite a few types of circumstances in which departures from his precepts are unequivocally desirable. Nevertheless, although there will not be moral reasons for officials to adhere *pertinaciously* to the principles of legality, the moral reasons that do favor compliance with those principles will probably call for a higher level of compliance with some of them than will most prudential reasons. After all, when a regime abides by the Fullerian principles on the basis of appropriate moral concerns, the rule of law which it upholds is expressive as well as promotive of worthy ideals. That expressive dimension engenders moral reasons that will probably warrant a greater degree of conformity with some of the principles of legality than will be warranted on prudential grounds under repressively exploitative regimes. An acknowledgment of this point is perfectly consistent with my claim that the Fullerian precepts are not inherently moral in their bearings. While advancing such a claim, I have always readily allowed that the fulfillment of those precepts can be a vehicle for communicating and achieving commendable nonprudential aspirations. Everything depends upon the context in which the fulfillment occurs.

motivations. When we recognize that the legal systems on which we should be concentrating for present purposes are hardly characterized by much squeamishness, we can discern that the difference of degree mentioned in my last paragraph is not sizeable.

A second reason for doubting the sizeableness of the difference is that the hypothetical critic has failed to distinguish adequately between two sets of actual motivations: motivations for governing, and motivations for governing in accordance with the rule of law. It might be that the actual motivations for governing, even among iniquitously power-hungry officials, are always nonprudential at least in large part. It might be, in other words, that no array of officials driven predominantly by prudential considerations could muster the tenacity and self-confidence needed for imposing their baleful dominion over the other people in their society. Perhaps only when evil officials are captivated by the allure of some twisted nonprudential objective, such as racial supremacy or religious purity or socialist revolution, will they be filled with sufficiently ruthless determination to place themselves in charge of the direction of their society. So, at least, someone might conjecture. Although a hypothesis along those lines would in my view be far from compelling, a rejection of it would require some elaborate empirical investigation. We need not reject it here, in any event. For the sake of argument, we can leave it unassailed. Much more dubious, however, would be a kindred hypothesis that relates not to the actual motivations for governing *tout court* but to the actual motivations for governing in accordance with the rule of law.

In order to train our attention on the latter set of motivations, we should take as given that some wickedly repressive officials have gained sway over a society. We should also take as given, *arguendo*, the truth of the empirical hypothesis broached in the preceding paragraph. That is, we should assume that the wicked officials are motivated chiefly by some hideous nonprudential aspirations rather than mainly by selfish concerns. Are we obliged to infer that the actual motivations for the officials' sustainment of the rule of law (if indeed their regime is a regime of law) are likewise nonprudential? Especially when we recall that the sustainment of the rule of law by autocratic officials will typically not be marked by fastidiousness, we can see that the answer to this question is negative. Even if *ex hypothesi* the aims that have prompted the officials to take or retain control of their society are nonprudential, the motivating factors that lead them to abide by rule-of-law principles can very credibly be the strictly instrumental considerations that also render the rule of law serviceable for the ends of exploitative officials who are motivated to govern by thoroughly prudential concerns. That is, when repressive officials driven to govern by nonprudential objectives have opted to adhere to the rule of law, their actual motivations for doing so can very credibly reside in the direction-providing and incentive-promoting and coordination-facilitating advantages of the rule of law—advantages that would be just as noteworthy in the eyes of the officials if their motivations for governing were instead entirely prudential. They need not look upon the rule of law as per se expressive of their objectives or indeed of any nonprudential aspirations. They might instead very credibly regard it as valuable only instrumentally. To be sure, their reliance on the rule of law for the tightening of their grip over their society is ultimately in the service of nonprudential goals, or so we are assuming. Nevertheless, they can very credibly view the rule of law not as an integral element of those goals but simply as an instrument for the effective realization thereof. In adopting such a view, they will be embracing the rule of law on the basis of the same considerations—wholly instrumental considerations—that would militate in favor of their embracing it even if their underlying concerns were utterly selfish. In any such credible circumstances, the nonprudential tenor of the evil officials' actual motivations for governing is not matched by the tenor of their actual motivations for governing through the rule of law.

In short, the relevant empirical issues are by no means as straightforward as the hypothetical critic's latest riposte has implied. The difference of degree highlighted in that riposte is indeed at most a difference of degree, which turns out to be much more tenuous than it might at first seem. My response to the critic's original challenge therefore stands. His challenge can salvage the inherently moral status of the rule of law only by trivializing that status. Unless we are prepared to attribute such a status to homicidal shootings and to wagers on cards, we should not attribute it to the conformity of officials with rule-of-law precepts.

II. Simmonds and the Rule of Law

In a textbook which in its second edition has become an estimably imaginative and perceptive work of legal philosophy in its own right,[7] Simmonds replies forcefully to my strictures on his account of the rule of law. That powerful account, which he presented in the first edition of his textbook in the course of his discussion of Fuller's writings, came under critical scrutiny by me in *In Defense of Legal Positivism*. Indeed, some of my central arguments concerning the moral status of the rule of law have evolved partly in reaction to Simmonds's ruminations on that status. Accordingly, his defense of his position against my queries will have to be countered if my positivist theory of law is to be fully vindicated herein.

Let us begin by noting that Simmonds often tends to obscure one of the principal distinctions highlighted in the preceding section of this chapter: the distinction between actual motivations and reasons-for-action. As has been observed, reasons-for-action obtain as such even when they do not actually motivate people to behave in certain ways. Simmonds obfuscates this potential

---

[7] N.E. Simmonds, *Central Issues in Jurisprudence* (London: Sweet & Maxwell, 2002) (2nd edn) [hereinafter cited as Simmonds, *Issues*].

divergence between motivations and reasons when he writes that '[m]uch of the debate relating to Fuller's theory... revolves around rival assertions regarding the probable or possible behaviour of wicked regimes. Would they have good reasons for establishing and respecting the institutions of law?'[8] As should be apparent from what has been said already in this chapter, only the second sentence in this quotation identifies the key question addressed by my critique of the moral status of the rule of law. The first sentence, by contrast, adverts to an empirical question from which my critique prescinds. To be sure, Simmonds speaks of probable or possible behavior rather than of probable or possible motivations. However, that difference makes no difference in the present context. Largely because reasons-for-action obtain independently of their efficacy in actually motivating anyone to seek to adopt certain courses of conduct, they likewise obtain independently of anyone's actual adoption of those courses of conduct. Thus, for example, the officials in vilely repressive and exploitative regimes have solid reasons (solid prudential reasons) for abiding by rule-of-law requirements to a considerable extent, whether or not they grasp those reasons and act on the basis of them. Even if the officials in all or most such regimes are somehow too obtuse to heed those reasons—and even if they attenuate and abbreviate their grip on power as a result—the strong prudential reasons in favor of their compliance with rule-of-law principles will exist. Because those reasons will exist as such, the sustainment of the rule of law is not an inherently moral pattern of behavior. This conclusion about the moral status of the rule of law derives entirely from reflections on evil officials' reasons-for-action, and not from any surmises about the ways in which the officials will be inclined to behave. Consequently, only the second sentence in the quotation from Simmonds accurately pinpoints the paramount issue around which the debates arising from Fuller's work have revolved.

A. Simmonds's First Major Retort: The First Strand

In his first main rejoinder to my enquiry into the moral bearings of the rule of law, Simmonds conjures up a scenario in which some Taliban-like despots have imposed a stifling religious orthodoxy on the society over which they exercise power. He adduces this scenario in order to recount a situation in which a grimly repressive regime can hold sway on a large scale for a long period without abiding by rule-of-law precepts to any significant extent. A 'pure regime of terror may work perfectly well' under the circumstances outlined in the scenario, or so Simmonds contends (Simmonds, *Issues*, 230). Quite a lengthy quotation from his argument is necessary here in order to set the stage for my rebuttals:

Suppose, for example, that a group of religious fundamentalists has the sole aim of discouraging the propagation of atheism, being content to leave all other aspects of social

---

[8] Ibid., at 226. For a passage that similarly elides the distinction between actual motivations and reasons-for-action, see ibid., at 230.

life (such as the operation of markets and the protection of property rights) to be sustained (or not, as the case may be) by informal customary practices unsupported by official rules and sanctions. Unregulated brutality towards anyone suspected of sympathy for atheism would serve such a regime perfectly well. Atheists and potential atheists would be deprived of the opportunity to exploit the interstices of liberty that are inherent in any meticulously enforced set of rules; they would know that the only way to be safe was to avoid doing anything that might annoy the regime's supporters, or arouse their suspicions. (Simmonds, *Issues*, 230)

Let us begin our examination of this passage by considering a few minor points, before we turn to the chief weakness in the argument. In the first place, as should be evident from some of my remarks in the first main section of this chapter, Simmonds's use of the word 'meticulously' near the end of the quoted passage is ill-advised. Although in some respects the officials in an oppressive regime may well have solid prudential reasons for being more meticulous than a liberal-democratic regime in following the Fullerian precepts—for example, in enforcing prohibitions with stern unflinchingness—they will probably have prudential reasons for being less meticulous in some other respects. Nowhere in any of my writings have I intimated that wickedly exploitative officials will have strong reasons for complying punctiliously with every one of the Fullerian principles. They must comply to a considerable degree with each principle if their regime is to operate as a system of legal governance at all, but the optimal extent of the conformity will undoubtedly fall short of punctiliousness (as it certainly will under any benign system of law, where the optimal extent is determined by moral considerations rather than by prudential considerations). Hence, insofar as Simmonds is arguing that the officials in the Taliban-like regime will not have weighty prudential reasons for adhering *assiduously* to every rule-of-law precept, he is knocking down a straw man. What he instead should be trying to show is that the officials will have no such reasons for adopting the somewhat looser level of adherence which I have described as promotive of the ruthless effectiveness of authoritarian rulers.

Another minor shortcoming in Simmonds's example lies in the nature of the regime on which it focuses. Whereas my discussions have trained attention primarily on rulers for whom starkly prudential considerations are of dominant importance, all or most of the Taliban-like rulers are driven predominantly or exclusively by heinous nonprudential concerns of religious purity. Still, as should be apparent from the first main section of this chapter, the inappositeness of Simmonds's example in the respect just mentioned can be pretermitted here. After all, by taking due account of the distinction between motivations for governing and motivations for governing through the rule of law (or between reasons for governing and reasons for governing through the rule of law), we can perceive that even officials whose retention of their grip on power is animated by nonprudential aspirations will have instrumental reasons for abiding by rule-of-law requirements—instrumental reasons that might constitute their actual motivations for upholding the rule of law (if the officials do indeed uphold it). As was argued earlier, the fulfillment of rule-of-law requirements can be directly motivated by strictly instrumental considerations even when it is ultimately in the service of nonprudential objectives. Thus, if we concentrate on the direct reasons for governing through the rule of law, and if we are careful to distinguish them from the ultimate motivations for governing, my critique of the moral status of the rule of law will work as well with Simmonds's example of the Taliban-like despots as with the examples of selfishly exploitative officials on which I have generally focused.

Of greater significance is another dubious feature of Simmonds's example. It is not clear in what sense the example's religious zealots have formed a governing regime. They are not regulating most aspects of life in their society in any way, and they are not providing an infrastructure that facilitates any basic governmental functions. Instead, they are much more like bandits who are endeavoring to enforce their will in one quite narrow area of life while leaving everything else ungoverned. (Indeed, given the extreme unlikelihood that any sizeable society will stay together if it is virtually anarchic, the example could more realistically have been presented as a depiction of a situation in which the overbearing zealots' campaign against atheism is conducted within the framework of the operations of some genuine government—perhaps a government just as harshly repressive as the coterie of religious zealots.) Accordingly, the fact that the anti-atheistical militants do not run a legal regime is due to their not running any veritable regime at all; the fact that they do not govern in accordance with the rule of law is due to their not governing, period.

Of still more importance is a tension between two of the statements in the passage quoted above. On the one hand, Simmonds declares therein that the religious fanatics are pursuing 'the sole aim of discouraging the propagation of atheism'. On the other hand, at the end of the passage he submits that the fanatics' policy of unregulated brutality will lead people to 'know that the only way to be safe [is] to avoid doing anything that might annoy the regime's supporters, or arouse their suspicions'. The fanatics' sole aim of snuffing out atheism is by no means most effectively achieved through the engendering of a state of affairs along the lines described in the second of these quoted statements. That state of affairs is fully consistent with a situation in which the unregulated brutality is very frequently inflicted on devout believers who have been falsely accused by the regime's supporters (maybe out of personal animosity and vindictiveness, or perhaps out of ignorance and hysteria, or maybe out of sheer corruption). If the brutality of the religious fanatics is indeed unregulated, then the opportunities for efficacious false accusations will abound. Insofar as the persecution of many devout believers does ensue, it will certainly not strengthen the fanatics' hold over the populace—since it will very likely antagonize and eliminate people who would otherwise be inclined to support the harsh imposition of religious uniformity. Even more clearly, such persecution by the coterie of religious zealots will not help them to attain their sole aim of discouraging the propagation of atheism. On the contrary, although that aim might still be realized if the terrible penalties inflicted on pious believers are combined with the infliction of terrible penalties on atheists, the former set of penalties will at best do nothing to advance the desired objective. What is more likely is that the penalties imposed on believers will set back the coterie's sole objective. For one thing, as has just been noted, people who would otherwise have been favorably disposed toward the cadre of zealots will have become alienated therefrom. They might still cooperate with the fanatics out of fear, but they will no longer be inclined to cooperate in an enthusiastic manner bred of sympathy. They—like Macbeth's subordinates—move only in command, nothing in love. Moreover, the atheists in the society may well adopt a 'nothing to lose' attitude when they perceive that they will stand a significant chance of undergoing severe punishment even if they abstain from any atheistic practices. The prospect of escaping such punishment by forgoing such practices is constitutive of a strong incentive to forgo them; inasmuch as that prospect is impaired, the concomitant incentive is likewise impaired. If an atheist who might refrain from giving expression to his views would not very much lower his chances of being subjected to ferocious treatment, he may well wonder why he should refrain.

Of course, it is not inevitable that the upshot of the use of unregulated brutality by the religious militants will include the frequent perpetration of violence by them against pious believers. Nor is it inevitable that their conformity with rule-of-law requirements would avert such a state of affairs. Nonetheless, the probability of the occurrence of counterproductive violence by the fanatics against devout individuals is considerably higher in what Simmonds describes as 'a pure regime of terror' than in a regime of law. Consequently, there are strong reasons for the militants to abide by rule-of-law principles to quite a substantial degree—instrumental reasons concerning the effectiveness with which the militants can achieve their sole aim of discouraging atheism. Whether or not the religious despots recognize that there are those reasons for them to adhere to rule-of-law precepts, and whether or not they act on the basis of those reasons, the reasons obtain as such. If the lone objective of the despots is to stanch the propagation of atheism, they are most apt to succeed if their ruthless pursuit of that objective is channeled through the rule of law. (This conclusion would of course be underscored if we were to take account of the fact that a pure regime of terror which operates through unregulated savagery will not only be prone to punish many compliant people but will also be prone to leave many disobedient people unpunished. More precisely, its proneness to errors in each direction will in typical circumstances be greater than the error-proneness of a legal regime. Nevertheless, throughout his discussion of the religious extremists, Simmonds appears to envisage a situation in which the enforcement of anti-atheistical mandates is markedly overinclusive without being significantly under-inclusive. Since my replies to his discussion are adequate without my having to challenge his assumption on that particular point, I shall indeed leave the assumption unimpugned here.)

B. Simmonds's First Major Retort: The Second Strand

Simmonds allows that the anti-atheistical zealots will very likely extend their sway into areas of life other than that of religious practices. He therefore allows that they will establish a full-fledged legal system. Furthermore, he readily accepts that the propagation of atheism will be dampened if the legal system includes norms that prohibit atheistical activities and if those norms are stringently enforced when breached. However, he maintains that the religious fanatics will have no reasons to refrain from punishing people for engaging in various atheistic practices or utterances that do not infringe the prohibitory norms. On the contrary, he contends, the fanatics will have strong reasons for disregarding the terms of such norms by cracking down on any manifestations of atheism irrespective of whether the manifestations violate those terms. At least in their regulation of the spiritual side of people's lives, then, the religious extremists will have strong reasons for declining to satisfy Fuller's eighth principle of legality (relating to the need for congruity between the formulation and the implementation of legal norms). Simmonds argues for this claim as follows:

But why should the regime treat as *immune* from officially organised violence those atheistic activities that do *not* violate any published and prospective rule? After all, some atheistic activities may emerge in forms not anticipated by the religious regime, but they may be just as obnoxious to the regime (and just as much to be discouraged) as those activities that were indeed anticipated and prohibited. By ordering or permitting ad hoc official violence against the perpetrators of such obnoxious activities, the regime would not only discourage the particular activities in question, but would also discourage the expenditure of intellectual effort in dreaming up further innovative forms of atheistic practice aimed at escaping the existing prohibited categories. (Simmonds, *Issues*, 231)

Now, although this quoted passage should be read in conjunction with the paragraph that immediately follows it (on which we shall concentrate presently), we should pause here to note *en passant* two questionable features of this extract. First, in arguing that punishments for lawful atheistic activities will be serviceable for keeping people docile, Simmonds strangely assumes that the legal norms which prohibit atheistic undertakings will each be quite narrowly framed and will thereby leave open the possibility of atheistic practices that are not covered by the norms. Much more likely is that a broad prohibition on atheistic practices will be included among those norms. Just as the Hebrew Scriptures lay down both narrowly targeted bans on idolatrous practices and wholesale bans on idolatry, so too the Taliban-like extremists will almost certainly issue blanket proscriptions of atheism as well as more narrowly defined proscriptions of specific activities associated with godlessness. Such an approach by the extremists need not involve any departures from Fuller's precepts of legality; and, in comparison with the approach sketched by Simmonds, it will more directly and perspicuously convey to potential atheists the message that their proclivities will not be tolerated. Accordingly, the Taliban-like tyrants have strong instrumental reasons for adopting the strategy outlined here, in preference to the strategy recounted by Simmonds. Whether or not the tyrants grasp those reasons and act upon them, the reasons obtain as such.

Second, in any event, I have never maintained that no deviations or hardly any deviations at all from rule-of-law principles will be serviceable for the entrenching of an evil regime's power and the accomplishment of its objectives. Weighty though the direction-providing and incentive-promoting and coordination-enabling advantages of the rule of law are, a vile regime will typically have to leaven them with the advantages of flexibility that come with departures from rule-of-law requirements. As was readily acknowledged in my earlier book on legal positivism (*IDLP*, 70), even very substantial departures from such requirements during quite a brief period or within quite a confined geographical or substantive area can consolidate the dominance of an iniquitous regime without depriving it of its general character as a regime of law (and therefore without depriving it of the advantages attendant on that general character). Thus, if Simmonds's only point were that transgressions of rule-of-law precepts can sometimes reinforce a heinous regime's grip on power, his argument would not really clash with anything said here or in my previous writings on legal positivism.

However, it straightaway becomes plain that Simmonds is putting forward a much bolder thesis. He brands as 'straightforwardly false' my claim that a wicked regime will tend to sap incentives for compliance with its mandates if it does not abide by rule-of-law requirements to a considerable extent. He declares that 'such a situation would not be brought about by the scenarios [relating to the Taliban-like fanatics] that I have described above; nor does the avoidance of such an undermining of incentives require compliance with Fuller's eight principles' (Simmonds, *Issues*, 231–2). He endeavors to support these assertions by asking us to contemplate two situations. In the first of those situations, the citizens governed by a repressive regime are punished for violating the regime's promulgated norms, 'but they also suffer on a very frequent but irregular basis, random acts of violence perpetrated by officials of the regime'. In the second situation, the citizens are punished for violating the regime's promulgated norms, 'but, with equal frequency, they are also punished for activities obnoxious to the ruling powers, although not prohibited in any published and prospective rule' (Simmonds, *Issues*, 232). Having delineated these two sets of circumstances, Simmonds proceeds to deliver his central line of argument against me:

In neither of these situations would incentives for compliance with the rules be reduced by the occurrence of official acts of violence not provided for in the rules, or provided for only in retrospective rules. For, by violating the rules, I would be greatly increasing my chances of incurring a punishment, or my chances of incurring an additional punishment.

Even if unregulated official violence is so widespread that citizens can all expect to be its victims from time to time, it is difficult to see how this would undermine their motives for complying with the rules. The fact that you will beat me if I break the rules gives me a good reason for complying with them even if you frequently beat me at random: after all, the beating in consequence of breaking the rules will be an additional beating that I could have avoided by compliance. (Simmonds, *Issues*, 232)

Before assailing the line of reasoning in this extract, I should mention preliminarily a couple of points on which there is no disagreement between Simmonds and me. First, in any thorough examination of punishment-centered incentives for conformity with legal mandates, two main factors are of key relevance: the probability and the severity of the threatened punishments for nonconformity. Incentives for obedience will be increased if either of those two factors is increased, and the incentives will be diminished if either factor is diminished. Nonetheless, purely for ease of exposition, my discussion here (like Simmonds's discussion) will concentrate on the probability of one's undergoing punitive measures and will put aside the matter of the severity of the measures. In other words, my rejoinders to Simmonds will proceed as if the probability of punishment were the only variable factor and as if the severity were constant. Nothing whatsoever of substance hinges on this simplifying assumption, which is operative solely for reasons of stylistic clarity.

A second preliminary point on which there exists no disagreement between Simmonds and me is that strictly speaking the incentives for one's compliance with mandates are determined not by the probability of one's undergoing penalties for non-compliance, but by the *perceived* probability of such penalties. Unlike reasons-for-action, which obtain whether or not the person for whom they are reasons is aware of them, incentives are awareness-dependent. A person will not be induced to modify his behavior by reasons-for-action of which he remains ignorant. All the same, like Simmonds, I will for present purposes set this matter aside and will assume that the perceived probability of punishment is the actual probability thereof. Such an assumption is warranted chiefly on stylistic grounds of clarity and smoothness. In addition, the actual probability and the perceived probability will correspond pretty well under most circumstances, especially if the actual probability is high. At any rate, once again, nothing of any philosophical importance hinges on my simplifying assumption. My analyses below could stand up perfectly well even if they took explicit account of the potential for discrepancies between actual probabilities and perceived probabilities; however, nothing of substantive interest would be added to the analyses, and they would become stylistically much more gnarled. Let us, then, disregard the potential for such discrepancies.

Now, in coming to grips with Simmonds's argument, we should straightaway observe that the relevant probabilities are comparative. That is, the probability of one's undergoing some detriment as a disobedient person is only one key element; also of crucial importance is the probability of one's undergoing some detriment even though one has been obedient. Suppose that, if Joe significantly violates a legal norm during a certain period, the probability of his being apprehended and imprisoned during that period is 90%. Suppose further that, if he does not significantly violate any such norm during that period, the probability of incarceration is only 1%. In these circumstances, Joe manifestly has a strong punishment-centered incentive to comply with the norms of the legal system under which he lives. The incentive resides not simply in the highness of the 90% level but in the disparity between 90% and 1%. To see as much, let us suppose that the 1% figure were instead 90%. In that case, Joe would have no punishment-centered incentive at all to adjust his conduct in order to comply with the prevailing legal mandates. The probability of his under-going some punishment would not be lowered even slightly by his compliance. If the original 1% level were increased to 95%, then Joe would actually have a punishment-centered incentive to flout the norms of his legal system. By dis-obeying those norms, he would lower the probability of his being penalized.

In short, as can easily be discerned, the punishment-centered incentives for conformity with legal norms will vary directly with the probability of a person's being penalized in the aftermath of his nonconformity and inversely with the probability of a person's being penalized despite his eschewal of nonconformity. The overall punishment-centered incentive consists in the gap between those two probabilities. In my arguments concerning the tendency of the rule of law to promote punishment-centered incentives for obedience, one of my claims has been that those incentives decrease as the aforementioned gap decreases. The smaller the disparity between the two specified probabilities, the weaker the inducement for complying with the prevailing legal norms.[9] If for example the second of the two probabilities relating to Joe has increased from 1% to 50% while the first of the probabilities has remained at 90%, his punishment-centered incentive for restraining himself from transgressing the mandates of his legal system will have waned considerably. If his restraint of himself is burdensome, then the impairment of his punishment-centered incentive for obedience may well have tilted the balance of his motivations in favor of non-compliance. Much the same will be true, of course, in comparable situations involving other people. Thus, given that a legal system with its regularized effectuation of its mandates will generally keep low the probability of the infliction of punishments on people who heed those mandates, and given that it will generally keep high the prob-ability of the infliction of punishments on people who contravene the mandates, it will tend to foster incentives for obedience. It will typically fare much better in fostering such incentives than will a system of governance that persistently fails to effect a congruence between its norms as articulated and its norms as enforced.

---

[9] I am assuming here that the disparity will remain positive; that is, I am assuming that for a noncompliant person the probability of undergoing some officially inflicted detriment will remain higher than the probability for a compliant person.

On the basis of the last two paragraphs, we can now detect the central fallacy in Simmonds's line of reasoning. Before we look at that fallacy, however, we should glance at two minor objectionable aspects of his pronouncements. First, in statements that have been quoted above and in one statement that has not been quoted, Simmonds thrice refers to the *undermining* of incentives for obedience. In so doing, he conveys the impression that my arguments about the incentive-promoting advantages of the rule of law have suggested that substantial deviations from Fuller's eighth principle of legality will do away altogether with each person's punishment-centered incentives for compliance. In fact, my arguments have adverted to the *impairing* or *weakening* of such incentives rather than to the wholesale destruction of them. Only in extreme circumstances will any system of governance be so sweepingly erratic or so wildly incompetent as to undermine thoroughly everyone's punishment-centered incentives for conformity with its directives. In respect of such extreme circumstances, indeed, we can rightly query whether a system of genuine governance would be operative at all. Much more credible are situations in which the punishment-centered inducements for obedience have been attenuated rather than eliminated. Such situations—rather than the far less credible circumstances in which the inducements have been entirely eliminated—are what I have usually had in mind when pointing to the eventualities which the incentive-promoting tendency of the rule of law will help to avoid. My arguments which highlight that tendency have not implied that a regime's significant departures from the rule of law will perforce generate a state of affairs in which the disparity between the expected level of punishment for each disobedient person and the expected level of punishment for each obedient person is reduced to a ratio of 1:1. Rather, those arguments have more mildly and realistically indicated that such departures will lessen that disparity.

A second minor shortcoming in Simmonds's discussion surfaced briefly at the end of my last subsection. In his quotations from *In Defense of Legal Positivism* and in his own analyses, Simmonds glosses over the fact that the disparity just mentioned can be diminished not only by the frequent imposition of penalties on obedient people, but also by the frequent failure to impose penalties on disobedient people. This point is of some importance because a regime that falls markedly short in its adherence to rule-of-law principles will tend to impair incentives-for-compliance in each of these two directions. Both because of the relatively low level of coordination among its officials and because of the relatively abundant opportunities for corruption on their part,[10] such a regime

---

[10] I should note that corruption, in the sense of one's willingness to accept payments or other inducements in return for declining to enforce the norms which one is supposed to enforce, will in some contexts be morally preferable to one's unwavering performance of one's official role. When a guard in a Communist gulag or a Nazi concentration camp takes bribes in return for conniving at transgressions of the odious rules which he is supposed to enforce, he acts less appallingly than if he were to give effect to the rules with flinty unsparingness.

will typically be significantly underinclusive in its punitive measures against uncompliant people. Hence, even if Simmonds were correct about the effects of overinclusiveness, he would still have to confront the incentive-sapping effects of underinclusiveness.

In fact, however, Simmonds is wrong about the effects of overinclusiveness. His analysis of the matter, let us recall, is presented by reference to the two situations which he delineates: situations in which people are very frequently thrashed even if they have committed no infractions of the norms which they are called upon to obey. Let us suppose that—in application to each person during some period of time—the probability of undergoing a beating for any significant instance of disobedience is 90%, while the probability of undergoing a random beating is 50%. For the sake of simplicity, we should assume that nobody will engage in more than one significant violation of the prevailing norms, and we should further suppose that the 50% probability of anyone's undergoing a random beating is independent of the 50% probability of her undergoing some other random beating. We shall also initially assume that the probability of anyone's undergoing more than two random beatings during the specified period of time is 0.

To see how shallow Simmonds's understanding of the matter is, we should ponder the calibrated probabilities that obtain in the presence of extensive extra-legal brutality, and we should then compare them with the calibrated probabilities that would obtain under a regime that adheres quite steadily to the rule of law. Given the figures specified in my last paragraph, the probability of a law-violating person's undergoing exactly one beating is 27.5%, while the probability of a law-abiding person's undergoing exactly one beating is 50%. The probability of a law-violating person's undergoing exactly two beatings is 47.5%, while the probability of a law-abiding person's undergoing exactly two beatings is 25%. The probability of a law-violating person's undergoing exactly three beatings is 22.5%, while the corresponding probability for a law-abiding person is 0.

To contrast the situation just delineated with the situation that would obtain under the rule of law, we should now assume that the probability of each person's undergoing any random beating is 1% rather than 50%. For the moment, the other assumptions made in the penultimate paragraph above will remain intact. Given as much, the probability of a law-violating person's undergoing exactly one beating is 88.407%, while the probability of a law-abiding person's undergoing exactly one beating is 1.98%. The probability of a law-violating person's undergoing exactly two beatings is 1.783%, while the probability of a law-abiding person's undergoing exactly two beatings is 0.01%. The probability of a law-violating person's undergoing exactly three beatings is 0.009%, while the probability of a law-abiding person's undergoing three beatings is 0.

Thus, under the regime that frequently departs from Fuller's eighth principle, a law-violating person will encounter an expected level of beatings of $[(0.275 \times 1) + (0.475 \times 2) + (0.225 \times 3)] = 1.9$. (An expected level of beatings is a mean figure, like a life expectancy or an average number of children per family.) A law-abiding person under such a regime will encounter an expected level of beatings of $[(0.50 \times 1) + (0.25 \times 2)] = 1$. By contrast, a law-violating person under the regime that adheres more persistently to Fuller's eighth precept will encounter an expected level of beatings of $[(0.88407 \times 1) + (0.01783 \times 2) + (0.009 \times 3)] = 0.92$. A law-abiding person under such a regime will encounter an expected level of beatings of $[(0.0198 \times 1) + (0.0001 \times 2)] = 0.02$. Accordingly, if 'RL' designates the rule of law, and if 'ELB' designates the regime of numerous extra-legal beatings, and if 'LV' and 'LA' designate each law-violating person and each law-abiding person respectively, and if the numbers represent the expected levels of beatings during some period of time, Table 6.1 delineates the situation that confronts each person.

In short, although as an absolute quantity the disparity between the expected level of beatings for a law-violating person and the expected level of beatings for a law-abiding person is 0.90 under each regime, the disparity as a ratio is far greater under the regime of steady adherence to Fuller's principles than under the regime of frequent extra-legal violence. Under the latter regime the ratio is 19:10, whereas under the former regime it is 46:1. Consequently, by engaging in extra-legal brutality, officials will have weakened citizens' punishment-centered incentives for compliance with the law. Such brutality will have markedly lessened the difference between the prospects of disobedient people and the prospects of obedient people, as a proportionate matter. A citizen's conformity with the law under the regime that cleaves to Fuller's eighth principle will lower her expected level of beatings by nearly 98%, whereas her conformity with the law under the regime of procedurally aberrant violence will only lower her expected level of beatings by approximately 47.4%.

The upshot of my riposte to Simmonds is fully generalizable, and is not dependent on the specifics of the assumptions that have been adopted here. For example, let us now suppose that anyone during some period of time may undergo as many as three random beatings rather than only two. Let us further assume that the probability of each random beating is 50% under the regime of extra-legal violence and 1% under the regime of persistent adherence to Fuller's principles of legality. Under either regime, the probability of any random beating is independent of the probability of each of the other random beatings. If we retain the rest of our assumptions, the relevant calibrated probabilities are as follows. Under the regime of extra-legal brutality, the probability of a

Table 6.1.

	RL	ELB
LV	0.92	1.9
LA	0.02	1.0

law-violating person's undergoing exactly one thrashing is 15%, while the probability of a law-abiding person's undergoing exactly thrashing is 37.5%. The probability of a law-violating person's undergoing exactly two thrashings is 37.5%, and the probability of a law-abiding person's undergoing exactly two thrashings is likewise 37.5%. The probability of a law-violating person's undergoing exactly three thrashings is 35%, whereas the probability of a law-abiding person's undergoing exactly three thrashings is 12.5%. The probability of a law-violating person's undergoing exactly four thrashings is 11.25%, while the probability of a law-abiding person's undergoing four thrashings is 0.

Under the regime of steady adherence to the rule of law, the probability of a law-violating person's undergoing exactly one thrashing is 87.62094%, whereas the probability of a law-abiding person's undergoing exactly one thrashing is 2.9403%. The probability of a law-violating person's undergoing exactly two thrashings is 2.64924%, while the probability of a law-abiding person's undergoing exactly two thrashings is 0.0297%. The probability of a law-violating person's undergoing exactly three thrashings is 0.02674%, while the probability of a law-abiding person's undergoing exactly three thrashings is 0.0001%. The probability of a law-violating person's undergoing four thrashings is 0.00009%, while the probability of a law-abiding person's undergoing four thrashings is 0.

Hence, under the regime of frequent extra-legal violence, a law-violating person will encounter an expected level of thrashings of $[(0.15 \times 1) + (0.375 \times 2) + (0.35 \times 3) + (0.1125 \times 4)] = 2.4$. Under such a regime, a law-abiding person will encounter an expected level of thrashings of $[(0.375 \times 1) + (0.375 \times 2) + (0.125 \times 3)] = 1.5$. By contrast, under the regime of persistent adherence to the rule of law, a law-violating person will encounter an expected level of thrashings of $[(0.8762094 \times 1) + (0.0264924 \times 2) + (0.0002674 \times 3) + (0.0000009 \times 4)] = 0.93$. Under such a regime, a law-abiding person will encounter an expected level of thrashings of $[(0.029403 \times 1) + (0.000297 \times 2) + (0.000001 \times 3)] = 0.03$. The situation is encapsulated in Table 6.2.

Once again, then, the disparity between the expected level of thrashings for a law-violating person and the expected level of thrashings for a law-abiding person is a far higher ratio under a regime of law than under a regime of lawlessness. Under the former regime the ratio is 31:1, while under the latter regime the ratio is 8:5. Officials' acts of extra-legal violence will have weakened the punishment-centered incentives for citizens to conform to the law, because those acts will

Table 6.2.

	RL	ELB
LV	0.93	2.4
LA	0.03	1.5

proportionately have lessened the difference between the well-founded expectations of law-flouting citizens and the well-founded expectations of law-obeying citizens. A person's compliance with the law under the regime of procedural regularity will lower his expected level of thrashings by nearly 97%, whereas his compliance with the law under the regime of procedurally aberrant violence will lower his expected level of thrashings by only 37.5%. Simmonds has gone badly astray by failing to comprehend that lawless violence will lead in this fashion to a substantial impairment of citizens' punishment-centered incentives for obedience to the law.

Of course, the impairment of the punishment-centered incentives is not tantamount to their elimination. Though their force will be weakened under a regime whose officials indulge in a lot of random acts of brutality, they will continue to exist. Those incentives will undoubtedly still be strong enough to induce many people to comply with repugnant laws. However, for some people, the balance of motivations—the balance between the disagreeableness of complying with repulsive laws and the agreeableness of avoiding disobedience-triggered punishments—may well be tilted decisively in favor of disobedience, as a result of the attenuation of the punishment-centered incentives. At any rate, even if nobody's overall balance of motivations is tilted decisively in favor of disobedience, the punishment-centered incentives will have been diminished. What my previous writings on the rule of law have claimed is that ruthlessly self-interested officials will have strong reasons to maximize the punishment-centered incentives for citizens to conform to legal directives, and that the officials can best act upon those reasons by cleaving to Fuller's eighth principle. That claim stands, and Simmonds's attempted refutation of it is unsustainable.

To be sure, any situation in the real world will be less tidy than the scenarios which I have sketched. For one thing, the occurrence of some beating might impinge on the likelihood of the occurrence of another. Indeed, the potential ways in which the occurrence of one beating could affect the probability of the occurrence of another are myriad. We certainly cannot know a priori which of those ways—if any—will prove to be actual in any particular system of governance. Still, the basic point of my rejoinder to Simmonds would be wholly unimpeached by such possibilities, though the calculations underlying the rejoinder might become considerably more complicated. Thus, while recognizing that the occurrence of a punishment of either type (disobedience-triggered or random) could lower or raise the probability of the occurrence of another punishment of either type, we need not enquire here into those effects. Whether there will be any such effects in some particular system of governance, and whether they will be augmentative or diminutional, and how intense they might be, are plainly empirical questions that cannot be answered in the abstract. Fortunately, these and other untidy empirical questions can be put aside, since any answers to them will not detract at all from the correctness of my response to

Simmonds. Let us join him, then, in exploring these empirical complexities no further.

Before moving on to probe Simmonds's additional lines of reasoning, we should briefly examine his two scenarios in order to determine whether there are any significant differences between them. My remarks in the past several paragraphs have concentrated implicitly if not explicitly on the situation outlined in his first scenario, a situation of very frequent acts of random punishment. His second scenario, which adumbrates a regime that punishes people for 'activities obnoxious to the ruling powers' as well as for violations of the regime's promulgated norms, may be quite different. On the one hand, if the regime's categorization of ostensibly permissible activities as obnoxious is itself unpredictably capricious and continually shifting, then the second of Simmonds's scenarios does not differ from the first. On the other hand, the regime's categorization of ostensibly permissible activities as obnoxious might not be random at all. There might be clear and established patterns that are discernible by citizens who acquaint themselves with the regime's punitive measures. If so, then the regime's operations may well be sufficiently regularized and ascertainable to constitute a regime of law—at least after those operations have been running for some time. To be sure, as Simmonds indicates, the ostensibly permissible activities deemed by the regime to be obnoxious are 'not prohibited in any published and prospective rule'. Nevertheless, the practice of wreaking penalties on people who engage in those activities might be patterned and predictable to such an extent that the penalties are manifestations of implicit norms which can be grasped by any moderately intelligent citizen who observes the practice. Officials' acts of imposing the penalties would in effect be the means by which those norms are promulgated. Even when punishing people for engaging in ostensibly permissible activities, then, the regime would be operating in accordance with the Fullerian purpose of subjecting human conduct to the governance of norms. In that event, its workings cannot serve as the grounds for any conclusions about the tenability or vibrancy of a regime that does not govern through the rule of law. After all, those workings in such circumstances would amount to governance through the rule of law.

C. Simmonds's Second Major Retort

The next major retort by Simmonds pertains to my criticisms of his arguments about the securing of freedom through the rule of law. In the first edition of *Central Issues in Jurisprudence*, he delineated two regimes that are equally guilty of human-rights violations. One regime adheres quite closely to the Fullerian principles of legality, whereas the other departs from those principles frequently. Simmonds presumed that his readers would regard the first regime as morally superior to the second, and he traced that superiority to the inherent moral worth of the rule of law. As he rehearses the argument in the new edition of his book:

[C]ompliance with the eight [Fullerian] principles is a morally desirable feature of a legal regime because, amongst other reasons, it provides interstices of liberty within which the citizen can act freely, without the risk of interference. This not only provides the necessary framework for purposeful and creative activity, but also provides secure areas of freedom which may be exploited for the purpose of opposing the existing regime (which is, of course, one reason why evil regimes are unlikely to favour Fuller's principles). (Simmonds, *Issues*, 238)

Simmonds submits that I have responded to his example by claiming that the moral inferiority of the second regime must be due to the malignity of the regime's procedural deviations. Such a characterization of my response is simplistic, however. The fundamental point of my response has been that substantive factors, rather than the content-independent statuses of the procedural deviations as procedural deviations, are the key to the relative moral postures of Simmonds's two regimes (*IDLP*, 56–8). My contention to that effect has not been fixated on the moral tenor of the procedural deviations. Although that moral tenor is indeed a substantive factor that can be determinative in some contexts, different substantive factors—explored in my original discussion of this matter—are determinative in other contexts. Regardless of whether the procedural deviations of Simmonds's second regime are malevolent or benevolent, its moral standing vis-à-vis the first regime is attributable to substantive considerations rather than to the sheer fact that it has committed procedural aberrations.

Simmonds now seems to have gone quite a way toward embracing my view, since much of his reply on this matter is devoted to maintaining that some putatively benign procedural aberrations can turn out to be morally regrettable in the light of certain substantive considerations. By developing this point, with an example which we shall examine presently, he hopes to show that 'one may pay a moral cost even when wicked laws are left unenforced, or are enforced only sporadically; official deviations from legality may have consequences adverse for liberty even when they are motivated by benevolence' (Simmonds, *Issues*, 238). Although Simmonds strangely implies that the statement just quoted is at odds with my own position, it is in fact fully compatible therewith. For one thing, the modality of the quoted sentence—its twofold use of 'may' to denote possibility, in lieu of 'must' to denote necessity—is entirely apposite. Whereas Simmonds in the first edition of his book contended that procedural deviations *must* be morally regrettable at least prima facie, he here declares simply that they *may* be morally regrettable. That shift from the modality of necessity to the modality of possibility is very much in keeping with my own emphasis on the role of contingent substantive factors in determining the moral bearings of any procedural aberrations. Likewise in keeping with that emphasis is Simmonds's effort to substantiate his assertion with a textured scenario which highlights some of the complexities that might have to be taken into account by a moral assessment of any given departure from the Fullerian principles of legality. His adducing of such a scenario tallies nicely with my insistence that the moral status of any procedural deviation is a complicatedly context-specific matter that cannot be known a priori or in abstracto.

Simmonds asks us to ponder the plight of somebody who lives in great dissatisfaction under a repressive regime. Surrounded by neighbors who are all loyal supporters of the autocracy, the dissident is unwilling to hazard their wrath by expressing his opposition openly. He therefore resorts to a furtive maneuver through which he takes advantage of a harsh 7:00pm curfew that has been imposed by the oppressive regime. Knowing that the strict enforcement of the curfew will deter his neighbors from strolling outside and seeing what he is doing, the dissident releases carrier pigeons from his window each evening for the purpose of dropping subversive leaflets onto his neighbors' lawns. Were instead the curfew unenforced or only laxly enforced, he would not be able to carry out his rebellious endeavors with a similar sense of security against being detected. What this story illustrates, then, is that even the enforcement of a stiflingly severe law can generate morally salutary effects; conversely, the non-enforcement of such a law can generate morally detrimental effects. As Simmonds writes, 'even in the case of such a law, the regular enforcement of the law enables me to form stable expectations about the conduct of my fellow citizens; and those stable expectations are an important bulwark of my freedom' (Simmonds, *Issues*, 239). Though Simmonds forthrightly acknowledges that an official's refusal to enforce a draconian law such as the 7:00pm curfew might be morally beneficial on the whole, 'such benign deviations come at a general moral cost, in so far as they undermine the ability of law to encourage stable mutual expectations, such stability being itself a precondition for the pursuit of individual projects' (Simmonds, *Issues*, 239).

Now, on the one hand, a reader could rightly challenge the specific example which Simmonds has adduced. After all, if an iron-fisted regime monitors people's movements sufficiently closely to enforce a suffocating curfew rigorously, then the likelihood of its detecting the dissident's release of carrier pigeons will doubtless be at least as high as the likelihood of detection by a stray pedestrian or motorist in more relaxed circumstances. Hence, if the lack of security against detection in the latter set of circumstances would be regrettably freedom-impairing, much the same can be said *a fortiori* about the lack of security against detection in the former set of circumstances. (The dropping of the subversive leaflets is almost certainly illegal under a grimly repressive regime. Even in the overwhelmingly improbable event that the dropping of the leaflets is lawful, the regime's officials can inform the dissident's neighbors about his activities in order to arouse their ire.) Furthermore, given that the dissemination of insurrectionary leaflets is almost certainly illegal under a heavy-handedly repressive regime, the very situation which Simmonds depicts is a situation in which the law is not being enforced—in other words, a situation of procedural irregularity that is essential for the preservation of the dissident's freedom to spread his maverick literature.

On the other hand, although the specific example offered by Simmonds is open to major objections, the general point illustrated by it is unexceptionable. That point, of course, is that the moral status of any particular procedural deviation is often a complicated matter which we can ascertain only by keeping an eye out for the possible existence of several interacting substantive considerations. My own original analysis of procedural aberrations sought to establish just such a point.

Simmonds, however, appears to draw a rather different message from his scenario. To be sure, he does allow that 'laws can reduce personal security as well as protect it. The same regime that imposes the 7 p.m. curfew may also confer upon Party members a right to search my home, and may enact laws prohibiting me from offering any physical resistance to their actions.' He further allows that '[i]f the judges deviate from a law of this type (whether by penalising the Party members or by refusing to punish me for my resistance to their actions) they will to that extent respect and protect my security on this occasion'. But he immediately adds: 'Precisely in being unregulated, however, such official deviations are unpredictable. They consequently fail to provide me with any domain within which I can confidently feel free from potential interference.' He contrasts such a precarious state of affairs with that established by a legal system which adheres to Fuller's principles and which consequently 'will (simply in virtue of being such a system of laws) inevitably provide the citizen with certain domains where interference is predictably excluded' (Simmonds, *Issues*, 239–40).

Two key contentions in these quoted statements—two closely related contentions—should receive some critical scrutiny here. First, Simmonds maintains that procedural deviations are never sufficiently predictable to enable anyone to feel confidently free from interference. Such a claim is an unconvincing dogma, however. On the vast majority of roads in virtually any English or American municipality, the probability of being penalized for violating a jaywalking ordinance is effectively zero. The probability of no penalties is much higher than the probability that one's rights against the theft of one's computer will be given effect through the apprehension and punishment of anybody who violates those rights. Even if we assume that the enforcement of those rights against theft is sufficiently predictable to be in compliance with Fuller's eighth principle of legality, the probability of such enforcement in relevant sets of circumstances will be considerably lower than the probability of the non-enforcement of laws that prohibit jaywalking. Admittedly, not all procedural deviations will be as solidly predictable as the non-enforcement of the jaywalking ordinances. However, the degree of predictability for sundry deviations is a variable empirical matter, rather than something that can be known and sweepingly proclaimed without any empirical investigation. If the procedural deviations described in the quotations from Simmonds in my last paragraph are highly predictable—as they might be—then they offer some highly predictable protection for the person whose premises would otherwise be subject to untrammeled searches. The predictability of that protection could well be greater than the predictability of the protection afforded by the effectuation of many of the person's legal rights.

Second, an equally dubious claim by Simmonds is his assertion that every legal system will inevitably provide each citizen with 'certain domains where interference is predictably excluded'. For one thing, as has already been remarked, his own example of the dissemination of subversive leaflets via carrier pigeons does not reveal a domain where interference is predictably excluded. Instead, it points to a domain in which the interference of intrusive governmental officials is highly likely as they watch for misbehavior while monitoring people's obedience to curfew-establishing dictates. Even if we put that objection aside for the moment, moreover, Simmonds's assertion is demonstrably false. Simmonds tries to ensure its truth by stipulating that people who enjoy no legal protections at all within some society are 'not . . . governed by law, but excluded from the scope of the legal system' (Simmonds, *Issues*, 240 n.9). Yet we can discern the falsity of his thesis without having to contemplate a setting in which somebody enjoys no legal protections at all. Let us simply think back to his scenario in which some person's premises and body are subject to being searched at any time by Party members. Let us suppose that that person enjoys ample legal protections against people who are not Party members, and that he accordingly is by no means 'excluded from the scope of the legal system'. Notwithstanding those protections, the person is legally unshielded against continual searches by the devotees of the Party. As a result, his life is susceptible to constant disruption. He cannot avail himself of any 'domains where interference is predictably excluded'. Wherever he ventures and whatever he does within his society, he is liable to undergo inspections at any moment by Party functionaries.

A woman can experience a comparable plight in a deeply patriarchal society. Suppose that a wife in such a society does not enjoy any legal protections at all against beatings and searches and other forms of mistreatment undertaken by her husband or his servants. She is legally forbidden to put up any resistance. We may further suppose that she is legally shielded against all such forms of mistreatment undertaken by people outside her household, and that she is therefore not excluded from the protective ambit of the legal system under which she lives. Nonetheless, her legally ordained exposure to the attacks perpetrated by her husband and his servants is a state that leaves her perpetually vulnerable to the thwarting of any projects that she might pursue. Were she to try to fend off those attacks, she would not only suffer further onslaughts but would also render herself liable to legal punishment. She lives her life in constant insecurity, as her legal system ensures that she cannot find any refuge in which she can escape the tribulation of worrying about the domineering interference that persistently besets her.

Many other examples could be adduced to reveal the falsity of Simmonds's claim about the salutary consequence that will inevitably follow from the existence of a legal system. Let us move on, however, to plumb two important sentences in which Simmonds synopsizes the message to be gleaned from his discussion: 'Human nature and human circumstances being what they are, things will generally be best when we have clear, published, prospective rules that are consistently enforced. Only in this way can we enjoy domains of liberty secure from official interference, and the interference of other citizens; only in this way can we form reliable expectations about the conduct of others that are sufficient to permit the formulation and pursuit of individual plans and projects' (Simmonds, *Issues*, 240). In his arguments contested by my last couple of paragraphs, Simmonds characterizes the existence of law as a sufficient condition for certain salutary consequences. In these two new sentences, he instead much more sensibly characterizes the existence of law as a *necessary* condition for certain salutary consequences. The first of the quoted sentences is indeed wholly unexceptionable, for it articulates a point which I myself have elsewhere highlighted in an even stronger form. As is declared in *In Defense of Legal Positivism*, the existence of law in any society larger than a handful of families is indispensable for the attainment of basic orderliness and coordination, which are desiderata of enormous moral importance (*IDLP*, 209). Insofar as the second of the two sentences in the extract above is a recapitulation of the first sentence, it too is unobjectionable—though it comes uncomfortably close to reiterating the fallacious claim that procedural deviations can never be sufficiently predictable to enable anyone to feel confidently free from potential interference.

What should be queried, then, is not the two quoted sentences in themselves, but the use to which they are put by Simmonds. He includes them in support of his contention that compliance with the Fullerian principles of legality is inherently a moral virtue. Those principles, he believes, are indeed the inner morality of law. In fact, however, the two quoted sentences do not support such a position. Let us reflect on two considerations.

First, and less important, the initial sentence in the quoted passage would be equally true if it were about roads—and about other channels of transportation such as waterways, which substitute for roads in some societies—rather than about conformity with the Fullerian precepts. Yet it would be silly rather than illuminating to describe the principles of road-building or of road-maintenance as the inner morality of roads. Much the same can be said about the principles of crop-growing.

Second, and more important, the two quoted sentences together are insufficient to generate the conclusion which Simmonds attempts to derive from them. They correctly indicate that the rule of law is essential for the realization of desiderata of great moral importance, but a premise affirming that very fact is not a basis from which we can validly conclude that the rule of law is inherently a morally worthy state of affairs. After all, as has been argued at length in *In Defense of Legal Positivism*, the rule of law is essential for the prosecution of wicked oppression on a large scale over long periods. If Simmonds's premise were sufficient to warrant his conclusion, then this point about wicked oppression would be sufficient to warrant the conclusion that the rule of law is inherently evil. In actuality, of course, we should draw neither of these conclusions. From the fact that the rule of law is indispensable for the perpetration of large-scale projects of evil over long periods, we should not infer that it is intrinsically deplorable or suspect. Equally, from the fact that the rule of law is indispensable for the attainment of orderliness and coordination and solid individual freedom, we should not infer that it is intrinsically commendable. Its moral status is determined by the varying roles which it performs, rather than by its sheer nature as the rule of law.

When bringing to a close the interrelated lines of argument which we have been probing in this subsection, Simmonds emphasizes the uncertainties under which our moral judgments have to be made. He chides philosophers for 'dreaming up hypothetical scenarios where all the circumstances and consequences of my actions are known', and he somewhat condescendingly sighs that 'life is not so simple, nor are we ever so well-informed as in the examples of philosophers'. In elaboration of this point, he refers back to his example of the dissemination of subversive leaflets through carrier pigeons:

We act under uncertainty, and the moral standards that guide us are intended for such conditions. Thus we must say that, even in the case of a wicked law, there is a moral cost in the deviation from standards of legality. The judge called upon to enforce an unjust curfew may feel that he sacrifices nothing of value by allowing the accused to escape punishment; but, by contributing to a situation wherein enforcement of the curfew cannot be relied upon, he may expose the author of subversive leaflets to hostile action of a kind sufficient to curtail his freedom. (Simmonds, *Issues*, 241)

For present purposes, let us leave aside the fact that the scenario of the carrier pigeons does not in fact illustrate the specific point which Simmonds hopes to demonstrate with it. That is, as has already been observed, it does not reveal to us a situation in which a beleaguered dissident enjoys a domain of secure freedom. All the same, as has also been observed, the general message of the example survives the failure of its specific point. What Simmonds helps to underscore is that our moral evaluations of procedural aberrations will often involve a host of difficulties and subtleties as we have to remain alert to the potential presence of sundry substantive considerations that may countervail one another. My criticisms of him should not obscure the correctness of that general message—a message which indeed can and will be turned against him.

One shortcoming in Simmonds's remarks is his apparent assumption that attentiveness to moral complexities will inevitably redound to the benefit of his anti-positivist position. His slightly supercilious posture of worldly-wisdom is undoubtedly appropriate in response to some positivist accounts of the moral status of procedural deviations, but it is likewise appropriate in response to many anti-positivist accounts. In fact, one of the chief aims of my analyses of these matters in *In Defense of Legal Positivism* was to call attention to complicating factors that have frequently been overlooked by theorists who submit that the compliance of legal-governmental officials with Fullerian principles is invariably promotive of freedom. For example, although Simmonds contends that I 'ignor[e] the fact that my actions may be impinged upon by the acts of other citizens, and the ability of other citizens so to interfere with my liberty is in part dependent upon the regularity with which the law is enforced' (Simmonds, *Issues*, 238), my earlier book actually laid stress on that very fact in order to expose some of the oversimplifications in anti-positivist arguments (*IDLP*, 55). An alertness to complexities of that sort is at least as serviceable for the legal-positivist approach to the rule of law as for any opposing approach.

Furthermore, the sheer imaginability of additional complexities does not always mean that they are present. It is false to suggest that we must inevitably be omitting some relevant consideration(s) when we pass judgment on this or that instance of a procedural deviation. Simmonds swerves disconcertingly from the modality of possibility to the modality of necessity when discussing this matter. He initially asserts that, even in ostensibly clear-cut cases, 'the fact *may* remain that there *are* conflicting considerations in such cases, even if some are relatively insubstantial by comparison with others' (Simmonds, *Issues*, 241, first emphasis added). In this statement, the modal auxiliary verb 'may' aptly signals a possibility to which any assessment of a procedural aberration should be attuned. However, just a few sentences later—in a statement quoted above—Simmonds proclaims that 'we *must* say that, even in the case of a wicked law, there is a moral cost in the deviation from standards of legality' (Simmonds, *Issues*, 241, emphasis added). This switch to the modality of necessity is unsustainably dogmatic. Our attentiveness to the possibility of multiple competing substantive considerations in our moral appraisals of procedural deviations does not commit us to the conclusion that substantive factors militating against the deviations are invariably present. In other words, it does not commit us to the conclusion that legal positivism is wrong. On the contrary, just such attentiveness has been a prime weapon wielded by positivists against the unduly sweeping assertions of their opponents.

Indeed, despite his relapse into dogmatism, Simmonds has effectively conceded the gist of the legal-positivist position. In *In Defense of Legal Positivism*, the question posed by my original critique of his comments on the moral status of procedural deviations was whether such deviations are at all morally objectionable purely on the ground that they are procedural deviations. My critique endeavored to show that the answer to that question is negative; in circumstances where procedural aberrations are at all wrong, they are so because of their substantive character or because of other substantive factors. By focusing on substantive complications that might be operative in situations where legal mandates have gone unenforced, Simmonds evinces a proper orientation. He directs attention to the same considerations that would be viewed as decisive by a legal positivist. His only misstep lies in assuming that substantive complications which tell prima facie against the correctness of procedural deviations will always be operative.

Simmonds leaves himself prone to such a misstep partly because of the example of a wicked law on which he concentrates. Although a 7:00pm curfew is plainly a repressive mandate, one can quite readily imagine circumstances in which it would be morally desirable (if only as a short-term or medium-term measure), and—along with Simmonds—one can even more readily imagine circumstances in which the non-enforcement of such a mandate would be morally detrimental as well as morally valuable. To concentrate on such a law is hence to make the task of the anti-positivist theorist far too easy. If Simmonds had instead concentrated on a much more rebarbative legal directive, he would not have been able to maintain persuasively that some complicating factors which tell prima facie against departures from that directive will always be present. Especially if the departures have become regularized, but even if they have not, they will often be unequivocally benign. To be sure, conditions are conceivable under which the effectuation of even the most flagitious legal mandate will produce some morally commendable results (which will undoubtedly be out-weighed by the morally deplorable results of the effectuation). However, a claim that such conditions will invariably or typically be present is an implausible dogma rather than an insight.

Simmonds resorts to one further tack in the closing portion of the discussion on which we have trained our scrutiny in this subsection. He seeks to uphold the status of the rule of law as something of inherent moral worth by analogizing it to basic moral virtues such as promise-keeping and kindness. Acknowledging that compliance with Fuller's principles of legality will sometimes lead to morally regrettable outcomes, he writes:

Analogously, honesty is a moral virtue; but telling the truth does not always lead to the best outcome, nor is it always the right thing to do (*e.g.* a mad axeman, with obvious intent, asks me for your whereabouts). To demonstrate that honesty or promise-keeping or kindness is a virtue we need to show that human nature and circumstances being what they are, things will generally go better if the truth is told, promises are kept, and kindness exhibited. Sometimes, it is right to tell a lie, break a promise, or cause pain that could have been avoided. In each such case, however, something of moral importance is sacrificed. (Simmonds, *Issues*, 240)

We should straightaway notice again that Simmonds's consequentialist test for identifying something as a moral virtue is plainly too broad. After all, it would classify road-maintenance and crop-growing and electricity-generation as moral virtues. Simmonds offers no reason for thinking that the rule of law is to be assimilated to promise-keeping rather than to road-building.

Moreover, even if we put aside that test, the analogy between the rule of law and the moral virtues mentioned by Simmonds is inapposite. Let us begin with promise-keeping. Unlike the rule of law (from a positivist perspective), that virtue contains a built-in moral component. That is, an undertaking is not a promise unless its substance and circumstances are such that there is at least one prima-facie moral reason in favor of its being fulfilled. If there is no such prima-facie moral reason, then an undertaking is not a genuine promise at all. For example, if Joe indicates to Mary that he will torture and murder some man who has annoyed her by wearing a blue shirt with brown trousers, there is no prima-facie moral reason whatsoever in favor of Joe's acting in accordance with his undertaking. Mary may have formed eager expectations on the basis of the undertaking, but she has proceeded illegitimately in so doing. The dashing of her expectations through the nonfulfillment of the undertaking is not a consideration that militates in favor of its fulfillment at all. Accordingly, the undertaking is not a genuine promise, and the practice of promise-keeping does not encompass the actions by which Joe would effectuate his pledge to Mary. Precisely because an undertaking is a genuine promise only if in its substance and circumstances it satisfies a threshold test of prima-facie moral commendability, the practice of promising and of promise-keeping is crucially different from the rule of law as understood by legal positivists. That practice is inherently moral in its bearings, whereas the rule of law is not. Hence, an analogy between them for Simmonds's purposes is inappropriate.

Note that the point made in the last paragraph goes markedly beyond something which Simmonds himself concedes and indeed emphasizes: namely, the fact that the keeping of a promise will not always lead to a morally optimal outcome. Simmonds's acknowledgment of that fact *sans plus* leaves fully intact his view that the practice of abiding by undertakings is a moral virtue in that there will always be some prima-facie moral reason(s) in favor of any instance of that practice. What my example of Joe and Mary is meant to disclose is that countless situations can arise in which there are not even prima-facie moral reasons in favor of the keeping of ostensible promises. Exactly because there are no such reasons, those ostensible promises must be ruled out as promises—if the practice of promise-keeping is to be analyzed as inherently virtuous. Whereas Simmonds's acknowledgment is wholly compatible with the notion that all undertakings impose prima-facie obligations of fulfillment, my argument has maintained that only promises impose such obligations and that promises are only a proper subset of undertakings.

To be sure, my example of Joe and Mary or any relevantly similar scenario could be embellished to include some complicating factor that would involve a moral reason for the fulfillment of an iniquitous pledge. For instance, the story of Joe and Mary might be amplified to include a significant possibility of harm to some innocent third party in the event of Joe's failure to act in accordance with his pledge. Or perhaps Joe will become more inclined to renege on important promises in the future, if he retreats from his current undertaking to Mary. Albeit such a cause for concern would undoubtedly be hugely overtopped by the moral reasons against his adherence to that undertaking, it would be a consideration weighing in favor of his torturing and murdering the blue-shirted man. Nevertheless, although there can in some circumstances be prima-facie moral reasons for carrying out wicked pledges, we have no grounds for thinking that there will be such reasons in all circumstances—just as we have absolutely no grounds for thinking that some complicating factors which militate against benign departures from the terms of pernicious legal mandates will always be present. In a situation like that of Joe and Mary, indeed, the existence of creditable moral reasons in favor of the fulfillment of his undertaking will be exceptional rather than typical. In such a situation, then, there will typically not be any prima-facie moral consideration that supports the keeping of an ostensible promise. Hence, unless we are prepared to accept the outlandish thesis that an action can be the exercise of a moral virtue even though there are no moral reasons whatsoever for performing the action, we shall have to conclude that some ostensible promises are not genuine promises despite meeting all the formal conditions for that status. Substantive moral constraints must be satisfied, on top of those formal conditions.

Of course, we could adopt a positivist approach to the practice of promise-keeping and could submit that that practice does not include any necessary moral component along the lines suggested here. According to such an approach, Joe has indeed made a genuine promise to Mary, and his slaying of the hapless man with the blue shirt will indeed be an instance of the practice of promise-keeping. No substantive constraints avert such a classification, as the only conditions required for the occurrence of a promise are formal. Though an approach of that type would be perfectly coherent, it would not tally with the characterization of promise-keeping as a veritable moral virtue. When combined with such a characterization, the positivist approach would yield the unacceptable conclusion that the torturing and the murdering of the man with the blue shirt are acts whereby Joe exercises a virtue. Thus, while the adoption of a purely formal approach to the practice of promise-keeping would allow Simmonds to draw analogies between that practice and the rule of law as understood by legal positivists, it would disallow him from invoking the analogies as grounds for deeming the rule of law to be an inherent moral virtue.

Should we embrace an anti-positivist conception of the rule of law as well as of promises? Such a tack would enable the drawing of analogies between the two and would also enable the designation of the rule of law as something inherently of moral value. This hypothetical question can be construed in either of two ways, neither of which will elicit a very long reply here. First, it can be construed as asking why anyone should become or remain a legal positivist rather than a natural-law theorist. There is not really any need for me to address such an inquiry sustainedly in this chapter, since *In Defense of Legal Positivism*—especially in its methodological sections (*IDLP*, 179–82, 232–9)—is a book-length answer. Alternatively, the hypothetical question can be understood as asking why one should differentiate between one's analytical approach to the rule of law and one's analytical approach to the practice of promise-keeping. Though any full-scale answer to this inquiry would lead us much too far afield, a very terse reply can address the first inquiry as well.

As I have argued at length in my earlier book on these matters, a positivist conception of law is to be commended on theoretical-explanatory grounds. We should opt for such a conception in preference to any natural-law approach because our doing so will advance various analytical objectives, such as the ferreting out of the reasons-for-action that confront legal officials or the pin-pointing of relationships among different types of social institutions. Theoretical desiderata such as clarity and precision and explanatory comprehensiveness and elucidative power and parsimony and coherence are the touchstones for deeming the legal-positivist perspective to be superior to the natural-law viewpoint. By contrast, those theoretical objectives would not similarly be furthered by the selection of a positivist perspective for one's analysis of the practice of promise-keeping. In particular, the distinctive reasons-for-action operative in that practice would not best be unearthed through the adoption of such a perspective.[11] Although these assertions about an optimal understanding of promise-keeping will not receive any substantiation within the confines of this chapter—in which my main positivist contentions about law do not hinge in any way on these ancillary assertions about promises—some of the salient differences between law and promises should signal the correctness of what has been said here. Most notable, of course, is the fact that promise-keeping does not typically involve operations of large-scale governance and dominance, whereas law does indeed typically involve such operations. The respective reasons-for-action that are applicable, and the best ways of becoming and remaining attuned to those reasons, are bound to differ between the legal domain and the promissory domain.

A number of the general points made in my last several paragraphs about the practice of promise-keeping are straightforwardly transferable to a discussion of acts of kindness, *mutatis mutandis*. Notwithstanding that some such acts are regrettable on the whole—for example, a generous donation of alms to a beggar who proceeds to spend the money on drugs and alcohol—there are always prima-facie moral reasons for engaging in such acts. Indeed, the invariable existence of such reasons is plainer in connection with deeds of kindness than in connection with promises. Whereas the act of promising can be described in purely formal terms, and whereas a positivist approach to the analysis of promises and promise-keeping is therefore perfectly feasible, the very characterization of something as a deed of kindness conveys that it is impelled by a substantively worthy motivation. Given such an underlying motivation, there will inevitably be some prima-facie moral consideration in favor of each kind deed. The prima-facie consideration

---

[11] In this discussion, I am using the phrase 'reasons-for-action' without the restrictions attached to it in the earlier portions of this chapter.

may be markedly outweighed by countervailing factors in this or that context, but the sheer status of some instance of behavior as an act of kindness entails that there is something to be said for it. To ascribe that status to some portion of a person's conduct is to indicate at the very least that what the person has done is not entirely bad. Hence, there is no germane parallel between acts of kindness and the acts whereby officials give effect to legal norms in accordance with Fuller's eighth principle. Whereas all actions of the former type are supported by prima-facie moral considerations in their favor, not all actions of the latter type are so supported. Some deviations from the terms of wicked legal norms are unequivocally benign, in that nothing whatsoever of moral significance is lost through them. A failure to engage in one of those utterly harmless and benevolent deviations would be unequivocally bad. By contrast, a kind deed is never unequivocally bad, even when it is bad on the whole. Consequently, Simmonds cannot rightly invoke kind deeds as illuminating analogues of official acts of compliance with Fuller's principles.

Honesty is rather different from promise-keeping and especially from kindness, in that its status as an inherent moral virtue is quite doubtful. (For present purposes, there is not really any need to distinguish systematically between a narrower conception of honesty as sincerity in communication and a broader conception of honesty as the avoidance of lying.) On the one hand, the mere fact that telling the truth will sometimes yield an undesirable outcome is not in itself sufficient to negate the status of honesty as a moral virtue. Simmonds is correct to contend as much. On the other hand, there are numerous sets of circumstances in which one's refusal to communicate sincerely is unequivocally good. Nothing of moral value is lost through such a refusal. In each of those sets of circumstances, that is, there are no prima-facie moral reasons at all in favor of communicating sincerely. Simmonds himself adverts to one type of situation—discussed frequently since the time of Plato—in which there will typically be no such moral reasons. Suppose that Jane is confronted by a madman with a plainly murderous intent, who asks her to specify the whereabouts of Ken (of which Jane is cognizant). In the absence of special complicating factors, Jane will be unequivocally justified in declining to tell the truth. Whether she prevaricates or simply says nothing, she will not be acting athwart any prima-facie moral considerations that weigh in favor of her revealing Ken's location. She will not be using the madman purely as a means by lying to him, since she will be preventing him from debasing himself by stooping to the crime of murder; consequently, the consideration that she should never use somebody else purely as a means is inoperative here as a factor that militates against her lying.[12] Nor will her dashing of the madman's expectation of her veracity count against her telling an untruth. In the circumstances, any such expectation on his part is utterly illegitimate, and

---

[12] Indeed, although Jane probably is primarily concerned to save Ken, it is conceivable that she is primarily concerned to preserve the moral integrity of the madman.

thus there is no reason for her to satisfy it. In the absence of somewhat far-fetched complexities, such as a likelihood of harm to innocent parties arising from her mendacity, Jane will be unreservedly justified in departing from her normal practice of speaking truthfully. Such a departure will not involve a sacrifice of anything that is morally valuable. Telling the truth to the madman would not amount to the exercise of a moral virtue, even prima facie. In this respect, then, deviations from the practice of truthful communication and deviations from the terms of laws are on a par. Though most deviations of either type are regrettable at least prima facie, some deviations of each type are not regrettable to the slightest degree. (In case these contentions about sincere communication might seem to rest unduly on one rather shopworn scenario, I should mention that many other scenarios would serve just as well. For example, innumerable situations involving disclosures by blackmailers or revelations of classified infor- mation to terrorists can very plausibly be such that there are not even any prima- facie moral reasons in favor of such instances of truth-telling.)

Note, incidentally, that sometimes the option of remaining silent will be unequivocally unacceptable, albeit not as often as the option of speaking sin- cerely. Suppose that the madman knows that Jane is aware of the path down which Ken has fled. The madman says to her sincerely and fiercely: 'If you tell me that Ken has fled down the left-hand path, then I shall infer that he has indeed gone down that way, and I will chase after him. If you tell me instead that he has fled down the right-hand path, *or if you say nothing*, then I shall infer that he has gone down that way, and I will chase after him in order to slay him.' Let us suppose that Ken has fled down the right-hand path. In this situation, Jane's saying nothing would be as disastrously misguided as her telling the truth. In the absence of special complicating factors, there are no considerations in favor of her speaking sincerely, and there are likewise no considerations in favor of her remaining reticent. In the absence of special complexities—which, though they might be present, will certainly not inevitably be present—all the applicable moral reasons militate in favor of her telling the madman a lie. As has been contended in my last paragraph, his expectation of her veracity does not carry any moral weight whatsoever in the circumstances, and her lying to him will not consist in her using him purely as a means (since the deception will spare him from sullying himself with the degrading crime of murder, and will thereby help to preserve his moral integrity). Consequently, nothing of moral value is sacrificed through her telling him an untruth. Far from constituting the exercise of a virtue, her refraining from prevarication would in the circumstances be a course of conduct for which there are no valid moral reasons at all.

In sum, whereas promise-keeping and kindness are inherent moral virtues— any departure from which is bound to involve a sacrifice of something morally significant, even if the departure is justified on the whole—honesty in either its narrower sense or its wider sense does not partake of a similar status. In that respect, of course, it is fundamentally akin to the rule of law and to compliance with Fuller's principles. Just as some deviations from the strict enforcement of legal norms by officials are unequivocally good, much the same is true of some deviations from truthfulness. Thus, although Simmonds is correct in suggesting a homology between complying with Fuller's principles and being honest, he is wrong to think that the homology warrants our classifying the strict enforcement of legal mandates as a moral virtue. The homology obtains precisely because neither honesty nor the strict enforcement of legal mandates is such a virtue. Whenever dishonesty or the non-enforcement of a legal requirement is morally regrettable (at least prima facie), it is so because of substantive considerations rather than because of anything intrinsic to honesty or to conformity with Fuller's eighth principle.

Of course, somebody enamored of a natural-law approach to legal systems and legal norms might feel inclined to adopt a similar approach to instances of dishonesty. That is, such a theorist might insist that apparent instances of dishonesty must be subjected to a moral test before we can conclude that they are genuine instances of dishonesty. Under that test, any apparent instance will not count as a genuine instance if there are no moral considerations at all that militate against it. Such a test will therefore generate the conclusion that Jane has not departed from strict honesty when she lies to the madman about Ken's location. Now, although such an approach is not incoherent, it is weirdly dogmatic and wooden. We can of course meaningfully say that Jane has not evinced the personality-trait of dishonesty in uttering her untruth (if she is generally a truthful person), but it is bizarre to deny that she has not been honest in her statement to the madman. In other words, it is bizarre to deny that somebody on the occasion of telling a lie has not been honest about the state of affairs concerning which she has deliberately deceived someone else. In order to avoid such bizarre implications, we should eschew anything along the lines of a natural-law approach to honesty and should accept that honesty in either its broader sense or its narrower sense is not inherently a moral virtue.

Accordingly, Simmonds fails in his attempt to bolster his position by drawing parallels between the effectuation of legal norms and the keeping of promises or the manifesting of kindness or the telling of truths. Exactly because the keeping of promises and the manifesting of kindness are inherently moral virtues, there are no relevant parallels between them and the strict effectuation of legal directives. By contrast, some relevant affinities do obtain between the effectuation of legal mandates and the telling of truths; but the affinities reside precisely in the fact that neither the effectuation of mandates nor the telling of truths is something that will never be unequivocally wrong. Like the moral status of any instance of honesty, the moral status of any instance of compliance with Fuller's eighth principle is determined by substantive factors whose presence or absence is not ordained by the sheer nature of the instantiated property.

D. Simmonds's Third Major Retort

Simmonds launches a final piquant challenge to legal positivism by asking us to contemplate an imaginary society called 'New Monia' (Simmonds, *Issues*, 244–9). Drawing creatively on the work of Max Gluckman, he recounts a very small and simple society in which the means of giving effect to settlements of disputes are highly limited. Because of the absence of police forces and prisons, and because of the dense multifacetedness of people's relationships with one another, the dominant manner of dealing with disputes is to press the parties toward compromise and reconciliation. The focus for defusing any conflict will lie on the overall relationship between the parties and on the need for give-and-take, rather than on the specific point of contention that has kindled strife between them. Each party will be expected to concede some ground on that specific point in order to sustain and improve his overall ties with the other party.

Simmonds conjures up his scenario of New Monia in order to compare the arrangements for dispute-resolution in such a society with the corresponding arrangements in modern liberal-democratic societies. Parties to a dispute in a liberal-democratic country such as the United Kingdom or the United States might be able to resolve their differences through negotiation and compromise, but they might instead end up in court. If their conflict does become the object of legal proceedings, their respective entitlements will be settled by reference to norms that are applicable to the specific point of contention between them. The focus of the court will not lie on the overall relationship between the parties; rather, the specific controversy will be treated largely in isolation from broader contexts. Nor will the court's primary aim be to effect a compromise-based reconciliation between the parties. Although a settlement of the differences between them will remain a possibility especially in the early stages of the proceedings, the principal task of the court is to find in favor of one party or the other by fixing the respective entitlements of each. Instead of seeking harmony through a process of give-and-take, the court is in the business of producing winners and losers.

Although Simmonds views the society of New Monia quite favorably, he observes that its approach to dispute-resolution is not without drawbacks. 'New Monia pays a price for its desirable features, and the price is paid in individual liberty' (Simmonds, *Issues*, 246). Within a legal system like that of England, he maintains, individuals will be able to ascertain with considerable confidence and precision the things which they are at liberty to do. Moreover, they will be permitted to do those things irrespective of the feelings and sensibilities of other people. There is no need for compromise or concessions on the part of anyone, so long as she is within the scope of her entitlements. Things are quite different in New Monia. Whenever somebody there behaves in a way that annoys somebody else to more than a trivial extent, he or she may well be authoritatively pressured to desist from the behavior in order to avert a deeper rift. New Monians favor cohesion and stability over individual freedom. 'My ability to stand foursquare within my established rights and to tell the world to go to the devil is severely reduced' (Simmonds, *Issues*, 247). Simmonds proceeds to deliver a general statement of the dissimilarities between the posture of the individual in an advanced legal system and the posture of the individual in New Monia:

Clear, published, prospective rules that are meticulously enforced by officials therefore serve liberty. No matter how narrowly the content of the rules may constrain my freedom, the very fact that they are ascertainable rules, and are reliably enforced, is likely to give me certain areas of entitlement within which I will be free from interference. In the world of New Monian compromise, by contrast, I will never be wholly free to behave in a manner that my fellows consider unacceptable or obnoxious. (Simmonds, *Issues*, 247)

Before we go on to consider why Simmonds has introduced the contrast that is epitomized in this passage, we should investigate the contrast itself. Although Simmonds has written competently elsewhere on Wesley Hohfeld's analysis of the four main types of entitlements that are commonly designated as 'rights',[13] he here uses the term 'rights' quite loosely. He describes the situation of the individual under the English legal regime as follows: 'I know that I can behave in eccentric ways that my neighbours may object to: but, if I am acting within my legal rights, the law will protect me' (Simmonds, *Issues*, 247). This quoted sentence is correct if 'rights' is a reference to claim-rights against interference with one's engaging in some activities, or (more likely) if it is a reference to such claim-rights combined with legal liberties to engage in those activities. So long as claim-rights against interference with one's performance of some action are operative, the law will indeed protect that performance. However, at this juncture in his discussion, Simmonds is focusing on legal liberties rather than on claim-rights. He is pondering a scenario in which two neighbors annoy each other by using their respective premises in irritating ways. Unable to reach a compromise, they wind up in court where each sues the other. 'The court will seek to decide who is and is not acting within their rights' (Simmonds, *Issues*, 246)—by which is meant that the court will seek to decide whether each party is or is not legally at liberty to use her premises in the annoying manner for which she has opted. Thus, the reference by Simmonds slightly later to the protective role of rights is at best misleading. When entitlements designated as 'rights' are legal liberties, they are protective only in the sense that legal enforcement mechanisms cannot successfully be mobilized to prevent their exercise.

The point made in the foregoing paragraph is more than a terminological quibble. Once we recognize that many legal liberties are not accompanied by claim-rights against all types of interference with their exercise, we can see that

---

[13] Simmonds, *Issues*, chap. 8; N.E. Simmonds, 'Rights at the Cutting Edge', in Matthew H. Kramer, N.E. Simmonds, and Hillel Steiner, *A Debate over Rights* (Oxford: Oxford University Press, 1998), 113, 146–95.

Simmonds's statements about the solid freedom of the individual under the rule of law are unduly sweeping. To discern as much, we should probe a lightly modified version of his own example. Suppose that a landowner Leonard plants a hideous shrub near the boundary between his plot of land and an adjacent plot that belongs to Michael. Michael complains bitterly about the eyesore that has been introduced by Leonard, but his expostulations come to nought. Michael therefore sues Leonard. He fails, however, as the court decides that Leonard is legally at liberty to plant and keep the shrub on his land. Unable to counteract Leonard's avocation through the courts, Michael instead erects a high fence that blocks off the sunshine which the shrub needs in order to flourish. The shrub withers and dies, as Leonard fumes. He brings a lawsuit against Michael, but he loses as the court decides that Michael is legally at liberty to build the fence and to obscure the sunlight. Thus, although Leonard has been found to be acting 'within his rights' (that is, within his legal liberties), he has discovered that he cannot with impunity 'behave in eccentric ways that my neighbours may object to' or 'tell the world to go to the devil'.

Of course, the failure of the lawsuit by Leonard was hardly inevitable. Had the law been different, the court could have found him to be endowed with legal rights against interference with his shrub-growing (either against interference generally or against the specific sort of interference undertaken by Michael). The point of this example has certainly not been to indicate that there will never be any protected leeway for eccentric behavior by individuals under the rule of law. Rather, the point has been to highlight the fact that there are countless areas of *damnum absque injuria* within the law. Leonard is akin to other people in being frequently doomed to failure if he seeks to avail himself of the protective force of the law against somebody else's interference with his idiosyncratic pursuits.

Although Leonard can know that he will not be prevented by legal officials from indulging his penchant for hideous shrubs, he cannot be similarly confident about a lack of obstruction from his fellow citizens such as Michael. Simmonds's neglect of this instance and the myriad other instances of *damnum absque injuria* in the law is one respect, then, in which his comments about the posture of the individual under the rule of law are too sweeping. (In an earlier section of his replies to me which we have already examined, Simmonds himself offers a good example of *damnum absque injuria*. When the votaries of some political party are legally at liberty to search a dissident's home at any time, her privacy will not be legally protected against their intrusions.) Perhaps even more important, however, are two other respects—overlapping respects—in which Simmonds has exaggerated the connection between the rule of law and individual freedom.

First, a legal system can bestow a suffocatingly extensive degree of protection on each individual against the eccentric behavior of other people. Suppose that, instead of failing in his lawsuit against Leonard, Michael has prevailed. With the backing of the enforcement mechanisms of the state, he has effectively obliged

Leonard to uproot the ugly shrub. Suppose further that Michael decides none-theless to erect a garish fence on the border between his plot of land and Leonard's plot. Outraged by the fence, and thirsting for revenge in any event, Leonard seeks an injunction against the implementation of Michael's plan. Let us suppose that he succeeds. In this new version of the Leonard/Michael scenario, then, neither man is permitted to behave in an eccentric fashion that irritates his neighbor. Whereas the initial version of the scenario involves legal liberties on each side of the dispute, this new version involves legal duties. Each man is obligated to conform his behavior to the sensibilities of the other. If the obliga-tions extend over many potential facets of their conduct, then each of them probably enjoys less latitude for idiosyncratic projects than is enjoyed by the typical inhabitant of New Monia. To be sure, it should go without saying that such a state of affairs under the rule of law is not inevitable; but such a state of affairs is indeed possible, and accordingly Simmonds's contrast between the promotion of harmony in New Monia and the promotion of freedom under the rule of law is simplistic.

Second, equally important as a ground for querying Simmonds's stark contrast is the fact that the rule of law will typically be administered by an elaborate governmental apparatus, which can monitor and regulate people's behavior with stifling efficiency. If officials use that apparatus for the squelching of dissent and the exploitation of the citizenry, they may well limit the freedom of most people even more stringently than does the emphasis on solidarity in New Monia. In the principal passage quoted above, Simmonds maintains that a system of legal norms will secure certain domains of freedom for each person regardless of how severely the norms curtail the range of things which each person is legally permitted to do. He juxtaposes that situation with the situation of individuals in New Monia, who are 'never...wholly free to behave in a manner that [their] fellows consider unacceptable or obnoxious'. His comparison is eminently plaus-ible in connection with liberal-democratic regimes of law, which undoubtedly intrude less into people's lives than does the conformity-inducing peer pressure in New Monia. However, the comparison is much less cogent in connection with repressively illiberal regimes, where the regularized enforcement of harshly restrictive mandates tends to ensure that individuals enjoy even less freedom than do New Monians. Because the relations among the New Monians are egalitarian to quite a considerable extent, each person will have reasons for putting up with some objectionable modes of behavior on the part of his fellows; each can thereby incline his fellows to put up with his own peculiarities. Contrariwise, evil officials wielding dominance over hapless citizens do not have similar reasons to adopt a live-and-let-live stance of forbearance. They need not look to citizens for tolerance, and thus they have no reasons to endeavor to elicit it through reciprocal indulgence. Consequently, Simmonds's blanket comparison between the New Monian system and every legal system is far from compelling. We have no grounds for thinking that every credible legal system will endow individuals with more solid freedom than will the New Monian system of peer pressure.

Let us now explore why Simmonds has drawn his contrast between the reconciliatory processes in New Monia and the rule of law. He explains that he is addressing the question whether officials' compliance with the Fullerian principles of legality is a genuine moral virtue. For that purpose, he rightly contends, we should not be comparing two full-fledged legal regimes of differing degrees of benignity. Instead, the baseline for comparison should be a mode of governance that does not operate through the rule of law. New Monia is ideally suited to serve as that baseline, for it is 'a reasonably attractive society which is just and humane but which attaches little or no importance to the meticulous enforcement of clear, published and prospective rules' (Simmonds, *Issues*, 249).

Simmonds is plainly correct in maintaining that the germane contrast is not between two legal regimes, and he is likewise correct in submitting that the New Monian system of governance is an excellent baseline for comparison. What is objectionable is the other side of his contrast. That is, although his resort to New Monia as a baseline for a comparison with a legal system is unexceptionable, his implicit resort to a morally commendable legal system as the counterpart for a comparison with New Monia is open to criticism. If we are seeking to gauge whether the rule of law is morally worthy, we must be careful not to mistake the worthiness of the contents of certain legal norms for the inherent worthiness of the rule of law itself. To avoid the prejudicing of our enquiry in that fashion, we should compare the arrangements in New Monia with those of an iniquitous legal system. Given that the contents of the norms in such a system are deplorable, we can be confident that any respects in which the arrangements of New Monia prove inferior will be due to the moral significance of the rule of law itself. Only by proceeding in this manner can we be sure that the outcome of our enquiry has not been distorted by the presence of substantive elements of worthiness (in a legal system) that are extrinsic to the principles of legality.

Yet, as has already been observed, a comparison between New Monia and an odiously repressive legal regime will by no means inevitably reveal that the scheme of governance in New Monia is less promotive of individual freedom than the dissent-stifling legal system with which it is being compared. On the contrary, the strict effectuation of the mandates in that legal system will tend to ensure that individuals within its jurisdiction are cramped even more severely in their activities than are the New Monians. If the officials in the system were considerably more relaxed in their enforcement of the especially draconian directives laid down by their regime, the situation of the people subject to those directives would perhaps compare favorably with the situation of the people subject to peer pressure in New Monia. Precisely because the officials are not relaxed in their enforcement of the draconian directives, however, the individuals governed by the repressive legal regime are very likely possessed of less leeway than the individuals in New Monia.

In short, Simmonds's latest line of argument has turned out to be as unavailing as his previous rejoinders. His efforts to defend an account of the Fullerian principles as the inner morality of law are dexterous and illuminating, as can be inferred from the length of my replies. Nevertheless, those efforts have foundered. Because compliance with the Fullerian principles is strongly service-able for the aims of evil officials who are driven by purely prudential consider-ations relating to the bolstering of their own exploitative power, and because such compliance is not inherently a moral virtue in any of the senses broached by Simmonds, the designation of those principles as the 'inner morality of law' is inapposite. Such a designation is untenable regardless of whether morality is understood in contradistinction to prudence or is instead understood in contra-distinction to badness.

III. Soper on the Claims of Law

In a powerfully impressive book that refreshingly sheds light on an array of topics in legal and political philosophy,[14] Soper has argued that an essential feature of any veritable legal system is that it presents itself as morally legitimate and its mandates as morally correct. On the one hand, the principal target in the jurisprudential chapters of his book is the quite widespread view (associated most notably with Joseph Raz) that any veritable legal system presents itself not only as morally legitimate but also as morally obligatory. On the other hand, Soper's additional main target is my positivist view that a legal system need not present its mandates and operations as either morally obligatory or morally legitimate. His arguments against his primary target are largely cogent; but, as will be maintained here, his arguments against legal positivism are less successful.

Soper declares that an ostensible legal system making no claim either to obligatoriness or to legitimacy would amount to an enterprise of 'purely coercive power' (Soper, *Ethics*, 54). He suggests that such a system would not be norma-tive at all and that it would therefore lack an essential dimension of any genuine legal regime—a dimension which, he maintains, has been recognized by legal positivists such as H.L.A. Hart. However, like David Dyzenhaus in my fifth chapter, Soper is clearly using 'normative' interchangeably with 'moral'; as a consequence, both his contention about Hart and his contention about norma-tivity as an essential feature of any legal system are unsustainable. Contrariwise, if we instead construe 'normative' more broadly to mean 'concerning what ought to be' or 'concerning what is required by general standards of conduct', then we should endorse Soper's claim about Hart and his claim about normativity as an essential property of every legal regime. However, we should then reject his

---

[14] Philip Soper, *The Ethics of Deference* (Cambridge: Cambridge University Press, 2002) [hereinafter cited as Soper, *Ethics*].

suggestion that an apparent legal system which makes no claim to moral legitimacy is not a normative system and is therefore not a genuine legal system.

In accordance with Fuller's first and eighth principles of legality, any veritable legal system will operate through the creation and effectuation of general norms. Those norms specify the patterns of conduct which people are required to adopt or eschew in order to avoid being subject to penalties imposed by the system. The specifications of the patterns of conduct are general standards by reference to which the officials who run the legal system can gauge each person's behavior. Whether the norms of the system present citizens with punishment-independent reasons for obedience or not, they do indeed constitute general standards which the citizens are called upon to heed. In this key respect, then, every veritable legal system is normative rather than purely coercive. Instead of governing solely through situation-specific orders in the manner of a typical gunman, a legal regime governs through general norms that apply to innumerable circumstances. Those norms might not bespeak any more solicitude for the well-being of citizens than do the typical orders of a gunman, but their form is quite distinct.

Thus, by complying with Fuller's first principle of legality and also with each of his other principles, a wicked legal regime that advances no claim to moral legitimacy will be operating as a normative system. Its functioning is very different from the typical issuance of behests by a gunman to his victims, even though the attitudes of the regime's officials toward the citizenry are doubtless just as callously exploitative as the gunman's attitude toward his victims. To glimpse another salient respect in which an evil legal system's functioning is normative rather than purely coercive, we should turn our attention to the interaction among the officials of the system. As has been argued at length in my earlier book on legal positivism (*IDLP*, 62–71, 94, 99–100), the interaction among officials will inevitably be normative in that they will have to coordinate their activities by assessing the actions and decisions of one another and by articulating prescriptions on the basis of their assessments. Given that the officials in the heinous regime here envisaged are motivated purely by prudential considerations, the tenor of the prescriptive statements which they address to one another—the tenor of the 'ought' in each such statement—will be prudential rather than moral. Nevertheless, as has been remarked in my fifth chapter's rejoinders to Dyzenhaus, prudential normativity is indeed one major variety of normativity. Prudential prescriptions express judgments concerning how things ought to be. Hence, not only do officials exert their sway through a normative apparatus when they have recourse to general standards of conduct in order to determine the legal consequences of people's doings; in addition, their exhortative and argumentative exchanges with one another imbue their regime with normativity.

In short, even if an apparent legal system does not put forward any claim to moral legitimacy, its workings are normative through and through. The power that is wielded by way of those workings is mediated and coordinated through their normativity. Let us now ponder whether an apparent legal system of the sort just described is credibly classifiable as a genuine legal system. Soper offers three arguments against such a classification, which we shall consider in turn.

First, he contends that no legal-governmental system outside the comical fantasies of Monty Python would ever designate its own mandates as unjust or morally illegitimate. No minimally credible legal regime would be managed in part by a Ministry of Injustice, and no such regime—however evil it might be— would proclaim the reprehensibleness of its own directives. Every full-fledged legal system will present its directives and operations as morally irreproachable. Whether those directives and operations are in fact morally irreproachable is of course always a live question; however, whether a regime of law will *present itself* as morally legitimate is a question to which the answer is invariably and knowably affirmative, or so Soper maintains. No tenable regime ever systematically expresses disapproval of its own workings (Soper, *Ethics*, 56–8).

Soper is surely correct in believing that no realistic legal system, however rebarbative, will continually denounce itself as morally abhorrent. Although some maverick officials might give voice to an attitude of revulsion when discussing their regime or some of its mandates, the regime as a whole will not persistently condemn itself and its workings—if it is to remain a viable regime. Systematic self-condemnation is a logical possibility, of course, but it is not a minimally credible possibility. Soper is right to dismiss it as undeserving of serious contemplation. However, he errs in thinking that his dismissal of such a scenario is sufficient to vindicate his view that every genuine legal system will claim to be morally legitimate. He fails to distinguish adequately between claiming legitimacy and not disclaiming it. Although it is true that every realistic legal regime will not deny its own legitimacy, we should hardly infer that every such regime will claim to be legitimate. 'Affirming' and 'not denying' are not equivalent; the former entails the latter, but not vice versa. An iniquitously exploitative legal regime might credibly deal with the question of its own moral status by disregarding the matter altogether. No such regime will disavow all legitimacy by characterizing itself as deplorable, but some regimes might well display complete indifference to the issue. When officials do exhibit such indifference, they will not have advanced a claim to legitimacy either in their pronouncements or in the substance of their mandates. Their regime will not *repudiate* such a claim, but it need not *put forward* such a claim, either. Indeed, the officials in many a wickedly exploitative legal system will probably be strategically well advised to leave unaddressed the question of the legitimacy of their dominion, since any pretensions to justice on their part would sound unconvincingly hollow and would thus merely draw attention to their lack of legitimacy. A posture of wholesale indifference, which ignores all questions of justice instead of highlighting them and their importance by addressing them unpersuasively, can be the optimal stance for the officials in a legal system that patently does not show solicitude for citizens. Such a posture of disdainful indifference could credibly be found outside the world of Monty Python.[15]

Soper resorts to a second line of argument in support of his thesis that an apparent legal system is not a veritable legal system unless it purports to be morally legitimate and presents its mandates as morally correct. He declares that, if any mode of governance does not so present its mandates, its workings will be inconsistent with some basic attributes of any legal system. Most notably, by effacing the distinction between having an obligation and being obliged (that is, being coerced), it will disallow the use of deontic language in its operations. Since the use of such language is an elementary feature of any legal system, we should realize that professions of moral correctness on the part of the people who run each system are likewise such a feature. So Soper argues. He seeks to drive his point home by quoting some vivid statements from Raz, who wrote them for a somewhat different purpose: 'We are to imagine courts imprisoning people without finding them guilty of any offense. Damages are ordered, but no one has a duty to pay them. The legislature never claims to impose duties of care or of contribution to common services. It merely pronounces that people who behave in certain ways will be made to suffer.'[16] Soper submits that we cannot fathom the ludicrousness of Raz's deliberately absurd scenario unless we grasp that the modes of governance which he deems 'purely coercive' are not genuine legal systems at all. Precisely because every genuine legal system commends itself as morally legitimate and its directives as morally correct, it employs deontic language in the creation and implementation of those directives.

The main shortcoming in the argument just summarized is that it begs the question by taking as given a key premise that has been assailed by Hart and by me.[17] That is, the argument presupposes that the terminology of 'obligation' or 'duty' carries the same meaning in legal contexts as in moral contexts. If that assumption is granted, then the rest of the argument follows. After all, if Soper is right in contending that legal regimes do not profess to engender content-independent moral obligations, then any such regime that purports to be imposing and applying moral obligations must be claiming in effect that the

---

[15] For a longer version of this riposte to Soper, see *IDLP,* 103–8.

[16] Joseph Raz, *The Morality of Freedom* (Oxford: Clarendon Press, 1986), 27, quoted in Soper, *Ethics,* 70.

[17] For a discussion of Hart's views on the matter, see *IDLP,* 81–3. For my own views, see ibid., at 78–112. Soper later suggests that '[s]tatements of legal obligation are at most only statements about what one ought to do, not statements about the [moral] obligations that subjects have' (Soper, *Ethics,* 90). However, his discussion at that subsequent juncture is puzzling in itself and is inconsistent with his earlier analyses, which admittedly deny that statements of legal obligations are statements of *content-independent* moral obligations but which affirm that they are indeed statements of moral obligations. At any rate, even if the sentence just quoted were to be regarded as the definitive expression of Soper's view, my response in the text would not have to be altered very much. Instead of highlighting the fact that the language of 'obligation' carries meanings in legal discourse that are importantly different from its meanings in moral discourse, I would make a largely parallel point about the language of 'ought' (which in a legal context can be centered purely on the prudential desideratum of avoiding punishment).

contents of its mandates are morally correct. Thus, if a regime advances no such claim of moral correctness, it does not purport to be imposing and applying moral obligations, and it accordingly does not employ deontic language when invoking its norms.

However, there is no reason to grant Soper's assumption. Although the meaning attached to the terminology of 'obligation' or 'duty' in a legal context clearly overlaps with the meaning attached to that terminology in a moral context, the dissimilarities are even more important. On the one hand, a legal obligation is like a moral obligation in being a requirement established by some authoritative norm(s). To fulfill a legal or moral obligation is to act in accordance with the terms of the legal or moral mandate(s) by which it has been imposed, and to breach a legal or moral obligation is to act at odds with the terms of the aforementioned legal or moral mandate(s). To breach a legal or moral obligation is to commit a legal or moral wrong. In these respects, the implications of deontic language in the legal domain and in the moral domain are cognate.[18] On the other hand, however, those several formal homologies are accompanied by a conspicuous divergence. Whereas the moral principles that impose moral duties always stand as objectively valid moral reasons for compliance with what they require, the legal directives that impose legal duties do not always constitute such reasons. Some legal directives, indeed, do not provide any punishment-independent reasons for compliance on the part of their addressees. Not all legal obligations are moral obligations, and not all legal wrongs (that is, not all breaches of legal obligations) are moral wrongs.

Thus, the language of 'obligation' or 'duty' is fully available to legal regimes that do not make any pretensions to moral correctness. When used by any legal regime—whether benign or malign—such language denotes requirements imposed directly or indirectly by the regime's general mandates. Exactly because the requirements are grounded directly or indirectly in those mandates, they are normative in the sense of following from general standards for conduct. When deontic language is used by an evil legal regime that does not purport to be laying down morally correct directives, the language indicates normativity only in the sense just specified. The deontic terminology does not bespeak or suggest any substantive correspondence between the legal directives and moral principles. All the same, that language is perfectly appropriate for requirements stemming from general norms that are generated and sustained by the normative interactions of officials. Those requirements can be invoked as such by officials who apply the norms and who need to specify why they are inflicting penalties on people who have behaved in certain ways. (The felt need to specify the normative grounds for the penalties does not perforce derive from the ascription of any importance to moral accountability. Rather, it can arise from the aim of giving people effective direction and palpable incentives for obedience.) Accordingly, while we should

---

[18] For a discussion of some further similarities, see Hart, *Concept*, 166–8.

agree with Soper and Raz that an apparent legal system would not be a genuine legal system if it made no use of deontic language, we have no grounds for thinking that such language will be eschewed by a repressive and exploitative regime that does not claim to be imposing morally correct requirements. We therefore have no grounds for thinking that such a regime cannot be a full-fledged system of law.[19]

Soper falls back upon one further argument. He pursues a methodological tack by explaining that, if anyone adopts the optimal theoretical stance for a political and legal philosopher, he or she will reject the notion that a regime which advances no claim to moral legitimacy or obligatoriness is classifiable as a regime of law: 'By designating as legal only regimes that claim a certain kind of authority, we at least preserve the possibility of justifying obedience to law and defending the legitimacy of state coercion. To preserve that possibility, which underlies such a long history of theoretical inquiry and debate, is enough by itself to explain why coercive systems are distinguished in practice and language from legal systems' (Soper, *Ethics*, 71). Soper correctly remarks that this methodological line of reasoning does not presuppose that the only modes of governance classifiable as legal systems are those which are endowed with moral legitimacy or moral obligatoriness. He thus feels confident that he has not damagingly begged any questions:

Note that this explanation—insisting that our current understanding of the concept of law is one that requires preserving the *possibility* of defending the legitimacy of the state and/or citizen obligation—does not beg the question. We are not saying that legal systems must be such as to ensure moral fidelity or state legitimacy. . . . We are only preserving the possibility of showing legitimacy, thus making plausible the continued attempts to ground citizen obligation or state legitimacy. The coercive system, which dooms from the start any ability to establish moral legitimacy, is for that very reason worth differentiating from legal systems. (Soper, *Ethics*, 71 n.38, emphasis in original)

Soper is right in asserting that he has not begged the question in the manner which he has outlined. Yet he has begged the question in a deeper and subtler fashion. He takes for granted that the proper methodological stance for any legal philosopher is fundamentally justificatory. In his eyes, the role of the legal philosopher is to distil the essential properties of law in such a way that the attribution of moral legitimacy or moral obligatoriness to each legal system is a live possibility. Although that justificatory project does not flagrantly beg the question by withholding the designation of 'legal system' *ab initio* from every mode of governance that lacks moral legitimacy or moral obligatoriness, it begs the question less obtrusively by withholding that designation *ab initio* from every mode of governance that does not stand any serious chance of turning out to

---

[19] Raz offers additional arguments for so thinking, but I have endeavoured to rebut each of them in the fourth chapter of *In Defense of Legal Positivism*.

possess legitimacy or obligatoriness. For Soper, such a move is warranted because the chief aim of legal philosophy is to vindicate the moral status of law.

As should be evident from the methodological sections of *In Defense of Legal Positivism* to which the present chapter has already adverted,[20] my own orientation in these matters is strikingly different from that of Soper. Instead of starting from the premise that the role of legal philosophy is fundamentally justificatory, my approach is resolutely theoretical-explanatory. What counts in favor of a conception of law is not its serviceability for a justificatory endeavor, but its serviceability for the enterprise of understanding the complex functions of various social phenomena. Of particular interest, as has already been noted, are the reasons-for-action faced by the officials who run legal institutions. We can best fathom those reasons-for-action, and we can best come to grips with the diversity of the functions of those institutions, if we opt for a wider conception of law in preference to a more restrictive conception. Most notably, we can grasp that the very features of law which in liberal-democratic societies render it expressive and promotive of worthy moral ideals are features which in illiberal societies render law essential for the continuation of oppression and exploitation on a large scale. Because of the followability of legal mandates, which ensues from their satisfaction of the Fullerian precepts of legality, it behooves just rulers and unjust rulers alike to govern through legal institutions. Such an insight may not be compatible with a justificatory approach to law, but it alerts us to the rich multifariousness of law's effects. It thereby enhances our understanding of social phenomena more generally.

A full substantiation of these methodological remarks is neither possible nor necessary within the confines of this chapter. It is not possible, because it would amount to quite a lengthy book; and it is not necessary, because *In Defense of Legal Positivism* has already undertaken the task. What should be emphasized here, then, is simply that the methodological position taken up by Soper is not a neutral standpoint from which he can avoid begging the question. In plumping for a justificatory orientation, he has preordained his arrival at an anti-positivist conclusion about the proper restrictiveness of the concept of law. An austerely theoretical-explanatory orientation would lead to quite a different conclusion.

In sum, admirable though Soper's overall account of law is in many respects, it is no more successful than Simmonds in repelling legal positivists' challenges to the moral bearings of the rule of law. When those challenges are judged by reference to their own ambitions, rather than by reference to profoundly anti-positivist ambitions, they prove to be resilient.

---

[20] See *IDLP*, 179–82, 232–9. Soper states that I have not addressed the methodological question which he is posing (Soper, *Ethics*, 65, 71 n.38). Though I do not squarely tackle the question in either of the two chapters of *In Defense of Legal Positivism* on which he focuses, I do address it elsewhere in that book.

7

On the Separability of Law and Morality

If there is one doctrine distinctively associated with legal positivism, it is the separability of law and morality. Both in disputation with classical natural-law thinkers and in response to more recent theorists such as Lon Fuller and Ronald Dworkin, positivists have endeavored to dissolve any number of ostensibly necessary connections between the legal domain and the moral domain. Although jurisprudential positivists characteristically occupy themselves with quite a few other analyses and contentions as well, of course, their principal aim has been to establish that the essential properties of law do not include moral bearings (irrespective of whether morality is understood in contrast with immorality or with prudence or with factuality). Such is the prevailing view of legal positivism among people familiar with jurisprudence, and the prevailing view is correct.

During the past couple of decades, however, that prevailing view has come into question among some estimable legal positivists. In particular, Joseph Raz and his disciples have queried the importance and the very tenability of an insistence on the separability of law and morality. Some other positivists, influenced to varying degrees by Raz, have likewise queried whether such an insistence is a key component of the positivist outlook. In the present chapter, we shall examine the most prominent lines of argument which these theorists have marshaled in opposition to the traditional image of the orientation of legal positivism. As will be maintained, those lines of reasoning do not succeed in throwing any serious doubt on either the sustainability or the significance of the notion that law and morality are disjoinable. When that notion is properly understood as a multiplicity of theses, it proves to be resistant to the challenges that have been mounted against it. Neither reproaches nor dismissals have inflicted any serious damage on it.

I. Missed Connections

Let us begin by looking at a rather curious argument from the Razian camp. John Gardner, a staunch and perceptive defender of Razian positions, has recently derided any ascription to legal positivism of the thesis that there are no necessary connections between law and morality. Asserting that the attribution of such a thesis to jurisprudential positivism is the propagation of a myth, Gardner writes: 'This thesis is absurd and no legal philosopher of note has ever endorsed it as it stands. After all, there is a necessary connection between law and morality if law and morality are necessarily *alike* in any way. And of course they are. If nothing else, they are necessarily alike in both necessarily comprising some valid norms.'[1] Exactly why someone as astute as Gardner has opted for such a wooden approach to the matter is not clear. He treats an approximation or a slogan as if it were propounded as a precisely true statement, and he thereby proceeds to discredit it in a dismayingly captious fashion.

We can tell that something has gone amiss, by the fact that Gardner's argument would support the postulation of necessary connections between morality and absolutely anything else. For example, morality and the third-largest moon of the planet Jupiter are alike in that neither of them is a custard pie. They are further alike in that neither of them is a piece of blank paper. And so forth; the similarities between morality and the third-largest moon of Jupiter are truly innumerable, and therefore by Gardner's lights the necessary connections between the two are innumerable. Much the same can be said, of course, about the necessary connections between morality and anything else (such as a custard pie or a piece of blank paper or an umbrella). Hence, any claim that there are no necessary connections between morality and the third-largest moon of Jupiter is false, strictly speaking. Yet, in most contexts, to gainsay such a claim would be more risibly misleading than to affirm it. If there is ever an occasion for a denial of necessary connections between morality and the third-largest moon of Jupiter, the denial will almost certainly be put forward as an approximation that is illuminating and true in all germane respects. It need not and will not be put forward as something that is strictly true in all conceivable respects. It is a convenient bit of shorthand that suitably draws attention to the features of the third-largest moon of Jupiter—such as a lack of any nontrivial bearing on the satisfaction of human interests—which endow that moon with the status of a non-moral phenomenon. Only somebody regrettably unattuned to the purpose of such a shorthand formulation could think that anything worthwhile is achieved by one's pointing out that the formulation is not strictly true in every conceivable respect. (Note that this paragraph's point about 'negative' likenesses can easily be extended to encompass 'affirmative' likenesses. For example, Gardner's argument leads to the conclusion that there are many necessary connections between morality and the number 31, on the ground that every proposition of morality is like the number 31 in being an abstract object and thus in being possessed of all the properties of any abstract object. Much the same can be said

---

[1] John Gardner, 'Legal Positivism: 5½ Myths', 46 *American Journal of Jurisprudence* 199, 223 (2001) [hereinafter cited as Gardner, 'Myths'], emphasis in original, footnote omitted. For a similar view, see Joseph Raz, 'About Morality and the Nature of Law', 48 *American Journal of Jurisprudence* 1, 2–3 (2003) [hereinafter cited as Raz, 'Morality'].

about the necessary connections between morality and the number 32. And so on.)

To be sure, the connections between morality and law are considerably more salient than the connections between morality and any of the non-moral phenomena mentioned in the preceding paragraph. Law is by no means a non-moral phenomenon.[2] Gardner is correct when he declares that 'there are many other necessary connections between law and morality on top of this rather insubstantial one [namely, the fact that each of them consists of norms]', and he is likewise correct in observing that 'legal positivists have often taken great pains to assert [some of the law-morality connections]' (Gardner, 'Myths', 223). Nevertheless, his misstep is basically the same as the misstep committed by somebody who would balk at the claim that there are no necessary connections between morality and a blank piece of paper or a planetary moon. That is, Gardner is dismissing an approximation as if it had been articulated as something other than an approximation. In the case of the relationship between law and morality, the precise truth behind the slogan of 'no necessary connections' is that positivists deny the necessity of nearly every one of the major law-morality links that have been postulated by natural-law theorists of varying persuasions. Anyone familiar with the debates between positivists and their opponents should have no difficulty in construing the aforementioned slogan appropriately. To be acquainted with those debates is to be acquainted with the sundry theses that together constitute the positivist insistence on the separability of law and morality (theses about which more will be said later). So long as the 'no necessary connections' formulation is understood with reference to those debates, it will be recognized as an approximate recapitulation of the positivist theses rather than as a boldly independent affirmation that goes untenably beyond them. In its broadly recapitulatory role, which can readily be grasped by someone attentive to its context, the 'no necessary connections' motto is undeserving of scorn. It is no worse than the many other approximations that sum up complex philosophical positions.

---

[2] Leslie Green suggests that somebody who insists on the separability of law and morality will be obscuring the fact that law is not a non-moral phenomenon. See Leslie Green, 'Legal Positivism', in Edward Zalta (ed.), *Stanford Encyclopedia of Philosophy* (Spring 2003 edn), URL =<http://plato. stanford.edu/archives/spr2003/entries/legal-positivism/>. As I have endeavored to emphasize in my earlier book on legal positivism, however, such a suggestion is mistaken. See Matthew H. Kramer, *In Defense of Legal Positivism* (Oxford: Oxford University Press, 1999) [hereinafter cited as *IDLP*], 122–5, 189–91, 200–4. When legal positivists insist on the separability of law and morality, they are referring to morality in three senses: morality contrasted with immorality, morality contrasted with prudence, and morality contrasted with factuality. They are not also adverting to a division between moral matters and non-moral matters, and therefore they are not submitting that law belongs on the non-moral side of such a division. That is, nobody has ever maintained that legal norms and decisions have no significant bearing on the interests of the people affected by them. Nor, consequently, has anyone ever maintained that legal norms and decisions are not appropriately subject to moral appraisal. Silly theses asserting the non-moral character of law can be eschewed, and are eschewed, by theorists who affirm the separability of law and morality. We can easily see as much when we disentangle the different ways in which morality is to be understood.

(Similarly, it is no worse than the countless approximations that crop up in other contexts. If a historian contends that there were no connections between the assassination of James Garfield in the United States in 1881 and the assassination of Indira Gandhi in India in 1984, a Gardnerian interpreter will pronounce such a statement to be false. After all, each assassination occurred in the ninth decade of a century; each involved a victim whose English surname begins with 'G'; each consisted in the killing of the leader of a large nation; neither of the killings was a custard pie; and so forth. By contrast, when the historian's statement is properly construed—that is, when it is construed as a pithy disaffirmation of many specific links that might be posited between the two murderous events—it is very likely true. Anyone who genuinely engages with the historian as an interlocutor will opt for the latter construal of his claim, and will perceive any Gardnerian riposte to that claim as mystifying rather than enlightening.)

Dealing in a heavy-handed manner with the 'no necessary connections' formulation, Gardner reproves H.L.A. Hart for using that formulation. He writes that Hart's 'apparent endorsements of [the "no necessary connections" slogan] must be read as bungled preliminary attempts to formulate and defend [a much narrower version of legal positivism]' (Gardner, 'Myths', 223). Instead of upbraiding Hart for bungling, we should recognize that his employment of the 'no necessary connections' language was intended in the same spirit as his repeated invocation of the phrase 'separation of law and morals'.[3] That is, he used such expressions as shorthand for an array of theses with which he denied 'that there are any important necessary connections between law and morality'.[4] Undoubtedly most prominent among those theses was an affirmation of the distinction between the law as it is and the law as it should be—a distinction which, in its Razian guise, is central to Gardner's own understanding of legal positivism. However, Hart went beyond that affirmation and contested many other supposedly necessary links between law and morality. For example, he persistently maintained that the motivations underlying officials' compliance with rule-of-law requirements can credibly be prudential rather than moral.[5] He likewise assailed Fuller's contention that the basic formal characteristics of legal norms and legal systems constitute an inner morality of law.[6] We shall

---

[3] H.L.A. Hart, 'Positivism and the Separation of Law and Morals', in *Essays in Jurisprudence and Philosophy* (Oxford: Clarendon Press, 1983) [hereinafter cited as Hart, 'Positivism'], 49.

[4] H.L.A. Hart, 'Introduction', in *Essays in Jurisprudence and Philosophy* (Oxford: Clarendon Press, 1983) [hereinafter cited as Hart, 'Introduction'], 1, 6.

[5] See, e.g., H.L.A. Hart, *The Concept of Law* (Oxford: Clarendon Press, 1961) [hereinafter cited as Hart, *Concept*], 198–9.

[6] See, e.g., H.L.A. Hart, 'Lon L. Fuller: *The Morality of Law*', in *Essays in Jurisprudence and Philosophy* (Oxford: Clarendon Press, 1983), 343. Gardner, cleaving to a narrow conception of legal positivism, appears to endorse a Fullerian position. Gardner, 'Myths', 210, 226. (The narrow conception of legal positivism has become *de rigueur* among Razians. See, e.g., Andrei Marmor, 'The Rule of Law and its Limits', 23 *Law and Philosophy* 1, 41–3 (2004).) Gardner cites the tepid approval of Fuller's stance in Hart's early work, but he omits to mention that Hart accepted Fuller's claims chiefly in order to

consider further examples of Hartian challenges to ineluctable law-morality connections presently.

Hart made clear from the outset that he was advancing more than a single thesis in his role as a champion of the legal-positivist insistence on the separability of law and morals. In the opening paragraph of the essay to which Gardner principally refers, Hart set the stage for his defense of positivism as follows:

> Contemporary voices tell us we must recognize something obscured by the legal 'positivists' whose day is now over: that there is a 'point of intersection between law and morals', or that what *is* and what *ought* to be are somehow indissolubly fused or inseparable, though the positivists denied it. What do these phrases mean? Or rather which of the many things that they *could* mean, *do* they mean? Which of them do 'positivists' deny and why is it [ostensibly] wrong to do so? (Hart, 'Positivism', 49–50, emphases in original, footnotes omitted.)

Hart pursued a similar approach in his discussion of law and morality in the ninth chapter of *The Concept of Law*. After his famous account of the minimum content of natural law, he indicated how the rest of his discussion would proceed:

> [T]he claim that there is some further way in which law *must* conform to morals beyond that which we have exhibited as the minimum content of Natural Law, needs very careful scrutiny. Many such assertions either fail to make clear the sense in which the connexion between law and morals is alleged to be necessary; or upon examination they turn out to mean something which is both true and important, but which it is most confusing to present as a necessary connexion between law and morals. (Hart, *Concept*, 198, emphasis in original)

As Hart stressed, his positivist confrontations with natural-law thinking were not confined to a single set of issues. He engaged in those confrontations on a variety of fronts, in order to expose the unsustainability of a medley of purportedly necessary connections between morality and law. Undertaking such a project, he wielded phrases such as 'no necessary connections' and 'the separation of law and morals' as sweeping encapsulations of the diverse points which positivists make in reply to their opponents. He hardly intended those phrases to be construed as a preposterous denial of the necessary ties between law and morality that are readily acknowledged by any jurisprudential positivist.

An alertness to the multifariousness of legal positivists' rejoinders to their foes is, then, the key to grasping the role of some of Hart's sloganeering phrases—phrases that are innocuous and indeed valuable as rough-hewn summations of those rejoinders. To be sure, near the outset of the ninth chapter of *The Concept of*

---

remark that their truth 'is unfortunately compatible with very great iniquity' in a legal system (Hart, *Concept*, 202). Nor does Gardner note that Hart later expressed grave misgivings about the line of thought that had led him in his early work to an unenthusiastic alignment with Fuller. See Hart, 'Introduction', 18.

Law, Hart did submit that the status of moral soundness as a necessary or sufficient condition for legal validity 'may still be illuminatingly described as the issue between Natural Law and Legal Positivism, though each of these titles has come to be used for a range of different theses about law and morals'. He added that '[h]ere we shall take Legal Positivism to mean the simple contention that it is in no sense a necessary truth that laws reproduce or satisfy certain demands of morality, though in fact they have often done so' (Hart, *Concept*, 181–2). However, in singling out this matter as the prime point of controversy between the proponents of natural-law thought and the proponents of positivism, he was merely highlighting the fact that traditionally the thinkers in those two camps had indeed crossed swords on precisely that point. Although classical natural-law theories have been less common in recent decades than in past centuries, they abide in some quarters to the present day.[7] Earlier instances of such theories, urging that moral soundness is always a necessary or sufficient condition for the status of norms as legal norms, were certainly the targets of classical legal positivism in the eighteenth and nineteenth centuries. Hart was warranted in suggesting as much. In so doing, however, he was scarcely indicating that his other challenges to putatively indissoluble links between legality and morality lay outside his positivist conception of law. On the contrary, he launched those challenges—some of which were mounted in *The Concept of Law* and some in his later work—chiefly in the course of responding to critics of legal positivism such as Fuller and Dworkin and John Finnis. As Hart emphasized in one of his final essays, he as a legal positivist oppugned many 'different forms of the claim that there is a conceptual connection between law and morality which are compatible with the distinction between law as it is and law as it ought to be' (Hart, 'Introduction', 8).

Gardner opts for a much more restrictive conception of jurisprudential positivism. Closely adhering to the ideas and terminology of Raz, he articulates the following proposition as the sole distinctive tenet of legal positivism: 'In any legal system, whether a given norm is legally valid, and hence whether it forms part of the law of that system, depends on its sources, not its merits (where its merits, in the relevant sense, include the merits of its sources)' (Gardner, 'Myths', 201). In Razian garb, this thesis enunciated by Gardner rehearses the traditional positivist separation between the law as it is and the law as it ought to be. Gardner's thesis is certainly a positivist tenet. However, should we go further

---

[7] See, e.g., Michael Detmold, *The Unity of Law and Morality: A Refutation of Legal Positivism* (London: Routledge & Kegan Paul, 1984); Deryck Beyleveld and Roger Brownsword, 'The Practical Difference between Natural-Law Theory and Legal Positivism', 5 *Oxford Journal of Legal Studies* 1, 2 n.1 (1985); Michael Moore, 'Law as a Functional Kind', in Robert George (ed.), *Natural Law Theory* (Oxford: Clarendon Press, 1992), 188, 198; Philip Soper, *The Ethics of Deference* (Cambridge: Cambridge University Press, 2002), chap. 4. See also Ronald Dworkin, 'A Reply by Ronald Dworkin', in Marshall Cohen (ed.), *Ronald Dworkin and Contemporary Jurisprudence* (London: Duckworth, 1984), 247, 256–60.

and agree with Gardner that it captures the whole of the positivist message? Is he justified in ignoring the sundry other respects in which a number of positivists such as Hart have endeavored to rebut assertions of necessary connections between law and morality? And should we consequently concur with Gardner's view that the 'no necessary connections' formulation is unacceptably misleading with reference to a school of thought that denies only one necessary link between the legal domain and the moral domain?

For several reasons, the answer to each of these questions is negative. First, even though Hart and some of his successors have gone beyond his great legal-positivist predecessors in the breadth of their contestation of ostensibly ineluctable ties between law and morality, Gardner and other followers of Raz likewise go beyond those predecessors by espousing the Exclusivist variety of legal positivism in preference to the Inclusivist and Incorporationist varieties. As Hart himself observed long before the controversies between Inclusivism/Incorporationism and Exclusivism arose, his positivist forebears favored the Inclusivist position *avant la lettre* (Hart, 'Positivism', 54–5). Like Hart and me, and unlike Raz and Gardner, they eschewed the view that it is *necessarily not* the case that the status of norms as legal norms ever depends on moral tests. They instead took the view that it is *not necessarily* the case that that status depends on such tests in any particular legal system. Hence, if confining oneself to the doctrines of eighteenth- and nineteenth-century positivism is essential for the classifiability of one's jurisprudential stance as positivistic, the Razians face at least as much difficulty as the Hartians in securing that classification.

More important, a principal reason for Hart's expansion of the range of positivist attacks on putatively necessary connections between law and morality was his keen attentiveness to the normative dimension of law, which had been largely obscured by his positivist predecessors. Precisely because Hart highlighted the normative tenor of officials' pronouncements and interaction, he had to confront and repel the notion that their activities inevitably amount to an enterprise of moral deliberation. His greatest advance over John Austin—his attunedness to law's normativity—posed new challenges for him as a legal positivist, which he met by parrying arguments that equate law's normativity with moral normativity. He had to engage in battles that were never similarly pressing for Austin.

The fact that Hart engaged in those crucial battles is another reason for rejecting (or, rather, hugely amplifying) Gardner's conception of legal positivism. If we were to uphold Gardner's narrow understanding of legal positivism, we would thereby render quite mysterious a lot of the disputes that have preoccupied legal positivists and their opponents during the past five decades. Theorists such as Fuller and Dworkin and Finnis and Stephen Perry and Gerald Postema and Philip Soper and Nigel Simmonds and Roger Shiner and Robert George have all taken themselves in varying ways to be casting doubt on tenets of legal positivism, while positivists such as Hart have taken themselves to be defending positivism against those critics. Since most of the disputation has not centered on the thesis which Gardner regards as the lone distinctive doctrine of jurisprudential positivism, one's endorsement of his view of the matter would commit one to the conclusion that most of the exponents and detractors of positivism in the past half-century have been deeply confused. They have been confused not only about specific points, but also about the general nature of the debates in which they are participants. Now, although such a conclusion is not incoherent, it is outlandish. We are well advised to conclude instead that Gardner's conception of legal positivism is unacceptably cabined.

At any rate, as Gardner himself quite rightly remarks, we should not quarrel prolongedly over a label. 'In philosophical argument it matters not which proposition is given which name; it matters only which is true' (Gardner, 'Myths', 199). Razians are at liberty to stipulate whatever meaning they wish to associate with the phrase 'legal positivism'. On the one hand, their stipulation results in a strange characterization of the last fifty years of legal-philosophical controversy. On the other hand, any protracted squabbling here at the level of terminology would be arid. Let us simply note, then, that some legal philosophers who are positivists by any reckoning—including Gardner's reckoning—have in recent decades sought to expose the contingency of motley links between law and morality that are often perceived as necessary. Whether or not one joins the Razians in stipulating that most of the endeavors of those positivist legal philosophers are not integral to any school of thought to which the phrase 'legal positivism' should be applied, one can hardly fail to notice that those endeavors have figured saliently in modern jurisprudential wrangling. Regardless of the label we affix thereto, a multifaceted insistence on the separability of law and morality is what Hart and other legal positivists have undertaken. It would not greatly matter if we were to designate most of the elements of that insistence as 'legal schmositivism' rather than as 'legal positivism', so long as we recognize their correctness and importance.

Though the language of 'no necessary connections' is unquestionably rough as a means of summarizing the upshot of an insistence on the separability of law and morality, its vividness largely offsets its brashness. Hence, the 'no necessary connections' formulation is acceptable as a slogan that can catchily synopsize some major lines of reasoning developed by legal positivists. Like any slogan, it has to be construed with a modicum of generosity—rather than in an unresponsively caviling fashion—if its purpose is to be realized.

II. Positivism Unbound

Unlike Gardner, Jules Coleman does not hesitate at all in ascribing to legal positivism the claim that there are no necessary connections between law and morality. '[T]he separability thesis is the claim that there is no necessary connection between law and morality. That claim does express a tenet of positivism.'[8] Coleman recognizes that the language of such a claim cannot be taken entirely at face value, and that it is therefore in need of interpretation. In offering an interpretation, however, he severely limits the scope of the legal-positivist insistence on the separability of law and morality.

As has already been suggested, the aforementioned insistence resides in a multifaceted array of challenges to anti-positivist theories. Unfortunately, Coleman recounts just one of those challenges as if it were in fact the only one. Moreover, the challenge which he singles out is less interesting than most of the other positivist ripostes to natural-law theories, because it is no longer very controversial. Accordingly, we should not be surprised to find that Coleman believes that the positivist affirmation of the separability of law and morality is quite jejune. His discounting of that affirmation as largely trivial is present in his early work,[9] but it surfaces again in his important recent book *The Practice of Principle*. There he writes as follows:

The separability thesis is the claim that there is no necessary connection between law and morality. Interpreted as a claim about the relationship between substantive morality and the content of the criteria of legality, the separability thesis asserts that it is not necessary that the legality of a standard of conduct depend on its moral value or merit. Thus, the claim it makes is true just in case a legal system in which the substantive morality or value of a norm in no way bears on its legality is conceptually possible. The truth of this claim seems so undeniable as to render it almost entirely without interest; the claim it makes so weak, no one really contests it. (Coleman, *Practice*, 151, footnotes omitted)

Having evinced such disdain for the so-called separability thesis, Coleman opines that that thesis is not distinctively positivistic. Although it is undoubtedly a tenet of legal positivism, it is endorsed as well by just about every legal philosopher. Or so he contends: 'We cannot usefully characterize legal positivism in terms of the separability thesis, once it is understood properly, because virtually no one— positivist or not—rejects it' (Coleman, *Practice*, 152). Coleman concludes that the hallmark of jurisprudential positivism lies not in an insistence on the separability of law and morality, but in an insistence on the conventionality of law.[10] He has indeed argued for that conclusion since his first major contribution to the literature on legal positivism more than two decades ago.

---

[8] Jules Coleman, *The Practice of Principle* (Oxford: Oxford University Press, 2001) [hereinafter cited as Coleman, *Principle*], 104 n.4.

[9] See Jules Coleman, 'Negative and Positive Positivism', in *Markets, Morals and the Law* (Cambridge: Cambridge University Press, 1988), 3, 12. See also Jules Coleman, 'Authority and Reason', in Robert George (ed.), *The Autonomy of Law* (Oxford: Clarendon Press, 1996), 287, 316 n.5.

[10] See also Kenneth Einar Himma, 'Law's Claim of Legitimate Authority', in Jules Coleman (ed.), *Hart's Postscript* (Oxford: Oxford University Press, 2001), 271, 286 ('[I]t is the emphasis on law's conventionality that distinguishes positivism from other conceptual theories of law'); Kenneth Einar Himma, 'Ambiguously Stung: Dworkin's Semantic Sting Reconfigured', 8 *Legal Theory* 145, 166 (2002) ('[T]he view, which represents the theoretical core of legal positivism, [is] that the grounds of law are exhausted by conventional criteria of legal validity'); Kenneth Einar Himma, 'Substance and Method in

Coleman espouses a position quite closely similar to that of Gardner, though he arrives at it by a markedly different route. Whereas Gardner repudiates and ridicules the 'no necessary connections' formulation, Coleman embraces that formulation but then interprets it as substantially overlapping with the one tenet which Gardner attributes to legal positivism. The only conspicuous difference between their standpoints is that Coleman cashes out the 'no necessary connections' language in a manner that bespeaks his allegiance to Inclusive Legal Positivism and Incorporationism, whereas Gardner's tenet is expressed in Exclusivist terms. In the key respect relevant to the focus of this chapter, by contrast, Coleman and Gardner are basically at one. Each of them synopsizes legal positivism in a fashion that gravely curtails the reach of its resistance to the postulation of necessary connections between law and morality. Each of them submits that that resistance is confined to the matter of legal validity.

In fairness to Coleman, we should note that at a later juncture in his book he acknowledges that the debates between positivists and natural-law theorists are considerably richer and more complicated than might be inferred from his discussion of the so-called separability thesis (Coleman, *Practice*, 193 n.21). Moreover, he himself sophisticatedly adopts an austerely positivistic stance on several points of contention, particularly in connection with methodological issues. Nevertheless, these manifestations of his fundamentally positivist outlook make especially puzzling the fact that he so narrowly and denigratingly construes the positivist insistence on the separability of law and morality when he broaches it directly in the passages quoted above. His elaboration of his credo is to be commended for not fully practicing what he preaches—that is, for departing from his highly restrictive interpretation of the 'no necessary connections' language—but we can wonder why he does not preach what he adeptly practices.

To see how regrettable are the pronouncements by Coleman that have been quoted above, we should glance at a number of the diverse forms which the positivist insistence on the separability of law and morality has taken. For this purpose, my terse account here will follow my earlier book on positivism by distinguishing among different conceptions or dimensions of morality: morality versus immorality, morality versus prudence, and morality versus factuality. With reference to morality-in-opposition-to-immorality, one of the most familiar positivist themes is the traditional distinction between the law as it is and the law as it ought to be. Contrary to what Coleman declares, that distinction is not wholly uncontroversial. As has already been remarked in this chapter, the traditional natural-law attack on that distinction has not vanished without a trace from the present-day jurisprudential scene. Philosophers as eminent as Dworkin and Soper and Michael Moore have pursued traditional natural-law

---

Conceptual Jurisprudence and Legal Theory', 88 *Virginia Law Review* 1119, 1152 (2002) ('The most fundamental of positivism's core commitments is the idea that law is, in essence, a social creation or artifact').

attacks, in varying ways and to varying degrees. Still, although the standard positivist riposte to such attacks is not completely uncontroversial, it has attained widespread acceptance (or, at least, acquiescence). Not many theorists continue to assail it. If the 'negative' side of legal positivism is to be piquantly worthy of sustained attention, then, it must extend beyond the matter of legal validity which Coleman has singled out. It does in fact extend well beyond that matter.

With the focus still on morality-as-contrasted-with-immorality, another area of disputation between positivists and their opponents is concerned with the general function of law. Theorists seeking to establish a necessary connection between law and morality have maintained that the central function of law is inherently commendable and that any regime of law is itself therefore inherently commendable. Whether the function is deemed to be the securing of basic orderliness and coordination or the governance of human beings as rational agents or the expression of reciprocity between the rulers and the ruled—or some other desideratum, or some combination of these desiderata—the claim by anti-positivist theorists is that law is necessary and/or sufficient for the attainment of morally vital states of affairs. Those theorists accordingly conclude that law is endowed with an intrinsic moral worth.

In rebuttal, positivists have in some cases challenged the premises of the anti-positivist arguments, and have in other cases accepted the premises while rejecting the conclusions drawn from them. The latter strategy is effective, for example, in reply to theorists who ascribe moral obligatoriness to law on account of its indispensable role in securing public order and social coordination. Positivists can best respond not by denying that indispensable role, but by assailing the unwarranted comparison that implicitly underlies the inference about the prima-facie moral obligatoriness of law.[11] Such an inference presupposes that the relevant baseline for a comparison with each particular legal regime is a state of lawless anarchy; a comparison along those lines will generate an imputation of prima-facie moral obligatoriness to the norms of any such regime, on the ground that those norms are the sole alternative to chaos. Jurisprudential positivists impeach this implicit comparison by contending that instead the appropriate baseline is other realistically attainable legal regimes, some of which may well be morally superior to the regime under consideration. With such a move, the positivist can block any general inference of prima-facie moral obligatoriness. That is, he can refute the view that the mandates of every legal system are possessed of such obligatoriness simply by dint of their status as legal mandates.

Yet another focus for the positivist resistance to moralized accounts of law is the self-presentation of any legal system. As we have seen in Chapter 6, theorists such as Soper believe that any legal system presents itself as morally legitimate and its mandates as morally correct. Although these theorists are positing a necessary connection between law and morality at the level of discourse rather

---

[11] I develop this point at length in *IDLP*, 204–9, 254–307.

than at the level of underlying substance, they do indeed maintain that officials' legal pronouncements are inextricably bound up with moral assurances (albeit usually implicit assurances). Moreover, under Soper's view, those pronouncements cannot retain minimal credibility if their assurances of moral legitimacy are wildly outlandish; consequently, under his view, nothing can count as a genuine legal system unless it surpasses some modest threshold of moral acceptability (Soper, *Ethics*, chap. 4). His reflections on the presuppositions of official legal assertions lead readily into his espousal of a traditional natural-law position. Thus, for more than one reason, positivists are well advised to contest Soper's claims about the self-presentation of every legal system. My sixth chapter—along with my earlier book on legal positivism—has indeed contested those claims.

Let us now turn to morality-defined-in-contrast-with-prudence. In this connection, perhaps the most commonly bruited notion to which the positivists have retorted is that the only substantial reasons for officials' adherence to rule-of-law principles are moral rather than prudential. Fuller and Finnis and Simmonds and many other theorists have sought to uphold just such a thesis. In so doing, they have endeavored to establish that the rule of law is inherently moral in its bearings. My ripostes to such arguments have been outlined in Chapters 5 and 6 (and have been presented fully in my earlier book on positivism). By indicating that there are strong prudential reasons for compliance with rule-of-law requirements on the part of evil officials who are devoid of moral compunctions, I have aimed to counter the attribution of intrinsic moral significance to the rule of law.

Another line of argument involving the moral/prudential distinction, to which legal positivists have responded, is concerned with the reasons-for-action which officials implicitly or explicitly invoke when they adduce legal norms in explanation of their decisions. According to this line of argument, propounded most notably by Raz, officials' invocations of legal directives presuppose that there are moral reasons for conformity therewith by the people to whom the directives are applied. Whether or not the officials believe the implications of what they are saying, their official references to legal mandates as the bases for their decisions do imply that the addressees of the decisions have been morally bound to obey those mandates. In adverting to legal requirements as grounds for demanding that people behave in specified ways, the officials are adverting to interest-independent reasons-for-action—that is, reasons-for-action which are moral rather than prudential. So runs Raz's argument, in a number of interesting variations. While my rejoinders have likewise been multiple, they have concentrated on the credible possibility of legal regimes in which no punishment-independent reasons-for-action are presented or presupposed by officials' invocations of legal mandates. Challenges to Raz's lines of reasoning on this matter are crucial, since his lines of reasoning are problematic for legal positivism in largely the same ways as Soper's. (The potential for the appropriation of Raz's position by a Soperian natural-law theorist is especially evident, given that Raz himself has denied that legal officials can be systematically deluded or mendacious in the claims which they make concerning the authoritativeness of their pronouncements.[12])

Also eliciting resistance from legal positivists are some arguments based on the observation that law and morality share a deontic terminological structure. Both in morality and in law, key terms such as 'right' and 'obligation' and 'authority' and 'permission' are prominently operative. For some theorists, the terminological affinities between law and morality are indicative of deeper connections between the two domains. As we have seen in Chapter 6, Soper advances just such a view in his efforts to establish that every genuine legal system will have presented itself as morally legitimate and its mandates as morally correct. Like Raz, Soper takes for granted that the terminology of 'duty' or 'obligation' carries the same meaning in legal contexts as in moral contexts. On exactly that point, Hart and I have raised queries—not by maintaining preposterously that the terminological correspondences are unaccompanied by any conceptual overlap, but by contending that the conceptual overlap is formal rather than substantive. That overlap is not sufficient to warrant Soper's conclusion, and it is not sufficient to warrant our concluding that the reasons-for-action invoked by officials in their authoritative pronouncements are perforce moral rather than prudential. It is consistent with the existence and operations of a credible legal system in which the only reasons invoked by many of the statements from officials to citizens are punishment-centered prudential reasons.

Let us finally turn to the distinction between morality and factuality. Here one principal source of disagreements between legal positivists and their foes is the issue or set of issues singled out by Coleman in his so-called separability thesis. That is, positivists submit that the endeavors of officials in ascertaining the existence and contents of legal norms are not necessarily guided by any moral assumptions. Those endeavors can concentrate strictly on matters of observable fact. In this or that particular legal system, it can be the case that moral soundness is neither a necessary condition nor a sufficient condition for the status of any norm as a legal norm. (As we have noted, Exclusive Legal Positivists go further by asserting that moral soundness cannot ever be such a necessary condition or such a sufficient condition.) In reply to Dworkin and other theorists who characterize the process of law-ascertainment as ineluctably an enterprise of

---

¹² See Joseph Raz, *Ethics in the Public Domain* (Oxford: Clarendon Press, 1994) [hereinafter cited as Raz, *Ethics*], 201. On the one hand, this denial by Raz has been quite persuasively impugned in Kenneth Einar Himma, 'The Instantiation Thesis and Raz's Critique of Inclusive Positivism', 20 *Law and Philosophy* 61 (2001). On the other hand, Himma's critique is forceful insofar as its target—the aforementioned denial—is linked to Raz's particular conception of authoritativeness. The critique would cease to be compelling if that denial were instead linked to the general notion of authoritativeness (as opposed to Raz's particular conception thereof). A Soperian natural-law theorist could and would opt for the latter way of fleshing out the denial, rather than for the Razian way.

moral deliberation, the Incorporationists and Inclusive Legal Positivists have held that the role of moral judgments in the law-ascertaining process is a contingent matter determined by each legal system's particular Rule of Recognition. The criteria for law-ascertainment can include, but need not include, moral standards.

Another area of debate centering on the morality/factuality dichotomy has been touched upon in each of my last two chapters. Many positivists (including me) have insisted not only on the separability of morality and law, but also on the separability of morality and legal philosophy. Notwithstanding that every theory must unfold on the basis of evaluative judgments in order to be an intelligible account of its explanandum, the values that inform a philosophical theory of law can be strictly theoretical-explanatory rather than moral-political. In the construction of such a theory, one's decisions about the relative importance of various phenomena are not perforce moral in their tenor. Instead, a claim about the importance or unimportance of something can derive from a judgment about the extent to which that thing should be taken into account by a comprehensive yet parsimonious analysis of sociopolitical life. Contrary to what some philosophers such as Perry and Postema have proclaimed, then, the inevitably evaluative enterprise of subjecting law to philosophical investigation is not inevitably moral-political in its orientation.

So ends my laconic survey of the paramount lines of confrontation between legal positivists and their opponents. This survey has not in itself presented any full-scale arguments in support of the positivist insistence on the separability of law and morality. Rather, it has simply sketched some of the chief points of contention that have led positivists—including me—to develop such arguments. Nonetheless, although this conspectus has merely described some debates instead of entering into them directly and sustainedly, it should suffice to convey their rich multifariousness. It should therefore suffice to indicate how much is omitted when Coleman or anyone else suggests that the positivist insistence on the separability of law and morality is reducible to a single thesis. To be sure, as has already been mentioned, the restrictiveness of Coleman's comments on the so-called separability thesis is not matched by any similar cramping of his methodological and substantive analyses. Although Coleman does not adopt a positivist stance in every one of the controversies delineated in my last several paragraphs, he does adopt such a stance in quite a few of them. All the same, his dismissive remarks about the so-called separability thesis are damaging to legal positivism. Those remarks tend to obscure some of the best positivist insights (which Coleman himself elsewhere helps to elaborate), and they render opaque most of the recent conflicts between positivists and their adversaries. When the positivist affirmation of the separability of law and morality is grasped in its expansive variegatedness—rather than only in its most pallid formulation—its centrality and profundity become clear. To slight that affirmation is to darken counsel.

III. Raz and Separability

At a number of junctures during the past three or four decades, Raz has written about the positivist insistence on the separability of law and morality. His attitude has almost always been wary and has sometimes been downright hostile. To be sure, Raz in *Practical Reason and Norms* critically assessed some natural-law theories in ways not wholly dissimilar from the approach favored by this chapter (and by my other writings on legal positivism).[13] In much of his work, however, he has expressed skepticism about the separability of law and morality—at least insofar as their separability is understood as broadly as it has been here.

Like Coleman, Raz suggests that the multifaceted positivist insistence on the separability of law and morality can be reduced to a single thesis (the 'separability thesis'). In two important respects, however, Raz disagrees with Coleman. First, he singles out a different and more capacious tenet as the separability thesis. Second, he rejects that tenet as unsustainable. Let us here very briefly consider each of these points.

As we have seen, Coleman construes the separability thesis as a claim that the criteria for legal validity in any particular legal system need not include moral tests. Such tests may be present in this or that particular system, but their presence is contingent rather than a necessary feature of everything that counts as a legal regime. To assert the contingency of the role of moral tests as criteria for legal validity is to affirm the separability of law and morality, according to Coleman. Raz takes a contrary view: 'Coleman's rendering of his own separability thesis is mistaken. A necessary connection between law and morality does not require that truth as a moral principle be a condition of legal validity. All it requires is that the social features which identify something as a legal system entail that it possess[es] moral value' (Raz, *Ethics*, 210). Although the wording in this quotation is not entirely unequivocal, Raz does not appear to be repudiating Coleman's version of the separability thesis outright. He appears to accept that the truth of Coleman's tenet—or the truth of an Exclusivist variant of that tenet—is a necessary condition for the truth of the separability thesis. What he then maintains, however, is that the truth of Coleman's tenet is not sufficient for the truth of the separability thesis. That latter thesis can be false even if Coleman's tenet (or an Exclusivist variant of that tenet) is true. In other words, Coleman's error resides in his having construed the separability thesis too narrowly. Raz puts forward a more expansive construal, whereby that thesis will be false not only if Coleman's tenet is false but also if any of law's defining features entail its possession of some degree of moral worthiness. Raz's

---

[13] See Joseph Raz, *Practical Reason and Norms* (Princeton: Princeton University Press, 1990) [hereinafter cited as Raz, *Reason*], 162–9.

position in the quotation above, then, is much the same as his position in an early essay:

The claim that what is law and what is not is purely a matter of social fact still leaves it an open question whether or not those social facts by which we identify the law or determine its existence do or do not endow it with moral merit. If they do, it has of necessity a moral character. But even if they do not, it is still an open question whether, given human nature and the general conditions of human existence, every legal system which is in fact the effective law of some society does of necessity conform to some moral values and ideals.[14]

Having opted for a broader specification of the separability thesis, Raz proceeds to announce that the thesis is false: 'The separability thesis is ... implausible. ... [I]t is very likely that there is some necessary connection between law and morality, that every legal system in force has some moral merit or does some moral good even if it is also the cause of a great deal of moral evil.' He adds: 'It is relevant to remember that all major traditions in Western political thought, including both the Aristotelian and the Hobbesian traditions, believed in such a connection' (Raz, *Ethics*, 211). He articulates a similar view in a quite recent essay, when he denies 'that a legal system may exist which implements no moral values'.[15]

Raz is on solid ground, of course, in censuring Coleman for conceiving of the separability thesis too restrictively. His only fault in that respect is that he does not go nearly far enough. As should be evident from the preceding section of this chapter with its terse synopsis of some of the clashes between positivists and their opponents, Raz enlarges the scope of the separability thesis far too modestly. Indeed, the chief problem lies in the notion that legal positivism's insistence on the separability of law and morality can aptly be recounted as a single thesis (albeit a rather complex thesis). Like Coleman, Raz implicitly relies only on the morality/immorality and morality/factuality dichotomies in cashing out the separability thesis, and he consequently obfuscates the fact that many of the liveliest debates over the separability of law and morality have in recent decades been centered primarily on the morality/prudence dichotomy. (Admittedly, Raz has been on the anti-positivist side in some of those debates.) Moreover, even in connection with the morality/immorality and morality/factuality contrasts, the controversies over the separability of law and morality have been more wide-ranging than Raz suggests. Though he wisely moves beyond the confines imposed by Coleman, he still conveys the false impression that the matter of separability is reducible to a very small set of issues that can be captured adequately in a univocal thesis.

More objectionable than the undue pinchedness of Raz's version of the separability thesis is his renunciation of that thesis. On the one hand, to be sure, his position in this respect is quite mild. While forswearing 'the view that the facts which determine the existence and content of law do not guarantee it

[14] Joseph Raz, *The Authority of Law* (Oxford: Clarendon Press, 1979), 38–9.
[15] Joseph Raz, 'On the Nature of Law', 82 *Archiv für Rechts-und Sozialphilosophie* 1, 16 n.17 (1996).

any moral value', Raz adds: 'What does appear true is that the necessary connection between law and morality which is likely to be established by arguments...is a weak one. It is insufficient e.g. to establish a prima-facie obligation to obey the law.'[16] On the other hand, even such an attenuated rejection of the separability thesis is too strong. For one thing, Raz does not do justice to the comparative character of any genuine moral assessment—a comparative character to which I have fleetingly adverted in this chapter's short discussion of the obligation of each citizen to obey the law. Moreover, his remarks do not suitably take account of the fact that some morally good results can be devoid of moral value. Nor do those remarks adequately acknowledge that the role of law as a necessary condition for certain moral desiderata is insufficient to vest law with any inherent moral worth. Let us ponder each of these shortcomings.

Raz himself is far from unaware of the comparative character of any moral appraisal. In *Practical Reason and Norms*, for example, he includes some pithy observations on the obligation-to-obey-the-law that are roughly akin to my own (Raz, *Reason*, 167). Nevertheless, his comments in the quotations above go too far toward contending that every legal system is endowed with some moral merit by sheer dint of its having secured some morally worthy aspect of the society over which it holds sway. The example which he uses to illustrate his point about law's possession of moral value is highly revealing: 'For example, assume that the maintenance of orderly social relations is itself morally valuable. Assume further that a legal system can be the law in force in a society only if it succeeds in maintaining orderly social relations. A necessary connection between law and morality would then have been established' (Raz, *Ethics*, 210–11). To detect the unsoundness of Raz's conclusion, we should glance at a variant of a scenario which I probed at some length in my earlier book on legal positivism (*IDLP*, 206–9).

Suppose that some gangsters operate a community-wide protection racket that has the effect of warding off other criminals—designated here as 'the Devils'—who would engage in even worse persecution of the hapless people in the community. The protection racket is grossly extortionate and ruthlessly enforced, and is run solely on the basis of the gangsters' selfish interests (which encompass the exclusion of their even more nefarious rivals). In these circumstances, the sustainment of the protection racket produces the morally beneficial effect of keeping the Devils out of the community. Nevertheless, we should not jump to the conclusion that the racketeers' oppressive activities are endowed with some moral value. Everything hinges on the pertinent baseline for comparison. If the only such baseline is a situation in which the Devils carry out murderous rampages and a host of other wrongs, then the protection racket does possess

---

[16] Raz, *Ethics*, 211 n.12. In some of his most recent reflections on the topic, Raz appears to move even closer to my own position; see Raz, 'Morality', 13.

some moral merit as the lone feasible alternative to that hideous situation. However, it may well be that a preferable state of affairs—marked neither by the misdeeds of the racketeers nor by the more heinous misdeeds of the Devils— is also available as an alternative. If such a state of affairs is attainable without significant moral costs (beyond the costs that would arise directly from the racketeers' own resistance to any attempts to alleviate their exploitative practices), it is the germane baseline for comparison when we gauge the moral worthiness of the protection racket. In that case, we should conclude that the racket is possessed of no positive moral value at all. Its only morally beneficial effects are also realizable through a plainly preferable state of affairs that is a reasonably attainable alternative to it.

Insofar as a morally worthy legal system is reasonably attainable as an alternative to an evil legal regime that is currently operative, the moral status of that evil regime is similar to the moral status of the protection racket just described. In such circumstances, that is, the evil legal system is devoid of any positive moral value. Its performance of the morally salutary function of maintaining orderly social relations is not sufficient to endow it with any such value, since the relevant baseline for comparison in our moral appraisals of the wicked legal regime is also characterized by the fulfillment of that function. Of course, if the germane baseline were instead a situation of anarchic tumult or other serious upheaval, the orderliness-promoting and coordination-enabling function of the repressive legal system would per se be sufficient to invest that system with some moral commendability. However, because the germane baseline is (*ex hypothesi*) a decent legal regime which not only avoids most of the iniquities of the repressive legal system but which also discharges its orderliness-promoting and coordination-facilitating function, that function cannot appositely be singled out as something which counts in favor of the repressive system.

To be sure, if the circumstances were different, our conclusion on this point would likewise have to be different. If for example the only realistically attainable alternative to the evil legal system were an even direr system operated by even more brutal officials, the orderliness-securing and coordination-facilitating function of the existing system would indeed count in its favor as something that confers moral value upon it. Much the same conclusion would follow if the only realistically attainable alternative were a situation of chaotic turbulence. In fact, the same conclusion will sometimes follow when a morally superior legal system is attainable. Although the alternative system may be morally more commendable in most respects, its capacity to fulfill the orderliness-promoting function might be less than that of the existing regime—in which case the effective discharge of that function is something which counts in favor of the existing regime, notwithstanding that it is outweighed by the regime's vices.

In other words, to some degree the moral status of an evil legal system's operations will vary across contexts. In a context in which the pertinent baseline for comparison is an even worse situation, or in which it is a better situation where basic public order would nonetheless not be as effectively secured, the maintenance of orderly social relations by the evil legal system does indeed endow it with some moral worthiness. Contrariwise, in a context in which the pertinent baseline for comparison is a better situation where the securing of basic public order would be at least as effective, the maintenance of orderly social relations by the evil legal system does not endow it with any moral worthiness. In such a context, that morally commendable function does not count in favor of the evil regime at all—since the function would be at least as effectively carried out by a morally superior regime that stands as a reasonably attainable alternative.

In sum, the upshot of these remarks is that no inherent moral worth attaches to law simply by virtue of the fact that (in Raz's words, quoted above) 'a legal system can be the law in force in a society only if it succeeds in maintaining orderly social relations'. Whether the orderliness-sustaining effects of a legal system invest it with any moral value is a question to which the answer depends on the baseline for the comparisons that underpin any apt assessments of the system's merits. An appropriate identification of that baseline in turn depends on the moral entitlements of people and on the feasibility of alternatives. If a morally superior system of law is accessible as an alternative without the infliction of significant harm on people's legitimate interests (beyond any harm that would directly ensue from the current regime's efforts to thwart improvements), then it stands as the baseline against which the moral worth of the existing legal system is to be evaluated. If no superior system of law is feasible, then some inferior system or a state of anarchy is the operative baseline. That is, the selection of a baseline, which will heavily affect one's conclusions about the moral value of the prevailing legal regime, will hinge on context-specific factors rather than on anything intrinsic to the nature of law. Though the worthiness attaching to law by dint of its orderliness-providing and coordination-enabling functions can correctly be designated as a connection between law and morality, the connection is contingent rather than necessary—even though those morally salutary functions are characteristic of everything that is classifiable as a legal system. (Note that, in order to address Raz's argument, my comments here have concentrated on the level of whole legal systems rather than on the level of individual legal norms within those systems. We typically proceed at the latter level when we are enquiring into the existence of an obligation to obey the law, but we fittingly proceed at the former level when we are enquiring into the moral fiber of each legal system as an overall array of institutions.)

Furthermore, even if we leave aside the point just made concerning the comparative orientation of our moral appraisals of legal regimes, we should resist the line of argument through which Raz reaches his conclusion. Let us grant his assumption that every legal system produces some morally estimable results, and let us additionally assume that no superior alternative way of producing those results is realistically attainable. Still, his rejection of the separability thesis does not perforce follow. Morally estimable results can themselves be morally un-acceptable if they are achieved through unacceptable means. In such a case, the results do not warrant any ascription of some positive moral value to the insti-tution or process that has brought them about.

Suppose, for example, that an oppressive government in an overpopulated country resorts to genocide in its treatment of some downtrodden minority. As a consequence of the slaughter of millions of people, the problem of overcrowded-ness in the country is significantly alleviated. Pressures on public services, and on the use of land and other natural resources, have substantially abated. The danger of the onset of famines has likewise diminished considerably. All of these effects of the policy of genocide are morally valuable developments by any ordinary reckoning. We would be foolish to deny as much. Nevertheless, those effects do not warrant our ascribing any moral worthiness to the policy that has engendered them or to the government. Because they have come about through an utterly unacceptable means, they do not count in favor of the government and its measures at all. Considered in isolation from their origins, the effects recounted above are plainly salutary; however, their origins have a crucial bearing on the question whether those effects contribute positively in any respect to the moral standing of the regime under which they have been accomplished. It is not the case that some good results and some horrific results have simply occurred alongside each other, and that they can be balanced against each other accord-ingly. Rather, the good results have ensued only because of the horrific results. Given the background circumstances, the latter have constituted the former. Consequently, there is no room for the good results to have an independent moral status that can militate in favor of a policy which is horrendous in other respects. Rather, the respects in which the genocidal policy is horrendous are constitutive of the respects in which it is beneficial.[17]

By the same token, we have to enquire into the means by which an oppressive legal-governmental regime discharges the morally valuable function of maintain-ing orderly social relations. If that function is fulfilled through odious measures, then it does not contribute favorably to the moral status of the regime by which it is effected. Suppose for example that the norms and the punitive mechanisms of the regime impose stiflingly harsh penalties on people for numerous innocuous acts and omissions. Everyone who engages in any mode of disorderly conduct is savagely tortured or executed, as a monitory example to others. Because of the draconian punishments that await anyone who steps out of line, and because of the public displays of the ruthlessness of the regime's officials in suppressing and deterring obstreperousness, virtually everybody is highly submissive and peace-able. Now, when we look at the prevalence of pacific dispositions among citizens

---

[17] I have elsewhere described the sort of constitutive connection that is operative between the heinous effects and the beneficial effects. See Matthew Kramer, *The Quality of Freedom* (Oxford: Oxford University Press, 2003), 280: 'S_1 amounts to S_2 if S_2 is entailed by the combination of S_1 and some aspect(s) of the prevailing circumstances other than any causal laws'.

in abstraction from the origins thereof, we shall no doubt conclude that it is a morally valuable development. However, once we take account of the etiology of those dispositions, we can see that the cultivation of them by the iron-fisted legal regime does not warrant our ascribing any moral worthiness to that regime. We can recognize that the peaceableness of the citizens is an index of their down-troddenness, rather than something to be admired. Orderliness is generally commendable, but the orderliness of subjugation is not. That is, because the orderliness has been elicited by iniquitous means—in other words, because the fact that people have been cowed into sheep-like submissiveness is constitutive of the fact that their relations are peaceable—the smoothness of the interaction among the citizens is thoroughly tainted.

This example can be brought even closer to the scenario of genocide. Suppose that the docility of the citizens is due not principally to the severe punitiveness of the legal regime that regulates their behavior, but mainly instead to the over-whelmingly manipulative inveiglements of the institutions and devices which that regime uses unremittingly in order to propagate its sinister ideology. Or, somewhat more fancifully, suppose that the citizens have each been rendered submissive by a lobotomy or some other type of brain surgery which each of them has been legally required to undergo at an early age. Or, again somewhat more fancifully, perhaps their unresistant willingness to comply with the harshly onerous legal requirements of their society is due to the continual administration of a potent mind-altering drug or the continual transmission of mind-controlling electronic impulses. In any of these circumstances, the morally valuable function of sustaining orderly social relations is carried out through the very shaping of the psyches of citizens in nefarious ways. Just as a policy of genocide comes to grips with the inordinate size of a population in a profoundly illegitimate fashion, a policy of effectively taking over people's minds in order to secure their placidity is a wholly unacceptable regimentation of their thoughts and actions. That regi-mentation is constitutive of the orderliness of their dealings with one another and with the legal-governmental apparatus that exerts its sway over them—which is why their orderliness, the orderliness of puppets, does not count morally in favor of that apparatus. Once again we behold a situation in which the beneficial aspects and the deplorable aspects of a legal system's governance over its citizens are not simply co-occurrent. Instead, the latter aspects constitute the former. Whenever the peaceableness of social relations is so constituted, it does not contribute positively at all to the moral value of the legal regime that sustains those relations.

Let us close by briefly pondering Raz's passing reference to the Aristotelian and Hobbesian traditions in Western political thought. Raz is unquestionably correct in declaring that past and present political thinkers have believed that law as such does inherently partake of some degree of moral worthiness. In most if not all cases, however, they have believed as much because they have further believed that the rule of law is necessary for the realization of extremely important moral desiderata such as the preservation of public order and the coordination of social life and the promotion of individual freedom. This latter belief is entirely accurate, as I have unhesitatingly acknowledged more than once in this book. Nonetheless, it does not support the thesis that law partakes of some inherent moral worthiness. As has been remarked in Chapter 6 (and as has been argued in my earlier writings on legal positivism), the rule of law is indispensable for the continuation of wickedly exploitative and repressive governmental institutions on a large scale over a long period. Ergo, if we were to ascribe inherent moral worthiness to law because of its status as a necessary condition for the attainment of key moral desiderata, we should likewise ascribe inherent moral iniquity to law because of its status as a necessary condition for the successful long-term pursuit of heinous purposes by evil regimes that rule over sizeable societies. Now, manifestly, we should not engage in either of those inconsistent ascriptions. We should instead conclude that the moral bearings of law are not inherent but are determined by its contingent substance and by the uses to which it is put in various settings. With such a conclusion, of course, we reaffirm legal positivism's insistence on the separability of law and morality.

IV. A Short Recapitulation

Whereas Chapters 5 and 6 have sought to rebut challenges posed by theorists who set themselves against legal positivism, the present chapter has balked at the unduly narrow conception of legal positivism to which several major positivist theorists have disconcertingly subscribed. On some occasions those theorists have suggested that certain important strands of the positivist insistence on the separability of law and morality are in fact outside the scope of jurisprudential positivism, and on other occasions they have squarely impugned certain elements of that insistence. Whatever may be their reasons for discounting central tenets of legal positivism that have been elaborated in tussles with natural-law theorists of sundry stripes, they have indeed de-emphasized or abjured a number of those tenets. To be sure, an unswerving allegiance to those tenets is not a necessary condition for the applicability of the 'positivist' label. For example, Raz is surely a legal positivist even though he has eschewed any such allegiance. Nevertheless, the vibrant heart of legal positivism (at least during the past five decades) is a far-reaching insistence on the separability of law and morality, from which these positivists have distanced themselves.

On the one hand, any minimally sensible person should accept that there are countless similarities between law and morality. The vast majority of those similarities are utterly trivial, but a small proportion of them (such as the normativity of legal propositions and moral propositions) are significant. On the other hand, when we distinguish among morality-contrasted-with-immorality and morality-contrasted-with-prudence and morality-contrasted-with-factuality, we can discern that nearly all of the important and ostensibly necessary connections between law and morality—in any of the three specified senses of 'morality'—are contingent at most. During the past five decades, natural-law theorists of differing persuasions have proclaimed quite a few of those contingent connections to be ineluctable bonds. Legal positivism has developed fruitfully in response to those proclamations, as its proponents have endeavored to expose the untenability of the natural-law arguments. Their endeavors have doubtless expanded the ambit of legal positivism beyond its historical contours, but the expansion has redounded to the great benefit of positivism by underscoring the soundness and versatility of its general insights.

An insistence on the separability of law and morality is pertinent not only in reaction to natural-law theories, but also in application to the most prominent intrapositivist disputes: the debates between Inclusivists/Incorporationists and Exclusivists, into which this book's first four chapters have ventured. After all, as the Introduction to this volume has remarked, the Inclusivist/Incorporationist positions in those debates uphold the separability of law and morality. Inclusivists and Incorporationists contend that moral principles *can* enter, but *need* not enter, into any particular society's law (as criteria for legal validity or as legal norms). Exclusive Legal Positivists, by contrast, maintain that law-ascertaining enquiries and moral enquiries are strictly separate rather than merely separable. In this key respect, then, the focus of the current chapter tallies nicely with the focus and contentions of Part I. My espousal there of Inclusivist/Incorporationist positions and my defense here of a wide-ranging insistence on the separability of law and morality do not entail each other, but they do fit together well. Legal positivists' altercations with natural-law thinkers can shed light on the battles that take place among positivists themselves.

PART III

FROM LEGAL PHILOSOPHY TO MORAL PHILOSOPHY

Affinities between Law and Morality

Moral Rights and the Limits of the 'Ought'-Implies-'Can' Principle: Why Impeccable Precautions are No Excuse

In a section of *The Concept of Law* that has not elicited as much scholarly commentary as some of the other parts of that classic text, H.L.A. Hart outlined four main dissimilarities between moral requirements and legal requirements.[1] He maintained that moral obligations are unlike legal obligations in that they invariably pertain to matters of considerable importance; he argued that legal norms are susceptible to abrupt and deliberate change, whereas moral norms are not similarly susceptible; he declared that there is no such thing as strict liability in morality, whereas some legal norms do impose liability irrespective of fault; and he contended that the law's typical form of compliance-inducing pressure is the threat and application of sanctions, whereas the characteristic form of moral pressure is exhortation. Each of these claims by Hart is open to challenge in certain respects, but the present chapter will concentrate on the third of them. Was he correct in thinking that impeccable intentions are always fully exonerative in morality? In arguing for a negative answer, this chapter will tackle some knotty issues in moral philosophy and legal theory.

Chief among those issues is the soundness of the 'ought'-implies-'can' principle within the realm of morality. Hart was of course correct in affirming that such a principle is not always determinative within the domain of law. People and corporations are sometimes held legally liable for their actions even if they have not been malicious or knowingly indifferent or reckless or careless in any way. Culpability is not always an element of legal wrongdoing. Hart went astray, however, in believing that morality is fundamentally different from law in this regard. Whether departures from fault-based liability are rarer or more

---

[1] H.L.A. Hart, *The Concept of Law* (Oxford: Clarendon Press, 1961) [hereinafter cited as Hart, *Concept*], 168–76. I should note two points of terminology at the outset. First, I use the terms 'duty', 'obligation', and 'requirement' interchangeably. Second, the phrase 'strict liability' refers to liability that is imposed without regard to the presence or absence of culpability. Further terminological points—such as my distinction between 'wrongful' and 'wrong'—will become apparent as this chapter unfolds.

common in morality than in law, they are by no means absent altogether. Wrongfulness (culpability) is by no means invariably a precondition for wrongness (impermissibility).[2]

The 'ought'-implies-'can' principle can be construed in a number of ways. This chapter will not assail that principle insofar as it is understood as a denial that anyone can be morally obligated to do something that is utterly unintelligible. We cannot make any sense of the statement that somebody is morally obligated to induce green ideas to sleep furiously or to cause the number seven to become swarthier than a nonexistent baseball game. If we take the 'ought'-implies-'can' principle simply as an admonition that the content of any genuine moral obligation must be minimally intelligible, then it undoubtedly stands beyond any reasonable contestation. More common renderings of the 'ought'-implies-'can' precept are markedly more vulnerable, however. Still, not all of those renderings will be directly impugned here.

For example, this chapter will not need to defend the view that a person can be morally obligated to do something that is logically impossible. To be sure, one does not contradict oneself when one affirms that a person is morally duty-bound to perform X and to abstain from performing X.[3] If somebody has promised somebody else that he will draw a round square, then he may well be morally obligated to do so. Nevertheless, the focus of this chapter will not lie on such moral obligations; that is, we shall not train our attention on moral obligations with which it would be logically impossible to comply. Nor will the chapter concentrate on moral requirements of which the fulfillment would be *physically* infeasible. Although my arguments will tend to support the view that such requirements are entirely possible and sometimes actual, my focus will lie elsewhere.

Specifically, as has been suggested already, this chapter will be examining the notion that nobody should ever be held morally responsible for failing to avoid the infliction of any harm which he or she has not been able to avoid through all reasonably manageable precautions in the carrying out of some worthwhile activity. In other words, according to the version of the 'ought'-implies-'can'

---

[2] My distinction between wrongness and wrongfulness clearly overlaps with Heidi Hurd's distinction between wrongdoing and culpability in her 'Justification and Excuse, Wrongdoing and Culpability', 74 *Notre Dame Law Review* 1551, 1557–72 (1999) [hereinafter cited as Hurd, 'Justification']. However, despite the terminological similarity between the two distinctions, they are substantively different in certain respects (which need not be recounted here). Philip Soper's dichotomy between moral error and culpability, drawn at a number of junctures in his *The Ethics of Deference* (Cambridge: Cambridge University Press, 2002), is roughly similar terminologically to my wrongness/wrongfulness distinction. In fact, however, Soper adopts a Hartian position on the exonerative effects of good intentions. See, e.g., ibid., at 61, 75, 85, 96.

[3] I agree here with Ruth Barcan Marcus, 'More about Moral Dilemmas', in H.E. Mason, *Moral Dilemmas and Moral Theory* (Oxford: Oxford University Press, 1996) [hereinafter cited as Mason, *Dilemmas*], 23, 28. Note, incidentally, that the structure of a conflict between moral duties does not consist in one's being obligated to do X and to abstain from doing X. Rather, it consists in one's being obligated to do X and one's being obligated to abstain from doing X.

precept that is controverted here, 'can' means 'be able to achieve through the scrupulous exercise of care and goodwill', and 'cannot' therefore means 'be *un*able to achieve through the scrupulous exercise of care and goodwill'. In the eyes of Hart and many other theorists, a person will not have acted wrongly if she has earnestly exercised fastidious caution. Hence, in the sense of 'cannot' just indicated, no one is morally required to accomplish things which he or she cannot accomplish. (Note, incidentally, that the specified sense of 'cannot' goes beyond stark physical impossibility. Some outcomes that cannot be attained through the scrupulous exercise of care and goodwill are nonetheless attainable as a sheer matter of physical possibility. For instance, a mountain climber might not be able to avoid a fall even if he ascends a slope with meticulous circumspection and skill, yet he could have avoided the accident by altogether forgoing the activity of climbing mountains. Suppose that everyone is morally required not to become involved as a driver in any automobile accident. Although a person might not be able to live up to such a requirement through punctiliously careful driving, he can live up to it by declining to get behind the steering wheel of an automobile at all. What he can achieve as a matter of sheer physical possibility is more expansive than what he can achieve as a matter of impeccable precautions.)

This chapter will present a brief summary of Hart's argument, with attention to certain distinctions that are drawn there and elsewhere in his work. It will then explain why Hart's position is unsound. In so doing, the chapter will explicate the concept of a moral right in order to show why violations of moral rights can occur even when no one has acted wrongfully in any fashion. Having seen that strict liability does exist in morality as well as in law, we shall then look at several potential objections to my lines of reasoning. A consideration of those objections will take us into some prominent debates among moral philosophers—debates that can be illuminated with the aid of analyses developed by legal philosophers.

I. Hart on the Role of Good Intentions in Morality

Hart rightly took exception to the distortively simplistic idea that legal norms regulate only external behavior whereas moral norms regulate only inner sentiments and intentions. He felt that that idea had arisen as a mistaken response to the four dissimilarities between law and morality which he highlighted. He especially attributed the mistake to the presence of the third dissimilarity, on which we shall be focusing. In seeking to give a correct account of the matter, he indicated that there is an important difference between the conditions of moral responsibility and the conditions of legal responsibility. As he stated at the outset of his discussion of the divergences between law and morality:

If someone does something forbidden by moral rules or fails to do what they require, the fact that he did so unintentionally and in spite of every care is an excuse from *moral* blame; whereas a legal system or custom may have rules of 'strict liability' under which those who have broken the rules unintentionally and without 'fault' may be liable to punishment. So it is indeed true that while the notion of 'strict liability' in morals comes as near to being a contradiction in terms as anything in this sphere, it is something which may be merely open to criticism when found in a legal system. (Hart, *Concept*, 168–9, emphasis in original)

In his main exposition of this ostensible dissimilarity between law and morality, Hart began by reaffirming his view that a person is to be excused from moral responsibility if he or she has not behaved culpably in any manner: 'If a person whose action, judged *ab extra*, has offended against moral rules or principles, succeeds in establishing that he did this unintentionally and in spite of every precaution that it was possible for him to take, he is excused from moral responsibility, and to blame him in these circumstances would itself be considered morally objectionable'.[4] Hart then reiterated his claim that morality and law are fundamentally different in precisely this respect: 'It is . . . clear that legal responsibility is not necessarily excluded by the demonstration that an accused person could not have kept the law which he has broken; by contrast, in morals "I could not help it" is always an excuse, and moral obligation would be altogether different from what it is if the moral "ought" did not in this sense imply "can"' (Hart, *Concept*, 174).

Hart importantly clarified and amplified his argument by invoking a distinction between justifications and excuses. Although he regarded 'I could not help it' as a valid excuse in morality, he regarded it only as an excuse and not as a justification. For Hart and for manifold other theorists,[5] the distinction between the two is as follows. If conduct is justified, then it is at least permissible and is perhaps also laudable; someone engaging in such conduct has not thereby done anything wrong. By contrast, if the conduct of a person is excused, he has done

[4] Hart, *Concept*, 173. In a discussion of a somewhat different point in his *Punishment and Responsibility* (Oxford: Clarendon Press, 1968) [hereinafter cited as Hart, *Punishment*], 35–40, Hart similarly took as given that strict liability is excluded from morality.
[5] Hart, *Concept*, 174–5; Hart, *Punishment*, 13–14. See also J.L. Austin, 'A Plea for Excuses', 57 *Proceedings of the Aristotelian Society* 1, 2–3 (1956–7) [hereinafter cited as Austin, 'Plea']; Peter Cane, *Responsibility in Law and Morality* (Oxford: Hart Publishing, 2002) [hereinafter cited as Cane, *Responsibility*], 90; Joshua Dressler, 'New Thoughts about the Concept of Justification in the Criminal Law: A Critique of Fletcher's Thinking and *Rethinking*', 32 *UCLA Law Review* 61, 66–8 (1984); Kent Greenawalt, 'The Perplexing Borders of Justification and Excuse', 84 *Columbia Law Review* 1897, 1899–900 (1984) [hereinafter cited as Greenawalt, 'Borders']; Walter Sinnott-Armstrong, *Moral Dilemmas* (Oxford: Basil Blackwell, 1988) [hereinafter cited as Sinnott-Armstrong, *Dilemmas*], 42. The justification/excuse distinction is drawn somewhat differently by George Fletcher, the legal theorist who has written most extensively on it. See his *Rethinking Criminal Law* (Boston, MA: Little, Brown and Company, 1978) [hereinafter cited as Fletcher, *Rethinking*], chap. 10; 'Should Intolerable Prison Conditions Generate a Justification or an Excuse for Escape?' 26 *UCLA Law Review* 1355 (1979) [hereinafter cited as Fletcher, 'Conditions']; 'The Right and the Reasonable', 98 *Harvard Law Review* 949, 954–5, 977–8 (1985) [hereinafter cited as Fletcher, 'Right']. I do not here need to challenge Fletcher's understanding of the justification/excuse diremption. Nor do I need to consider the bearings of jurisdictional immunities, which operate in the law alongside justifications and excuses as liability-precluding factors.

something wrong but is absolved of responsibility for it. Justifiability consists in responsibility without wrongdoing, whereas excusability consists in wrongdoing without responsibility. An example of justified conduct is the action of a policeman in restraining a culprit who has committed a misdeed, while an example of excusable conduct (within the domain of criminal law) is the action of some person *P* who punches another person because a third party has credibly threatened *P* with death or other severe harm if he does not inflict the blow.

Now, before we explore the bearing of the justification/excuse dichotomy on Hart's argument about strict liability in morality, we should take account of another category to which Hart elsewhere adverted: the category of mitigations or extenuations (Hart, *Punishment*, 14–17). Though some theorists have distinguished between totally exonerative and partially exonerative excuses,[6] we are better advised to follow Hart in using a different term or set of terms for factors that are only partially exonerative. An extenuating factor is some feature of a person's behavior or circumstances that lessens the gravity of a wrong which the person has committed. Such a feature does not remove the character of the wrong as a wrong—that is, as something impermissible—and it might not entirely remove the wrongfulness thereof (that is, the status of the wrong as something impelled by malice or knowing indifference or recklessness or carelessness). Nevertheless, by reducing and perhaps eliminating the wrongfulness of what a person has done, any mitigating element will have lessened the blameworthiness of the person's conduct. It will thereby have softened the penalty or other remedy that is due. An example of a mitigating factor is offered by my last paragraph's illustration of an excuse. Although the harsh coercion employed to induce *P* to punch somebody else is undoubtedly sufficient to excuse his behavior in any criminal proceedings, it does not completely absolve him of moral responsibility. It heavily extenuates his behavior without fully exonerating him. In the absence of special circumstances, he will at least be obligated to apologize to the punched person when an opportunity arises.

Let us return to Hart's discussion of strict liability in morality. How does the justification/excuse dichotomy enter into that discussion? Hart maintained that, although 'I could not help it' is always an excuse in morality, it is only an excuse. When a person *P* has wronged somebody else in spite of exercising scrupulous care and goodwill, the exclusion of moral liability does not indicate that *P*'s action was justified. Rather, Hart argued, it indicates that holding *P* responsible for her unjustified action would be inappropriate in the circumstances. Moral norms do regulate *P*'s outward conduct—contrary to the simplistic view of morality as pertaining only to inner sentiments and intentions—but they also prescribe when it is or is not fair to hold *P* accountable for the injurious effects of

---

[6] See, e.g, Austin, 'Plea', 3. Because both justifications and excuses fully exclude criminal liability, quite a few criminal-law theorists do not attach very much importance to the justification/excuse distinction. For a recent example of such an attitude, see A.P. Simester and G.R. Sullivan, *Criminal Law: Theory and Doctrine* (Oxford: Hart Publishing, 2000), 537–40.

that outward conduct. Because of the latter role of moral norms, people are sometimes excused from moral responsibility for the wrongs which they have done to others. So Hart reasoned, as he concluded: 'Even in morals there is a difference between "He did not do the wrong thing" and "He could not help doing what he did"' (Hart, *Concept*, 175).

II. Moral Rights and Strict Liability

For my purposes, what is especially noteworthy about Hart's discussion of strict liability within morality is the absence of any references to extenuations. Though Hart in his philosophical writings on criminal law was well aware of the import of mitigating factors, he made no mention of them in the passages quoted above. Indeed, in the first of my extracts from *The Concept of Law*, he unwittingly brushed such factors aside by writing about blameworthiness and liability as if those two properties were equivalent. In my second quotation, he did much the same with blameworthiness and responsibility. This gap in his account is more than a gap; it is a far-reaching error. As will be argued in the rest of this chapter, there are no excuses in the domain of morality. Rather, the only relevant division in that domain is between justifications and extenuations. As a consequence, liability without culpability is present not only in some areas of the law but also in the realm of morals. With the aid of the conceptual demarcations which Hart himself carefully elaborated elsewhere, we can detect the shortcomings in his efforts to pin down the differences between legal responsibility and moral responsibility.

A. The Remedy Principle

To begin to substantiate the claims just made, this chapter will analyze what is involved in anybody's holding of a moral right. Though a number of objections will be parried as we go along, one query should be addressed straightaway. My analysis of moral rights, which will be presented below, can just as aptly be characterized as an analysis of moral duties. That is, my analysis takes for granted the correlativity of rights and duties. In other words, it takes for granted that a relationship of mutual entailment obtains between any moral right with a certain content held by some person X vis-à-vis some person Y and a moral duty with the same content owed by Y to X. X vis-à-vis Y holds a right to Y's ϕ-ing if and only if Y owes a duty to X to ϕ (where 'ϕ' represents any course of conduct by Y).[7] I have

---

[7] Sometimes the content of a moral duty pertains not to the duty-bearer's conduct but to the occurrence of some state of affairs (which will obtain or not obtain independently of his conduct). For example, if I earnestly and knowledgeably assure you that the sun will shine on a certain day, and if you reasonably rely upon my assurance, I shall have to apologize or otherwise make amends if the specified day turns out to be rainy. Purely for ease of exposition, I leave such duties out of consideration here.

argued at length elsewhere that every right is correlative with a duty and that every duty is correlative with a right. Nonetheless, such a view is not uncontroversial. Many theorists have contended that some duties are not correlated with rights.[8] Is my analysis in this chapter rendered dubious, then, by the controversial tenet that underlies it?

For two reasons, the foregoing question should be answered in the negative. First, anyone who denies the comprehensive correlativity of rights and duties can simply take this chapter's analyses to be confined to those duties that are manifestly correlated with rights. Only such duties will receive attention in the discussions below. Second, and more important, this chapter's explication of the nature of moral duties could quite easily be reformulated to eliminate any reliance on the thesis that rights and duties are invariably correlative. Likewise, my discussions which emanate from that explication could be suitably reformulated if necessary. Hence, somebody who rejects the idea of the thoroughgoing correlativity of rights and obligations can nevertheless accept all the central claims advanced in this chapter.

One further preliminary point should be noted. Thus far, I have referred only to persons as right-holders, and I shall largely continue to do so. On the one hand, this limitation is apposite partly because it facilitates stylistic simplicity and smoothness, and partly because the various scenarios explored in this chapter will all involve adult human beings as right-holders. There is no need for quarrels with theorists who insist that the universe of right-holders comprises only such human beings. On the other hand, the singling out of persons as right-holders is apposite solely for the reasons just mentioned. Nothing herein should lead anyone to infer that I myself regard the universe of right-holders as restricted to human adults. Quite the contrary; I have elsewhere argued sustainedly in favor of a more expansive conception.[9] (Worth remarking here is that the most prominent scenario in this chapter will involve a duty that is owed by an organization. Readers who recoil from a portrayal of a collectivity as a duty-bearer should reconstrue the scenario as involving a duty owed by a person—or by each of several persons—within the organization.)

Let us now look at my basic exposition of the situation that obtains when someone holds a moral right. That exposition consists in a *Remedy Principle*, in which 'X' and 'Y' designate persons and in which 'ϕ' designates some course of conduct by Y:

---

[8] For my view, see my 'Rights without Trimmings', in Matthew H. Kramer, N.E. Simmonds, and Hillel Steiner, *A Debate over Rights* (Oxford: Oxford University Press, 1998) [hereinafter cited as Kramer, 'Rights'], 7, 24–60. For citations to many writings that deny the thoroughgoing correlativity of rights and duties, see ibid., at 25 n.11.

[9] See Kramer, 'Rights', 49–70; Matthew H. Kramer, 'Getting Rights Right', in *Rights, Wrongs, and Responsibilities* (Basingstoke: Palgrave, 2001) [hereinafter cited as Kramer, 'Getting'], 28, 29–57.

If and only if X holds vis-à-vis Y a moral right against Y's ϕ-ing, Y's ϕ-ing will place Y under a moral obligation to X to remedy the resultant situation in some way.

This Remedy Principle is paralleled by a logically equivalent *Remedy Principle**, which encapsulates the situation that obtains when someone is under a moral duty:

If and only if Y owes X a moral duty not to ϕ, Y's ϕ-ing will place Y under a moral obligation to X to remedy the resultant situation in some way.

The key concept in each of these principles is obviously that of a moral remedy. A moral remedy is a measure undertaken or undergone in order to acknowledge the wrongness of what one has done to somebody else, and in order to deal adequately with the resultant situation. Among the most common types of moral remedies are apologies, acts of compensation or restitution, and punishments. Feelings of remorse also belong on this list. In every case, a remedy goes beyond merely taking steps to improve somebody else's situation or to lighten somebody else's hardships; such steps in themselves could appropriately be taken by a person who has not thitherto behaved impermissibly in any way and who therefore does not need to make amends for his conduct at all. Nor is a remedy the mere paying of a price or the paying off of a debt. When people hand over money to a restaurateur for a meal which they have just eaten, they are averting rather than correcting the commission of a wrong. A measure counts as a remedy only when it serves to indicate that some previous act or omission was impermissible and in need of rectification.

Before we proceed to ponder how the Remedy Principle and Remedy Principle* are connected with strict liability in morality, we should consider four objections that might be posed against those principles themselves. (We shall encounter additional objections later in the chapter.)

1. First, as some philosophers have pertinently recognized,[10] a duty-bearer is morally obligated to seek a waiver of his duty in advance when he knows that he will not be able to fulfill the duty and when he can reach the right-holder without incurring unreasonable costs. Yet, given the possibility of being released from one's duty ahead of time, it might seem that the Remedy Principle* is false. Someone can be morally obligated to abstain from ϕ-ing, yet his ϕ-ing will not impose any remedial obligations upon him. So a critic might assert. Any such objection to the Remedy Principle* will have foundered, for two reasons. In the first place, the waiving of a duty extinguishes it. By the time a duty-bearer behaves in some way that would have run athwart the waived duty if it had

---

[10] See, e.g., Judith Jarvis Thomson, *The Realm of Rights* (Cambridge, MA: Harvard University Press, 1990) [hereinafter cited as Thomson, *Realm*], 91–3 *et passim*; Walter Sinnott-Armstrong, 'Moral Dilemmas and Rights', in Mason, *Dilemmas* [hereinafter cited as Sinnott-Armstrong, 'Rights'], 48, 54. See also Terrance McConnell, 'Moral Residue and Dilemmas', in Mason, *Dilemmas* [hereinafter cited as McConnell, 'Residue'], 36, 42.

still existed, it will actually no longer exist. Consequently, the fact that the duty-bearer's behavior does not give rise to any remedial obligations is fully in accordance with the Remedy Principle*. After all, a corollary of that principle is that no such obligations are generated when somebody conducts himself in a manner which he is not duty-bound to eschew. No breach of duty, no remedy.

Furthermore, the obtention of a release from one's duty is itself an anticipatory remedy. An obligatory concomitant of a request for such a release is an apology for one's inability to abide by the specified duty. Indeed, something more than an apology might very well be obligatory if the granting of the waiver will be costly for the right-holder. Hence, the potential occurrence of waivers is perfectly consistent with the truth of the Remedy Principle*. (Of course, somebody might get released from a duty and might subsequently find that he is able to adopt the course of conduct which he was obligated to adopt. In such circumstances, he might opt for exactly that course of conduct. In that event, the anticipatory remedy turns out not to correspond to any actual act or omission that would have been a breach of duty in the absence of the release. To accommodate this point, the Remedy Principle and Remedy Principle* could be reformulated to link any post-hoc remedy with an actual breach, and to link any anticipatory remedy with an expected act or omission which would constitute a breach in the absence of a waiver and which might or might not turn out to be actual. However, the analytical benefits of such a reformulation would not be worth the stylistic convolutedness introduced by it—especially since all my examples in this chapter will involve obligations concerning post-hoc remedies rather than requests for waivers. Thus, although the role of waivers is unquestionably important, and although it could be taken into account within the main principles of my analysis, it will henceforth be pretermitted.)

2. A second criticism that might be leveled at my explication of moral rights and duties is that I have supposedly overlooked the myriad remedial arrangements that can be set conventionally.[11] For instance, vicarious liability in some of its guises might seem to reside beyond the ambit of my analysis.[12] Much the same might seem to be true of various third-party insurance policies which commit insurers to compensating people who have been harmed by the injurious conduct of the purchasers of the insurance. Although many arrangements for vicarious liability are not even ostensible counterexamples to my analysis—arrangements under which, for instance, employers are held

---

[11] Among the philosophers who have recognized the importance of conventionally established remedial arrangements are Jules Coleman, *Risks and Wrongs* (Cambridge: Cambridge University Press, 1992) [hereinafter cited as Coleman, *Risks*], 296–8; and Thomson, *Realm*, 95. When I designate the arrangements as conventional, I do not mean to suggest that all of them are introduced extra-legally. On the contrary, many such arrangements are required or authorized by legal norms. Because law itself is inherently conventional, the legally required or authorized status of various remedial schemes is fully consistent with their conventionality.

[12] For a recent account of vicarious liability in English tort law, see W.V.H. Rogers, *Winfield & Jolowicz on Tort* (London: Sweet & Maxwell, 2002) (16th edn), chap. 20.

responsible for the damage caused by employees who were acting within the scope of their jobs—other such arrangements are similar to the third-party insurance schemes in that they shift at least part of the burden of paying compensation onto parties who cannot plausibly be deemed to have caused the harms for which the compensatory payments are owed. Even more clearly will such a shift have occurred under a scheme of first-party insurance, whereby people take out policies that will compensate them for losses which they themselves suffer at the hands of others. Let us assume that, once these conventional schemes are established, the insurers or the vicariously liable parties are morally obligated to render the compensatory payments. In that case, those parties are morally obligated to remedy losses that have not been brought about by any breaches of duties on their part. Is such a state of affairs consistent with my conception of moral rights and duties?

To ascertain why the answer to this question is affirmative, we should initially probe the situation of the people from whom the compensatory responsibility is partly or wholly shifted. We should then examine the situation of the parties to whom the compensatory duties have been assigned. One minor point to be noted in connection with the former set of people is that in some circumstances the compensatory burdens will only have been partly transferred from them. For instance, under any plausible scheme of third-party insurance, the purchasers of the insurance will have to pay higher premiums if they cause mishaps that trigger the indemnification of injured parties. A much more important point is that sundry remedies—such as apologies, feelings of remorse, and punishments—can never properly be undertaken or undergone vicariously. An insurance company can take on the onus of compensating victims monetarily for their injuries, but it cannot appositely offer them an apology that originates with the company itself. If an apology is to function as an apology, it will have to come from the person who is causally and morally responsible for the injuries that have been suffered. That person is morally duty-bound to apologize, whether or not he has also retained the moral duty to furnish compensatory payments. (Of course, if more than one person is causally and morally responsible for the injuries, an apology from each of them is morally obligatory.) Even more obviously, if feelings of remorse are appropriate, they are appropriate only on the part of someone who is causally and morally responsible for the harm to which the remorse pertains. Somebody who is not so responsible can still naturally feel keen dismay over the damage that has occurred, but his harboring of the sentiment of remorse for that damage would amount to a delusion rather than to a morally requisite reaction. Equally unsuitable would be his undergoing of punishment for the damage. If the harm that has been inflicted is serious enough to warrant a resort to punitive measures, those measures should be taken against the person(s) responsible for the harm and against no one else. As Peter Cane declares: 'People should not be allowed to offload deserved punishments and penalties onto others.... So the fundamental question in this context concerns when the imposition of criminal sanctions is justified'.[13] Whatever one thinks about the notion of vicarious atonement expressed in the 'suffering servant' passages of the Book of Isaiah and in the New Testament's portrayal of Jesus, no tenable set of moral principles would yield the conclusion that the undergoing of a punishment due to a malefactor for his misdeeds can ever legitimately be delegated by him to somebody else. The Bible is correct in admonishing—in conflict with some other Biblical passages—that '[t]he fathers shall not be put to death for the children, nor shall the children be put to death for the fathers; every man shall be put to death [only] for his own sin' (Deuteronomy 24:16). To be sure, an extreme version of utilitarianism will prescribe that a person should undergo the penalties due for another person's misconduct whenever such an arrangement is promotive of utilitarian objectives. However, as has often been remarked, an extreme version of utilitarianism is unsound partly because it generates such a prescription.

In short, a remedy such as an apology or remorse or a punishment is not susceptible to being appropriately originated or undergone by anyone other than the person whose conduct has engendered the need for the remedy. Hence, given that the offering of an apology will be morally obligatory whenever a wrong has been committed, at least one morally requisite remedy will not lend itself to being initiated by anyone other than the wrongdoer. Consequently, the Remedy Principle* does indeed encapsulate what is true of anyone who has transgressed a duty. Such a person is morally obligated to remedy the resultant situation in some way, even if somebody else (such as an insurer) is morally obligated to rectify the situation in other ways. A chief source of the strength of the Remedy Principle*—and of the Remedy Principle—lies in the fact that it does not specify the remedy that is due in any particular context. Nothing is said therein about the type or extent of any remedy. Accordingly, so long as *some* rectificatory measure must be undertaken or undergone by everyone who transgresses a duty, the fact that in a particular context some additional such measure must be undertaken by someone else (such as an insurer) is perfectly compatible with my analysis. The possibility of shifting the responsibility for fulfilling compensatory obligations is consistent with the truth of the Remedy Principle* precisely because it is not the case that the responsibility for fulfilling every other remedial obligation can likewise be shifted.

We should now explore briefly the position of the parties to whom the task of fulfilling the compensatory obligations has been transferred. When an insurance company is called upon to indemnify the victims of any accidents that have been caused by its policy-holders, it does not thereby rectify any wrongs which it itself

---

[13] Cane, *Responsibility*, 249. For an excellent discussion of the inappositeness of insurance in the context of criminal law (as opposed to tort law), see ibid., at 245–9. As Cane observes, there are borderline cases of punishment. For example, some regulatory fines imposed on corporations cannot correctly be deemed morally justifiable unless they are understood as taxes on the corporations' activities rather than as punishments. In such cases, insurance covering the likely imposition of the fines is probably legitimate.

has perpetrated. Having never wronged the people to whom it is obligated to make compensatory payments, it furnishes the payments in order to keep itself from wronging them. In that respect, those payments are cognate with the payments made by diners to a restaurateur for the meals which they have consumed. Though the insurance company is helping to rectify wrongs, the wrongs which it is helping to rectify are not its own. Considered purely in relation to its own operations, its payments to any victim of a policy-holder's misbehavior are not a moral remedy at all in the sense which I have delineated. That is, the payments do not amount to any acknowledgment of wrongdoing, for there is no wrongdoing (on the part of the insurance company) to be acknowledged. The difference between the insurer's position and that of any of its miscreant policy-holders is captured straightforwardly in the Remedy Principle*. According to that principle, Y's doing or omitting to do something—his ϕ-ing— must be sufficient for the obligatoriness of a remedy if Y is to be classifiable as a duty-bearer. Whereas the culpably injurious conduct of a policy-holder (for example, someone's driving carelessly into a pedestrian) is indeed sufficient for the obligatoriness of a remedy, the sheer act of an insurance company in providing coverage to policy-holders is not similarly sufficient. Nor is the insurance company's action necessary for the obligatoriness of the remedy, of course. By contrast, in the prevailing circumstances the policy-holder's misconduct is both sufficient and necessary for the activating of remedial obligations. Thus, in connection with any such obligations to which a policy-holder's misdeeds have given rise, the Remedy Principle* correctly leads us to two firm conclusions: the policy-holder was duty-bound to avoid those misdeeds, and the emergence of the remedial obligations was not due to any breach of duty by the insurers who have provided the policy-holder with coverage and who have thereby committed themselves to discharging some of those obligations.

3. A third query that might be raised about the Remedy Principle or Remedy Principle* is that some counterexamples supposedly show that violations of moral rights and duties are not invariably associated with remedial obligations. Let us briefly investigate a few scenarios that putatively support this latest query.

Walter Sinnott-Armstrong, who is keenly alert to the links between breaches of moral duties and remedial obligations, nevertheless feels a need to concede that those links are not unfailingly present. To substantiate his view, he offers the following scenario: 'Suppose that I promise to meet you for a casual lunch, but I break my promise in order to save someone's life. Later you tell me that, if we had met, we would have both been killed by a bomb in the restaurant. It would then be odd for me to feel bad about breaking my promise or to say, "I'm sorry. I'll make it up to you"' (Sinnott-Armstrong, 'Rights', 54–5). Sinnott-Armstrong has constructed his example skillfully. The original duty in the example is palpably exceeded in importance by the far more pressing duty that countervails it, and the consequences of breaching the former duty are strongly positive on the whole for each of the people involved. If any scenario were to involve the transgression of a moral duty without the engendering of any remedial obligations, Sinnott-Armstrong's would surely be it. In fact, however, his scenario fails. Its fatal shortcoming is that—like Hart's discussion of the dissimilarities between legal liability and moral liability—it neglects the distinction between absolution and extenuation.

The circumstances recounted in Sinnott-Armstrong's scenario do not completely absolve the promisor of obligations to remedy his breach of duty, but they do very heavily extenuate that breach. Because of the extenuating force of those circumstances, neither of the remedies mentioned by Sinnott-Armstrong is apposite. Plainly, the promisor should not feel remorseful dismay over what he has done. Nor is he under the slightest obligation to make amends to the promisee beyond the mere offering of an apology. Rather, because of the exigency of the situation that impelled him to violate his promissory duty, and because of the remarkably gratifying consequences of the violation, the sole remedy required of him is the offering of an apology and a brief explanation. Any apology in this context will itself be a terse formality, accompanied no doubt by an expression of exhilarated relief. ('I'm sorry that I had to break my promise to meet up with you for lunch, but thank goodness that everything turned out so well for us as a result!') When presented with the apology and the explanation, the promisee might laughingly indicate that she is fully satisfied without them. Nonetheless, if the apology and explanation were not offered at all—not even as laconic formalities that will probably be laughed off by their recipient—their wholesale absence would bespeak insufficient respect for the promisee as a moral agent to whom a moral duty was owed.[14] The permissibility of their absence would imply that, whenever the contravention of a right of a promisee will fortuitously promote some of her own important interests and will not cause her any serious harm, the right can legitimately be altogether ignored for the sake of furthering the well-being of others. In sum, though the promisor's wrong was without wrongfulness and was morally optimal, it was a wrong that now has to be remedied. Mild though the requisite remedy is, it is the means of upholding the moral status of the promisee and is therefore something that cannot legitimately be forgone.

When we note that Sinnott-Armstrong's example is a variant of a scenario frequently discussed by Anglo-American tort lawyers, we can perceive more clearly that it fails to establish his point. Tort lawyers have posited a situation in which a pedestrian at an airport is injured by a speeding motorist who is driving carelessly or maliciously. As a result of the injuries and the attendant disruption, the pedestrian is unable to board her flight to a distant city. A bomb explodes on that flight, and everyone on the plane is killed. Now, although this scenario is quite closely parallel to Sinnott-Armstrong's example, it obviously

---

[14] This point is missed in Peter Railton, 'The Diversity of Moral Dilemma', in Mason, *Dilemmas* [hereinafter cited as Railton, 'Diversity'], 140, 154. However, for a valuable corrective, see ibid., at 166 n.23.

lacks one of the main extenuating features in the latter: the absence of culpability. Whereas Sinnott-Armstrong envisages a promisor who commendably adopts a morally optimal course of action in breaching a duty owed to a promisee, the motorist in this new scenario not only commits a wrong but also acts wrongfully (either carelessly or maliciously). Moreover, even the other major extenuating feature in Sinnott-Armstrong's example—the gratifyingness of the consequences that flow from the promisor's violation of his duty—is not fully paralleled in the tort lawyers' scenario. Though it turns out that the pedestrian is better off than she would have been if the motorist had not driven into her, she has suffered injuries that are almost certainly much more serious than the inconvenience occasioned by the breaking of a promise to meet for lunch. Thus, although the gravity of the wrong committed by the motorist is extenuated by the favorableness of the ultimate outcome for the pedestrian, it is not extenuated by an absence of culpability and is likewise not extenuated by a very low level of any detriment at all. In these circumstances, the need for some remedies is evident. Especially if the driving was malicious, the motorist is morally obligated to undergo some sort of punishment (perhaps a fine or perhaps some sterner measure). The motorist is also morally obligated to apologize for his misconduct, and to provide compensation for the pedestrian's wounds. To be sure, because of the exceedingly unusual upshot of the motorist's misbehavior, the compensation morally due to the pedestrian might well exclude certain items that would normally be compensable (such as her lost earnings, if any). Nevertheless, at the very least the motorist will be morally required to pay compensation for his victim's pain and distress. As we would expect, then, the differences between the scenario of the commendable promisor and the scenario of the blameworthy motorist are reflected in a large disparity between the remedies due in the one case and the remedies due in the other. Still, in a key respect the scenarios are fundamentally similar. In each case there has been a transgression of a moral duty, and in each case the transgressor of the duty is morally required to remedy the resultant situation. Factors present in the scenario of the promisor—and absent from the scenario of the motorist—greatly extenuate the breaking of the promise but do not eliminate entirely its nature as a breach of a moral duty. An acknowledgment of the occurrence of a wrong against the promisee is essential for a reaffirmation of her moral status, even though the fact that the wrong has proved to be hugely beneficial for her will sharply attenuate the extent of what is required for that reaffirmation. In this basic respect, the tale of the promisor is like the tale of the motorist in being crucially divergent from any scenario in which there has been no infringement of a moral duty. Dissimilarities between those two tales center on the degree to which the infringement in each has been mitigated, rather than on the questions whether an infringement in each case has occurred and whether a remedy of *some* sort is obligatory.

Let us move on to an example devised by Philippa Foot. In an important essay published more than two decades ago, she has conjured up a situation largely similar to the one imagined by Sinnott-Armstrong.[15] Somebody has promised to meet somebody else for lunch, but must instead rush an accident victim to a hospital. There is no opportunity for the promisor to alert the promisee to his inability to keep their appointment. All the same, the promisee does not suffer any sense of frustration, for she meets her future spouse (or somebody who offers her a splendid job) just as she is starting to wait. Having sketched this chain of events in which 'things turn out splendidly all around', Foot is initially intent simply on emphasizing that feelings of remorse on the part of the promisor would be out of place. 'Are we to say that . . . in the general rejoicing there should be an element of distress (moral distress) because after all a promise was broken and that is something bad, and therefore regrettable' (Foot, 'Realism', 387). As has already been indicated in my remarks on Sinnott-Armstrong's example, Foot's rhetorical question is wholly unexceptionable. Foot is correct in submitting that the promisor is in no way morally required to experience a sense of remorse for what he has done. Such a remedy would be quite unsuitable. However, having made this germane point, Foot slightly later adverts to a variant of her example in order to advance some bolder claims. Her pronouncements should be quoted at some length here, partly because they echo a bit of Hart's language and partly because they address the distinction between mitigation and exoneration:

[T]here is an imputation against which not only physical or mental but also moral necessity is a shield. How can this be denied? There is a clear place for the plea 'I couldn't help it' (couldn't help breaking the promise because I had to attend to the accident victim, and so on). Nor does this plea simply plead mitigation, as if the offense of breaking the promise was merely lessened. If you suffer because I cannot get to the appointment I have with you, I say that I am sorry, meaning that I regret it; but if it was not my fault I do not apologize, and I certainly do not have to 'make restitution' as some have suggested. If I *can't* keep the appointment it isn't my fault that you suffer, and it doesn't make any difference whether the necessity of breaking the promise was physical, mental, or moral. (Foot, 'Realism', 388–9, emphasis in original)

Insightful though Foot's essay is in most other respects, this passage is misconceived. As Judith Jarvis Thomson has pungently commented: 'This [passage] sounds remarkably cavalier to me. Can she really believe that *she* may at will make others pay the full costs of her altruism' (Thomson, *Realm*, 100 n.12, emphasis in original).

Let us first consider what Foot says about restitution. On that topic, Thomson again supplies a pertinent observation: 'But perhaps [Foot] is thinking of what is most common where an appointment is broken: the victim suffers only inconvenience, for which it is hard even to imagine what restitution would consist in' (Thomson, *Realm*, 100 n.12). In other words, Foot is doubtless correct about

---

15 Philippa Foot, 'Moral Realism and Moral Dilemma', 80 *Journal of Philosophy* 379, 387 (1983) [hereinafter cited as Foot, 'Realism'].

restitution but only because it is a remedy that is manifestly out of place in this context. Unless we stretch the notion of restitution to encompass virtually every other remedy—that is, unless we construe Foot's phrase 'make restitution' as if it were 'make amends'—we shall be hard-pressed to understand how anyone could suggest that restitution is an appropriate means of rectifying a failure to keep a luncheon engagement. On that specific point, no one has ever seriously espoused the view which Foot is contesting.

Compensation is a more plausible remedy, but in most situations of broken engagements it will not be obligatory. If the inconvenience incurred by the promisee is substantial, however, some compensation (perhaps in the form of a gift such as flowers or candy) might very well be morally required. Yet, under many circumstances, the sole obligatory remedy for a broken luncheon engagement is an apology accompanied by an explanation. It is precisely in connection with such a remedy that Foot's remarks are so puzzling. To be sure, her remarks would be sensible if it were true that an apology perforce amounts to an admission of culpability. In the circumstances envisaged, in which a promise to meet for lunch has gone unfulfilled because the promisor has had to rush somebody to a hospital, he has behaved admirably rather than culpably. He has patently not been malicious or knowingly indifferent or reckless or careless. Hence, if an apology were inevitably an expression of contrition for wrongful conduct, no such remedy would be apt in the situation which Foot sketches. In fact, however, an apology plays a quite different role in such a situation, where a wrong has been committed without wrongfulness. In a context of that kind, an apology serves as an acknowledgment that a duty owed by oneself to somebody else has been breached—even though the breaching was morally optimal and entirely well-intentioned. In the absence of an apology in Foot's example, as has already been argued, no adequate respect would be paid to the status of the promisee as someone who held a right that has been infringed; the promisee's right would in effect be entirely ignored. The ascribability of the infringement to a pressing emergency will have mitigated the extent of the requisite remedy (which can be a mere formality), but will not have done away with the need for a remedy completely.

Foot appears not to distinguish sufficiently between wrongness or impermissibility and wrongfulness or culpability. Both in the long quoted passage and in the accompanying parts of her essay, she repeatedly indicates that she is concentrating on the faultiness or the lack of faultiness of the promisor's conduct. While insisting correctly that the promisor is not at fault (that is, not culpable), she believes incorrectly that she has thereby established that his conduct gives rise to no remedial obligations whatsoever. Despite behaving nonculpably and indeed laudably, the promisor has committed a moral wrong in that he has failed to fulfill a moral duty which he owed to the promisee. That moral wrong, heavily extenuated though it is by the crisis that prompted it, must be rectified if the promisee's standing as a right-holder is to be shown due esteem. The absence of faultiness in the promisor's conduct will enormously affect the extent and nature of the required remedy, but will not affect its sheer status as something that is indeed required.

In the principal passage quoted above, Foot draws an unexplicated and quite elusive distinction between saying that one is sorry and apologizing. She apparently has in mind a division between the sort of consternation that should be expressed by a mere bystander and the sort of consternation that should be expressed by someone who is culpably responsible for harm to another person. Again, however, she is eliding the difference between responsibility and culpability. It is true that the promisor in her example has not behaved culpably, but it is not true that his position is morally equivalent to that of a mere bystander; unlike the bystander, he has failed to carry out a duty which he owed to someone else. Foot's verdict in the long quotation above is especially curious because her rehashing of her scenario of the promisor allows that the breaking of the luncheon engagement may have significantly inconvenienced the promisee. Given that the promisee may have suffered considerable hardships, the notion that the promisor has no obligation to apologize for the nonfulfillment of his duty is decidedly odd. Quite fitting is Thomson's harsh comment about the chilly hauteur of a Footian rescuer who does not deign to take account of the costs which his altruism imposes on others.

Let us move on to a clever example put forward by Simon Blackburn, who endeavors to reveal that moral remedies are sometimes required in circumstances where no wrongs have been perpetrated.[16] He posits a situation in which he needs to use a chainsaw and in which Alice has offered hers and Bertha has offered hers. He opts to use Alice's saw. Having accepted Alice's offer, Blackburn contends, he owes Bertha 'some friendly overture to show that I took her offer seriously, that I had no particular preference for Alice, and so on. . . . At the very least I have to show that I appreciated her offer' (Blackburn, 'Dilemmas', 131–2). He then draws his conclusion: '[I]t is sometimes argued that the need for reparation or apology to a side whose interests are not met after a dilemma shows that a genuine [moral] requirement has been violated. Here I simply point out that the phenomenon is more widespread, for similar apology and even reparation may be in order when no requirements have been violated' (Blackburn, 'Dilemmas', 132). What Blackburn in effect is challenging here is the biconditionality of the Remedy Principle*. Even if that principle is correct in

---

[16] Simon Blackburn, 'Dilemmas: Dithering, Plumping, and Grief', in Mason, *Dilemmas* [hereinafter cited as Blackburn, 'Dilemmas'], 127, 131–2. In addition to the example which I discuss in the text, Blackburn offers an example that involves the comforting of a lad by a coach who has not selected the lad for some team. See ibid., at 135–6. My approach to this latter example would be essentially the same as my approach to the example of Alice and Bertha. However, instead of distinguishing between apologies (or other moral remedies) and expressions of gratitude—the appropriate dichotomy for my analysis of the situation concerning Alice and Bertha—I would distinguish between apologies (or other moral remedies) and expressions of encouragement and solace. Like expressions of gratitude, expressions of encouragement and solace do not in themselves constitute any acknowledgment of wrongdoing.

declaring that every breach of a moral duty will give rise to remedial obligations, it might be wrong in declaring that every occurrence of remedial obligations will have ensued from a breach of a moral duty. Blackburn in effect is assailing the Remedy Principle* on precisely that point.

Fortunately, Blackburn's example fails to clinch his challenge. Let us presume that his assurances to Bertha are felicitous. Then, either they are an obligatory apology, in which case they rectify a moral wrong; or they are merely an expression of gratitude and friendship, in which case they are not a moral remedy and are not proffered in the context of any moral wrong. The first of these two possibilities can be actual in some circumstances. For example, Blackburn may have promised Bertha that he would accept her chainsaw. In that event, his decision to reject the saw in favor of Alice's is a breach of a promissory duty. Or, even in the absence of a promise, he may have had good grounds for believing that Bertha would be seriously offended if he were to decline her chainsaw. His snubbing of her might then be a minor wrong and consequently call for a mild apology.

Of course, on the basis of the facts of which we are apprised, we cannot say with certitude whether Blackburn has owed Bertha a duty in the circumstances just adumbrated. We would have to know more about the reasonableness of the grounds for her strong hope or expectation that he would take her chainsaw in preference to Alice's. The sheer strength of her hope or expectation is not necessarily determinative. After all, if Bertha has fervently hoped that Blackburn will propose marriage to her, that fact alone does not obligate him to do so. Only if he has culpably encouraged her fervent hopes, will he have placed himself under a duty to satisfy them. We need to know whether any comparable element of culpability is present in the scenario of the chainsaws, before we can judge with confidence whether Blackburn has been under an obligation to select Bertha's saw or not.

Naturally, if Blackburn has been under an obligation to Bertha, he may also have been under an obligation to Alice (perhaps because he has promised to take her chainsaw, or perhaps because he has encouraged her hopes in some other way). If he is indeed under an obligation to each of the two ladies, and if he is not able to take more than one of the chainsaws, then he confronts a situation of conflicting obligations. Whichever chainsaw he selects, he will be committing a wrong against the person whose saw he has not accepted. In such a situation of moral conflict, the wrong undertaken will be extenuated by the fact that the commission of it is necessary for the avoidance of another wrong. Nevertheless, although extenuated, the nonfulfillment of a moral duty engenders a remedial obligation. To comply with that latter obligation, Blackburn will have to apologize to the lady whose chainsaw he has declined.

More likely, however, is that the selection of Alice's saw by Blackburn has not amounted to the commission of a moral wrong against Bertha. If so, then no apology is required. Nonetheless, he still might be obligated to utter soothing words to Bertha. In such a situation, the obligatory assurances are not an apology but are instead an expression of gratitude. Instead of being morally required to say something along the lines of 'I apologize for the wrong which I have done to you', Blackburn will be morally required to say something along the lines of 'I'm extremely grateful for your generosity, but I can only take one chainsaw, and I have opted to take Alice's'. The key point here lies in what was observed earlier about the nature of moral remedies. Any such remedy is a way of acknowledging that one has done something impermissible. An obligatory expression of gratitude involves no such acknowledgment, for there has been no impermissible thing done. Instead, such an expression makes clear one's awareness of the generosity of someone else, and it conveys one's favorable reaction to that generosity—a reaction that can be sincerely felt even when, as in Blackburn's scenario, one elects not to take advantage of the generosity. An assurance of one's appreciation, which does not involve any intimation that one has acted wrongly in declining an offer, is singularly appropriate for a context in which the declining of the offer is indeed not wrong. An apology, which would indicate that one has acted impermissibly, would be inappropriate for such a context. No wrong, no remedy.

In short, the message of Blackburn's thought-provoking example is markedly different from what his discussion of the example implies. Blackburn appears to think that, in scenarios like the one which he concocts, we can always unproblematically distinguish between the presence and the absence of moral requirements. He similarly appears to think that we can always distinguish unproblematically between apologies and expressions of gratitude. After all, in the passages quoted above, his prime contention is that his scenario reveals the obligatoriness of an apology in a situation where no moral duty has been breached. The true lesson to be derived from his little narrative is in a contrary direction. What the narrative discloses is that we cannot always tell straightforwardly whether a duty has been breached or not. There is a gray area of borderline cases. We therefore cannot always tell straightforwardly whether an apology or an expression of gratitude is due. Indeed, if we were to listen to the soothing words uttered to Bertha, we might not be able to determine unequivocally whether they constitute an apology or an expression of gratitude. Like the extension of any philosophical distinction, then, the extension of the distinction between apologies and expressions of gratitude is subject to vagueness. Over a certain range of cases, that extension is not clear-cut. A healthy alertness to the existence of those borderline cases is what we can gain from musing on Blackburn's valuable example. At the same time, any such alertness should be combined with a clear-eyed awareness that—in situations like that of Alice and Bertha and Blackburn— an apology is due whenever a moral duty has been breached, and a mere expression of gratitude is due when no moral duty has been breached. Though the concrete question whether a transgression of a moral duty has occurred is not always susceptible to an unequivocal answer, we can always give an unequivocally affirmative answer to the more abstract question whether a moral remedy will be due when and only when a transgression has occurred.

Let us glance at one further example, which we have investigated for slightly different purposes in Chapter 6. Mary Mothersill has noted that, if someone has to lie to a would-be murderer in order to prevent him from ascertaining the whereabouts of his intended victim, any 'subsequent remorse would be irrational'.[17] Two quick observations are in order here. In the first place, Mothersill is of course correct in affirming that remorse would be foolish in this context. Even if one owed a moral duty to the murderer to abstain from prevaricating, one's breaching of that duty would plainly be morally optimal (in the circumstances) and would therefore not be a transgression for which remorse is a suitable remedy. What is more, as has been argued in Chapter 6, there are in fact no grounds for maintaining that the murderer holds a moral right against being told an untruth. His expectations of his interlocutor's truthfulness carry no moral weight in the special circumstances. Accordingly, not only would remorse be out of place, but any moral remedy at all would be inappropriate. No wrong, no remedy. Although Mothersill thinks that she has referred to a situation of conflicting duties, the person confronted by the murderer does not in fact face any genuine moral conflict. If telling a lie to the aspiring murderer about the location of the intended victim is necessary in order to save that victim's life, then telling such a lie is permissible as well as obligatory.

4. A fourth major objection that might be mounted against the Remedy Principle would highlight the fact that any remedial obligation envisaged by that principle is owed to the holder of the right that has been violated. What should we think about a situation in which the violation consists in a murder? Is the remedial obligation owed to a dead person? Indeed, some critics would balk even at the notion that a remedial obligation can be owed to the victim of an assault who has been left comatose. Are only some types of rights-violations covered by the Remedy Principle?

As was suggested near the outset of my discussion of the Remedy Principle, either of two responses to these questions is sufficient for my purposes. In many ways, the better response is to deny the premises that underlie the questions. I have argued elsewhere that dead people and comatose people are potential holders of moral and legal rights (Kramer, 'Rights', 32; Kramer, 'Getting', 29–31, 48–52). In light of those arguments and in light of the Interest Theory of rights which underpins them, a proponent of the Remedy Principle should feel no embarrassment about that principle's countenancing of the possibility of nonstandard right-holders. If dead people and comatose people can indeed hold moral rights, then the Remedy Principle is correct in implying that dead or comatose victims of attacks hold moral rights that are correlative to some of the remedial obligations of their attackers.

---

[17] Mary Mothersill, 'The Moral Dilemmas Debate', in Mason, *Dilemmas* [hereinafter cited as Mothersill, 'Debate'], 66, 79.

Still, as was stated earlier, the main lines of argument in this chapter can be detached from any embroilment in the controversies over the Interest Theory and the Will Theory of rights. While blenching from the notion that dead or comatose people can hold rights, the advocates of the Will Theory can nonetheless embrace a pertinently reformulated Remedy Principle*. A reformulation satisfactory to such theorists would remove the principle's current indication that all obligations (in particular, all remedial obligations) are correlated with rights. Revised in that fashion, the Remedy Principle* would then announce simply that Y is under a moral duty to ϕ if and only if Y's not ϕ-ing will place Y under a moral obligation to remedy the resultant situation in some way. Furthermore, any Will Theorist could retain my own favored wording of the Remedy Principle* as a formulation that specifically covers all cases involving moral duties that are correlated with rights. With that original principle and the broader revised principle in hand, a Will Theorist can endorse every line of reasoning in this chapter (perhaps with some terminological alterations here and there). Hence, although the Remedy Principle and the Remedy Principle* as currently worded are indeed expressive of my allegiance to the Interest Theory of rights, their betokening of that allegiance is a dispensable feature.

B. No Right without a Remedy

Legal theorists have often submitted that legal rights are invariably connected to remedies. 'No right without a remedy' or 'No remedy, no right' is a maxim frequently bandied about by jurisprudential writers.[18] Such a maxim, however, is too sweeping in application to legal rights. Contrariwise, as a bit of reflection on the Remedy Principle reveals, the 'no right without a remedy' apothegm is true in application to moral rights. In other words, although legal rights are often thought to be indissolubly linked to remedies, and although moral rights are often thought to be disseverable from remedies, the truth is precisely the reverse. Let us briefly probe this divergence between legal rights and moral rights, and ponder why it exists.

As I have argued elsewhere (Kramer, 'Getting', 65–78), some legal duties are purely nominal in that the legal mandates which establish them do not provide for any means of giving effect to them. Although the requirements articulated in those mandates instruct people to act or refrain from acting in specified ways, the instructions receive no backing whatsoever from any legally authorized penalties or punishments. Existing solely as formulations, nominal duties imposed by those mandates are not only unenforced but also unenforceable. The potential for the emergence of nominal duties within the law is attributable to the practice of articulating the law's requirements in written or spoken formulations. Such a

---

[18] See, e.g., Karl Llewellyn, 'Some Realism about Realism—Responding to Dean Pound', 44 *Harvard Law Review* 1222, 1244 (1931).

practice is operative in every legal system, though its specifics of course differ from system to system. Because all or some of the law's demands are presented in written or spoken formulations, gaps can arise between the demands that are expressed and the demands for which legal remedies are available. If no legal remedies are available at all for breaches of certain expressed requirements—that is, if legal remedies are wholly unprovided for rather than simply unused—then the legal requirements in question are purely nominal. The legal norms which lay down those requirements are thereby imposing legal duties and conferring legal rights that are not linked to any legal remedies whatsoever.

Within conventional or positive morality—that is, within the domain of moral precepts that emerge and obtain as such by dint of being widely accepted—there is similarly a potential for nominal duties. Because some or all of the requirements of conventional morality are set forth in written or spoken formulations, there can arise gaps between the duties articulated in those formulations and the duties of which any breaches will give rise to remedial obligations (within conventional morality). Some duties in the former sense might not be duties in the latter sense.

Things are quite different within the domain of critical or transcendent morality. Within that domain—that is, within the domain of moral norms whose status as binding mandates does not depend on their acceptance among the people to whom they apply—there is no room for nominal duties. Precisely because the norms of critical morality are always independent of conventional formulations, they do not give rise to duties that exist only as formulations. If a critical-moral duty does not exist in a formulation-independent mode, it does not exist at all. The formulation-independent mode in which any such duty exists, of course, is its standing as a requirement that will generate remedial obligations if it goes unfulfilled. Duties in the domain of critical morality are integrally and invariably connected to remedial obligations, whereas duties whose existence is not inherently formulation-independent (namely, duties in domains such as law and conventional morality) are disjoinable from remedial obligations.

Throughout this chapter, except where explicitly stated otherwise, my references to obligations and rights are references to critical-moral obligations and rights. The Remedy Principle and Remedy Principle* are explications of just such rights and obligations. What those principles are designed to capture is the stark vacuity of the notion of a moral right or duty that does not engender remedial obligations in the event of its being infringed. If someone is morally obligated to do x, and if his abstention from doing x will not impose any remedial duties upon him, then what exactly does his being obligated-to-do-x consist in? It cannot consist in a purely nominal state of requiredness, since the relevant norms of critical morality apply as such without ever having been articulated in writing or speech. What, then, would his being obligated-to-do-x consist in, if its nature is not encapsulated by the Remedy Principle*? The lack of any minimally satisfactory answer to this question is what vindicates that principle. (Obviously, nothing said here is meant to imply that the contents of the norms of critical morality will perforce remain unarticulated as guides to behavior. On the contrary, it is overwhelmingly likely that some such norms will be formulated as precepts of conventional morality in virtually every society. However, the bearings of those norms as mandates of critical morality are never derivative of their having been formulated and endorsed as mandates of conventional morality. Accordingly, when we ask what some state of moral obligatedness would be if it were not a state that engenders remedial duties in the manner outlined by the Remedy Principle*, we cannot fall back on the answer that it might exist simply in the form of a pronouncement. Any state of critical-moral obligatedness is independent of every pronouncement of conventional morality, and is therefore never reducible to any such pronouncement.)

C. Strict Liability in Morality

During my discussion of the Remedy Principle and Remedy Principle*, we have pondered some instances of wrongs without wrongfulness. We shall now study a more extended example that can underscore the unsustainability of Hart's belief in the fully exonerative effect of impeccable intentions.

Suppose that George is tried in a criminal court for a serious crime which he has not in fact perpetrated or attempted to perpetrate. The evidence against him is compelling, as reliable witnesses testify in good faith that they saw him perform the misdeed for which he has been charged. Various other items of evidence all militate in favor of a conviction. Thus, although the court abides scrupulously by all relevant requirements of procedural fairness, and although George is provided with ample opportunities to rebut the incriminating evidence if he can come up with contrary evidence, the decision of the court ultimately goes against him. He is convicted for a crime which he never carried out. He is sentenced to prison, where he spends six years. During his time in prison, he suffers no ill treatment at the hands of the officials or his fellow inmates; but, of course, he is deprived of his general liberty throughout the period of his detention. At the end of six years, some suitable exculpatory evidence becomes available. (Perhaps technological developments have made possible the discovery of his innocence through new forensic techniques, or perhaps the genuine culprit has confessed, or perhaps a previously reluctant witness has come forward to attest cogently to George's innocence. The precise factor behind the unearthing of his innocence is immaterial for my purposes.) With his conviction quashed, George is released from prison.

What should be done to George, according to tenable standards of morality? Should the authorities in the jail simply supply him with his belongings and direct him to the exit, and should that be an end of the matter? Should no further steps be taken? Or is some moral remedy—some measure acknowledging the wrongness of his long detention in prison—obligatory in the circumstances? Without seeking to pin down exactly what the authorities in the criminal-justice system are morally required to do in order to remedy George's situation, I shall take as given that at the very least they are morally required to extend a formal apology. Were no such measure to be taken, George would be thoroughly justified in feeling aggrieved. The wrong already done to him would be compounded by the nonfulfillment of the remedial obligations that are owed to him.

Yet, although a moral wrong has been committed against George, and although a moral remedy is therefore obligatory, the officials in the criminal-justice system have behaved impeccably. A formal apology to George will constitute an acknowledgment of the wrongness of his having been imprisoned for so long, but it will not carry any suggestion of wrongfulness. No official at his trial or in the prison has acted maliciously or recklessly or carelessly toward him. His trial was conducted with meticulous fairness, and his incarceration was the result of that fastidiously careful trial where the verdict was reached in accordance with the mass of evidence against him. The deprivation of his general freedom for several years was impermissible but not culpable. It was impermissible in that it has morally obligated the authorities in the criminal-justice system to make amends appropriately (at least by apologizing and probably also by taking further steps that will repair the contravention of his moral right-against-being-lengthily-confined-for-any-crime-which-he-has-not-committed). It was not culpable, however, in that it ensued from the workings of institutions that adhered scrupulously to all pertinent procedural safeguards. Contrary to what Hart maintained, then, worthwhile actions or activities can trigger moral liability even if the people engaging in them have exercised all reasonably attainable precautions. Contrary to what he affirmed, 'ought' does not imply 'can'. The organizations that operate the criminal-justice system have breached a moral duty through the lengthy incarceration of George, even though their operations which failed in that respect were impeccably careful.

To be sure, the remedial obligations that have descended upon the aforementioned organizations are clearly affected by the impeccableness of the procedural safeguards that attended the processes whereby George was imprisoned. However, the effect is to extenuate the wrong done to him, rather than to remove it altogether. The requisite remedies would be much stiffer if the internment of George had stemmed from malice or knowing indifference or recklessness or carelessness. Because none of those culpability-producing factors was present, the measures required for remedying the situation will be relatively light. Nonetheless, some measures are indeed required; extenuation is not exoneration. At the very least, an authoritative apology is due. After all, an innocent man has been deprived of his general liberty for six years.

The requisite apology will be more than simply an expression of solicitous consternation, for an expression of the latter sort is not an acknowledgment of the commission of a wrong by oneself and is therefore something that could just as aptly be uttered by an uninvolved observer. Nor, of course, will the requisite apology be simply an expression of encouragement and consolation. Again, such an expression, which might for example be offered to a lad who has suffered the disappointment of failing to land a place on his school's basketball team, is not an acknowledgment of any wrongdoing. An apology accepts responsibility for a certain state of affairs or chain of events, and admits that that state of affairs or chain of events is wrong. It admits, in other words, that one's treatment of somebody else has fallen short of minimally acceptable standards. Though the falling short may be heavily extenuated by one's having adopted all reasonable precautions or by one's having had to avert an even worse outcome, it remains a falling short. As such, it calls for a moral remedy or a set of moral remedies. An apology concedes as much, without denying the possible existence and weightiness of some mitigating considerations.

In the scenario of George and the criminal-justice system, a moral remedy in the form of an authoritative apology is morally obligatory. Further moral remedies may also be morally obligatory. What exactly is being remedied? One cannot very plausibly maintain that the sheer fact of the arrest of George for a crime which he had not perpetrated was sufficient to impose remedial obligations on the officials and institutions involved.[19] If the arrest was conducted in good faith on solid grounds—as we are assuming—then the moral duties owed to George by the relevant authorities were most likely satisfied at that juncture. Had his innocence quickly become apparent, or had the grounds for detaining him otherwise soon proved to be perceptibly inadequate, then the authorities would of course have been morally duty-bound to release him. However, the duty to release him in those circumstances would not have been a remedial obligation. The release would have averted, rather than remedied, a wrong; it would not have indicated that any wrong (as opposed to a permissible error) had been committed theretofore. No apology or compensation would have been morally required. Much the same can be said in connection with the other early stages of George's ordeal. If exculpatory evidence had come to light during his trial, or if doubts had been raised at that time about the incriminating evidence, then an acquittal and a subsequent release would have been obligatory. However, once again, the acquittal and release would have averted rather than remedied a wrong. What would have been corrected was a permissible mistake, rather than something impermissible for which an apology or some other moral remedy would be required. Yet, as time went on, the continued detention of George shifted from the realm of the permissible to the realm of the impermissible. Certainly by the end of the six years during which he was incarcerated, the loss of his general liberty had become a violation of his moral rights. Obviously, we cannot specify some talismanic moment at which the transformation from the permissible to the

---

[19] It should go without saying that my chief claims in this paragraph are substantive moral contentions rather than conceptual analyses.

impermissible occurred. There was no such moment, just as there is no magical point at which the accumulation of one grain of sand after another will suddenly yield a heap. Still, although a sorites problem like the shift in the moral standing of the treatment of George does not lend itself to the pinpointing of a moment of transition, we can be sure that that transition had taken place well before George had spent his sixth year in jail. By that time, his moral right-against-being-lengthily-imprisoned-when-innocent had unquestionably been infringed.

Now, since the scrupulous fairness of the workings of the criminal-justice system vis-à-vis George did not diminish or disappear during the period of his confinement, some other factor accounted for the change in the moral status of that confinement. Quite plainly, the determinative factor was the seriousness of the impact of the criminal-justice system's operations on George's basic interests. As that impact became more and more severe, the justificatory force (that is, the permissibility-sustaining force) of the impeccableness of the officials' procedures dissipated. We can safely conclude, then, that strict liability in morality is sometimes warranted because of the extent to which the unimpeach-ably careful actions of people impinge on the well-being or autonomy of other people. As Cane writes, '[i]n some situations, lack of fault seems a less than conclusive response to the harm suffered by a faultless victim' (Cane, *Responsibility*, 107).

However, we should not jump to the conclusion that strict liability in morality is never warranted in the absence of severe hardships for the people to whom remedial obligations are owed. For example, if Oliver is caught in a wholly unforeseeable and unprecedentedly large traffic jam, and if he is consequently unable to keep his promise to meet up with Susan at an appointed time, he is morally obligated to apologize to her. The circumstances heavily extenuate the breaking of the promise, but do not do away completely with the fact that a wrong has been committed against Susan and that a remedy is accordingly required. Yet, notwithstanding the sway of strict liability in such circumstances, the extent of the injury to Susan's well-being or autonomy is slight. We may presume that she has suffered no more than a bit of annoyance and inconvenience. Thus, although the chief message of the scenario of George is as it was stated in my last paragraph, we should not be misled into thinking that any easily isolable factor or set of factors will account for the division between the medley of situations within which strict liability in morality is applicable and the medley of situations within which such liability is not applicable. A thorough investigation of the sundry interacting determinants of that division is beyond the scope of this chapter, but we at any rate can see that many aspects of people's lives will indeed be covered by the reign of strict liability. Whatever may be the determining factors in this or that context, people will frequently be morally obligated to remedy states of affairs which they could not help bringing about. Once we discriminate carefully between extenuation and exoneration, we can perceive that Hart was wrong to insist that 'ought' always implies 'can'.

III. Potential Objections

In the course of the presentation of the Remedy Principle and Remedy Principle*, we have encountered some potential criticisms of my conception of moral rights and duties. We should now come to grips with some further potential objections. An examination of these queries will help to clarify and refine the various lines of argument that have been marshaled hitherto.

A. Frequently Rather than Invariably

Some philosophers, arguing that strict liability is decidedly unattractive, might question whether such liability is ever truly operative in morality. The putative unattractiveness of any rejection of the 'ought'-implies-'can' principle is traced to a diversity of considerations by different theorists. For many philosophers, including Hart, the basic intuition that motivates them to subscribe to the 'ought'-implies-'can' principle is the sense that it would be unfair to require people to remedy situations which they have striven with assiduous care and earnestness to avoid. That intuition imbues David Ross's remark, for example, that '[n]o one thinks that he has failed to do his duty if he has done his best, without success, to fulfil his promise'.[20] Other philosophers have concentrated on more technical considerations. For instance, Jules Coleman—who admittedly is writing principally about the moral foundations of legal liability rather than about moral liability itself—submits that strict liability is plagued by two major difficulties. It is excessively rigid as a general standard, and it leads to indeterminacy when we seek to apply it to concrete disputes.[21]

To the various arguments against the appealingness of strict liability in morality, three main replies—in an ascending order of importance—are germane. First, concerns about fairness are clearly double-edged at best. If it is unfair that somebody is morally required to remedy a harmful state of affairs which she could not avert despite her best efforts, it would be at least as unfair for someone else to have to bear the whole burden of that unremedied state of affairs. When theorists worry about the harshness of the imposition of remedial obligations on

---

[20] W. David Ross, *Foundations of Ethics* (Oxford: Clarendon Press, 1939) [hereinafter cited as Ross, *Foundations*], 108. For a view broadly similar to Ross's, albeit focused more on the guidance-providing and dignity-upholding roles of moral precepts, see Thomas E. Hill, Jr., 'Moral Dilemmas, Gaps, and Residues: A Kantian Perspective', in Mason, *Dilemmas* [hereinafter cited as Hill, 'Dilemmas'], 167, 175–9. For some much more favorable views of strict liability in morality, see, e.g., Fletcher, 'Conditions', 1362–3; Railton, 'Diversity', 143–4; Thomson, *Realm*, 171–3, 175.

[21] For the former accusation, see, e.g., Coleman, *Risks*, 316. For the latter accusation, see, e.g., Jules Coleman, *The Practice of Principle* (Oxford: Oxford University Press, 2001), 47–8.

people whose meticulous efforts have come to nought, they tend to overlook the harshness of the imposition of suffering on people who have been detrimentally affected by the failure of those efforts. To be sure, if the detrimental effects of any particular failure are diffusely distributed among members of the general public, then leaving the losses where they lie—without any measures to counteract them—is probably the fairest upshot. A blameless perpetrator of some harm will most likely not be obligated to take steps to undo the harm if such steps would be costly and if the consequences of the harm are so dispersed as to be virtually imperceptible by any individual affected. To allow as much, however, is simply to accept that the sway of strict liability in morality is limited in its reach (as it of course is). Yet the unwarrantedness of that sway in some settings does not mean that it is unwarranted in all settings. In application to any situation in which someone's impeccably careful conduct goes awry and produces harmful effects that fall upon one person or a small group of people, arguments about the unfairness of strict liability will generally be inconclusive.

Second, when we yet again take account of the distinction between extenuation and exoneration, we can see that concerns about fairness are largely misdirected. If the only two alternatives in every context were no remedy at all and a remedy that completely removes any hardships which have been occasioned by someone's faultless nonfulfillment of a moral duty, then the onerousness of such a sweeping remedy would indeed militate (to some degree) against the idea that it is morally obligatory. However, the alternatives are never so restricted. The faultlessness of a person's nonfulfillment of some moral duty is a strong mitigating factor that markedly lessens the extent of the moral remedy which the person will have to undertake in order to rectify what he or she has done. An apology might well be the sole remedy that is due, and an apology is not terribly burdensome for anyone (save perhaps in extreme circumstances of mutual antipathy between people). As was observed earlier, the Remedy Principle and Remedy Principle* leave open the substance and expansiveness of the moral remedy that is requisite in any particular case. Among the factors which bear on that substance and that expansiveness, the culpability or lack of culpability in a person's conduct is of particular importance. Though a wrong committed in the course of impeccably earnest striving is still a wrong, its lack of wrongfulness will have reduced significantly the extent of the remedy that is sufficient for the proper making of amends. As a result, the fairness-based objection to a standard of strict liability is easily accommodated and defused by such a standard. Any apprehension animating that objection should dissipate when one remembers the role of extenuative factors in the adjustment of remedial obligations. Given that role, the required remedy for any moral wrong will be set in accordance with the demands of fairness rather than athwart them.

Third and most important is a point that has emerged already to some degree in the preceding points. An affirmation of the possibility and actuality of strict liability in morality is perfectly compatible with a recognition of the frequent inappropriateness of such liability. As Sinnott-Armstrong has remarked, '[t]hose who deny that "ought" implies "can" can admit that "cannot" is sometimes a reason to deny "ought"' (Sinnott-Armstrong, *Dilemmas*, 115). There are plainly many circumstances in which the earnest diligence of people's precautions is exonerative rather than merely extenuative. In any such circumstances, it is not the case that the infliction of harm by one person on another is an excusable breach of a moral duty. Rather, if the facts are such that the faultlessness of the person who has inflicted the harm is exonerative, there has not been any transgression of a moral duty at all. Hence, there is no occasion for an excuse. As has already been declared, there are no excuses in the domain of morality; when an absence of culpability does not simply mitigate a breach of a moral duty, it averts such a breach and thereby obviates the need for any remedy.

An example of a situation not characterized by strict liability has already surfaced in this chapter. If policemen arrest George for some crime on the basis of solidly persuasive evidence, then, even if he has not actually committed the crime, they have not violated any duty owed to him. They are not morally obligated to apologize to him or to pay him any compensation. The relevant duty which they have owed to him is not a duty to forbear from arresting him for any crime which he has not carried out or attempted. Rather, the relevant duty is to exercise scrupulous care and good faith in assessing any evidence that might lead to an arrest and in executing any arrest itself. In common language, their duty is a duty of care rather than a duty of outright avoidance. If their meticulous efforts eventuate in the arrest of George for an offense which he has not perpetrated, they have not *pro tanto* committed any wrong against him.

The very coherence of the idea of a duty of care has recently come under challenge by Heidi Hurd in a piquant essay. She asserts that '[i]t literally makes no sense to maintain that an action is justified if and only if the actor reasonably believes that the action is justified' (Hurd, 'Justification', 1559). Now, although the proposition contested by Hurd is excessively sweeping as a general thesis, it is not incoherent if it is suitably construed. Hurd contends that that proposition falls prey to vicious circularity: '[F]or an actor to believe that an action is justified, he has to have a theory about when an action is justified, and on pain of circularity, that theory cannot consist solely of the formula that an action is justified if the actor believes that it is justified' (Hurd, 'Justification', 1559). The vicious circularity detected here by Hurd is escapable if we adopt a more generous approach to the thesis that an action is justified if and only if the actor reasonably believes that it is justified. Such a thesis so formulated is coherent—even though it is far too sweeping—if the first instance and only the first instance of 'justified' means 'permissible in light of all the relevant facts including the actor's reasonable ignorance of some of those facts (when the actor is indeed reasonably ignorant of some of those facts)', and if the second instance and only the second instance of 'justified' means 'permissible in light of all the relevant facts known to the actor'.[22] So construed, the thesis does not run afoul of vicious circularity. Of course, to say as much is not to endorse that thesis, which disregards the myriad situations where strict liability prevails in the moral realm. Given that this chapter has endeavored to highlight just such situations, any proclamation that disregards them in a blanket fashion is bound to be condemned here as erroneous. Nevertheless, if we are to reject the proposition which Hurd impugns, we should reject it for the right reasons. Although patently overbroad in implying that the impeccable circumspection of a person's beliefs and intentions is always fully exonerative—and in consequently ignoring the countless contexts within which such circumspection is merely extenuative—the aforementioned proposition is correct in implying that the impeccable circumspection of a person's beliefs and intentions is sometimes fully exonerative. Sometimes the only relevant duty owed is a duty to exercise reasonable care. Hurd errs in thinking that there is anything conceptually dubious in the postulation of such a duty.

She seeks to sustain her attack with another line of argument, which should be quoted here at some length:

[F]or an actor to *reasonably* believe that an action is justified, his beliefs must approach truth about the matter. There thus must be a truth about the matter separate from his beliefs about it. We cannot assess whether a person reasonably inferred from the evidence available to him that he would do no wrong without a nonepistemic theory of wrongdoing. For evidence is only evidence if it is evidence of *something*. We can only inquire into whether a person reasonably believed that a killing was justified if we have a theory of the conditions under which it is wrong to kill and can assess the evidence available to him concerning the existence of those conditions in light of that theory. (Hurd, 'Justification', 1559, emphases in original)

This additional strand of argument by Hurd is no more successful than her first strand, for it is subject to rebuttal in essentially the same way. We should readily accept that the reasonableness of a person's beliefs will hinge on his having acquired them through processes or sources that are normally reliable, and we should likewise accept that the reliability of those processes or sources will hinge on their generally leading to the truth about the matters to which they pertain. We should accordingly also happily grant that any adequate judgment about the reasonableness of a person's beliefs must rely on presuppositions concerning the objective facts to which the beliefs pertain. However, all of these points are consistent with the truth of the proposition which Hurd is assailing—the proposition that an action is justified if and only if the actor reasonably believes that it is justified—so long as we interpret that proposition in the manner advocated above. That is, so long as we construe each instance of 'justified'

---

[22] Under this construal of the statement that an action is justified if and only if the actor reasonably believes that it is justified, the qualifier 'reasonably' attaches not only to the actor's drawing of inferences from the known facts but also to his being unaware of other relevant facts. An otherwise impermissible action will never be rendered permissible if the choice made by the actor is based on an unreasonably circumscribed grasp of the situation confronting him.

along the lines suggested above, the thesis under assault from Hurd has preserved rather than elided the division between what is the case and what is believed to be the case. Wholly unproblematic, then, is the reliance of that thesis on presuppositions concerning whether particular actions are justified or not as objective matters of fact. Likewise unproblematic, therefore, is the idea of a duty of care. A person's actions are sometimes permissible precisely because they are undertaken with sedulous care. Though many moral duties require success on pain of strict liability, some other such duties require no more than an absence of culpability (that is, an absence of malice or knowing indifference or recklessness or carelessness).

B. Permissibility and Cases of Desperation

In response to examples such as my scenario of George's imprisonment, some theorists might seek to invoke a distinction developed by Thomson and by Joel Feinberg: the distinction between infringements and violations.[23] Under the terms of that distinction, all violations are infringements, but not all infringements are violations. An infringement occurs when someone has a right that *p* be the case—where '*p*' designates some proposition—and someone else causes *p* to be false. For example, if Henry has a right that Ron not bang him in the nose, then Ron infringes the right if he bangs Henry in the nose. A violation is a culpable infringement. If Ron's banging of Henry's nose is attributable to malice or recklessness or carelessness, then the infringement of Henry's right is a violation thereof. Contrariwise, if the banging occurs despite Ron's careful efforts to avoid it, the infringement is a mere infringement.

Proponents of the infringement/violation dichotomy generally maintain that mere infringements are permissible. Only violations are impermissible. In other words, these philosophers take culpability to be a necessary condition for impermissibility and thus for wrongdoing. Now, in light of the distinctions drawn in this chapter, such a view should plainly be eschewed as a conflation of wrongness and wrongfulness. Although wrongfulness is sometimes a necessary condition for wrongness (if the duty owed is a duty of care rather than a duty of outright avoidance), it frequently is not. Strict liability is often the operative standard in morality. Nonetheless, we should not simply brush aside the infringement/violation dichotomy. For one thing, that dichotomy will salutarily elicit here a clarification of the notion of permissibility, which this chapter has not really

---

[23] See Judith Jarvis Thomson, *Rights, Restitution, and Risk* (Cambridge, MA: Harvard University Press, 1986) [hereinafter cited as Thomson, *Restitution*], chaps 3–5; Thomson, *Realm*, 122; Joel Feinberg, *Rights, Justice, and the Bounds of Liberty* (Princeton: Princeton University Press, 1980) [hereinafter cited as Feinberg, *Rights*], 229–32. See also Cane, *Responsibility*, 107; Coleman, *Risks*, 282–3, 299–302; Fletcher, 'Right', 977; George Fletcher, 'The Nature of Justification', in Stephen Shute, John Gardner, and Jeremy Horder (eds), *Action and Value in Criminal Law* (Oxford: Clarendon Press, 1993), 175, 177; McConnell, 'Residue', 42; Sinnott-Armstrong, *Dilemmas*, 51–2.

elucidated so far. Moreover, as will be perceived shortly, some situations—in which people act out of desperation—can seem to vindicate the infringement/violation dichotomy as it has heretofore been understood. An exploration of those situations will reinforce my analyses of moral rights and duties by adding a layer of complexity to them.

1. Two Conceptions of Permissibility

Permissibility and wrongness are contradictories. An action or a state of affairs is permissible if and only if it is not wrong. Furthermore, under my analysis of moral rights and duties, an action is wrong (impermissible) for some person if and only if the performance of that action by that person will obligate him or her to remedy the resultant situation in some way. Given such an analysis, the notion that infringements are permissible is patently untenable. Everyone agrees that mere infringements—if they are indeed genuine infringements, rather than the ostensible infringements which we shall investigate presently—give rise to re-medial obligations. From my analysis of moral rights and duties, then, it follows that mere infringements as well as violations are impermissible. Such a conclusion is correct, as will be argued below; however, when we probe a bit more deeply into the notion of permissibility, we can discern a respect in which the champions of the infringement/violation distinction are also correct. The correctness of their position in that respect can readily be conceded here, since it will cast no doubt whatsoever on my own analyses.

If some person X is permitted to perform some action q, then X is not obligated to not perform q. (To avoid any ambiguities in my prose, my placement of 'not' in several of the sentences in this discussion will create some ugly split infinitives.) So much is clear, but we need now to take account of two ways in which someone can be morally obligated to do or not do something. The pertinent distinction here is between overtopping and non-overtopping obligations.[24] An overtopping moral requirement exceeds in importance all the moral requirements that run contrary to it, or is unopposed by any countervailing moral requirements. A non-overtopping moral requirement R does not exceed in importance all the moral requirements that run contrary to it. (Any competing moral requirements might be equal in importance to R, or they might exceed it in importance, or they might be insusceptible to any determinate comparisons with it because of problems of incommensurability.) With reference to these two broad types of obligations, we can apprehend two broad types of permissibility. First, in affirming that some person X is permitted to perform some action q, we might be maintaining that X is not under any overtopping obligation to not

---

[24] Some very closely related distinctions are brought to the fore in an illuminating, sustained, and sophisticated fashion in Sinnott-Armstrong, *Dilemmas*. Although the term 'overriding' is much more common than 'overtopping' in discussions of these matters, I disfavor the former term because it conveys the impression that less important duties are eliminated or canceled in conflicts with more important duties.

perform *q*. Such a claim is consistent with the possibility that *X* is under a non-overtopping obligation to not perform *q*. Second, we might instead be maintaining that *X* is neither under an overtopping obligation nor under a non-overtopping obligation to not perform *q*. Let us designate the first of these two types of permissibility as 'weak permissibility', and the second as 'strong permissibility'.

Throughout this chapter, I have invoked the notion of permissibility in the strong sense. My arguments have assumed that an action *q* is impermissible for a person *X* unless *X* is not under any obligation at all to not do *q*. For the purpose of gauging whether any particular course of conduct is impermissible, there has been no attempt in this chapter to discriminate between situations in which someone is under an overtopping obligation to eschew *q* and situations in which someone is merely under a non-overtopping obligation to eschew *q*. Precisely because I have not discriminated between those two kinds of situations, this chapter has contended that morally optimal courses of action can be impermissible. If two moral duties clash, and if one exceeds the other in importance, then compliance with the former is a morally optimal but impermissible course of conduct. The moral optimality of such compliance will extenuate but not eliminate the breach of duty involved; it will therefore not eliminate the impermissibility of the compliant course of action. My arguments on this point are sustainable because they rely on the strong conception of permissibility. Were this chapter instead drawing on the weak conception of permissibility, my arguments about the impermissibility of some morally optimal courses of conduct would be unsound.

By contrast, the proponents of the infringement/violation diremption have typically relied (at least implicitly) on the weak conception of permissibility when submitting that mere infringements of people's rights are permissible. They maintain that, so long as any person *X* is conducting himself in accordance with all the overtopping moral duties that are incumbent upon him, he is conducting himself permissibly. The fact that he might be contravening a non-overtopping moral duty—for example, by breaking an engagement for lunch in order to go to the aid of a seriously injured pedestrian—is perfectly compatible with the weak permissibility of his course of action. In their repeated affirmations of the permissibility of mere infringements, then, Thomson and Feinberg are not really committing any errors. Instead, they are exhibiting their adherence to a conception of permissibility that diverges from my own conception.

Which conception is to be upheld? Why should this chapter's reliance on the strong conception of permissibility be preferred? Clearly, any apposite choice in favor of the strong notion or the weak notion of permissibility will depend on the purposes and foci of one's analyses. For the purposes of my exposition and defense of the Remedy Principle and Remedy Principle*, the strong conception of permissibility is uniquely germane. After all, irrespective of whether a moral duty is overtopping or non-overtopping, any breach of it will give rise to remedial obligations. What the Remedy Principle* declares about the nature of any moral duty is true in application to overtopping and non-overtopping duties alike; thus, a pertinent defense of that principle will advance claims that are true of overtopping and non-overtopping duties alike. Of course, to say as much is not to suggest that the overtopping/non-overtopping distinction plays no role whatsoever in any of my analyses. In my very arguments about the impermissibility of some morally optimal courses of action, I have presupposed the overtopping/non-overtopping dichotomy by maintaining that the fulfillment of an overtopping moral duty is impermissible whenever it conflicts with the fulfillment of a non-overtopping moral duty. Still, the overtopping/non-overtopping dichotomy plays no role in determining whether some course of conduct will count as permissible or not—because it plays no role in determining whether the occurrence of that course of conduct will trigger the imposition of some remedial obligations. To be sure, the aforesaid dichotomy does play a role in determining the *severity* of the remedy required in the aftermath of a breach of some moral duty. A breach undertaken in order to avoid a transgression of an overtopping moral duty will be extenuated much more heavily than a breach undertaken in order to avoid a transgression of a non-overtopping moral duty. Nevertheless, the need for a remedy of *some* sort in the aftermath of the contravention of a moral duty is unaffected by the status of the contravened duty as overtopping or non-overtopping. To capture the irrelevance of the overtopping/non-overtopping distinction in that crucial respect, this chapter adheres to the strong conception of permissibility throughout.

One of the central principles of standard deontic logic, which I shall call the 'Permissibility Theorem', tends to cloud reflection on these matters.[25] According to that theorem, the obligatoriness of any occurrence or state of affairs entails the permissibility thereof; by contraposition, then, the impermissibility of any occurrence or state of affairs entails the non-obligatoriness thereof. Although there is a way of construing the Permissibility Theorem that renders it necessarily true, most construals of it falsify it. On the whole, it impedes rigorous thinking about the structure of deontic relations.

The Permissibility Theorem proclaims that everything obligatory is permissible. If we construe 'obligatory' as 'overtoppingly obligatory', and if we construe 'permissible' as 'at least weakly permissible', then the Permissibility Theorem is true. It is indeed the case that every overtoppingly obligatory course of action is at least weakly permissible, for, if some such course of action were not at least

---

[25] Many highly sophisticated philosophers endorse the Permissibility Theorem. See, e.g., Earl Conee, 'Against Moral Dilemmas', 91 *Philosophical Review* 87 (1982) [hereinafter cited as Conee, 'Dilemmas']; Feinberg, *Rights*, 235, 237; Hill, 'Dilemmas', 177; G.E. Hughes and M.J. Cresswell, *A New Introduction to Modal Logic* (London: Routledge, 1996), 43; Hillel Steiner, 'Working Rights', in Matthew H. Kramer, N.E. Simmonds, and Hillel Steiner, *A Debate over Rights* (Oxford: Oxford University Press, 1998), 233, 268 n.55; Peter Vallentyne, 'Prohibition Dilemmas and Deontic Logic', 117–18 *Logique et Analyse* 113, 119–20 (1987); Peter Vallentyne, 'Two Types of Moral Dilemmas', 30 *Erkenntnis* 301 (1989). For a fine critique, to which I am much indebted, see Sinnott-Armstrong, *Dilemmas*, 156–61. See also Sinnott-Armstrong, 'Rights', 52.

weakly permissible, then a person would be under an overtopping moral duty to do q and an overtopping moral duty to not do q. Given that an overtopping moral duty exceeds in importance any moral duties that conflict with it, each of the two duties just mentioned would be morally more important than the other. Such a state of affairs is impossible, since any coherent relation of superiority (such as 'more important than') is strictly non-symmetrical. Ergo, every overtoppingly obligatory course of action is indeed at least weakly permissible.

Construed in any other way, however, the Permissibility Theorem is false. It is not the case, for example, that every overtoppingly obligatory course of action is strongly permissible. One's moral duty to aid a badly injured pedestrian might well be overtopping in a given context, but the fulfillment of that overtopping duty might preclude the fulfillment of one's less important moral duty to keep one's promise to meet somebody else for lunch. In that event, one's going to the aid of the pedestrian is only weakly permissible rather than strongly permissible. Countless similar examples could be adduced.

Even more plainly, it is not the case that every non-overtoppingly obligatory course of action is strongly permissible. Indeed, no such course of action is strongly permissible. Furthermore, given that some non-overtopping moral duties conflict with overtopping moral duties, it is not even the case that every non-overtoppingly obligatory course of action is weakly permissible. Many such courses of action are impermissible in every sense. Hence, only under one interpretation is the Permissibility Theorem correct; under the three other available interpretations, it is false.

Because the only true variant of the Permissibility Theorem presupposes the distinction between overtopping and non-overtopping moral duties, and because the Remedy Principle* applies to overtopping and non-overtopping moral duties alike, the Permissibility Theorem is far more misleading than helpful for my purposes. As has already been explained, the fact that the Remedy Principle* applies to all moral duties is exactly what accounts for this chapter's reliance on the strong conception of permissibility. Yet the true variant of the Permissibility Theorem excludes the strong conception of permissibility; that theorem is true only if its reference to permissibility is construed as a reference to weak permissibility. Hence, the Permissibility Theorem cannot play any role—save as a false proposition—in this chapter's analyses. Far from encapsulating an essential feature of every relationship of obligation, that theorem encapsulates a feature of each relationship of obligation within a highly circumscribed range. To transcend such restrictiveness, this chapter sets the Permissibility Theorem aside.

2. Cases of Desperation

Certain types of situations have received attention in much of the literature on the infringement/violation dichotomy. Those situations are often designated as cases of necessity, but are more illuminatingly labeled as cases of desperation.[26] In any such case, somebody resorts to contravening somebody else's moral rights in order to avert a dire fate for himself or for another person. Suppose for example that a child develops a serious illness. Alas, the only antidote that can be reached in time to save her life is owned by Joe, who has placed it in his storage shed. Joe at present is sojourning inaccessibly in another country. To save the child's life, her father (who happens to be a doctor) breaks into the shed and removes the antidote, which he then administers to his daughter. In these circumstances, Joe upon his return is entitled to an apology and to compensation for the smashing of the shed and for the appropriation of the antidote. He might cheerily dismiss the apology, and he might decline to accept some or all of the compensation. Nevertheless, the child's father is morally obligated to extend the apology and to come up with the compensation if it is not waived.[27] Remedial obligations have descended upon the father because he has acted athwart the rights of somebody else. Yet it is clear that he has behaved in a morally optimal fashion. By infringing Joe's moral rights, the doctor has fulfilled an overtopping moral duty which he owed to his daughter.

Many of the philosophers who mull over situations of this sort have been tempted to rely (implicitly or explicitly) on the weak conception of permissibility. They have concluded that anyone in a desperate position akin to that of the child's father is acting permissibly when engaging in a morally optimal breach of duty. For instance, when discussing a case of desperation involving someone named 'Hal', Coleman writes that a 'right can be invaded permissibly.... Infringements are justified or permissible invasions of rights.... Hal has acted permissibly in the circumstances, and only someone who had no understanding of human need and motivation could think otherwise' (Coleman, *Risks*, 282).

By recognizing that pronouncements such as these from Coleman rely on the weak conception of permissibility, we can avoid branding them as false or incoherent. Nonetheless, precisely because such pronouncements depend on the weak conception of permissibility for their truth, they cannot be accommodated in my analyses. As has been stated, this chapter relies throughout on the strong conception of permissibility. We should consequently now investigate whether any satisfactory account of the deontic relations in cases of desperation is compatible with that strong conception. If the only effective way of expounding the nature of a desperate person's plight were to follow Coleman and other theorists in deeming some infringements of moral rights to be weakly permissible, then my own explications of moral rights and duties—which eschew the

---

[26] Several such cases are discussed in Coleman, *Risks*, chaps 14 and 15; Thomson, *Restitution*, chaps 3–5; and Thomson, *Realm*, chaps 3–7. See also Fletcher, *Rethinking*, 774–98. One of the most famous examples of a case of desperation is offered in Feinberg, *Rights*, 230.

[27] If the father is much less wealthy than Joe, his remedial obligation might not require him to pay the full market value of the antidote that has been taken.

weak conception of permissibility—would *pro tanto* be inadequate. Fortunately, however, two apt analyses of the deontic relations in cases of desperation are perfectly compatible with the strong conception of permissibility. One or the other of these two approaches may be more suitable in application to this or that particular situation, but each of them is effective in conveying the formal structure of a desperate person's predicament. Let us explore each of them, by reference to the scenario of the father and the antidote.

A first approach concurs with the proponents of the infringement/violation dichotomy in maintaining that the father has infringed some of Joe's moral rights by gaining access to the storage shed nonconsensually and by taking away the antidote. However, this approach further maintains that the father's infringements—like any other infringements of moral rights—are impermissible. We can know that they are impermissible, exactly because they obligate the father to remedy the resultant situation fittingly. All the same, the father's behavior is morally optimal, and his transgressions of moral duties are therefore heavily extenuated. Moreover, the behavior is rightful in that the father has a right against any deliberate interference by Joe with his appropriation of the antidote. If Joe had been present rather than abroad at the time of the emergency, he would have been morally duty-bound to acquiesce in the father's obtention of the antidote. Indeed, he would probably have been morally duty-bound to assist the father in getting the antidote. In short, while the father owes Joe a moral duty to abstain from damaging the shed and removing the antidote, he has a right against any deliberate interference by Joe with his performance of those actions (insofar as the actions are necessary in order to save the child's life). In other words, he has rights against interference with his commission of some wrongs.

Thus, although my analyses of moral rights and duties lead to a characterization of the father's conduct as wrong, they are consistent with several other characterizations that adequately reveal the moral effects of the dire straits in which the father finds himself. We can and should recognize that, although the father's behavior is wrong, it is in no way wrongful. Furthermore, we should perceive that the wrongness of his actions is greatly extenuated by the fact that they amount to the fulfillment of an overtopping moral duty. In addition, we should grasp that his behavior is rightful in the sense defined by my last paragraph; inasmuch as that behavior is necessary for forestalling the death of the child, the father has a right against any deliberate interference with it. Having recognized all of these points, we shall not be misled about the urgency of the father's plight when we also grasp that his forced entry into the shed and his procuring of the antidote are not strongly permissible (and that they are consequently impermissible in the only sense that is relevant within this chapter's analyses). By emphasizing the rightfulness of the father's conduct, this first approach to cases of desperation does justice to the gravity of his situation.

Equally good in that respect is a second approach to this matter.[28] In regard to some cases of desperation, we are perhaps best advised to conclude that apparent transgressions of moral duties turn out not to be genuine transgressions when they are plumbed more closely. We should initially examine this second approach in application to the scenario of Joe and the child's father, and then in application to a scenario for which the approach is somewhat better suited.

We might arrive at the verdict that, despite superficial appearances to the contrary, the father's nonconsensual entry into Joe's shed and his gaining possession of Joe's antidote do not infringe any of Joe's moral rights. Although the father is morally obligated to make payments to Joe, the payments are for the purpose of reimbursement rather than of compensation. They will avert, rather than remedy, a wrong. The relevant moral duty owed by the father to Joe is not a duty to abstain from damaging the shed and taking the antidote in an emergency; instead, it is a more complex duty-to-abstain-from-damaging-the-shed-and-taking-the-antidote-in-an-emergency-without-subsequently-paying-Joe-the-fair-market-value-of-what-he-has-lost. That is, the relevant duty is comparable to the duty-of-reimbursement owed by customers to a restaurant at which they dine. They pay for their meals not to rectify any wrongs, but to avoid the commission of the wrong of eating-without-paying-afterward. Similarly, according to this second way of coming to grips with cases of desperation, the father avoids the commission of any wrongs by reimbursing Joe for his losses. He avoids the commission of any wrongs, because the reimbursement fulfills the complex duty (specified above) which he has owed to Joe.

In application to the story of Joe and the child's father, the second way of analyzing cases of desperation is not entirely convincing. However, some other examples lend themselves far more persuasively to such an analysis. A scenario devised by Kent Greenawalt for a somewhat different aim, and slightly modified here, is a useful illustration (Greenawalt, 'Borders', 1908). Suppose that Roger is a fire-prevention officer who uses advanced techniques for predicting the speed and direction of the wind. He carefully judges that the only way of preventing the spread of a forest fire to a nearby town is to burn out some large fields of crops owned by a local farmer. After the crops have been burned, the wind abruptly and unforeseeably subsides. As a result, the forest fire dissipates before it ever reaches the burnt-out fields.

For present purposes, this scenario could be altered in its closing portion with no real change in its overall import. Suppose that, instead of abating, the wind continues and drives the forest fire into the fields. Only because of Roger's timely orders has the spread of the fire been stanched. Both in this new version and in the original version of the scenario, the local authorities (or the authorities at some other pertinent level of government) are morally obligated to pay the

---

[28] For a classic exposition of this approach, see Robert Keeton, 'Conditional Fault in the Law of Torts', 72 *Harvard Law Review* 401, 418–44 (1959).

farmer whose crops have been lost. In each case, however, the payments are for the purpose of eminent domain rather than of compensation. No moral wrong has been done to the farmer—especially if, though not only if, his own property has been protected through the burning of the fields—but a moral wrong would be done to him if he were not paid for the mandatory destruction of his crops. Having been required to let his fields be devoted to the furtherance of the public weal, the farmer now has a moral right to be reimbursed for some or all of the lost value of his crops. Of key importance here is that his right is indeed a right to eminent-domain reimbursement rather than to rectification. He has not suffered any wrong, and his condition is thus not in need of rectification, though of course he would suffer a wrong if he were not to be reimbursed.

When applied to circumstances of the kind just depicted, the second way of analyzing the deontic relations within cases of desperation is clearly germane. It is highly plausible that the relevant moral right held by the farmer vis-à-vis the local authorities is not a right-against-their-burning-of-his-crops-for-a-truly-urgent-public-purpose; rather, the relevant moral right is a right-against-their-*both*-burning-his-crops-for-a-pressingly-important-public-purpose-*and*-declining-to-remunerate-him-for-his-losses. That complex entitlement is not a remedial right that has arisen because of the authorities' breach of an anterior right. Instead, it is itself an anterior right against the authorities' combining a specified action with a specified omission. The action is not per se wrong, so long as it is not coupled with the omission. By enabling us to descry this aspect of the deontic relations within some cases of desperation, the second approach to such cases can capture what Coleman and others have sensed about the permissibility of many desperate measures. Some such measures are indeed permissible—strongly permissible—as long as they are not conjoined with certain instances of uncooperative niggardliness.

Before we leave this discussion, we should briefly ponder an interesting critique by Thomson of the second approach to cases of desperation (Thomson, *Restitution*, 71–7). She maintains that absurd conclusions follow from the analysis yielded by such an approach. She considers an example in which a desperate person—whom I shall designate as 'X'—has had to burn some furniture owned by somebody else, whom I shall designate as 'Y'. The owner plainly has a moral right to be paid for the loss of his furniture. With Thomson's semi-formal notation (somewhat modified here), Y's moral right to be paid by X can be rendered as follows:

Prop1 $R_{Y,X}$ X pays Y for the loss of the furniture.

The notation '$R_{Y,X}$' stands for 'Y has a right vis-à-vis X', and the sentence 'X pays Y for the loss of the furniture' specifies the content of the right which Y holds. Now, if the situation of X and Y lends itself to the second way of analyzing cases of desperation, the complex right originally held by Y is to be explicated as follows:

Prop 2 $R_{Y,X}$ If X burns Y's furniture out of desperation, then he pays Y for the loss of the burnt items.

When conjoined with the sentence 'X burns Y's furniture out of desperation', Prop2 entails Prop1—which means that the second approach to cases of desperation generates exactly the right result. Or so we should conclude. Thomson, however, demurs.

She takes as given a certain principle governing the relations among rights:

Prin1   '$R_{Y,X}\ p$' entails '$R_{Y,X}\ q$' if 'p' entails 'q'.

Here 'p' and 'q' designate the sentences that specify the contents of the respective rights. Thomson offers no defense of this principle. Rather, she 'simply assume[s] it true' (Thomson, *Restitution*, 72). She then posits the following principle, on which we rely when we infer Prop1 from the combination of Prop2 and the sentence 'X burns Y's furniture out of desperation':

Prin 2   '$[R_{Y,X}\ (p \rightarrow q)]$ & p' entails '$R_{Y,X}\ q$'.

(Here, of course, the symbol '$\rightarrow$' denotes the 'if... then' relationship of conditionality.) Thomson now pounces. She points out that, if both Prin1 and Prin2 are true, then '$(R_{Y,X}\ \text{-}p)$ & p' would entail '$R_{Y,X}\ q$'. After all, given that the truth of any conditional with 'p' as its antecedent is ensured by the truth of '$\text{-}p$', '$R_{Y,X}\ \text{-}p$' entails '$R_{Y,X}\ (p \rightarrow q)$' under Prin1; and, under Prin2, the conjunction of '$R_{Y,X}\ (p \rightarrow q)$' with '$p$' entails '$R_{Y,X}\ q$'. Thomson correctly complains that such a conclusion, which consists in the derivability of '$R_{Y,X}\ q$' from any proposition asserting a breach of a moral duty by X vis-à-vis Y, is preposterous. Because '$\text{-}p$' and 'q' can each designate any proposition, the truth of both Prin1 and Prin2 would mean that someone who contravenes any moral right is thereby obligated to do absolutely everything in order to remedy the situation. As Thomson remarks, '[t]his is, to say the least, an unacceptable consequence. You do not give me a claim against you to anything and everything simply by bringing about some one thing which I have a claim against you that you not bring about' (Thomson, *Restitution*, 73).

Strangely, Thomson submits that the upshot of her clever argument is that we must reject Prin2, on which the second approach to cases of desperation depends. We therefore have to reject that second approach, according to her. Such a verdict is exceedingly odd. Prin2 creates mischief only in combination with Prin1; in isolation from Prin1, it breeds no difficulties or peculiarities at all. Prin1, by contrast, is hopelessly problematic. In the absence of significant restrictions on its scope,[29] it carries any number of ludicrous implications. Under it, for example, my right against being punched in the nose by Arnold entails my having a right vis-à-vis him that $2 + 2 = 4$ and another right vis-à-vis him that today either is Tuesday or is not Tuesday. I likewise have a right (under Prin1) that either he

---

[29] The need for some restrictions is recognized in Sinnott-Armstrong, *Dilemmas*, 165–6, but the restrictions have to be more far-reaching than Sinnott-Armstrong suggests.

punches me in the nose or he does not punch me in the nose. Perhaps most damagingly, Prin1—in combination with my holding the aforementioned right vis-à-vis Arnold—assigns to me a right that Arnold must do-absolutely-everything-if-he-punches-me-in-the-nose. Even before that implication of Prin1 is conjoined with Prin2, it is outlandish. Manifestly, we should shun the principle that generates it.

In sum, Prin1—in the absence of significant restrictions on its scope—is to be rejected. Prin2, accordingly, can be embraced without any untoward consequences. Thomson's ingenious argument does not cast any genuine doubt upon that latter principle. Prin2 can thus serve perfectly well as a linchpin of the second approach to cases of desperation. Anyone wanting to gain a theoretical purchase on the complexities of such cases can avail himself of either of the two main approaches that have been expounded in this subsection. We can secure such a theoretical purchase without abandoning the strong conception of permissibility in favor of the weak conception.

C. Prima-Facie Duties and Rights

For a final challenge to my account of strict liability in morality, some theorists might be inclined to have recourse to the concept of prima-facie moral duties. Originally given expression by Ross, that concept has figured prominently in a number of debates concerning topics that have been broached in this chapter.[30] In the present context, some theorists might seek to object to my analyses on the ground that the moral duties transgressed by non-culpable behavior are merely

---

[30] The main discussion by David Ross is in his *The Right and the Good* (Oxford: Clarendon Press, 1930) [hereinafter cited as Ross, *Right*], chap. 2. However, the notion of prima-facie duties and rights also appears recurrently in Ross, *Foundations*. For some writings that invoke or discuss the distinction between prima-facie duties/rights and all-things-considered duties/rights, see Robert Audi, 'Intuitionism, Pluralism, and the Foundations of Ethics', in Walter Sinnott-Armstrong and Mark Timmons (eds), *Moral Knowledge?* (Oxford: Oxford University Press, 1996), 101, 103–6; Conee, 'Dilemmas'; Jonathan Dancy, *Moral Reasons* (Oxford: Blackwell, 1993), chap. 6; Alan Donagan, 'Moral Dilemmas, Genuine and Spurious: A Comparative Anatomy', in Mason, *Dilemmas*, 11, 18–21; Joel Feinberg, 'Supererogation and Rules', in *Doing and Deserving* (Princeton: Princeton University Press, 1970), 3, 8–9; J.N. Findlay, *Values and Intentions* (London: George Allen & Unwin, 1961), 336–8; Fletcher, 'Right', 978–9; Foot, 'Realism', 385–6; William Frankena, *Ethics* (Englewood Cliffs, NJ: Prentice-Hall, 1973) (2nd edn), 26–7 *et passim*; Hill, 'Dilemmas'; W.D. Hudson, *Modern Moral Philosophy* (Basingstoke: Macmillan, 1983) (2nd edn), 95–6; S.L. Hurley, *Natural Reasons* (Oxford: Oxford University Press, 1989) [hereinafter cited as Hurley, *Reasons*], chap. 7 *et passim*; Peter Jones, *Rights* (Basingstoke: Macmillan, 1994), 195–8; David McNaughton and Piers Rawling, 'Unprincipled Ethics', in Brad Hooker and Margaret Little (eds), *Moral Particularism* (Oxford: Oxford University Press, 2000), 256, 266–71; A.I. Melden, *Rights and Persons* (Oxford: Basil Blackwell, 1977), 4–16; Mothersill, 'Debate', 77–8; Frederick Schauer, *Playing by the Rules* (Oxford: Oxford University Press, 1991), 5–6, 113–14; Sinnott-Armstrong, *Dilemmas*, 97–102; W.J. Waluchow, *The Dimensions of Ethics* (Peterborough, ON: Broadview Press, 2003), chap. 8; Bernard Williams, *Problems of the Self* (Cambridge: Cambridge University Press, 1973), 176; Bernard Williams, *Ethics and the Limits of Philosophy* (Cambridge, MA: Harvard University Press, 1985), 176–7. Especially valuable for my purposes in the present chapter are the discussions by Audi, Foot, Jones, Melden, and Sinnott-Armstrong.

prima-facie rather than all-things-considered requirements. With reference to the story of the conviction and incarceration of George for a crime that he did not commit, for example, such theorists might contend that the only duties transgressed by the authorities in the criminal-justice system are prima-facie duties. Those authorities have admirably fulfilled their all-things-considered duties to carry out their professional roles with concern both for the safety of the general public and for scrupulous fairness to criminal defendants. Hence, the critics of my analysis might conclude, the story of George's imprisonment does not genuinely illustrate the possibility of strict liability in morality. It shows only that prima facie moral duties can be faultlessly contravened; it does not show that there can be faultless contraventions of any full-blown moral duties.

Such an objection trades confusedly on an equivocation in the distinction between prima-facie moral duties and all-things-considered moral duties—an equivocation which is maddeningly present in Ross's work and which has bedeviled some of the subsequent literature.[31] Sometimes in ordinary discourse, the phrase 'prima facie' is used to mean 'on first consideration' or 'at first glance'. When such a pattern of usage is operative, a person who declares that some state of affairs prima facie obtains is saying that an initial inspection of the matter indicates that the state of affairs in question does obtain. As Susan Hurley writes: '*Prima facie* reasons are like rules of thumb, that give us reasons provisionally but may turn out not to apply when we learn more about the situation at hand, in which case they have no residual reason-giving force' (Hurley, *Reasons*, 133). This pattern of usage carries over into the workings of legal institutions, where references to what is prima facie established are references to what is tentatively deemed to be established in light of the incomplete evidence that has been submitted. (In the law, the notion of prima-facie evidence is connected with issues relating to the distribution of the burden of proof between plaintiffs and defendants.) If this pattern of usage were likewise regnant in moral and political philosophy, then philosophers who discuss prima-facie moral duties would be referring to properties or states that are believed upon first inspection to be moral duties. No such property or state will qualify as a full-fledged moral duty unless the initial consideration of the factors that bear on its existence and force is confirmed by subsequent investigations of all further relevant factors (if any). In short, when prima-facie moral duties are understood in this fashion, only some of them are veritable moral duties. Many are mere appearances.

In fact, however, the meaning attached to 'prima-facie' in moral and political philosophy is generally quite different—though the foregoing sense of the phrase often lurks in the background and leads to muddles. 'Prima-facie' in philosophical discourse means 'susceptible to being overtopped' or 'subject to being surpassed in moral importance'. Hence, the distinction between all-things-con-

---

[31] I have previously drawn the distinction between two meanings of 'prima-facie' in my *In Defense of Legal Positivism* (Oxford: Oxford University Press, 1999), 267.

sidered moral duties and merely prima-facie moral duties is really at one with the distinction between overtopping and non-overtopping moral duties, which this chapter has already highlighted. That is, it amounts to a dichotomy between those moral duties that do exceed any competing moral requirements in importance and those moral duties that do not.

Two interrelated points should be stressed here. First, the status of a prima-facie moral duty as such has nothing to do with first appearances or tentative identifications. If someone is under a prima-facie moral duty, he is under it as a result of all relevant considerations. Insofar as 'all things considered' is contrasted with 'prima facie' in the first sense of the latter phrase—that is, insofar as 'all things considered' means 'in accordance with what would be found by a thorough investigation'—every prima-facie moral duty is an all-things-considered moral duty. The standing and scope of any such duty as a moral obligation are determined by the full array of circumstances in which the obligation obtains. Ross sometimes obfuscated this point, not least by proclaiming that any prima-facie moral obligation consists in a '[t]endency to be one's duty' (Ross, *Right*, 28). Such a formulation promotes confusion, for it fails to distinguish between a tendency to be a duty of any sort and a tendency to be an overtopping duty.[32] Certain considerations engender a tendency of the former kind. For example, the pain and indignity that would be suffered by Edward in the event of his undergoing a thrashing by Frank are factors that militate in favor of Frank's being under a moral obligation to forbear from thrashing Edward in any particular context. Those factors are not always conclusive, however. If Edward himself launches a serious and unprovoked assault against Frank, then Frank is morally at liberty to use as much force as is necessary to fend off Edward's attack. He is not under any moral obligation at all—not even a prima-facie duty, much less an overtopping duty—to abstain from landing blows on Edward in such circumstances. At first glance we might think that Frank is under at least a prima-facie moral duty to restrain himself from using violence against Edward, but a more detailed exploration of his predicament reveals that not even a prima-facie moral duty is applicable. There are factors that tend toward the existence of such a duty, but none of them actually eventuates in it. Such a situation is crucially different, then, from a situation in which a veritable prima-facie moral duty does exist and is overtopped by a weightier moral duty. A veritable prima-facie moral duty does not *tend* toward the existence of a duty; it *is* a duty. What it tends toward is the existence of an overtopping moral duty. Inasmuch as that tendency is realized in any particular context, the moral duty in question prevails over all contrary moral pressures. If the tendency is instead checked by the existence of some more important moral consideration(s), the prima-facie duty still obtains as

---

[32] This distinction is missed by Joseph Raz when he draws a parallel between (i) the liberty of courts in some circumstances to overrule precedents which they would in other circumstances be obligated to apply and (ii) the overtopping duty of a promisor to decline to abide by her promissory obligation in some circumstances. See Joseph Raz, *The Authority of Law* (Oxford: Clarendon Press, 1979), 114.

such. Even when overtopped, it is indeed a moral duty rather than a mere appearance or a mere factor (like Edward's pain) that contributes toward the existence of such a duty.

Second, the way in which a prima-facie moral duty continues to obtain as a moral duty—even when overtopped—is explicated by the Remedy Principle*. Any such duty is a normative state that imposes remedial obligations upon the person to whom it attaches, if he does not behave in accordance with it. When a moral duty is exceeded in importance by some conflicting moral obligation(s), it is not thereby canceled or eliminated. It remains a normative state of the type that has just been mentioned; that is, it remains a normative state of the type expounded by the Remedy Principle*. As has been emphasized already in this chapter, the Remedy Principle* applies equally to overtopping and non-overtopping moral duties. To be sure, as we have seen, the difference between non-compliance with an overtopping moral obligation and non-compliance with a non-overtopping moral obligation is not devoid of significance. Ceteris paribus, an instance of non-compliance of the latter sort will trigger a lighter remedial obligation than will an instance of non-compliance of the former sort. In other words, the overtopping or non-overtopping force of a moral duty affects the nature and stringency of the remedy that will be required in the event of any breach of the duty. Nevertheless, as we have likewise seen, a remedy of *some* kind will be required irrespective of whether the duty is overtopping or non-overtopping. In that basic regard, the difference between the two classes of duties does not make a difference.

Now, in mulling over the objection that was posited at the outset of this subsection, we should observe that the various examples adduced by this chapter in support of the Remedy Principle and Remedy Principle* have all involved veritable moral duties—whether prima-facie or overtopping—rather than mere factors that weigh inconclusively in favor of the existence of moral duties. Specifically in the scenario of the conviction and imprisonment of George, the duty owed by the authorities in the criminal-justice system is a duty not to deprive him of his general liberty over a long period for a crime which he has not committed. Despite their meticulous care in their procedures, they have breached that duty. To be sure, that duty may well have been overtopped by a conflicting duty to safeguard the public through the incarceration of people who have been convicted of serious crimes after scrupulously fair proceedings. Nonetheless, though the fault-independent duty owed to George is probably overtopped by the countervailing obligation owed to the public, it abides as a moral duty, and it has been contravened. We can know that it abides as a moral duty and that it has been contravened, precisely because the authorities have morally obligated themselves to remedy the situation that has been brought about by their six-year confinement of George. They obviously are morally obligated to release him promptly when they learn of his innocence, but they are also morally obligated to do more. At the very least, they must issue an authoritative apology that will serve as an acknowledgment of the wrongness of what has been done to George. In so doing, they will be remedying (or going some way toward remedying) their transgression of the moral duty which they have owed to George; a remedy is required because a moral duty has been breached, even though the conduct of the authorities has not been wrongful and even though it has indeed amounted to their fulfillment of a moral duty of superior importance. In the face of a more pressing duty, the duty owed to George has abided as a moral constraint on what the authorities can do without incurring remedial obligations. In that respect, *mutatis mutandis*, the moral duty owed to him is like every other prima-facie moral duty. Like every other such duty, it differs sharply from anything that only appears to be a moral duty and from anything that only contributes toward the existence of a moral duty. Though overtopped by a conflicting requirement, it is a full-blown moral obligation whose status as such is invested with the normative implications delineated by the Remedy Principle*.

IV. A Pithy Conclusion

As this chapter has tried to show, Hart was incorrect in declaring that strict liability is peculiar to law and is not to be found in morality. Indeed, not only was he incorrect, but the truth of the matter is nearly the opposite of what he contended. Although strict liability is present in the law, it is almost certainly more common in morality. In substantiation of this claim, two points deserve emphasis.

First, once we take account of the distinction between extenuation and exoneration, we can sense just how frequent the occurrence of strict liability in morality is. Because of the mitigating effects of impeccable intentions and precautions, the requisite remedy in many a case involving the innocent infliction of harm on one person by another is nothing more than an apology. Given as much, and given how often the innocent infliction of harm does call for nothing more *and nothing less* than an apology, we can quite safely presume that strict liability is not only present within morality but also widespread therein. Were there nothing between outright exoneration and onerous remedies that bespeak the culpability of wrongdoers, then exoneration would doubtless be the appropriate upshot for numerous people who faultlessly harm others. In fact, however, extenuating considerations such as faultlessness are reflected in the remedies which people are morally obligated to undertake in order to make amends for their wrongdoing. Hence, the prevalence of the principle of strict liability in morality is not unfair to the people who have to shoulder remedial obligations under that principle. Even people who have been fastidiously careful in their conduct are not inordinately burdened by being duty-bound to apologize for hardships which they have imposed on innocent victims. (Of course, nothing just said is meant to imply that every hardship imposed on an innocent victim must be remedied. Sometimes the occasioning of detriment to another person is not wrong, by any tenable reckoning. For example, if John falls in love with Mary, and if she has done nothing to encourage his love, she is not morally obligated to apologize for its unrequitedness. She is probably obligated to communicate regret over his disappointment—here the difference between expressing sorrow and apologizing is crucial—but she is not obligated to take any step that would constitute an acknowledgment of wrongdoing.)

Second, although mitigation is also operative in the punitive mechanisms of many legal systems, the application of legal penalties—even when the penalties are softened in response to the presence of extenuating factors—is generally something that stands in need of a more ample justification than does the accrual of remedial obligations in morality. The legal rectification of wrongdoing mobilizes the coercive power of governmental institutions against the person on whom the rectification is brought to bear. Most moral remedies, by contrast, do not activate the mighty power of those institutions at all. Admittedly, someone who behaves not only wrongly but also wrongfully will often thereby have morally obligated himself to undergo an appropriate legal punishment. However, a person's undergoing of punishment will very seldom if ever be a morally obligatory remedy for any wrong that is non-culpable. As Cane observes, 'punishment in the absence of fault is generally considered extremely difficult to justify... [P]unishment carries with it an implication of blameworthiness that is inappropriate in the absence of fault' (Cane, *Responsibility*, 109–10). Far more common are moral remedies such as apologies, which are implemented with no input from governmental institutions (save in unusual circumstances, including of course circumstances in which the people morally obligated to undertake such remedies are themselves governmental officials—as is true in the story of the incarceration of George). Thus, since the mechanisms of government will rarely be implicated in giving effect to any remedial obligations which are imposed by the sway of strict liability in morality and which would not be imposed by a culpability-based standard, the justification required for the existence of strict liability in the domain of morality is typically lighter than in the domain of law. Given that the heavy hand of government pervades the latter domain and is largely absent from the former, a major factor that weighs morally against the application of *legal* penalties to faultless people is hardly ever an obstacle to the incurring of remedial *moral* obligations by such people.

In sum, contrary to what Hart proclaimed, strict liability is almost certainly more prominent in morality than in the law. Though the impeccableness of one's efforts and safeguards is sometimes exonerative in morality, it more frequently is simply extenuative. When the plea 'I could not help it' does not establish that the prevailing moral requirements have been satisfied, it is only a plea in mitigation and is never an excuse. Morality contains no place for excuses.

Index